Social Psychology of Health

About the Editors

Dr. Urmi Nanda Biswas is presently working as a Professor in the Department of Psychology, the M.S. University of Baroda, Vadodara. She obtained her D.Phil. degree from Centre of Advanced Study in Psychology, Allahabad University. She has worked as a Commonwealth Academic Staff Fellow (CASF) in 2006-2007 with Commonwealth Fellowship from British Council, UK and has been the recipient of UK India Educational Research Initiative (UKIERI) Collaborative Delivery Award from British Council in the year 2008-2009 for development of a short-term course on Professional Development Course on Mental Health Assessment. She has also been associated with the Clinical and Health Psychology Research Centre, School of Life Sciences Roehampton University as an honorary senior research fellow from 2006-2009. She has been a Visiting Professor to Department of Work Science, and Department of Psychology, Gothenberg University, Sweden and has been appointed as a steering committee member of Sweden India Gender Network (SIGN). Prof. Biswas has been the Principal and Co-investigator in various national and international projects with grants from UGC, ICSSR, Population Council, New York; Education Department, Commonwealth Secretariat, London, SIDA, Sweden etc.

Dr. Biswas's broad research interest includes applied social and health psychology and organizational behaviour, with specific interest in psychosocial, behavioural interventions to promote health and well-being of individuals across context. She has been consistently publishing in these areas. She has been a part of the state level evaluation and monitoring mission of National Aids Control Programme for the Voluntary Counselling and Testing Centre, and Partnership in Sexual Health Projects. She has been working as a national level external evaluator for TI projects under Gujarat State AIDS Control Society for almost 10 years now which has enriched her understanding of socio-cultural issues in healthcare delivery system in India.

SOCIAL PSYCHOLOGY OF HEALTH

The Issues and Concerns in India

Edited by

Urmi Nanda Biswas

CONCEPT PUBLISHING COMPANY PVT. LTD.

NEW DELHI-110059

ISBN-13 : 978-93-5125-001-2

First Published 2014

Published and Printed by

Concept Since 1974

Concept Publishing Company Pvt. Ltd.
A/15-16, Commercial Block, Mohan Garden
New Delhi-110059 (India)
T: 25351460, 25351794, *F*: 091-11-25357109
E: publishing@conceptpub.com, W: www.conceptpub.com
Editorial Office: H-13, Bali Nagar, New Delhi-110 015, India.

Cataloging in Publication Data—*Courtesy:* D.K. Agencies (P) Ltd. <docinfo@dkagencies.com>

Social psychology of health : the issues and concerns in India / edited by Urmi Nanda Biswas.
p. cm.
Includes bibliographical references and index.
ISBN 9789351250012

1. Clinical health psychology—Congresses. 2. Social psychology—Congresses. 3. Social medicine—Congresses. 4. HIV infections—Psychological aspects—Congresses. 5. AIDS (Disease)—Psychological aspects—Congresses. I. Biswas, Urmi Nanda.

DDC 616.0019 23

Preface

The aim of the book is to explore the relationship of health psychology as being intimately involved with the problems of our changing social scenario. Since 1970s health psychology focused primarily on clinical issues. Health is increasingly being viewed as not a matter of personal responsibility and choice rather; as an interaction of individual characteristics with the social, cultural, economic and political environment. Thus, the future of health psychology research is directed towards understanding the complex relationship that exists between the social and individual dimensions that lead to health seeking behaviour of individuals which can be directed in creating effective interventions for disease prevention and health promotion, especially with reference to sexual health, diet, smoking, alcohol, inactivity and stress. The basic argument in this conceptualization is that the health behaviours are not just a product of individual responsibility, governed by freely taken choices. The choices adopted by people are constrained by the environment (both physical and social) that pushes people towards health aversive behaviours.

Health psychology is a rich interdisciplinary field requiring an understanding of the socio-political and economic roots of behaviour and experience. In India, as the gaps between 'haves' and have-nots, rich and poor is widening along with the economic growth and development, there has been a fragmentation in the society due to its failure in amalgamating the modern health care practices with the indigenous cultural values and practices leading to value conflicts and aversive health behaviours. For example, traditional health care practices are not integrated into the modern health care system. Some of these practices may have roots in our socio-philosophical context and thus matches the health belief system of the community members. When these belief systems have been embedded into the modern health care systems, health seeking behaviour and the health delivery system has improved significantly. Two of the chapters in this book address these issues.

Rapid urbanization and rural to urban migration is resulting in social isolation and alienation from the root culture. Moreover, as more and more people are migrating to cities, a growing aging population is left at the villages to look after themselves. These are becoming increasing salient feature of the society. In preparing to deal with these issues, all those concerned with health services and disease prevention require in-depth understanding, not only of the complexities of human behaviour in its social context, but of the lived experiences of health, illness and health care. The single male migrants in the sub-urban areas have been identified as the major high risk group for HIV/AIDS (National AIDS Control Planning-III, 2006). Similarly, young male and female migrants in low socio-economic and high crowding residential areas are at high risk of Sexually Transmitted Infections (STI) and diseases (STDs). In addition to that, the public health services for antenatal care may not be easily accessible for young migrant mothers residing away from the city limit. The migrant adolescents from low SES have also been reported to be at high risk for life style related health problem like smoking, alcoholism and drug abuse. Thus, disease prevention and health promotion efforts by health care practitioner and policy makers should take the socio-structural dimensions of health into active consideration.

Because AIDS is the leading cause of death worldwide, the need for health measures such as condom use and safe sex practices is readily apparent if we are to halt the spread of this disease. It can only be possible through effective social marketing. The large-scale change in attitudes and beliefs, and promotion of behaviour change in diverse socio-cultural milieu of India can only be addressed through tailor-made strategic social marketing programmes. Moreover, stigma, discrimination and rejection are the major barriers against health seeking, disclosure and compliance to regimen by the people living with HIV/AIDS. Without disclosure and treatment, HIV can spread like wildfire. Thus, psychosocial and educational interventions through carefully designed public health programmes can be immensely helpful. Chapters on Saksham project and family counselling for people living with HIV/AIDS address these concerns.

Health habits lie at the origin of our most prevalent disorders, like smoking, alcohol consumption and engaging in health risk behaviours. Obesity is now one of the world's leading health problems, which is also catching up Indian population. CHD has been the major cause of death in India in the last decade. The increasing physical inactivity among South Asians as a major cause of cardiovascular diseases, diabetes and other lifestyle related diseases. Inculcating health habits to reverse this trend is important. This can be addressed by developing a social norm of physical activity and exercises. The Indian traditions lays considerable emphasis on positive health and has provisions not only for the cure and prevention of diseases but also to enhance health. The indigenous systems of Yoga, Ayurveda and various folk traditions have delineated a number of practices and interventions to augment health and well-being. Reviving our age-old social tradition of indigenous practices of Yoga and Pranayam, and considering health as a value can be achieved by acknowledging these systems in our health habits and practices.

In this scheme, the state of health and well-being is dynamically located at the intersection of person and environment. That is why, Ayurveda and Yoga emphasized on *Samatva* or balance between the inner and the outer (person and environment) which share common properties. (*i.e.* Vata, Pitta and Kaf). This is based on the view that life depends on the continuous interchange between the body and the environment. (Dalal & Mishra, 2012). Thus; health needs to be understood from the perspective of social well-being, to accomplish holistic health.

In addition to working in clinical environments, health psychologists have a contribution to make in developing and evaluating health promotion interventions. Psychologists carry out these activities in close collaboration with communities, other health care practitioners and policy makers. Changes in policy and practices are urgently needed to increase equity and enhance well-being of the most vulnerable members of the society. For example, gender based violence, like female infanticide, feticide, domestic violence etc. has larger implications for health and well-being at the societal levels. Similarly, infant mortality and reproductive health of women from vulnerable sections needs to be addressed through health policies. Some of the chapters of the book evaluate the effectiveness of some of the health promoting initiatives by the government and funding agencies. This sheds light on the social psychological processes involved in the successful delivery and implementation of the programme. Gradually health practitioners and policy makers are realizing the importance of multilevel interventions, rather than having purely educational or behavioural interventions. Evidence suggests that such approaches alone are ineffectual and too small in scale (Marks, 2002a, 2002b). Thus the emerging need to plan large-scale interventions including the socio-cultural context and community characteristics are becoming popular to bring changes in health behaviour and practices.

Thus, the social psychology of health urges the health care professionals, practitioners and policy makers to adopt a preventive perspective by understanding the socio-structural, socio-demographic, psycho-social and socio-cognitive factors in the context, and to work on the socio-cultural traditions of societies and communities, ethnic and minority groups, with a focus on positive health enhancement through the use of multi-level strategies that take into account the whole context of health related experience and behaviour.

Acknowledgements

I am thankful to Prof. S.N. Biswas for the support he has provided throughout.

I am indebted to all the participants of my various research projects, who have provided me the insight and inspired me to look at 'health' differently, from the social psychological perspective.

Contents

Contributors's Profile

Ajit K. Dalal

Professor Ajit K. Dalal is a Ph.D. in Psychology (1978) from the Indian Institute of Technology, Kanpur. He is currently working as a Professor and Head, in the Centre for Advanced Study in Psychology, Allahabad University, Allahabad, U.P. and as the National fellow, ICSSR. He was awarded Fulbright Senior Research Fellowship at UCLA, he is a recipient of UGC Career Award (1989-92), Rockfeller Foundation Award (1992), and ICSSR Senior Fellowship (1999). He was a Scholar-in Residence at the Rockfeller Foundation Center, Bellagio, Italy (1992), Adjunct Associate Professor (1993-97) at the Queen's University, Canada and visiting Professor at the Indian Institute of Management, Ahmedabad (2002-03) and Calcutta university. Currently he is the Editor of the journal "Psychology and Developing Societies", published by the Sage India. He has published in the areas of information integration theory, causal attribution, research methods, health beliefs, folk healing, disability attitudes, and history and concepts in Indian psychology. His work has primarily focused on how cultural beliefs and attitudes play pivotal role in shaping behaviour and recovery from the chronic diseases. His present work focuses on traditional healing systems and their integration in the health care programmes. His major publications are *Attribution Theory and Research* (1988), *New Directions in Indian Psychology* (2001), *Social Dimensions of Health and Well-being* (2005) and *Handbook of Indian Psychology* (2008). He has edited the book, "*New Directions in Health Psychology*" in 2012.

Anuradha Sovani

Dr. Anuradha Sovani is working as an Associate Professor in the Department of Applied Psychology, University of Mumbai for 20 years. She has to her credit over 60 research papers and book chapters on mental illness and health related topics in National and International publications, and ten books in Marathi. Dr. Sovani's areas of interest include preventive programmes to promote family and child mental health, and rehabilitation of chronic mental illness. She currently serves on the Core Committee for Rehabilitation of Maharashtra State and has been a member of the Maharashtra State Mental Health Authority. She serves on the Academic Committee of NIMH, on several ethics Committees and advisory panels to State level bodies, and as Consultant and Trustee to the Institute for Psychological Health, Thane, Maharashtra.

Anuradha Shivramakrishnan

Dr. Anuradha has a Ph.D. in Psychology (Clinical) from the Maharaja Sayajirao University of Baroda, Vadodara, Gujarat. In 2008, she became the recipient of the Fulbright Doctoral and Professional Research Fellow, and has worked with the State University of New York, Buffalo. She has worked on projects in the area of Mental Health for the past few years. Her area of interest comprises learning disabilities, psychopathology, neuropsychology, social psychology of health and mental health.

Binu Sundas

He has Ph.D. degree from the Centre for Social Medicine & Community Health, Jawaharlal Nehru University, New Delhi, and is currently working as Assistant Professor in the Department of Social Systems and Anthropology, School of Humanities and Social Sciences, Sikkim University. He is the author of the books 'HIV and AIDS in Darjeeling: Emerging Socio Political Challenge' and 'A Heady Mixture: Culture, Economics, Health and Alcohol in Darjeeling.'

Fakir Mohan Sahoo

Prof. Fakir Mohan Sahoo is Research Professor in the Xavier Institute of Management (Bhubaneswar). He was the Professor in the Centre of Advanced Study in Psychology, Utkal University. He received Common Wealth Scholarship and obtained his doctoral degree from Queen's University, Canada. He was a recipient of University Grants Commission's Emeritus Fellowship, Career Award in Humanities and Social Sciences, fellowship offered by Shastri Indo-Canadian Institute and Professional Associateship offered by the East-West Center, Honolulu, Hawaii, USA. He has published several books in both English and Odiya.

Kalpana Jain

Dr. Kalpana Jain is presently working as Associate Professor and Head, Deptt. of Psychology, M.L. Sukhadia University, Udaipur. Completed M.A. and Ph.D. from M.L. Sukhadia University, Udaipur and Certificate Course in Career Development from University of Washington, Seattle, US. Published one book and 24 research papers in various journals. Editor of *Journal of Well Being* published by Academy of Well Being Society, Udaipur.

Nilamadhab Mohanty

Nilamadhav Mohanty is a Participant in the Fellow Programme in Rural Management (FPRM) at the Institute of Rural Management Anand (IRMA). Before joining IRMA, he worked as Veterinary Assistant Surgeon for The Department of Animal Husbandry and Fisheries, Govt. of Odisha. Currently pursuing his research in the field of consumer behaviour and marketing strategy.

Nivedita Das

She is presently working as a research Assistant at Xavier Institute of Management (OB/HR), Bhubaneswar is doing her Ph.D. from Utkal University after completing her Post Graduation from Delhi University in Clinical Psychology. The title of her research is "Psychosocial Adaptation of Destitute Women: Implications for Behavioural Intervention." She has also been running a destitute home in Cuttack, Odisha. She has also contributed articles in management journals and book chapters on issues of women.

Nitu Singh Bhadouria

She has completed her masters from the Department of Psychology, she worked with TI project in an NGO named Vikas Jyot Trust, where she had the opportunity to counsel the Commercial Sex Workers of Vadodara City. Presently she is working as a school counsellor, in Bright School, Vadodara.

Priyanka Behrani

Dr. Priyanka Behrani is working as a lecturer with the Department of Psychology, The M.S. University of Baroda. She has specialized in the field of Educational and Industrial Psychology. She is a practicing Psychologist and works with children having special needs She also works as a trainer for soft skills in various organizations.

Ravi Gunthey

Dr. Ravi K. Gunthey is an Associate Professor in Jai Narain Vyas University, Jodhpur since 1984 in Dept. of Psychology. His area of specialisation is mental health and children with special needs. Presently, he is working in GFATM, R7 and ICMR project. Is also coordinator of Centre for Differently Abled. He is running a special school in University for Mentally Challenged Children.

Renu Sharma

Dr. Renu Sharma is currently serving as an Associate Professor in the Department of Psychology, The M.S. University of Baroda, Vadodara. Her major research interests are, Indian psychology, counselling psychology and hypnotherapy.

Sashibala Rai Sharma

Sashibala Rai Sharma is a Participant in the Fellow Programme in Rural Management (FPRM) at the Institute of Rural Management Anand (IRMA). She is currently pursuing her research in the field of social marketing and public health.

Saswata Narayan Biswas

Dr. Saswata Narayan Biswas is a Professor of Organizational Behaviour and Human Resource Management at the Institute of Rural Management, Anand (IRMA). His academic interest is in understanding the relationship between micro and macro issues in organizational context. He has published and presented more than 60 research articles in several journals and written book chapters. He serves on the editorial boards of several journals; Community, Work and Family published (Carfax Publishing) from University of Manchester, UK and International Journal of Rural Psychology published from University of South Australia, Australia; Advances in Management, and KIIT Journal of management. He was also the founding Chief Editor of the International Journal of Rural Management published by Sage Publishers, India.

Swati Akshay Sachdeva

She is currently working as the Asst. Professor in the Department of Social System and Anthropology, Sikkim University Gangtok. She is the author of "Structural Analysis of Bhutia Society and Position of Bhutia Women in Society of Sikkim" (LAP, 2011). She has been Co-Investigator of project on Suicide in Sikkim: A Psycho-social Study.

Sunil K. Verma

Sunil K. Verma has done D.Phil. from Center for Advanced Study, Department of Psychology, Allahabad University, currently working as Asst. Professor in Vivekananda College, Delhi University. Earlier he taught at Department of Psychology studies, Sikkim University Gangtok, Sikkim. He was the Principle-Investigator of projects on Suicide in Sikkim: A Psycho-Social Study, and Subjective experience of Sikkim's Police Personnel: Role of Personnel and Organizational Factor.

Usha Chelani

Usha Chelani is a Research Scholar in the Dept. of Psychology, Jai Narain Vyas University, Jodhpur. Doing her Ph.D. on HIV pregnant females, she is working as a Resource Person in GFATM R7 Project.

Urmi Nanda Biswas

Dr. Urmi Nanda Biswas is currently working as a Professor in the Department of Psychology, The M.S. University of Baroda, Vadodara. She has been working in the area of applied social psychology, health psychology, and organizational behaviour. Her major research thrust is on psycho-social and bio-behavioural interventions for health promotion and maintenance across contexts.

Veena Panjwani

Ms. Veena Panjwani has done masters in Clinical Psychology from Department of Psychology, Faculty of Eduction and Psychology, The M.S. University of Baroda. She is the recipient of TKN Menon Gold Medal for her academic excellence in Psychology. She is doing her doctoral research in Self Regulation from the Department of Human Development and Family Studies, Faculty of Family and Community Sciences, The M.S. University of Baroda.

1

Social Psychology of Health: The Issues and Concerns in India

Urmi Nanda Biswas

Introduction

Health is the net outcome of the behavioural choices we make and lifestyle we adopt. Behavioural choices are not made in isolation. These choices are based on individuals' life experiences, understanding and interpretation of the reality, which involves the dynamic social interaction with other individuals, social-cultural contexts, and socio-structural variables. The individual is an active construction of his reality. Health behaviour can only be understood in the context of an individual's perception. The behavioural choices that the individual makes largely depend on his social construction and interpretation of the alternatives available. Talking about the principles that people rely on, to motivate the choices they make, McGuire (1991) proposed that there are at least 16 different goals that may shape people's behavioural choices. According to him people often act based on a desire to maximize their "expected utility." In order to attain this, most of the times they would act in the service of these various goals which may include maximization of immediate pleasure, minimizations of cost, distinguish themselves from others, confirm to others' expectations, or increase their acceptance of other people. However, people's assessment of these costs and benefits associated with behaviour at a given moment are filtered through these motives. Thus, what appears as cost and benefits associated with a particular behaviour may change from moment to moment and from situation to situation depending on what influences the person's motives and what is of value and subjective utility to a person at that moment in the particular situation (Salovey & Rothmen, 2003). Thus the social psychological factors in the context may also play a major role in understanding the choices that people make regarding their health practices and health decisions.

"Health behaviour can only be understood in the context of an individual's perceptions, construal, and resulting belief systems, and these behaviours are motivated by the individuals' dispositions and situational affordances. Moreover, a social psychological approach places health behaviour in the context of other social behaviours of the individual and considers the diverse set of human need that may underlie people's health practices." (Salovey & Rothman, 2003, pp. 4). Thus, it is suggested that focusing on the social psychological processes that underlie people's behavicural practices rather than the specific behavioural practices. (like focusing on the person who smokes rather than smoking behaviour *per se*) may make the development of interventions and public health programme more effective.

When the government is striving and spending major budget heads on developing the public health programmes and strategies to bring changes in health behaviour and practices of people, it can only be successful if we understand that the likelihood of significant advance in health behaviour changes are contingent on the identification of the psychological processes that facilitates or inhibits a health behaviour. For example, in India most of the significant surgical/treatment decision of the patient is taken in consultation with significant family members. Thus, if the doctor is trying to counsel for effective treatment regimen or convincing the patient for adherence to a suggested regimen, it will be more effective to include one or two significant family members in the counselling session.

It will be possible to reduce the disease morbidity effectively, only if individuals engage reliably in prevention behaviours such as regular physical exercise and screening behaviours such as mammography and pap smear testing. But the question is whether the target group has the awareness about these kinds of screening and its long- term benefits. Do we design and promote strategies for creating public awareness? Moreover, the health benefits that are to come from the overwhelming majority of advances of biomedical sciences critically depend upon people's behavioural decision making. For example, as evidenced by innovations in medical treatments for persons living with AIDS, people must adhere to their prescription if they are to experience the benefits of the drugs. In fact, poor rates of adherence may produce adverse health consequences, as not taking medications as prescribed allows the virus to become drug resistant (see Salovey & Rothman, 2003). Thus, what seems important for healthy living of AIDS patients is the adherence to prescribed regimen rather than availing the innovative and advanced medical treatment.

Although individuals can assume personal risk of engaging in unhealthy practices, like smoking or alcoholism, when aggregated for the whole population of India, the burden in terms of the morbidity, cost and other social and psychological implication for the society indeed seems unacceptable. Small changes in individual health behaviour may ramify and produce large benefits for the society. There are domains in which efforts to change behaviour have been successful to some extent. In case of India, dealing with HIV pandemic, behaviour change communication has been adopted as one of the most important components of National AIDS Control Programme-III along with integrated prevention through care, support and treatment. Behaviour change communication involves understanding and assessment of individual and group behaviours/practices which make an individual at risk for HIV, counselling through counsellors and creating enabling environment to reinforce safe practices. The strategies for behaviour change communication are educational programmes, repetitive media presentation of information about the disease, regular campaigns conducted on mass media, outdoor activities and interpersonal communication. This has been successful to some extent by arresting the spread of the epidemic.

Thus, understanding and appreciation of the social psychology of health would greatly benefit the primary care givers, health professionals and policy makers. The public health system can incorporate more sensitive and patient friendly strategies, effective social marketing and health communication plans can be drawn to enable the benefactors' access and utilization of the health services. It would also be helpful to enhance the individual health efficacy, by motivating them to engage in more health promoting behaviour and restrain from health damaging practices.

The Current Status of Health Care System in India

According to a recent article in *The Lancet*, the health care system in Southeast Asian countries needs urgent attention for review and reform. Deliberating on the factors associated with health care system, the authors identified some of the major causes which demands reform (Chongsuvivatwong, Hong, Yap *et al.,* 2011). Some of those factors which describe the current status of health care system in India are as follows:

The diversity of geography and history, including social, cultural, and economic differences, have contributed to highly divergent health status, health systems, health beliefs and practices across and within states of India.

Demographic transition is taking place at a faster pace, whether in terms of fertility reductions, ageing population, and rural-to-urban migration. Rapid epidemiological transition is also occurring, with the disease burden shifting from infectious to chronic diseases. Rapid urbanization, population movement, and high-density living raise concerns about newly emerging infectious diseases. The sprawling slums around the big cities, with its residential crowding with accompanying unhygienic environmental conditions are becoming major health concern for the nation.

India's long coastline and geo-climatic diversity, contributes to its being one of the most disaster-prone region in the world, more susceptible to natural and man-made disasters affecting health, including earthquakes, typhoons, floods, and environmental pollution. Climate change along with rapid economic development could exacerbate the spread of emerging infectious diseases. Health systems in the region are a dynamic mix of public and private delivery and financing, with new organizational forms such as corporate public hospitals, and innovative service delivery responding to competitive private health-care markets and growing medical tourism. However, along with all these modern developments exists its age-old traditional health care systems which caters to the educated and uneducated, urban and rural population equally.

Changing Patterns of Illness

According to the Global Burden of Disease report by WHO (as cited in Patel *et al.,* 2011), out of 10.3 million deaths that occurred in India in 2004, 1.1 million (11%) were due to injuries and 5.2 million (50%) were due to chronic diseases. The chronic diseases discussed in this report caused an estimated 3.6 million (35%) deaths. Mortality rates for people with age-specific chronic diseases are estimated to be higher in India than in high-income countries. In 2004, the overall age standardized mortality rates for chronic diseases were 769 per 1,00,000 men (56% higher than in high-income countries in 2004) and 602 per 1,00,000 women, which is 100 per cent higher than in high-income countries in 2004 (as cited in Patel *et al.*, 2011).

In India, the number of deaths due to communicable diseases and to maternal, perinatal, and nutritional causes is predicted to decrease between 2004 and 2030 (WHO report on Global Health Risks: Mortality and burden of disease attributable to selected major risks as cited in Patel *et al.,* 2011). As India's population ages during the next 25 years, the total number of deaths will increase substantially; this increase will be largely attributable to chronic diseases. Deaths caused by cancer are projected to increase from 7,30,000 in 2004 to 1.5 million in 2030, and those attributable to cardio vascular causes from 2.7 million in 2004 to 4.0 million in 2030. Overall, the projections suggest that chronic diseases will account for slightly less than three-quarters of all deaths in India by 2030. In India, the number of years of life lost because of coronary heart disease deaths before the age of 60 years will increase from 7.1 million in 2004 to 17.9 million in 2030, which means that, by 2030, more life years will be lost as a result of this disease in India than is projected for China, Russia, and the USA combined (as cited in Patel *et al.,* 2011 from WHO report on Global Health Risks). Cardiovascular diseases, especially coronary heart disease, are major contributors to the higher death rates in India, because Indians are more likely to develop coronary heart disease and have an earlier age of disease onset than are people in high-income countries, and because the case-fatality rate in India is higher than in high-income countries. Apart from this alarming change in the disease pattern in India, the reported health behaviour among Indian population is a major public health concern.

Health Behaviours

Analysing World Health Survey data (Ustun, Chatarjee, Mechbal, Murray, WHO collaborating Groups, 2003) shows that more than

20 per cent of the Indian population smoke daily. Data from the Indian Migration Study shows that men in urban areas are twice as likely to have low physical activity when compared with those in rural areas. The increasing use of tobacco by young people is of great concern; data from a study suggest that tobacco use among students from lower grades in urban schools seems to be increasing, signalling a worrying trend that needs to be investigated. About 2.5 per cent of men in the population report that they drink heavily (five or more standard drinks on at least 2 days in the previous week), 12.4 per cent of the population does not do sufficient physical activity, and the proportion increases with age, 7.3 per cent of the population are overweight, and 1.2 per cent of the population are obese. Physical inactivity and obesity are most common among individuals in the upper-income group urban residents, and elderly people. The overall levels of these risk behaviours reported in the World Health Survey might be underestimates, as suggested by an Indian study estimating that up to 35 per cent of a rural population and 56 per cent of an urban population does not engage in sufficient physical activity (Mohan *et al.*, 2008). Whether these discrepancies arise from differences in survey samples, measurement strategies, or study design is unclear. More than 80 per cent of the Indian population use solid fuel for cooking. Indoor air pollution from use of solid fuel for cooking affects nearly 90 per cent of rural households. This data-mine about the health behaviour in Indian population, urges immediate attention to design effective public health campaigns, and community as well as psycho-social interventions for changes in health behaviour and practices.

Social determinants: More than 20 per cent of the population has at least one chronic disease and more than 10 per cent have more than one. Chronic diseases are widespread in people who are younger than 45 years and in poorer populations. Whereas, socio-economic development tends to be associated with healthy behaviours (Gupta, 2006) rapidly improving socio-economic status in India is associated with a reduction of physical activity and increased rates of obesity and diabetes (Ramachandran, 2007; Reddy, Prabhakaran, and Jeemon, 2007). Physical inactivity increases the risk of many adverse health conditions, including major non-communicable diseases such as coronary heart disease, type 2 diabetes, and breast and colon cancers, and shortens life expectancy. Inactivity causes 9 per cent (range 5.1-12.5) of premature mortality, or more than 5.3 million of the 57 million deaths that occurred worldwide in 2008. Elimination of physical inactivity would increase the life expectancy of the world's population by 0.68 (range 0.41-0.95) years (Lee, Shiroma, Lobelo, Puska, Blair, and Katzmarzyk, 2012). The emerging pattern in India is therefore characterized by an initial uptake of harmful health behaviours in the early phase of socio-economic development. Such behaviours include increased consumption of energy-dense foods and reduced physical activity, increased exposure to risk factors for road traffic injury such as driving above the speed limit, after intake of alcohol, or without appropriate safety precautions like wearing seat belts or motorcycle helmets.

Table 1.1 presents top ten causes of death in India reported in one of India's topmost news weekly. When this article as well as other sources admits the non-availability of compiled country-wide authentic data on death-causes in India, the data presented from a large-scale study is quite representative of the present scenario. The results indicate a reversal in disease patterns in the country from communicable diseases to non-communicable or lifestyle diseases in last decade. About 25 per cent of deaths in the age group of 25-69 years occur because of heart diseases. In urban areas, 32.8 per cent

Table 1.1: Top Ten Causes of Death in India

Rank	*Disease*	*All Ages*			*Ages 25-69 yrs.*		
		Male	*Female*	*Total*	*Male*	*Female*	*Total*
1	Cardiovascular diseases	20.3	16.9	18.8	26.3	22.3	24.8
2	Respiratory Diseases	9.3	8.0	8.7	10.1	10.4	10.2
3	Diarrhoeal diseases	6.7	9.9	8.1	11.4	8.3	10.3
4	Perinatal condition	6.4	6.2	6.3	7.8	11.8	9.4
5	Respiratory infections	5.4	7.1	6.2	4.8	6.0	5.3
6	Tuberculosis	7.1	4.7	6.0	6.1	3.5	5.1
7	Malignant and other Tumours	5.4	6.0	5.1	4.0	6.6	5.0
8	Senility	4.0	6.5	5.1	5.0	4.1	4.6
9	Unintentional Injuries	5.2	4.5	4.9	3.3	2.6	3.0
10	Ill-defined Conditions	4.6	5.0	4.8	2.4	3.4	2.8

Source: Data reproduced from Sharma (2010), *http: //indiatoday. intoday. in/ story/India's+no. 1+killer: +Heart+disease/1/92422. html*

deaths occur because of heart ailments, while this percentage in rural areas is 22.9. Overall, 42 per cent of deaths in India are accounted for by non-communicable diseases, while communicable diseases and those associated with childbirth and nutritional disorders account for 38 per cent of deaths. Other causes of deaths in the 25-69 years age group - urban and rural areas taken together - are respiratory diseases such as asthma (10.2%), tuberculosis (10.1%), malignant tumours (9%), digestive diseases (5.1%) and diarrhoeal disease (5%) Malaria, which had been a leading cause of death, now accounts for only 2.8 per cent deaths. (Sharma, 2010).

Unlike deaths from communicable diseases or injuries having known causes, most non-communicable diseases can have multiple causes, out of which many are lifestyle related. For example, heart attack could be caused by smoking, high blood pressure, high cholesterol and other factors. Thus, understanding lifestyle related risks and socio-cultural determinants has a lot of implications for health maintenance and promotion.

Importance of Social Aspects in Indian Understanding of Health

In the traditional Indian conceptualization, health is conceived in a wider sense of total well-being and happiness (Sinha 1990 as cited in Dalal & Mishra, 2006). It is not only the absence of pain and suffering but includes cultivation of many personality attributes, emotional state, intellectual capacities, and moral values, such as inner peace, truthfulness, and self-knowledge. Dalal and Mishra (2006), conceptualize the Indian notion of a healthy person as an auto-locus person (*svastha*) who flourishes on the recognition of life force derived from the material reality (*mahabhutas*) and therefore, offers remedies for being healthy by opening a dialogue with its environment and observing one's duty (*dharma*). The nutrition (*ahar*), world of leisure (*vihar*), and thoughts (*vichar*) need to be synchronized in proper order. Health and well-being are both personal as well as social. Thus, in Indian context, health and well-being is contingent not only on the state of one's own self, but also on the state of other fellow beings in the family, community and society.

Integrating Traditional and Existing Health Practices

In any society, health and well-being is understood in its socio-cultural perspective and attributed to numerous factors. Particularly in South East Asian culture, most of the healing techniques emphasize holistic healing, thus: believe in treating the patient as embedded in his or her socio-cultural milieu. Khatoon (2012) divides the Indian healing structure into three domains – professional, popular (family, social network and community) and folk (non-professional healers). The third category constitutes of the temple healers, shamans, homeopaths, yoga practitioners, *vaids* and *ojhas* seem to be the most important and integral part of the Indian health system, who specialize in dealing with a variety of social, cultural and personal problems (Kakar, 1982; Kakar, 1991 as cited in Khatoon, 2012). In fact, in India where more than 70 per cent of the population lives in rural areas, the most widely used treatment processes are the folk healing methods.

Use of alternative medicinal systems apart from allopathy is another aspect of the healing scene in India. These systems include Ayurveda, Siddha, Unani, Yoga, and Homeopathy. These methods through their safe, effective and inexpensive treatments have made significant contributions to the Indian health care system.

Ayurveda literally means the science of life; it is the most prominent and well documented among all the systems of medicine. It derives its basic principles from the *Chraka Samhita* and the *Susruta Samhita* (ancient Indian scriptures on health care practices). This approach emphasizes life and health more than disease and treatment. The system is based on the belief that humans are miniature replicas of the universe. The individual and universe and both essentially comprised of the *panchabhoota* or the five basic physical factors (space, air, water, fire and earth). Any disharmony in the composition is the basic cause of disease and illness. Ayurveda speaks of a harmony between the *tridoshas* (*vata, pitta, kapha*) and the three *gunas* (*sattva, rajas* and *tamas*). All ailments arise out of the imbalance of these three *doshas*, or *humours*, and the *gunas*. The role of medicine is to help the natural healing of the body.

Though there are significant differences within the approaches of Indian medicine, there are certain fundamental similarities amongst all the systems which has been summarized as follows (Khatoon, 2012):

- All the systems adopt a holistic approach and aim at treating the patient as a whole.
- The systems are more life-oriented than disease-oriented.

- All the approaches adopt a belief that disease is a cause of disharmony between man and nature that disturbs the balance between the biological factors or humours. The main aim of therapy is the restoration of this balance.
- All systems use natural substances, predominantly herbal preparations for treatment.
- Diet is emphasized as an important component of healthy living.
- Health Psychology considers these indigenous perspectives of various socio-cultural milieus important to plan and deliver health care programmes and make the public health programmes effective for the target group. The concept of health, as construed in Indian culture, has been presented well in a model of Health and Well-being by Dalal and Mishra (2012).

Health and Well-being: A Schematic Model

Considering the Indo-Asian perspective of health and well-being, and the socio-cultural framework Dalal and Mishra (2012), presented a schematic and comprehensive model of health and well-being, which includes the whole gamut of psychological conditions which are linked with health as causes, concomitants, and consequences. This model builds on the three main domains of health, which are conceived as restoration, maintenance, and growth of life processes. The first domain represents the illness domain where the primary focus is on bringing the person back from the state of illness (incongruity/disjunction) to the state of health, or re-establishing the congruence and conjunction. Here, bringing back to health practically implies the process of recovery from the disease. Thus, it involves curative and healing interventions that can free the patient from the bodily suffering and pain. This basically concerns patients, health practitioners, caregivers, and hospitals and any health care services. The process of rehabilitation from disability can also be a part of this domain.

The second domain emphasizes maintenance of health. In Indian culture, this domain is largely unattended by the masses. The major concern of this domain is to engage in the activities to maintain good health and protect one's own self from diseases and disabilities, which basically implies health behaviour and practices. Health is not static or fixed, being a dynamic process and one's health status is subjected to change. People who primarily belong to this domain are agents of their health. They have to be motivated to act proactively to enhance their immunity or power of resistance to diseases, resilience, physical and mental vitality, and active participation in family and lives. Maintenance of health according to this model involves the personal as well as social or relational space. Thus, on the one hand, the person has to perform exercise, yoga, work, and take proper diet promoting positive health behaviour, and on the other hand he or she has to be active in continuing and nourishing the social relations with family, co-workers, and environment to promote his well-being.

The third domain of health is identified to be growth centred. Considering the psycho-philosophical context of the Indian culture and traditions growth has been referred to as psycho-spiritual health. The person evolves and goes beyond the isolated and limited self and his concept of health encompasses his total existence inclusive of his physical, social, and spiritual status, and needs to be established in both the physical as well as moral or ethical spaces. The person strives to achieve a level of functioning that ensures effective personal functioning to further harmony with others. The blossoming of inherent potential takes place and with energy, creativity, and efficiency which in turn, it helps the individual to maintain equilibrium. The journey with restoration from disease (*vyadhi*) moves towards the state of self-realization, equanimity, and calmness leading to bliss often conceptualized in terms of *Samādhi*. There is, in fact, a great deal of overlap and permeability in the three domains of health, though these are hierarchically organized.

According to Dalal and Mishra (2012), the salience of these domains in one's life space keeps shrinking or expanding. The model specifically demonstrates how the interaction of mind, body, and self is a crucial condition in all the three domains when health and well-being of the individual is considered. The model summarizes that, in the restoration domain the emphasis is more on the mental states affecting the body condition, in the maintenance domain, it is the harmonious relation between the two which is of prime importance, and in the growth domain, the focus is on psychological factors and a harmonious relation among mind–body–soul (self). The model emphasizes the social well-being as an important aspect of health in Indian conceptualization, which encompasses not only the well-being of the self, but also of the fellow beings like others in the family and community.

Social Psychological Concommitants of Health

Keeping all the above discussions and secondary data in perspective social psychology of health can be understood as a dynamic process which encompasses socio-cognitive, psycho-social, socio-demographic and socio-structural factors in the space of individual's existence.

Socio cognitive factors include the beliefs, attitudes about health and disease processes, perceived norms and social comparison, health awareness and health communication which largely affects the choices people make pertaining to the restoration of health, their health seeking behaviour, readiness for behaviour change and adherence to medical regimen among the target group. These factors have implications for the success of health policies and programmes.

Psychosocial factors include values, social relationships and support, patient-physician relationship, role of care giving etc. which has implications pertaining to the maintenance domain of health, like arresting disease progression, coping with chronic illness, or subjective well-being of the individual.

Socio-demographic factors comprise of factors like gender, education, age, religion and caste/tribal status. These factors have been extensively studied in psychology, and particularly in health psychology. Health risk behaviours, vulnerability to different diseases and prevalence of different health problems in societies and cultures have been persuasively explained with the help of socio-demographic factors.

Socio-structural factors in the context of India and other developing south-Asian countries have an important role in explaining health behaviour and practices of individuals. Socio-economic class, family structure and residential density and environmental hazards, rapid urbanization, rural to urban migration are examples of socio-structural factors. Although it is difficult to account for the role of distal social or structural determinants or early life determinants in the development of chronic diseases, still it can safely be assumed that early life determinants affect diabetes, hypertension, and chronic diseases—e.g., prenatal and infant food supplementation seems to improve adult outcomes (Kinra, Sarma, Ghafoorunissa *et al.*, 2008). However, evidence exists that distal social and structural determinants strongly affect the burden of chronic diseases and injuries. For example, rapid motorization along with the heterogeneous composition of road traffic and infrastructural deficiencies are directly linked to the increased number of road traffic injuries. Similarly, large number of suicides among farmers has been linked to a combination of factors, such as drought, increased competition from cheap food imports, and large-scale mechanized agricultural practices, which make local small-scale agriculture economically unviable and restrict access to formal credit for marginalized farmers. Powerlessness, as experienced by these farmers, or women entrapped in violent marriages, is a major social determinant of suicide (See Patel *et al.*, 2012).

Socio-cognitive Factors

Health Beliefs and Attitudes: Attitudes and beliefs about health determine subsequent health behaviour. Health beliefs and attitudes determine the perceived susceptibility; perceived severity; perceived benefits; perceived barriers; and cues to action regarding any particular health problem and available behavioural choices. The Health Belief Model attempts to explain the widespread failure of people to participate in programmes to prevent or detect asymptomatic disease, people's responses to experienced symptoms and their behaviour in response to professionally diagnosed illness, particularly compliance with medical regimens (Rosenstock, 2000). From a social psychological perspective, it is important to understand whether there are styles in how individuals approach an opportunity to engage in or modify a healthy or unhealthy practice.

Social Norms and Social comparison: It is also important to understand the objective features of the social context which affect people's health. Individual's perceptions of social norms and their reliance on social comparison process affect how they think and reason about their health. For example, adolescents and young adults' health risk behaviour (sexual, alcohol and smoking) and health seeking behaviour largely depend on perceived social norms and social comparisons. Adjustments and coping behaviour of people suffering from chronic illnesses also depend on the social comparison process and awareness.

Health Communication and Social Marketing: Health care and health promotion are complex human endeavours. While communication research focuses on messages, psychological research focuses on meanings. Social psychology of health deal with the issue of how message and meaning interrelate in the pursuit of health and well-being. The health communications field has been rapidly changing over the past two decades. Social marketing was "born" as a discipline in the 1970s, when Philip Kotler and Gerald Zaltman realized that the same marketing principles that were being used to sell products to consumers could be used to "sell" ideas, attitudes and behaviours (Kotler & Zaltman, 1970). Kotler and Andreasen define social marketing as "differing from other areas of marketing only with respect to the objectives of the marketer and his or her organization. Social marketing seeks to influence social behaviours not to benefit the marketer, but to benefit the target audience and the general society." (as cited in Weinreich, 2010). Social Marketing is an approach used to develop activities aimed at changing or maintaining people's behaviour for their benefit. Social marketing is the systematic application of marketing, along with other concepts and techniques, to achieve specific behavioural goals for a social good. For example, this may include asking people not to smoke in public areas, asking them to use seat belts, or prompting to make them follow speed limits. This technique has been used extensively in international health programmes, especially for contraceptives and oral rehydration therapy (ORT), and is being used with more frequency in the United States for such diverse topics as drug abuse, heart disease and organ donation. In India, AIDS controlling programmes are largely using social marketing. Also, Indian government has been successful in eradicating polio through social marketing. Successful social marketing strategies can work wonders in the field of public health and can ensure the success of public health campaigns by motivating large-scale behaviour change in the general public. Moreover, successful social marketing can promote health as well as prevent incurable health complications. Some of the recently launched social marketing initiatives are to get a blood assay done to check against thalassemia before tying the nuptial knot and urge to donate blood by healthy individuals above the age of 18.

Health Awareness and Behaviour: Health behaviour is influenced by health related cognitions like knowledge and awareness about the diseases. Awareness studies are significant since they provide information on the current status of knowledge of people, about ethology of a disease, and lifestyle factors in illness prevention (Parasher, 2000). In case of coronary patients, knowledge about the disease and health behaviour/practices is found to be significantly related to each other (Latha & Suresh, 2002). Jejebhoy (1998) reviewed research concerning sexual and reproductive behaviour including reproductive morbidity, abortion seeking and reproductive choice. Other factors determining family planning and reproductive health behaviour are: religiosity, value orientation, fatalism, women empowerment, and future orientation in family planning behaviour (see Sharma & Mishra, 2010). Social taboos, misconceptions about sex and sexuality, sex related myths and unsafe sexual behaviour are seen as pressers to marital distress and life threatening diseases like HIV/AIDS. A large gap has been documented between actual and deserved knowledge and beliefs and practices about reproductive health (Kumar, Raizada, Agarwal, Kaur, 2000), and sexual health (Biswas & Daftuar, 2000). Thus, awareness and knowledge about infections/communicable as well as non-communicable diseases have implications for health behaviour and practices of individuals.

Psycho-social Factors

Social Relationships and Support: Talking about social psychology of health, the effect of social relationships and social culture on health behaviour, decision making, and health consequences cannot be undermined. Our social relationships can both inspire us to engage in salubrious behaviour and motivate us to take necessary risks. Social support particularly may be health enhancing and sometimes health damaging in clinical and indirect ways. Particularly, in case of chronic illness, the support from spouse, children and families can play a major role in terms of health well-being of individuals.

Care-giving and Health: Support and care giving on the other hand, may prove itself quite damaging from the health point of view of the caregiver. A chronic illness affects and get affected by the family context, specifically in Indian settings. As the care providers are mostly women (spouse or mothers), there is a tremendous emotional and physical cost to the caring. Mothers and primary caregivers of physically and mentally challenged children are more vulnerable to stress incurred health problems and their well-being is seriously threatened (Bhan, Mehta, and Chhaproo, 1998; Dalal and Pande, 1997; Tripathi and Agarwal, 2000). Parental psychological adaptation to such chronic illnesses in their children largely depends on the severity of child's illness, satisfaction with available social support and the strength of religious beliefs (Pal, Choudhury, Das and

Sengupta, 2002). Prema and Kodandaram (1998) have highlighted the severity of the burden experienced by family members (especially by female members) of caring for the patients suffering major affective disorders. Counselling to the primary caregivers through professionals about realistic expectations and ramification of these chronic illnesses can be helpful. Thus, when on one hand, positive and task oriented coping with the help of family and friends may play a protective factor for these primary caregivers, on the other hand; broader socio-structural contexts should be sensitized to the issues of gender inequalities in family caregiving, and addressed through issues of public health policies.

Physical Activity as a Social Value: Physical inactivity has a major health effect worldwide. Decrease in or removal of this unhealthy behaviour could improve health substantially. Physical inactivity increases the risk of many adverse health conditions, including major non-communicable diseases such as coronary heart disease, type 2 diabetes, and breast and colon cancers, and shortens life expectancy (Lee, Shiroma, Lobelo, Puska, Blair, & Katzmarzyk, 2012). Because much of the India's middle class and upper class population are inactive, this link presents a major public health issue. Developing health as a value and integrating it in the socio-cultural existence of the individual may help promote exercise and other indigenous health enhancing practices like yoga and meditation in the population, thus, protecting against lifestyle related health problems.

Stigma: "Stigma is typically a social process, experienced or anticipated, characterized by exclusion, rejection, blame, or devaluation, which results from experience or reasonable anticipation of an adverse social judgment about a person or group. This judgment is based on an enduring feature of identity conferred by a health problem or health-related condition, and the judgment is in some essential way medically unwarranted". (Weiss and Ramakrishna, 2004, p. 13). It is not only applied to persons or a group, the discriminatory social judgment may also be applied to the disease or designated health problem itself with repercussions in social and health policy. Other forms of stigma, which result from adverse social judgments about enduring features of identity apart from health-related conditions (e.g., race, ethnicity, sexual preferences) also, play a major role in the health choices of individuals. When the individual suffers from a stigmatized disease and belong to a discriminated group, the person has to bear the cumulative effect of the both.

The emotional impact of social and cultural meanings of illness indicates the various ways by which stigma operates. Social science research on stigma regards it fundamentally as a problem arising from social interactions. But Goffman and other researchers (as cited in Weiss & Ramachandran, 2004) have also recognized self-perceived stigma, or the impact of anticipated interactions, which may be as distressing as actual interactions. Each of these various aspects of stigma may impair quality of life from experiences or concerns about disclosure, and effects on work, education, marriage, and family life. Stigma contributes to what a WHO fact sheet identifies as the hidden burden of mental illness (WHO, 2001), and it constitutes a hidden burden for other stigmatized conditions as well. Research also shows that stigma and labelling may affect the course of recovery (Link *et al.*, 1991; Wahl, 1999). Although denial may relieve the emotional discomfort that results from stigma, denial is a problem when it interferes with timely and appropriate help seeking and treatment.

The stigmatization of HIV/AIDS and specific groups at risks such as men, who have sex with men, drug users using untreated needles, etc., shy away from voluntary testing, counselling and treatment. Timely treatment, benefits the individual and society by reducing suffering, improving health and productivity, and limiting opportunities for spread (Chesney and Smith, 1999). For example, leprosy, one of the most stigmatized diseases, may progress late in its course to preventable deformities. Tuberculosis not only becomes more serious for the infected individual, but also poses a threat for contacts and further spread, and it may also promote development of drug resistance. For diseases that require a relatively long course of treatment (like leprosy and TB), or chronic disorders that require chronic treatment (like epilepsy), stigma constitutes an obstacle to continuing or remaining in treatment.

People living with HIV are stigmatized leading to severe social consequences related to their rights, health care services, freedom, self-identity and social interactions. It also severely hampers the treatment and diagnosis of HIV contributing to further spread of the disease (Bharat, 1999; Mawar & Paranjape, 2002; Piot, 2002). AIDS-related stigma has had a profound effect on the epidemic's course. The WHO cites fear of stigma and discrimination as the main reason why people are reluctant to be tested, to disclose HIV status or to take antiretroviral drugs (World Health Organization, 2008). These factors all contribute to the expansion of the epidemic (as a reluctance to determine HIV status or to discuss or practice safe sex means that people are more likely to infect others) and a higher number of AIDS-related deaths. An unwillingness to take an HIV test means that more people are diagnosed late, when the virus has already progressed to AIDS, making treatment less effective and causing early death. Thus, the importance of accounting for particular features of stigmatised health problems and their socio-cultural contexts needs to be studied. This will further help to identify the determinants and effects of the stigma associated with the particular health problems and would recognize its practical significance for specific health policies.

Patient-Physician Relationship: Patient-physician relationship, trust and reported satisfaction of the patients are off-shoots of the social context of health care systems. Patients' trust in their physicians is vital for a successful treatment relationship, which is important for achieving desired treatment outcomes. Trust is especially salient in critical medical situations, such as serious side-effects, hospitalizations, and diagnoses of serious medical conditions Hospitalization, perceived seriousness of condition, and concerns about the risks of medications were found to be associated with patient trust in physicians or the medical profession. These findings highlight the salience of trust in serious physician-patient encounters and the role that patient vulnerability plays in determining patient trust (Shenolikar, Balkrishnan, & Hall, 2004). Trust in physicians is a positive acceptance of a vulnerable situation in which patients believe that physicians will care for their interests.

One of the most important and thoroughly researched aspects of health behaviour is the patient's adherence (or compliance) to the physician's advice or prescribed medical regimen. More often than not, it has been reported that a good patient-physician relationship is a precursor to the adherence of the regimen by the patient. Examining the extent to which patients' trust their physicians may moderate the impact of economic constraints and other risk factors for cost-related adherence problems, research findings have suggested that a trusting patient-physician relationship may moderate the impact of cost pressures on patients' medication adherence (Piette, Heisler, Krein, & Kerr, 2005). Therefore, creating awareness among the doctors and patients about the factors which may lead to good patient-physician relationship and trust in various cultural contexts will lead to adherence to medical regimens and thus, to health promoting behaviour.

Socio-structural Factors

***Socio-economic Status**:* In most of the developing countries the social rubric is uneven and disparity in socio-economic status affects life styles and life courses very differently. In India, persons in the lower socio-economic class have been found to display poorer physical and mental health and well-being as indicated by self-repost measures of efficacy, adjustment, life satisfaction, coping and quality of life. Studies have reported that chronic preoccupations of very poor illiterates living in remote villages include, livelihood stress, sexual conflicts (extramarital relations) and familial conflicts (Chakroborti, Kulhara & Verma, 1992). Moreover, tribal status also contributes to stress systems of poor quality of living (Singh, 1993). Thus, the social class and status may be indicative of health behaviour and practices adopted by the individuals.

Family Structure: Social relations in Indian context need to be understood structurally as the social-networks, and functionally as the nature of social support. (Sharma & Misra, 2010). The family or household is the most important social sub-system which regularizes several domains of behaviour including health behaviour and practices. Some studies have dealt with the efficacy of nuclear and joint families or environment. In a study of 50 cardiac patients admitted in ICU for cardiac care, when patients were asked about their post-surgery or post-hospitalization health related decisions or behaviour change, it was indicated by most of them that the changes in health behaviour and practices would be decided jointly by the family members or with the spouse and children (Panchakshri, 2010). Nonetheless in the collectivist societies where health behaviours are largely contingent upon socio-cultural construction of health beliefs and practice, the functional content of family relations seems important as compared to structural aspects of the family for explaining and promoting health behaviour. However, the role of family and social relations in shaping health behaviour and practices needs to the further explored, which would strengthen the health care systems in the socio-cultural context of the society.

Residential Density and Environmental Hazards: Slums, suburbs and other residential areas which cater to the low socio-economic group population are generally associated with residential crowding, pollution and are devoid of facilities for basic civic amenities. Living in such a habitat has got long-term negative consequences on physical and psychological health of the residents. (See Sharma & Mishra, 2010). Environmental hazards, specifically biological pathogen, physical hazards, chemical pollutants, and shortage of specific natural resources are proving to be crucial factors affecting the physical and mental health of residents of these locations. Moreover, contaminations of human environment, air, water, oil etc. with these biological pathogens have indications for water-borne diseases, respiratory infections, tuberculosis etc. Since food, fuel, fresh water and hygienic living conditions are central to health, the environmental dimension has got serious impact on health behaviour and practices of individuals. In a study of 10 to 12 year old children in Pune city (Evans, Lepore, Shejwal & Palsane, 1998), reported that chronic residential crowding is associated with difficulties in adjustment at school, elevated blood pressure, helplessness and poor academic achievement. Several researches in India substantiate the impact of crowding and environmental hazards on health behaviour and practices (Arora & Sinha, 1998, Pandey, 2003).

Rural to Urban Migration and Urbanization: The potential health impacts of rural to urban migration experience have not been thoroughly and systematically explored. Still, it is believed to significantly affect various dimensions of the migrants' well-being. VanLandingham (2003) conducted a multidimensional health assessment of migrant population to systematically investigate these potential impacts. Migrants are disadvantaged with respect to non-migrants on several of these dimensions of health status, including physical functioning; role limitations due to physical health problems; bodily pain; general mental health; role limitations due to emotional problems; and general health perceptions. These differences are maintained in models that control for differences in distributions of age, sex, and socio-economic status between the two groups. (VanLandingham, 2003). In yet another study carried out to examine whether permanent settlement and within-province migration patterns are linked to mental health diagnoses among adolescents (15 to 19 years old), young adults (20 to 30 years old), and adults (30 years old and older) who grew up in rural or urban communities or migrated between types of community (N = 8,502), Maggi and her associates (2010) conclusively reported that, mental health diagnoses were selectively associated with stability and migration patterns. Specifically, adolescents and young adults who were born in and grew up in the same rural community were at lower risk of being diagnosed with acute reaction to stress and depression compared to their matched controls that were not born in and did not grow up in the same rural community. Furthermore, adolescents and young adults migrating between rural communities were at lower risk of being diagnosed with adjustment reaction than those not migrating between rural communities. The study provides some compelling evidence of the protective role of rural environments in the development of specific mental health conditions (*i.e.*, depression, adjustment reaction, and acute reaction to stress) among the children of sawmill workers in Western Canada (Maggi *et al.*, 2010).

Migrants who migrate from rural to urban areas, experience the environmental changes associated with rapid urbanization, thus enabling epidemiologic transitions. Recent data on rural-urban migrants in India have shown that migration is associated with marked increases in obesity and diabetes (Ebrahim *et al.*, 2010). The diets of migrants of rural origin, their rural dwelling sibs, and those of urban origin together with their urban dwelling sibs were assessed by Bowen *et al.* (2011) and they concluded that, rural to urban migration appears to be associated with both positive (higher fruit and vegetables intake) and negative (higher energy and fat intake) dietary changes. These changes may be of relevance to cardiovascular health and warrant public health interventions.

Not only rural to urban migration, but large scale urbanization also leads to public health outcomes. The range of disorders and deviancies associated with urbanization is enormous and includes psychoses, depression, sociopathy, substance abuse, alcoholism, crime, delinquency, vandalism, family disintegration, and alienation (Trivedi, Sareen and Dhyani, 2008). Negative impact is also experienced by behaviour constraints practiced or imposed upon the urban people. If behaviour is unduly suppressive, it may result in learned helplessness leading to stress-related disorders (Stokols, 1978). The mental health problems which results from urbanisation and rural to urban migration, in turn affects the physical health of the individuals.

Rapid urbanization puts immense pressure on both physician and patient. Sound doctor-patient relationship becomes almost impossible in busy clinics. In view of large number of patients, time constraints and wide range of diseases, making accurate diagnosis and proper follow-up are almost impracticable. This leads to a high rate of clinical errors and superfluous diagnostic tests. During the visits to the slums, and sub-urban residential areas in Ahmedabad, Surat and Vadodara (the major cities of Gujarat) to evaluate the Target Intervention Projects funded by National AIDS Control Society for HIV risk reduction and behaviour change communication among the high risk target groups, the author discovered the stark reality of available quality of health care services to these migrant populations. Mostly, the service of trained MBBS doctors was not accessible to people living in these extended city areas, and slum communities. Unethical medical practices are rampant in these areas. In order to avoid the cost and distance that they have to visit, migrants and slum dwellers keep visiting these medical practitioners and their clinics which lack basic facilities and infrastructures where half the time wrong diagnosis and treatment complicates the cases and the treatment continues for months without any effective results.

In addition to this, cities extend beyond the limits of the municipality area as a result of rapid urbanization. Because of lack of civic amenities, like drinking water etc., these in-state and out-state migrants are susceptible to malaria, typhoid, diarrhoea etc.

Urbanization alters the dynamics of society at large and family in particular. Rapid urbanization has created a huge population of older men and women left to fend for themselves in the rural areas while the young make their living in the cities. This also means less availability of caregivers when older people fall ill. In developed countries, with their comprehensive health and social care systems, the vital caring role of families, and their need for support, is often overlooked. Conversely, in developing countries, the reliability and universality of the family care system is often overestimated; older people are among the most vulnerable groups, in part because of the continuing myths that surround their place in society (see Trivedi *et al.*, 2008). Urbanization affects young and old alike as far as the health implications are concerned. Children and adolescents in socio-economically deprived urban areas are often drawn to antisocial behaviour. Moreover, being away from the native villages and kinship networks gives a feeling embarking on lack of socio-cultural identity and a sense of anonymity to the migrants and slum adolescents. The slum adolescents are more vulnerable to high risk behaviours, e.g., drug and alcohol abuse, high risk sexual activities etc. which leads to serious health implications (Daftuar & Biswas, 2000).

Therefore, considering the social psychological perspective of health, all the efforts for developing effective health care services and systems for promotion of health and prevention of diseases, particularly; communicable and infectious diseases should account for the health implications of rural to urban migration and urbanization. Health problems in these communities can be successfully avoided by arresting the precursors early, e.g., high health risk behaviours like smoking, alcoholism, drug abuse, high risk sexual practices, and irregular, erratic lifestyles. Moreover, promoting health seeking behaviour among these communities by making public health services available at their door-step can save the nation a lot of resources, financial, and human as well.

Conclusion

As it has been understood by now, health and disease processes cannot be deliberated and dealt with only focusing on individual's health habits, practices, behaviours, attitudes and beliefs about health. Individuals' choices, practices, beliefs and attitudes are strongly rooted in their socio-cultural context, mediated by ecological and structural issues. Sharma & Mishra (2010) argue that health needs to be understood in the ecological context of people, which is critical to the construction, and experience of health and illness. This becomes more pertinent in view of the current realization that health is not simply the absence of illness. It is closer to the Indian view that treats health holistically as a state of delight or a feeling of spiritual, physical and mental well-being. Yet, the lived meaning of health is quite diverse, depending on the social world of people and their perception. This makes understanding the socio-cultural construction of causation of illness and well-being relevant. Therefore, all efforts made by the individuals, health practitioners and public health policy makers to prevent diseases and promote health and well-being should be aligned with the paradigmatic shift from clinical diagnosis, treatment and maintenance in a clinical context to preventive and promotive measures in the socio-cultural, ecological context.

The nature and pattern of illnesses are changing along with socio-economic growth and resultant socio-structural changes. The development in modern medical sciences, and affordability to these medical privileges, has rather made the effect of chronic diseases more pronounced and widespread in Indian society. Moreover, the growing ageing population, weakening joint family system, the quantum increase of women in the workforce, and changing societal values have made the role of caregiving and health delivery system more pertinent for maintenance and sustenance of health in the society. In this context, integrating the traditional health care systems into the public health care and delivery system may prove beneficial. The problems of accessibility to primary health care as faced by the ageing population living alone in villages and remote places can be dealt by promoting Ayurvedic medicines, *yoga*, *pranayama* and other indigenous systems.

Reviving the traditional preventive health care measures like meditation, *yoga*, and *pranayama* as a part of the daily life can be an effective strategy against all life-style related diseases. Habits are inculcated early in life. The national curriculum for pre-school/ primary school education may integrate these indigenous practices as a part of life-skills training to inculcate health habits that not only acts as a preventive measure but also integrate seamlessly with the socio-cultural milieu. Though sporadic efforts are made intermittently, there is a lack of systematic efforts in building it into school level curricula and make it part of the educational process. This can be done through policy level decisions. The ramification of physical inactivity which is regarded as the prime cause for growing prevalence of CHD as a major cause of death can be fought back systematically by inculcating physical activity as a value in the society by encouraging sports/athletics in schools, and in social life.

Understanding health at individual level raises three main questions. 'Who becomes sick and why?', 'among the sick who recovers and why?', 'who succumbs to the faster disease progression and why?' Research has demonstrated that, the level of health and illness are jointly determined by socio-structural environment and psychosocial factors. Research related to issues of coping with chronic illness have identified some of the factors as social support, future complication in dealing with work and social life, emotional and sexual problems, perceived rejection and stigma. In an earlier study, Wahengbam (2003), in her research on institutionalized HIV positive people, and drug addicts, has reported that, individuals who express their emotions more, and who ask for support actually receive more support, whether it is social, financial or medical. This, implies that support seeking, as well as having a support network, helps people cope better with diseases and health problems. Thus, establishing networks with people with similar health problems, eliminates the fear of future complications, results in more disclosure, and promotes more health seeking behaviour. For example, it has been successful in case of '*positive people's network*', meant for HIV positive people in different cities and states. It has helped them to fight the fear of stigmatized existence, rejection, vent out their emotional problems and conflicts, have better subjective well-being and cope better. Health care practitioners should facilitate to develop these networks among people suffering from various life threatening chronic diseases, and other stigmatized health conditions, in order to promote subjective well-being and social well-being among them.

At the community level, the pertinent issues are, 'how disease disclosure can be encouraged', 'how health seeking behaviour can be improved?', and 'how can illness be prevented and health be promoted?' Lack of awareness, stigma, and discrimination are the three major barriers to the disclosure of disease status to family members and doctors. Moreover, denial and undermining the implications of the disease, impairs health seeking behaviour. Particularly, mental health disorders, reproductive health problems, if overlooked at the initial stages can lead to complications later on leading to complex process and longer duration of treatment.

Thus, creating awareness and psycho-education about implications of diseases can promote health seeking behaviour. Similarly, certain health problems can be prevented by taking precautionary measures. Working on strategies to prevent high risk behaviour among adolescents can reduce the risk of sexual health related problems, problems of tobacco use, alcoholism, drug-abuse, etc.

Illness prevention and health promotion initiatives include: (i) individual based interventions and (ii) community based interventions – programmes aimed at the prevention of illness and promotion of health. Now these initiatives have an added facet of social marketing. Social marketing of public health campaigns, and programmes have brought significant differences in behaviour change, at individual as well as at community level. If such programmes could be based on the understanding of traditions, belief systems, pattern of family and community interactions and indigenous resources, it can appeal the individual's convictions. Culturally sensitive therapeutic techniques can be used to promote health and well-being effectively. Social psychology of health emphasizes the importance of multi-level interventions. Individual based interventions in clinical context should be supplemented with community level interventions, and large-scale social marketing for disease prevention and health promotion.

REFERENCES

Arora, P. & Sinha, P. (1998). A study of relationship between perception of residential crowding, personality characteristics and need pattern among adolescents. *Social Science International,* 14, 46-59.

Bhan, S.; Mehta, D. & Chhaproo, Y. (1998). Stress experienced and coping methods used by mothers of children with cerebral palsy. *Prachii Journal of Psycho-Cultural Dimensions*, 14, 15-19.

Bharat, S. (1999). *HIV/AIDS related discrimination, stigmatization and denial in India - A study based in Mumbai and Bangalore* (sponsored by UNAIDS, Geneva, TISS Mumbai).

Biswas, U.N., & Daftuar, C.N. (2000). Adolescence, sexuality and health: Awareness and perceived constraints among out-of-school slum children. In U. Vindhya (Ed.), *Psychology in India: Intersecting Cross-Roads* (pp. 176-201). New Delhi: Concept.

Bowen L.; Ebrahim S.; De Stavola B.; Ness A.; Kinra S.; Bharathi, A.V.; Prabhakaran, D. & Reddy, K.S. (2011). Dietary Intake and Rural-Urban Migration in India: A Cross-Sectional Study. PLoS ONE 6 (6): e14822. doi: 10.1371/journal. pone. 0014822

Chakraborti, S.; Kulhara, P. & Verma, S.K. (1992). Extent and determinants of burden among families of patients with affective disorders. *Acta Psychiatrica Scandinavica*, 86, 247-252.

Chesney, M.A. & Smith, A.W. Critical delays in HIV testing and care: the potential role of stigma. *Amercian Behavioural Scientist*, 42 (7): 1162-1174, 1999.

Chongsuvivatwong, V.; Hong, K.; Yap, M.T.; Pocock, N.S.; Hashim, J.H.; Chhem, R.; Wilopo, S.A.; & Lopez, A.D. (2011). Health and health-care systems in Southeast Asia: Diversity and transitions. *The Lancet*, Volume 377, Issue 9763, 429-437.

Dalal, A.K. & Mishra, G. (2006). The Psychology of Health and Well-being: Some emerging perspectives. *Psychological Studies*, 51 (2-3), 91-104.

Dalal, A. & Mishra, G. (2012). Psychology of Health and Well-being: Emergence and Development. In A. Dalal and G. Mishra (Eds.), *New Directions in Health Psychology*, pp. 1-45. New Delhi: Sage.

Dalal, A.K. & Pande, N. (1997). A community intervention programme for changing attitude with disability. *The Social Engineer*, 4, 16-25.

Dalal, A.K. & Pande, N. (1999). Cultural beliefs and family care of the children with disability. *Psychology and Developing Societies*, 11, 55-75.

Ebrahim S.; Kinra S.; Bowen L.; Andersen E.; Ben-Shlomo Y.; Lyngdoh, T.; & Reddy, K.S. (2010). The Effect of Rural-to-Urban Migration on Obesity and Diabetes in India: A Cross-Sectional Study. PLoS Med 7: e1000268

Evans, G.W.; Lepore, S.I.; Shejwal, B.R. & Palsane, M.N. (1998). Chronic residential crowding and children's well-being: An ecological Perspective. *Child Development*, 69, 1514-1523.

Gill, A. & Singh L. Farmers' suicides and response of public policy: evidence, diagnosis and alternatives from Punjab. *Economic and Political Weekly*, 27662–68.

Gupta, R. (2006) Smoking, educational status and health inequity in India. *Indian Journal of Medical Research*; 124, 15-22.

Jejebhoy, S.J. (1998). Adolescent sexual and reproductive behaviour: A review of the evidence from India. *Social Science and Medicine*, 46, 1275-1290.

Kakar, S. (1982). *Shamans, Mystics and Doctors. A Psychological Inquiry into India and its Healing Tradions.* Oxford University Press, New Delhi.

Khatoon, N. (2012). *Health Psychology*. The Pearson-ICFAI University Series. Pearson Education, New Delhi.

Kinra S.; Rameshwar Sarma; K.V., Ghafoorunissa, *et al.,* (2008). Effect ofintegration of supplemental nutrition with public health programmes in pregnancy and early childhood on cardiovascular risk in rural Indian adolescents: long term follow-up of Hyderabad nutrition trial. *Behavioural Medicine Journal*, 337: a605.

Kotler, P. & Zaltman, G. (1971). Social marketing: an approach to planned social change. *Journal of Marketing*, 35, 3-12.

Kumar, R.; Raizada, A.; Agarwal, A.K. & Kaur, M. (2000). Adolescent behaviour regarding reproductive health. *Indian Journal of Pediatrics*, 67, 877-882.

Latha, K.S. & Suresh, A. (2002). Knowledge, Attitude and Practice (KAP): A study in coronary artery disease. *Psychological Studies*, 47, 100-105.

Lee, I.; Shiroma, E.J.; Lobelo, F.; Puska, P.; Blair, S.N. & Katzmarzyk, P.T. (2012). Effect of physical inactivity on major non-communicable diseases worldwide: an analysis of burden of disease and life expectancy. *The Lancet*, 380 (9838), 219-229.

Link, B.G. & Phelan, Jo C. (2001). Conceptualizing stigma. *Annual Review of Sociology*, 27: 363-385.

Maggi, S.; Ostry, A.; Callaghan, K.; Hershler, R.; Chen, L.; D'Angiulli, A. & Hertzman, C. (2010). Rural-urban migration patterns and mental health diagnoses of adolescents and young adults in British Columbia, Canada: a case-control study. *Child and Adolescent Psychiatry and Mental Health*, 4: 13 doi: 10.1186/1753-2000-4-13

Maselko, J. & Patel, V. (2008). Why women attempt suicide: the role of mental illness and social disadvantage in a community cohort study in India. *J Epidemiol Community Health*, 62: 817-22.

Mawar, N.; & Paranjape, R.S. (2002) Live and Let Live: Acceptance of people living with HIV/AIDS in an era where stigma and discrimination persist. *Indian Council of Medical Research Bulletin*, 32: 105-14.

McGuire, W.J. (1991). Using guiding idea theories of the person to develop educational campaigns against drug abuse and other health threatening behaviour. *Health Education* Research, 6, 173-184.

Mohan V.; Mathur P.; Deepa R. *et al.,* (2008). Urban rural differences in prevalence of self-reported diabetes in India—the WHO-ICMR Indian NCD risk factor surveillance. *Diabetes Research and Clinical Practice*, 80, 159-68.

National Crime Records Bureau. *Accidental deaths and suicides in India.* New Delhi: Ministry of Home Affairs, Government of India; 2007. http://ncrb. nic. in/adsi/data/ADSI2007/home. htm (accessed August, 2012).

Pal, D.K.; Chaudhury, G.; Das, T. & Sengupta, S. (2002). Predictors of parental adjustment to children's epilepsy in rural India. *Childcare, Health and Development*, 28, 295-300.

Panchakshari, D. (2010). *Perception of Trust in Patient-Physician Relationship*. Unpublished Masters Dissertation submitted to Department of Psychology, The M.S. University of Baroda, Vadodara, Gujarat, India.

Pandey, S. (2003). An empirical study of the role of perceived control in coping with residential crowding. In A. Agarwal and A.K. Saxena (Eds.), *Psychological Perspectives in Environmental and Developmental Issues* (pp. 170-183). New Delhi: Concept.

Parasher, R.P. (2000). Lifestyle for perfect health. *Psychological Studies*, 45, 167-172.

Patel V., Araya R., Lewis G. & Swartz L. (2001). *Socio-economic factors and mental health. Mental Health: a call for action by World Health Ministers.* Geneva: World Health Organization.

Patel, V.; Chatterji, S.; Chisholm, D.; Shah, E.; Gopalakrishna, G., Mathers, C.; Mohan, V.; Prabhakaran, D.; Ravindran, R.D. & Reddy, K.S. (2011). India: Chronic diseases and injuries in India: Towards Universal Health Coverage (3), *The Lancet*, 377 (9763), 413-428.

Piette, J.D.; Heisler, M.; Krein, S. & Kerr, E.A. (2005). The role of patient-physician trust in moderating medication non-adherence due to cost pressures. *Archival International Medicine*, Aug. 8-22; 165 (15): 1749-55.

Prema, T.P., & Kodandaram, P. (1998). Impact of mental health education on "distress experience" by the family members of the chronically mentally ill. *Indian Journal of Clinical Psychology*, 25, 174-177.

Ramachandran, A. (2007). *Epidemiology of diabetes in India*. New Delhi: Jaypee.

Reddy K.S.; Prabhakaran D.; Jeemon P., *et al.*, (2007). Educational status and cardiovascular risk profile in Indians. *Proc Natl Acad Sci.*, USA; 104: 16263-68.

Rosenstock, I.M. (2000). Health Belief Model. In Kazdin, Alan E. (Ed), Encyclopedia of Psychology, Vol. 4., pp. 78-80. New York, NY, US: Oxford University Press, WHO (2008) Towards Universal Access: Scaling up priority HIV/AIDS interventions in the health sector: Progress Report, 2008.

Salovey, P. & Rothman, A.J. (2003). Social Psychology of Health Key Readings in Social Psychology: An Overview. In P. Salovey & A.J. Rothman (Eds.) *Social Psychology of Health Key Readings*, pp. 1-4. Psychology Press, New York.

Sharma, D.C. (2010). India's no. 1 killer: Heart disease. *Mail Today*, India Today (New Delhi, April 12) retrieved from *http://indiatoday.intoday.in/story/India's+no.1+killer: +Heart+disease/1/92422.html* on 30th June, 2012.

Sharma, S. & Mishra, G. (2010). Health Psychology: Progress and Challenges. In G. Mishra (Ed.), *Psychology in India*, Vol. 3, pp. 265-316. ICSSR Survey of Advances in Research. New Delhi: Pearson.

Shenolikar, R.A.; Balkrishnan, R. & Hall, M.A. (2004). How patient-physician encounters in critical medical situations affect trust: results of a national survey. *BMC Health Services Research*, 4 (24).

Singh, A.K. (1993). Impact of acculturation on mental health of the tribal. *Psychological Studies,* 38, 55-58.

Stockols, D. (1978). A typology of crowding experiences. In: Baum A., Epstein Y, (ed.) *Human Response to Crowding*. Hill Sadale NJ: Erlbaum.

Tripathi, I.; and Agarwal, A. (2003). Coping with chronic illness, symptoms and efficacy in children as related to some psychological charecteristics of mothers. *Psychology and Developing Societies*, 12, 31-42.

Trivedi, J.K.; Sareen, H. & Dhyani, M. (2008). Rapid urbanization - Its impact on mental health: A South Asian perspective. *Indian J. Psychiatry* Jul-Sep; 50 (3): 161–165.doi:10.4103/0019-5545.43623 PMCID: PMC2738359

UNAIDS World AIDS Day message: Dr Peter Piot (1 December 2002) Available at *http: //www.unaids.org/whatsnew/speeches/eng/2002/WAD02PPmessage_en.html*.

UNAIDS, Geneva. World Health Organization. *The 'undefined and hidden' burden of mental health problems*. Fact sheet Number 218. Revised November 2001.

Ustun, T.B.; Chatterji S.; Mechbal A. & Murray, C.J.L. (2003). W.H.S.

Collaborating Groups. The world health surveys in health systems performance assessment: debates, methods and empiricism. Geneva: World Health Organization.

VanLandingham, M. (2003). Impacts of Rural to Urban Migration on the Health of Young Adult Migrants in Ho Chi Minh City, Vietnam. Paper prepared for Conference on African Migration in Comparative Perspective, Johannesburg, South Africa, 4-7 June, 2003.

Wahengbam, J. (2003). *A Study of Emotional Quotients, Spiritual Quotients and Social Support Network among the Drug Addicts and HIV Positive Individuals.* An unpublished Master's Dissertation, Department of Psychology, The M.S. University of Baroda, Vadodara, India.

Wahl, Otto F. (1999). Mental health consumers' experience of stigma. *Schizophrenia Bulletin* 25 (3): 467-478.

Weinreich, N.K. (2010). *Hands-On Social Marketing: A Step-by-Step Guide to Designing Change for Good* (2nd Edition). Sage Publications, New York.

WHO. Closing the gap in a generation (2008). *http: //whqlibdoc. who. int/hq/2008/WHO_IER_CSDH_08.1_eng. pdf* (accessed Nov. 9, 2010).

WHO. Global health risks: Mortality and burden of disease attributable to selected major risks. *http: //www. who. int/healthinfo/global_burden_disease/GlobalHealthRisks_report_full. pdf* (accessed July 4, 2012).

WHO. The global burden of disease (2004) update. *http: //www. who. int/healthinfo/global_burden_disease/GBD_report_2004update_full. pdf* (accessed July 4, 2012).

Yusuf S.; Hawken S.; Ounpuu S. *et al.* (2004), Effect of potentially modifiable risk factors associated with myocardial infarction in 52 countries (the INTERHEART study): case-control study. *The Lancet*; 364: 937–52.

2

Freedom and Reactance: The Case of Social Marketing for Public Health

Nilamadhab Mohanty and *Saswata Narayan Biswas*

Introduction

The utility of social marketing as a tool for addressing public health issues has been widely acclaimed by both government and non-government agencies in several countries. In USA, interventions to influence voluntary lifestyle behaviours, like; smoking, drinking, drug use and diet are being guided by the principles of social marketing (CDC, 2005). Department of Health, UK has recognized the impact of social marketing for public awareness, behaviour change and social good (Department of Health, UK, 2004). In a similar fashion National Consumer Council and the Department of Health has acknowledged the contribution of social marketing towards improvement of health and reduction of health inequalities (NCC/DH, 2005). In addition to the above programmes U.S. Department of Agriculture, U.S. Department of Health and Human Services, and many other federal, state, and local governmental and non-profit organizations are actively engaged in social marketing activities to accomplish public health objectives.

It has been more than four decades since the introduction of the concept of social marketing (Kotler & Zaltman, 1971) and more than two decades since it got established as a component of public health practice (Coreil, Bryant & Henderson, 2000; McDermott, 2000). But still social marketing is successful in carving out new areas of intervention in the field of public health. Application of the principles of social marketing has been reported in the promotion of increased fruit and vegetable consumption, physical activity, Special Supplemental Nutrition Programme for Women, Infants, and Children (WIC) and Food Stamps (Kotler, Roberto & Lee, 2002). Apart from these breast cancer screening (Bryant, Cole, 1996), breast feeding (Lindenberger & Bryant, 2000), physical activity and nutrition (Salazar, Lindenberger, 2001), condom use (Cohen *et al.,* 1999), nutrition education (Young, Anderson, Beckstrom, Bellows & Johnson, 2004), and physical activity among teens (Wong *et al.,* 2004) are some other public health programmes where social marketing principles are being used effectively for design, implementation and evaluation of the intervention.

The main principle underlying above public health intervention through social marketing has been behaviour change. Behaviour change is achieved through any of the four different appeals viz., behaviour modification, behaviour retention, behaviour development, or behaviour rejection. This process is accomplished through the use of tools and techniques of marketing and guided by the theories and principles of psychology, sociology, anthropology, and communication. The theories so far used are, health belief model, the theory of reasoned action, social cognitive theory, the trans-theoretical model of behaviour change (or "stages of change") and diffusion of innovations. These theories have been utilized to address the issue of rate of adoption of social marketing offer by evaluating the benefits and the barriers/costs associated with the behaviour change process as devised by the social marketing programme. In this process these theories are being related to marketing concepts like exchange theory and segmentation, targeting and positioning to design the social marketing offer in the form of 6Ps viz., product, price, place, promotion, person and policy. However, the research so far in the domain of public health social marketing has failed to address the subject of reactance associated with the behaviour change appeal.

It has been reported that any attempt to bring about a change in an individual's behaviour would lead to the violation of the freedom of choice of the customer which will cause reactance and rejection of the appeal (Brehm, 1966; Brehm & Brehm, 1981; Clee & Wicklund, 1980; Wicklund, 1980). Thus, it is essential for the public health interventions through social marketing approach to take into consideration two factors, namely, the freedom of choice and psychological reactance before formulating any intervention. However, the theories so far guiding social marketing interventions for public health programmes have not addressed properly the role of individual's freedom of choice in acceptance or rejection of behaviour modification offer.

In the backdrop of this information the paper attempts to provide an introductory exposure to the role of freedom of choice and reactance in the process of behaviour change and with an objective to explore the possible scope for the use of theory of reactance in the design, implementation and evaluation of social marketing programmes with public health importance.

Social Marketing

Social marketing has been conceptualised as a process of behaviour change targeted at societal and individual benefit accomplished through the use of marketing tools and techniques. Grier & Bryant (2005) and Lamptey & Price (1998) advocated that under social marketing the behaviour change is voluntary and targeted at a priority population. Others (Andreasen, 2002; Bryant, DeWalt, Courtney & Schwartz, 2003; Glanz & Rimer, 1995; Maibach, 2003; Smith, 1997) characterised this approach as a research driven consumer centred process based on the fundamentals of marketing like notion of exchange and the marketing mix, assessment of competition, branding, audience segmentation, consumer orientation, and careful, continuous monitoring and revision of programme activities. The marketing mix incorporated considerations for product, price, place, promotion, people and policy elements. The formulation of the mix is a long-term planning outlook (Andreasen, 1995) focusing on the consumer orientation (Lefebvre and Flora, 1988; Lefebvre, 1992b; Andreasen, 1995) and guided by the principles of exchange theory (Leathar and Hastings 1987; Lefebvre and Flora, 1988; Lefebvre, 1996; Smith 1997).

Thus, social marketing has been propagated as a practice to aid voluntary behavioural change (Grier and Bryant, 2005; Lamptey & Price, 1998). This is initiated by a social agent who proceeds with some social mission and a specific behavioural goal (Andreasen, 1995). The process is consumer oriented that is the behaviour goal is set considering the audience and the social problem to be addressed and the social marketing interventions are developed taking the consumer had into account (Andreasen, 2002; Grier & Bryant, 2005; Maibach, 2002; Smith, 1997). This attempt of social change through social marketing is based on the concepts of exchange of value (Leathar and Hastings, 1987; Lefebvre and Flora, 1988; Lefebvre, 1996; Houston & Gassenheimer, 1987; Smith, 1997) where the behaviour change is considered to be a process of exchange where costs born and benefits availed by the target audience determine the approach of social marketing. The second concept which social marketing brings to the process of social change is the process of segmentation (Grier & Bryant, 2005), where people are approached after they are grouped or segmented by their values related to a specific behaviour because individuals value different things at different times in exchange for different values (Smith, 2002). The third aspect of social marketing which has tremendous impact on the social change process is the notion of competition. People have choices. Therefore, almost all behaviours compete against other behaviours to provide competitive value to the individual (Smith, 2002). Thus social marketing plan design focuses not only to provide benefits which compensate for the cost incurred by the customer but also surmount the attraction of other competitive behaviours.

Behaviour Change—The Central Concept of Social Marketing

Behaviour change has been conceptualised as the central theme of any social marketing intervention. This could involve acceptance of a new behaviour, rejection of a potential behaviour, modification of a current behaviour or abandonment of an old behaviour (Kotler, Roberto & Lee, 2002). From the marketing intervention standpoint the targeted behaviour could be categorized into a positive (desired) or a negative (undesirable) behaviour and an old or a new behaviour. Thus resulting into four possible options of behaviour intervention viz.: (1) helping the customers to maintain the behaviour: applicable for a desired and old behaviour, (2) developing a new behaviour: for desired and new behaviour, (3) behaviour modification: strategy adopted for an undesirable old behaviour, (4) resisting the development of the behaviour: in case of a undesirable new behaviour. This is shown in Table 2.1.

Table 2.1: Options of behaviour intervention

	Desired Behaviour	*Undesirable Behaviour*
Old Behaviour	Maintain	Change
New Behaviour	Develop	Resist

To aid this process the (social) marketer designs the social marketing mix (Rothschild & Gaidis, 1981), on the basis of fundamental marketing principles which acts as a stimulus to invoke transaction by eliciting the desired behavioural response. Thus, marketer's responsibility in this regard is to design stimuli which are to be used by the individuals to persuade themselves (Simons, 1971) as per the requirement *i.e.,* development of new behaviours, inhibition of "undesired" behaviours and facilitation of the occurrence of desired behaviours which are currently being practiced by the customer (Nord & Peter, 1980). However, any attempt to change behaviour is resisted by the individual. Moreover, before adopting any behaviour modification people evaluate the proposed behaviour in terms of their expectation and the cost and benefit associated with the behaviour change. This prompts the marketer to consider and device mechanisms to help the prospective customer overcome barriers to adopt the proposed behaviour. Different strategies in application in this regard could be enlisted as reinforcement and punishment under Stimulus Response Theory (Skinner, 1953), empowerment under Theory of Freeing (Freire, 1973), provision of benefits which overcomes the perceived barriers under Health Belief Model, or HBM (Rosenstock, Strecher & Becker, 1988) and provision of high levels of information, motivation and behavioural skills by making provisions for knowledge, attitudes, and both generic self-efficacy and instrumental behavioural skills (Fisher, Fisher, Bryan & Misovich, 2002). These strategies thus help the customer avail benefits of exchange, consumption, information availability, and engagement. However, the benefit of marketing which the customer is stripped of due to the behaviour modification process is the choice and the degrees of freedom to buy and consume as per their own preferences. Moreover, the theories serving as the guiding principles for the design of social marketing plans have so far inadequately raised this issue. Considering this as a gap in the research it is attempted, in the following sections, to identify the theories and analyse their contribution towards the design and implementation of social marketing programmes in the context of public health. Subsequently, the debate is furthered using the theory of psychological reactance to discuss the role of freedom and choice in the behaviour modification process.

Theories and Models in Social Marketing

Social marketing, as evident from the above discussion, is an approach to behaviour change which has got two aspects viz., one a social aspect and the second a marketing aspect. The issues of behaviour change targeted at individual and societal welfare are dealt with the help of marketing tools and techniques which are predicted on theories of consumer behaviour. Thus, social marketing draws knowledge from other disciplines like psychology, sociology, and anthropology and communications theory to understand, explain and transform people's behaviour (Kotler & Zaltman, 1971). These theories are utilized to decide upon the selection of target audiences, formulation of questions for formative research studies, selection of intervention strategies, design and implementation of programme elements, and evaluation and measurement of outcomes. In the following section, it is attempted to organise the social marketing programmes targeted at public health context with a focus on the theory utilized and the marketing concept addressed (Table 2.2 and Table 2.3).

Table 2.2: Theories and models in social marketing

Behaviour	*Model*	*References*
Alcohol/Drug Use (Giving Up)	Prochaska and Di Clemente's Transtheoretical Model ('Stages of Change')	Prochaska and Velicer, 1997
Condom Use	Theory of Planned Behaviour	Ajzen, 1991
Preventative Health Behaviours	Rosenstock's Health Belief Model	Becker *et al.*, 1977
Smoking (Giving Up)	Prochaska and Di Clemente's Transtheoretical Model ('Stages of Change')	Prochaska and Velicer,1997
Smoking (Giving Up)	Protection Motivation Theory	Rogers, 1975
Smoking (in Public)	Social Learning Theory (social proof)	Dawnay and Shah, 2005
Taking Exercise	Theory of Planned Behaviour	Ajzen, 1991
Using Contraception	Prochaska and Di Clemente's Transtheoretical Model ('Stages of Change')	Prochaska and Velicer, 1997
Using Sunscreen	Prochaska and Di Clemente's 'Stages of Change': decisional balance	Shepherd, 2006

Table 2.3: Theories and models used in public health interventions

Theory	*Reference*	*Context*
Health Belief Model (HBM)	Strecher & Rosenstock, 1997; Janz & Becker, 1984	Receiving flu shots, practicing breast self-examinations, using seat belts, attending screening programmes compliance with medication regimens, self-help behaviours among people with diabetes, addressing issues for "at risk" populations who may not perceive themselves as such
Theory of Reasoned Action (TRA)	Sutton, Balch & Lefebvre, 1995	Fruits and vegetables eating habit
Social Cognitive Theory (SCT)	Lefebvre, Olander & Levine, 1999	Team nutrition programme for 4th graders
The Transtheoretical Model of Health Behaviour Change	Marcus, Banspach, Lefebvre, Rossi, Carleton & Abams, 1992	To increase physical activity levels of community residents
Health belief model, information-seeking research), information processing models, consumer involvement models, and a typology for consumer motivation	Morris, Tabak & Olins, 1992	Segmentation analysis of prescription drug information-seeking motives among the elderly
Social cognitive theory, the health belief model, and the theory of reasoned action	Slater & Flora, 1991	Healthy lifestyle
Concepts drawn from the fields of anthropology, advertising research and communications literature	Williams & Flora, 1995	Hispanic health

(Contd.)

Table 2.3 (*Contd.*)

Theory	*Reference*	*Context*
Political science and public opinion research and theories	Murray & Douglas, 1988	Alcohol policy arena — to shape social policies about alcohol
Community organization theories	Farquhar, Maccoby & Solomon, 1984	Stanford Five-City Project — community health
Community organization theories	Lefebvre, Lasater, Carleton & Peterson, 1987	Pawtucket Heart Health Programme
Social marketing with social mobilization strategies	McKee, 1992	
Combined community organization theories and social marketing principles	Bryant *et al.*, 1999	"Community-Based Prevention Marketing" model
Steps to Behaviour Change (SBC) an adaptation of diffusion of innovations theory and the input/output persuasion model	Piotrow, Kincaid, Rimon & Rinehart, 1997	Reproductive health and family planning overseas
Social cognitive or social learning theory	Baranowski, *et al.*, 2003; Beech, *et al.*, 2003, Story & Sherwood, 2003	

Identified by Lefebvre, (2001) and as seen from the above analysis, health belief model, the theory of reasoned action, social cognitive theory, the trans-theoretical model of behaviour change (or "stages of change") and diffusion of innovations are found to be the most prominent theories in use for the design of social marketing interventions. All these theories have been used to formulate strategies for increasing the rate of adoption of the social marketing offer. Health belief model, the most widely used model of all has been utilized for designing programmes for receiving flu vaccine shots, practicing breast self-examinations, using seat belts, attending screening programmes (Janz & Becker, 1984). The core components of HBM include: perceived susceptibility, perceived severity, perceived benefits, perceived barriers, cues to action and self-efficacy. These components have been used to identify explanations for people's reluctance to participate in preventive programmes and disease diagnosis programmes. Using the explanation from the perceived barrier and perceived benefit component of the model, social marketers have used the exchange theory to design message themes, pricing strategy and placement decisions (Lefebvre, 2001).

The Theory of Reasoned Action alongwith its variant the Theory of Planned Behaviour explain the individual's attitude towards the proposed behaviour on the basis of his/her belief about behavioural outcomes and the evaluation of those outcomes (Lefebvre, 2001). Under social marketing approach, the TRA has been used to relate the predictors of one's behaviour to the outcomes and attributes associated with the behaviour and the beliefs regarding the appraisal of the behaviour by referent people. And the TPB has been utilized for its additional components like "control beliefs" (the presence or absence of resources and impediments to engage in the behaviour) and "perceived power" – (the weighing/evaluation of each resource and barrier) to address the issues of public health importance (Lefebvre, 2001). These theories have thus been used along with the principles of exchange theory and segmentation, targeting and positioning for determining the focus of the intervention effort (teen tobacco use prevention) and establishing proper image of the public health programmes (5 A Day for Better Health programme) (Sutton, Balch & Lefebvre, 1995).

Social Cognitive Theory (SCT) argues that an individual's behaviour is an outcome of the interaction of his/her environment, personal characteristics and his/her response to the environment. As a result of which any decision regarding behaviour modification would depend upon the individual's perception of his/her ability to perform the desired behaviour, the anticipated outcome of the behaviour and the value he/she associates with this outcome. This has led to the formulation of different message channels for Team Nutrition messages aimed at children. The theory advocates for processes governing observational learning and motivates social marketers to consider attention, retention, production and motivational processes while designing interventions targeted at effective learning and performing of new behaviours (Lefebvre, 2001).

Another theory widely used to guide the public health social marketing intervention includes The Transtheoretical Model of Health Behaviour Change or the "stages of change" model (Marcus, Banspach, Lefebvre, Rossi, Carleton & Abams, 1992). It argues that people's decision regarding a particular behaviour modification is based on their assessment of pros and cons of any action. The pros and cons change as people progress through the behaviour modification process. Hence social marketers should design their intervention according to the stages of change. Basically it argues for effective utilisation of segmentation, targeting and positioning strategies.

Thus, a major outcome of this review has been the emphasis of various theories and models of social marketing on the concepts of exchange and the process of segmentation, targeting and positioning. Exchange theory has been utilized to explain the phenomenon of exchange in terms of assessment of costs and benefits. HBM has explained this phenomenon of exchange in terms of barriers and benefits which has been used in many social marketing programmes to guide price and placement decisions. According to this, inclination towards a particular behavioural modification comes from perception of susceptibility and perception of severity, whereas transformation of interest into action depends on the perception of benefits and barriers and the action is triggered by bodily or environmental events — thus design of any social marketing plan directed towards public health intervention should try to generate awareness regarding the susceptibility and severity, emphasize the perception of benefit and highlight the intervention's utility in overcoming the negative aspects (barriers) of taking specific actions.

The Theory of Reasoned Action (TRA) addresses the concept of exchange theory by arguing that people's decision to go for a behavioural modification is dependent on their assessment of the cost and benefits they will be incurring of this transformation. Thus, making the social marketing intervention to emphasise on the perception of benefits and minimizing the perception of severity of barriers and also creating a better social image of the proposed behaviour among the peers and the referent people

The Trans-theoretical Model of Health Behaviour Change Theory assumes that the adoption of behaviour modification is based on people's judgment of the benefits and barriers of that particular action. People's perception of the number of benefits or "the pros" and the number of barriers or the "cons" changes. At the end an individual comes to a stage when the perception of the benefits is so high that it outnumbers the perception of number of barriers and thus making the customer to adopt the behaviour change. Hence, behaviour modification in a person occurs in stages and each stage is characterized by the individual perception of ratio of the number of benefits to the number of barriers. Thus, role of social marketing is to identify the stage of the customer and plan the movement of the customer to the successive stage by designing a social marketing offer where the perception of the benefit outnumber the perception of costs or barriers. In this fashion, this theory addresses the success of behaviour transformation to the exchange of benefits and costs. And the application aspect of the theory emphasizes on the segmentation targeting and positioning concept of marketing.

A comparative analysis of these theories gives us the information as shown in Table 2.4.

Research pertaining to the social marketing application in public health context has so far been directed towards the understanding of acceptance or rejection of behaviour change appeal from the point of view of positioning of product or behaviour change appeal. Thus, the outcome has been the identification of the barriers to overcome in the form of product, price, place and promotion. Theories guiding social marketing interventions have focused on the increasing acceptability of the social marketing offer. Therefore, they have emphasized on the exchange theory which is nothing but an assessment of cost and benefits in the context of social marketing. And the outcome of this analysis is utilized to segment the audience, select target population and position accordingly the social marketing offer so as to increase its adoption rate. In this process most of the theories used in the context of public health under social marketing approach have addressed the segmentation issue on the basis of

Table 2.4: Summary of the theories and models in social marketing

Theory	*Factors Affecting Consumer Response*	*Marketing Concept Addressed*
Health Belief Model	Consumer fear towards the risk of developing a disease or severity or the outcomes of a preventive measure Demographic, social, psychological and structural variables affecting individual perception	Perceived barrier and perceived benefit concept (EXCHANGE THEORY)
Theory of Reasoned Action	The presence or absence of resources and impediments to engage in the behaviour (control beliefs) and the weighing of each resource and barrier (perceived power)	Positioning strategy to create the image of the campaign to counter the negative attitudes of people towards the programme (STP & EXCHANGE THEORY)
Social Cognitive Theory (SCT)	Behaviour is determined by the environment, audience's personal character, and how they respond to their environment. Audience perception of their ability to perform the desired behaviour, the anticipated consequences of that action and the value they place on that consequence determines their decision to follow a behaviour	EXCHANGE THEORY
Trans-Theoretical Model	STAGES OF CHANGE Weighing the pros and cons of the change People utilize specific processes in different stages	Matching interventions to the stage a person is in STP*
Diffusion of Innovation	Different types of adopters in different target audience group Perception of advantages and disadvantages of the behaviour adoption.	EXCHANGE THEORY STP*

* STP—Segmentation. Targeting, Positioning

perceived benefits and perceived costs or the resources and the barriers. However, these theories have failed to address the role of freedom of choice which has been identified as one contributing factor in shaping individual's response (acceptance or rejection) towards any marketing offer.

Freedom of Choice, Reactance and Social Marketing of Public Health Programmes

Customer's decision about attention and liking for a product is a subconscious activity (the pre-attentive stage of analysis) which depends on the analysis of significance of the information regarding the marketing offer (Janiszewski, 1988). Jacoby & Olson (1977) describe it as a cognitive process where the consumer first perceives the stimuli in the form of marketing offer and then interprets it to draw inferences (Geistfeld, Sproles & Badenhop, 1977). Thus, the consumer response formation is a process of confirming compatibility (Higgins, Rholes & Jones, 1977) where the consumer compares the exposed stimuli to his knowledge and memory and then establishes links between self and the stimulus. However, in case of novel, incongruous, or complex stimuli, people develop resistance upon initial exposure (Berlyne, 1970). Similarly, Fabrigar & Petty (1999) argue any mismatch between the nature of the appeal and the basis of the attitude may lead to the rejection of persuasion because of contrast effect (Herr, Sherman & Fazio, 1983; Herr 1986). Sawyer (1981) identifies counter-arguments and source derogation as consumer strategies to deal with manipulative intent of the marketer. Koslow (2000) also confirms that consumers respond in the form of "defence motivation" to vested interests, persuasion for change in attitudinal components or to protect other preferences like freedom of choice.

Thus, any attempt to change the behaviour of the consumer in the form of persuasive communication may lead to the generation of negative response from the customer if it is experienced as a potential threat to the freedom of the customer (Brehm, 1966; Brehm & Brehm, 1981). These are nothing but psychological alloy of emotion and cognition (Dillard & Shen, 2005) adopted to justify man's innate need to affect his or her own environment (Grandpre, Alvaro, Burgoon, Miller & Hall, 2003) or his control over decision making process. This negative response has been explained by the theory of psychological reactance as a process of reactance formation whose strength depends on the importance of a specific behaviour to the individual and the degree of threat against the behaviour (Brehm, 1966). Because of this, the individual under consideration may act against the proscribed behaviour which threatens his/her freedom and engage in the forbidden behaviour (Henriksen, Dauphinee, Want & Fortmann, 2006). The reactance may lead to the generation of aggressive and hostile behaviour among the consumers (Wicklund, 1974) against the marketer and the marketing offer which ultimately may end up in the rejection of the proposed behaviour. However, if people are given the freedom to make their own choices then these negative consumer responses can be avoided. Supporting the argument is the study by Kalda, Põlluste, & Lember, (2003) which suggests that patients' satisfaction with their medical care is associated with their freedom of choosing the physician and (Kao, Green, Davis; Koplan, Cleary, (1998) suggest this freedom can also help them exhibit higher levels of trust.

Threats to freedom can have two sources; impersonal sources or the barriers and the interpersonal sources or the influence attempts. While impersonal threat like product scarcity may increase the attractiveness of the product (Brehm, 1966) or cause derogation of the product which is unavailable (Hammock and Brehm 1966; Wicklund, 1970) and make the consumer to indulge in the forbidden behaviour, interpersonal influence induces the customer to react in a manner opposite to the prescribed way and thus get engaged in the prohibited behaviour. This type of behaviour is ascribed to the motivational state of the person and defined as "reactance". This reactance is a pre-decisional condition associated with the stage of decision making. The strength of the reactance is dependent on the choice, freedom, expectation of freedom of the customer, the faith of the individual on the expert and the awareness of the expertise of the person indulged in the act of persuasion (Clee & Wicklund, 1980).

The reactance generation through interpersonal influence can occur not only through personal influence attempts but can occur through mass media appeal also (Robertson and Rossiter, 1974). These types of communication influences can have two aspects: on one hand if the persuasion aspect of the communication is high then it results in reactance on the other hand if the communication is helpful and has interpersonally appealing qualities then it may lead to successful persuasion (Clee & Wicklund, 1980).

Conversely, the sources of impersonal threats could be related to product, price or the place elements of the marketing mix. The threat include product shortages, discontinuations, long waiting lines, and physical distances which inhibit (partially or fully) the decision alternative for the customer and thus increase the customer motivation to obtain that alternative (Clee & Wicklund, 1980). Under impersonal source of threat to freedom related to price, an increase in price may lead to reactance because of creation of barrier to the free choice and make the expensive alternative more attractive. These findings are summarised in Table 2.5.

Table 2.5: Summary of Social Marketing Tactics and its Impact on Individual Response

Social Marketing Tactics	*Freedom Expected*	*Individual Response*
Non-availability of product	Yes	Reactance arousal – increases the attractiveness of the product
	No	Product derogation
Steep increase in price	Yes	Reactance arousal – increase in the attractiveness of the product
	No	Product derogation
Place of availability is far from reach	Yes	Reactance arousal – increase in the attractiveness of the product
	No	Product derogation
Pressure to purchase (persuasive communication)	Yes	Boomerang effect – Reactance and rejection of the offer
	No	No reactance

Thus, any of the marketing mix element; product, price, place or promotion can cause threat to the freedom of the customer and lead to the generation of reactance resulting in the rejection of the proposed behaviour (marketing offer). Hence, social marketer should take ample care to design social marketing mix so as to minimize the reactance generation. Some of the practices undertaken by the marketers could be related to the communication part of the marketing mix - an impersonal source of reactance. For making a high pressure appeal for change factors that promote positive influence are being used in the past with an objective of minimizing the chances of generation of negative effect. These positive influence elements are related to the style or content of the persuasive communication which is instrumental in minimizing the perception of external influence or control on the individual's behaviour (Clee & Wicklund, 1980). The pressure laden communication can make use of informative features (persuasive arguments) and select a communicator from the reference group to minimize the reactance.

However, the most important implication for the social marketing from the analysis of freedom of choice and reactance emerges for the segmentation, targeting and positioning strategic decisions. As seen from Table 2.5, the audience can be segmented on the basis of the expectation of the freedom. Presence or absence of expectation of freedom determines the future course of action of customer in the form of resource derogation or the reactance generation. While reactance generation makes the prohibited option attractive and steers the consumer towards the achievement of the prohibited option, source derogation makes the consumer forbid the use of the prohibited behaviour. Hence, an *a priori* understanding of possible consumer response can help take decision on social marketing mix tactics.

Conclusion

Thus, expectation of freedom and threat to freedom can give the behaviour modification approach an altogether different direction. These can generate reactance in response to any attempt of behaviour modification realized under varied contexts like promotional influence resulting from persuasive communication, manipulative advertisements, product unavailability, censorship or government regulations. Information overload and consumer protection regulations can also lead to reactance generation by depriving one from making his own mistakes. Hence, any intervention aimed at behaviour change should take into consideration the freedom and reactance of the individual involved before devising any strategy or policy. Especially in the context of public health where behaviour modification approaches are at the centre of any intervention consideration of freedom and reactance to design public health interventions can help minimize the unintended effects of the interventions. Moreover, development of marketing strategies to deal with social marketing issues of public health importance under the framework of freedom and reactance can augment the efficacy of the strategy by giving a new direction to the segmentation, targeting and positioning tactics being followed in the current scenario.

REFERENCES

Ajzen, I. (1991). The theory of planned behaviour. *Organizational behaviour and human decision processes*, 50 (2), 179-211.

Andreasen, A.R. (1995). *Marketing social change: Changing behaviour to promote health, social development, and the environment*: Jossey-Bass San Francisco.

Andreasen, A.R. (2002). Marketing social marketing in the social change marketplace. *Journal of Public Policy & Marketing*, 3-13.

Baranowski, T.; Baranowski, J.C.; Cullen, K.W.; Thompson, D.I.; Nicklas, T.; Zakeri, I.E., *et al.* (2003). The Fun, Food, and Fitness Project (FFFP): the Baylor GEMS pilot study. *Ethnicity & disease*, 13 (1 Suppl 1), S30.

Becker, M.H.; Maiman, L.A.; Kirscht, J.P., Haefner, D.P., and Drachman, R.H. (1977). The Health Belief Model and prediction of dietary compliance: a field experiment. *Journal of Health and Social Behaviour*, 348-366.

Beech, B.M.; Klesges, R.C.; Kumanyika, S.K.; Murray, D.M.; Klesges, L.; McClanahan, B., *et al.* (2003). Child-and parent-targeted interventions: the Memphis GEMS pilot study. *Ethnicity & disease*, 13 (1 Suppl 1), S40.

Berlyne, D.E. (1970). Novelty, complexity, and hedonic value. *Attention, Perception, & Psychophysics*, 8 (5), 279-286.

Brehm, J.W. (1966). A Theory of Psychological Reactance. New York.

Brehm, S.S.; and Brehm, J.W. (1981). *Psychological Reactance: A Theory of Freedom and Control*: Academic Press, New York.

Bryant, C.A.; Cole, S.; Salazar, B.; Lindenberger, J.; Perrin, K.; R.; Sorrell, C., *et al.* (1996). Breast cancer screening: A social marketing study. *Social Marketing Quarterly*, 3 (1), 24-35.

Bryant, C.A.; Forthofer, M.S.; Brown, K.M.C. and McDermott, R.J. (1999). Community-based prevention marketing. *Social Marketing Quarterly*, 5 (3), 54-59.

Bryant, C.; DeWalt, K.; Courtney, A. and Schwartz, J. (2003). *The cultural feast: An introduction to food and society*. Belmont, CA: Wadsworth/ Thompson Learning.

Centres for Disease Control and Prevention (CDC) (2005), Communication at CDC, Practice Areas: Social Marketing. Available: http: //www. cdc. gov/communication/practice/socialmarketing. htm.

Clee, M.A.; and Wicklund, R.A. (1980). Consumer behaviour and psychological reactance. *Journal of Consumer Research*, 389-405.

Cohen, D.A.; Farley, T.A.; Bedimo-Etame, J.R.; Scribner, R.; Ward, W.; Kendall, C., *et al.*, (1999). Implementation of condom social marketing in Louisiana, 1993 to 1996. *American Journal of Public Health*, 89 (2), 204-208.

Coreil, J.; Bryant, C. and Henderson, J.N. (2001). *Social and behavioural foundations of public health*, Sage Publications, Inc.

D., R.C.L.P. (1996). 25 years of Social Marketing: looking back to the future. *Social Marketing Quarterly*, 3 (3-4), 51-58.

Dawnay, E. and Shah, H. (2007). *Behavioural Economics: Seven Principles for Policy Makers*.

Department of Health, H.M. Government, UK (2004). Choosing Health: Making heal their choices easier. Public Health White Paper, Series No. CM 6374, London, The Stationery Office.

Dillard, J.P., and Shen, L. (2005). On the Nature of Reactance and its Role in Persuasive Health Communication. *Communication Monographs*, 72 (2), 144-168.

Fabrigar, L.R. and Petty, R.E. (1999). The role of the affective and cognitive bases of attitudes in susceptibility to affectively and cognitively based persuasion. *Personality and Social Psychology Bulletin*, 25 (3), 363-381.

Farquhar, J.; Maccoby, N. & Solomon, D. (1984). Community applications of behavioural medicine. *Handbook of behavioural medicine*, 437-478.

Fisher, J.D.; Fisher, W.A.; Bryan, A.D. & Misovich, S.J. (2002). Information-motivation-behavioural skills model-based HIV risk behaviour change intervention for inner-city high school youth. *Health Psychology*, 21 (2), 177.

Freire, P. (1973). *Education for critical consciousness* (Vol. 1), Continuum Intl Pub Group.

Geistfeld, L.V.; Sproles, G.B. & Badenhop, S.B. (1977). The concept and measurement of a hierarchy of product characteristics. *Advances in Consumer Research*, 4 (1), 302-307.

Glanz, K.; Rimer, B.K. & Institute, N.C. (1995). Theory at a glance: A guide for health promotion practice: United States Department of Health and Human Services. *Public Health Service*. National Institutes of Health.

Grandpre, J.; Alvaro, E.M.; Burgoon, M.; Miller, C.H. & Hall, J.R. (2003). Adolescent reactance and anti-smoking campaigns: A theoretical approach. *Health Communication*, 15 (3), 349-366.

Grier, S. & Bryant, C.A. (2005). Social marketing in public health. Annu. Rev. *Public Health*, 26, 319-339.

Hammock, T. & Brehm, J.W. (1966). The attractiveness of choice alternatives when freedom to choose is eliminated by a social agent1. *Journal of Personality*, 34 (4), 546-554.

Henriksen, L.; Dauphinee, A.; Wang, Y. & Fortmann, S. (2006). Industry sponsored anti-smoking ads and adolescent reactance: Test of a boomerang effect. *Tobacco control*, 15 (1), 13-18.

Herr, P.M. (1986). Consequences of priming: Judgment and behaviour. *Journal of Personality and Social Psychology*, 51 (6), 1106.

Herr, P.M.; Sherman, S.J. & Fazio, R.H. (1983). On the consequences of priming: Assimilation and contrast effects. *Journal of Experimental Social Psychology*, 19 (4), 323-340.

Higgins, E.T. (1997). Beyond pleasure and pain. *American psychologist*, 52 (12), 1280.

Higgins, E; Rholes, W.S. & Jones, C.R. (1977). Category accessibility and impression formation. *Journal of Experiment of Social Psychology*, 14(1), 8.

Houston, F.S. and Gassenheimer, J.B. (1987). Marketing and Exchange. *Journal of Marketing*, 3-18.

Jacoby, J. & Olson, J.C. (1977). Consumer response to price: an attitudinal, information processing perspective. *Moving ahead with attitude research*, 39, 73-97.

Janiszewski, C. (1988). Preconscious processing effects: The independence of attitude formation and conscious thought. *Journal of Consumer Research*, 199-209.

Janz, N.K. & Becker, M.H. (1984). The health belief model: A decade later. *Health Education and Behaviour*, 11 (1), 1-47.

Kalda, R.; Pölluste, K. & Lember, M. (2003). Patient satisfaction with care is associated with personal choice of physician. *Health Policy*, 64 (1), 55-62.

Kao, A.C.; Green, D.C.; Davis, N.A.; Koplan, J.P. and Cleary, P.D. (1998). Patients' trust in their physicians. *Journal of General Internal Medicine*, 13 (10), 681-686.

Koslow, S. (2000). Can the truth hurt? How honest and persuasive advertising can unintentionally lead to increased consumer skepticism. *Journal of Consumer Affairs*, 34 (2), 245-267.

Kotler, P.; Roberto, N. and Lee, N. (2002). *Social Marketing: Improving the Quality of Life*, Sage Publications, Inc.

Kotler, P. and Zaltman, G. (1971). Social marketing: an approach to planned social change. *Journal of Marketing*, 3-12.

Lamptey, P.R. and Price, J.E. (1998). Social marketing sexually transmitted disease and HIV prevention: A consumer-centred approach to achieving behaviour change. Aids.

Leathar, D. and Hastings, G. (1987). Social marketing and health education. *Journal of Services Marketing*, 1 (2), 49-52.

Lefebvre, R. (1992). The social marketing imbroglio in health promotion. *Health Promotion International*, 7 (1), 61-64.

Lefebvre, R.C. (1996). 25 years of Social Marketing: Looking back to the future. Social Marketing Quarterly. Special Issue: 51-58.

Lefebvre, R.C. (2001). Theories and models in social marketing. *Handbook of Marketing and Society*. London and New Delhi, Sage Publications.

Lefebvre, R.C. and Flora, J.A. (1988). Social marketing and public health intervention. *Health Education & Behaviour*, 15 (3), 299-315.

Lefebvre, R.C.; Lasater, T.M.; Carleton, R.A. and Peterson, G. (1987). Theory and delivery of health programming in the community: The Pawtucket Heart Health Programme. *Preventive medicine*, 16 (1), 80-95.

Lefebvre, R.C.; Olander, C. & Lewvine E. (1999). The impact of multiple channel delivery of nutrition messages on student knowledge, motivation, behaviour: results from the Team Nutrition Pilot Study. *Social Marketing Quarterly*, 5(3), 90-98.

Lindenberger, J.H. and Bryant, C.A. (2000). Promoting breastfeeding in the WIC program: a social marketing case study. *American Journal of Health Behaviour*, 24 (1), 53-60.

Maibach, E.W. (2003). Explicating social marketing: What is it, and what isn't it? *Social Marketing Quarterly*, 8 (4), 7-13.

Marcus, B.H.; Banspach, S.W.; Lefebvre, R.C.; Rossi, J.S.; Carleton, R.A. and Abrams, D.B. (1992). Using the stages of change model to increase the adoption of physical activity among community participants. *American Journal of Health Promotion*, 6 (6), 424-429.

Mc Kee, N. (1992). Social Mobilization: Social Marketing in Developing Communities, Lessons for Communicators.

McDermott, R.J. (2000). Social marketing: A tool for health education. *American Journal of Health Behaviour*, 24 (1), 6-10.

Morris, L.A.; Tabak, E.R. and Olins, N.J. (1992). A segmentation analysis of prescription drug information-seeking motives among the elderly. *Journal of Public Policy & Marketing*, 115-125.

Murray, G.G. and Douglas, R.R. (1988). Social Marketing in the Alcohol Policy Arena. *British Journal of Addiction*, 83 (5), 505-511.

National Consumer Council (NCC) & Department of Health (DH) (2005). National Social Marketing Strategy for Health: Realising the potential of effective social marketing. London, July.

Neiger, B.; Thackeray, R.; Merrill, R.; Miner, K.; Larsen, L. and Chalkey, C. (2001). The impact of social marketing on fruit and vegetable consumption and physical activity among public health employees at the Utah Department of Health. *Social Marketing Quarterly*, 7 (1), 10-28.

Nord, W.R. and Peter, J.P. (1980). A behaviour modification perspective on marketing. *Journal of Marketing*, 36-47.

Piotrow, P.T.; Kincaid, D.L.; Rimon, J.G.; Rinehart, W., and Samson, K. (1997). Health communication: Lessons from family planning and reproductive health, Praeger Westport, CT.

Prochaska, J.O. and Velicer, W.F. (1997). The transtheoretical model of health behaviour change. *American Journal of Health Promotion*, 12 (1), 38-48.

Robertson, T.S. and Rossiter, J.R. (1974). Children and commercial persuasion: An attribution theory analysis. *Journal of Consumer Research*, 13-20.

Rogers, R.W. (1975). A Protection Motivation Theory of Fear Appeals and Attitude Change1. *The Journal of Psychology*, 91 (1), 93-114.

Rosenstock, I.M.; Strecher, V.J. and Becker, M.H. (1988). Social learning theory and the health belief model. *Health Education & Behaviour*, 15 (2), 175-183.

Rothschild, M.L. and Gaidis, W.C. (1981). Behavioural learning theory: Its relevance to marketing and promotions. *Journal of Marketing*, 70-78.

Sawyer, A.G. (1981). Repetition, Cognitive Response and Persuasion, In E.R.E. & T.O. Petty, and T. Brock, (Eds.), *Cognitive Responses in Persuasion*, pp. 237-261. Hillsdale, NJ: Erlbaum.

Shepherd, R. and Raats, M. (2006). The use of the stages of change model with dietary behaviours. *Frontiers in Nutritional Science*, 3, 345.

Simons, H.W. (1971). Persuasion and attitude change. In R.J. K.L. L. Barker (Ed.), *Speech communication behaviour: Perspectives and principles* (p. 232). Englewood Cliffs, NJ: Prentice Hall.

Skinner, B.F. (1953). *Science and human behaviour*, Free Press.

Slater, M.D. and Flora, J.A. (1991). Health lifestyles: audience segmentation analysis for public health interventions. *Health Education & Behaviour*, 18 (2), 221-233.

Smith, W.A. (1997). Social marketing: Beyond the Nostalgia. Social marketing: *Theoretical and Practical Perspectives*, 21-28.

Smith, W.A. (2002). Social marketing and its potential contribution to a modern synthesis of social change. *Social Marketing Quarterly*, 8 (2), 46-48.

Story, M.;, Sherwood, N.E.; Himes, J.H.; Davis, M.; Jacobs Jr, D.R.; Cartwright, Y., *et al.* (2003). An after-school obesity prevention programme for African-American girls: the Minnesota GEMS pilot study. *Ethnicity & disease*, 13 (1 Suppl 1), S54.

Strecher, V.J. & Rosenstock, I.M. (1997). The health belief model. *Cambridge handbook of psychology, health and medicine*, 113-117.

Sutton, S.M.; Balch, G.I. & Lefebvre, R.C. (1995). Strategic questions for consumer-based health communications. *Public Health Reports*, 110 (6), 725.

Tory Higgins, E.; Rholes, W.S. & Jones, C.R. (1977). Category accessibility and impression formation. *Journal of Experimental Social Psychology*, 13 (2), 141-154.

Wicklund, R.A. (1970). Prechoice preference reversal as a result of threat to decision freedom. *Journal of Personality and Social Psychology*, 14 (1), 8.

Wicklund, R.A. (1974). *Freedom and reactance*, Lawrence Erlbaum.

Williams, J.E. & Flora, J.A. (1995). Health behaviour segmentation and campaign planning to reduce cardiovascular disease risk among Hispanics. *Health Education & Behaviour*, 22 (1), 36-48.

Wong, F.; Huhman, M.; Asbury, L.; Bretthauer-Mueller, R.; McCarthy, S.; Londe, P. *et al.,* (2004). VERB™—a social marketing campaign to increase physical activity among youth. *Preventing Chronic Disease*, 1 (3).

Young, L.; Anderson, J.; Beckstrom, L.; Bellows, L. & Johnson, S.L. (2004). Using social marketing principles to guide the development of a nutrition education initiative for preschool-aged children. *Journal of Nutrition Education and Behaviour*, 36 (5), 250-257.

3

A New Paradigm for Integrated Primary Health Care Planning

Ajit K. Dalal

Providing health services to more than a billion of population is a colossal task. Given India's cultural diversity, plurality of health care practices, rural-urban divide and scarce resources, it is a daunting task for any national government to engage in planning health for all. One must view India's health care scenario keeping in mind the fact that India's 42 per cent of the population (456 million people) lives below the revised poverty line (income below $1.25 a day). A majority of this population lives in rural areas where medical care is scarce and inaccessible. With limited men and monetary resources, and crumbling infrastructure, it seems impossible for the government to provide even minimum health care to all citizens of the country.

It is ironical that where India lacks basic infrastructure for primary health care to reach out its 80-85 per cent of the population, it has best known worldwide to have super speciality centres comparable to anywhere in the world. India is a much sought after destination for medical tourism by the western countries. McKinsey and Company Report (May, 2008) has observed that India had 1,50,000 medical tourists from USA in 2002 which increased to 4,50,000 in 2007. The number was likely to be a million in 2010. There is a phenomenal increase in medical tourist from other developed countries, as well as patients from neighbouring countries. One reason for India to be such a favoured destination for orthopaedic and heart problems is that the cost is only 25 per cent than what they will pay in USA for the same quality of treatment. India currently has a booming health care industry at present.

The health care scenario for the common men is dismal. The India Health Report, released by Confederation of Indian Industry (CII) in 2010 has pointed out that there is a critical gap in the need and availability of infrastructure in terms of sheer health care sub-centres and trained staff even if the quality is not considered. This inadequate access to quality health care is particularly deleterious for the poor, lower caste, rural people and women. According to the Report, about 7–8 per cent of households are pushed below the poverty line because of expenses incurred on health care. National data reveal that 50 per cent of the bottom quintile sold assets or took loans to access private hospital care. In fact, nationwide survey of medical expenditure conducted by the National Council of Applied Economic Research revealed that, among the poor, expenditure incurred to meet the medical needs is the second most important cause of rural indebtedness after daughter' marriage (Banerji, 2003). Another study showed that in India 80 per cent of the health care expenses are borne by the users, 90 per cent of which are by the poor people (Krishnakumar, 2004). This scenario is corroborated by many recent health surveys.

Over the decades, a major shift in the health care is towards privatization. The recent India Health Report (CII, 2010) states that the contribution of the private sector in terms of the availability of hospital beds has gradually increased from about 28 per cent in 1973 to about 61 per cent in 1996. The Report estimates this number to have reached about 78 per cent in 2009. Health is increasingly reduced to an industry than a service sector.

India's Health Report

In the last fifty years India has many achievements in the health sector. All health indicators registered an improvement over time. Nevertheless, their levels are still unacceptable. Even though infant mortality rates have declined from a high of 110 in 1981 to 68 in 2000, it is still very high, *vis-à-vis* other countries at comparable or even lower levels of development. The fertility rate for India as a whole is 3.2, much above the replacement level. Overall life expectancy at birth has doubled for both males and females between

1941-1951 and 2000: from 32.4 years to 63.3 years for males and from 31.7 years to 65.6 years for females. Although female life expectancy is slightly higher than male life expectancy, achievements along other dimensions of women's health in India are very low. India has one of the highest maternal mortality rates in the world, registering as many as 407 maternal deaths per 1,00,000 live births in 2000. Another bitter statistic is the lopsided sex-ratio of 927 females per 1000 males, largely due to discrimination against girls and women in nutrition and medical care. This overall sex ratio has improved to 940.27 in 2011 (preliminary Census Report); a good part of this can be explained by the greater natural longevity of women and improvements in health care over the years. A disturbing statistics in this provisional population data (Census, 2011), however, is a steep fall in the child sex ratio, which measures the number of girls for every 1,000 boys in the 0-6 years age group. The sex ratio in the 0-6 age group has been continually declining since 1961 but the fall from 927.31 in 2001 to 914.23 in 2011 is the worst since Independence.

Malaria and Tuberculosis claim more than 5,00,000 lives every year. Added to this is the spectre of AIDS: there are an estimated 4 million HIV positive cases in India and their numbers are expected to grow rapidly. The average figures for India hide a great deal of variation in the performance of different states. While Kerala, Maharashtra and Tamil Nadu are doing better, the densely populated states of Orissa, West Bengal, Bihar, Rajasthan, Madhya Pradesh and Uttar Pradesh are way behind.

Health centres in urban area, are generally the populations' first point of contact with any health care personnel. As the bulk of the Indian population lives in rural areas, provision of essential health services through sub-centres and primary health care centres is crucial in determining any access to health care services for most people, especially women and children. All health indicators for rural areas compare unfavourably with those for urban areas; people belonging to Scheduled Castes and tribes have much poorer health compared to those who belong to the upper castes; and children and women in India suffer grossly from the burden of disease and ill-health. Morbidity among women and children is endemic in India.

In 1982, when the Government reformulated National Health Policy and officially adopted the WHO declaration of "Health for All by 2000", it made many significant changes at the policy level (Chatterjee, 1993). It brought forth the role of community and social sciences in promoting public health care. An apex committee of ICSSR and ICMR was formed to bring changes in the curriculum of medical education and to bring in more input from social science research.

Accordingly, rural health infrastructure development became a major activity in 1980s and a massive expansion of Sub-Health Centres took place with emphasis on maternal and child care, family welfare, and hygiene education. Each PHC was targeted to have one doctor and one community health officer (medical doctor, of course). This expansion was so rapid that the targets of developing infrastructure by 2000 were met in 1991 itself. In terms of manpower planning, a remarkable achievement was the training of 4 lakhs of community health workers (CHWs) within five years (1977-1982), almost one CHW for each village in the country, constituting the largest health care cadre in the world (Chatterjee, 1993).

These CHWs were trained by medical doctors to take care of common diseases and as a link between the community and medical staff. This rapid expansion did compromise in quality in many ways. Nobody knew what kind of training these CHWs should be imparted and very soon these workers began to perceive themselves as village medical practitioners. Later on, the Indian Medical Association opposed this scheme and termed these CHWs as quacks, who were indeed more popular than the medical doctors in many places. In 1981 when the Government of India transferred this scheme to the states, many states who did not commit to this scheme initially started backing out. Lack of availability of state funds made this scheme almost defunct. These workers were rechristened as Multipurpose Health Workers, and later, as health guides but no serious efforts were made to revive the scheme. The most ambitious scheme of the government lost its direction and relevance in the present time.

In 1990s, a major shift in the national health policy took place in which the management of health was turned over to the local self-government, the *panchayati raj*. Initially, there was a lot of enthusiasm and hope that it will make health services more accountable to local communities. But, like many other schemes, it also got mired in many controversies and rarely showed the desired results. Panchayats in India are not true representative of the people but are dominated by the powerful elite and power brokers. In the feudal system that still prevails in rural India, decentralization and bottom-up approach rarely succeed. It is anachronistic to the prevailing ethos and functioning of the Government.

In 2001, the Government announced a new health policy with the main objective of achieving an acceptable standard of good health of the general population. The policy aimed to strengthen the infrastructure, decentralize health care delivery through *panchayati raj*, setting up national accounting services and to regulate private practice. These were all laudable goals; but no proper mechanism was worked out to implement the provisions of this policy. In fact, this new policy was a kind of rundown for the already depleted primary health centres. The new policy ignored the earlier health policy's objectives of providing primary health care for all, especially to the underprivileged (Qadeer, 2001). The commitment of the earlier policy to create a well-worked out referral system was dumped to make way for privatization and commercialization of health services. The Government opened up the health sector for the private enterprises in a hope that with better monitoring and regulations the private sector will ease resource crunch in the health sector.

The National Rural Health Mission (NRHM) was launched by the Union Government in 2004 aimed to rectify the gross neglect of the health care needs of the rural masses. Though the funds allocated for this scheme are paltry (Rs. 320 crores), it raised the hope of strengthening health infrastructure, particularly the health worker scheme. It had reconceptualised this scheme as ASHA (Accredited Social Health Activist). The plan was to identify functionally literate women from the same village and train them for awareness building about health rights. In addition, ASHA was expected to implement national health programmes with the support of local panchayats. In 2009, the Government of India drafted a National Health Bill for the legal system to recognize the right to health and right to health care. It is yet to be implemented.

Primary Health Care: Coverage and Quality

On the 12th of September, 1978, the International Conference on Primary Health Care being held in Alma-Ata, in the erstwhile USSR, adopted the 'Declaration of Alma-Ata' which proclaimed a positive view of health as complete physical, mental and social well-being and a fundamental human right. The declaration envisaged primary health care as the first level of contact between individuals and families with their country's health system. According to this declaration, primary health care was to have its basis in the community it served; the notion of primary health care included maternal and child care including family planning, immunization against major infectious diseases, prevention and control of locally endemic diseases, appropriate treatment of common diseases and injuries, provision of essential drugs, education concerning prevailing health problems and ways to deal with them, provision of adequate food and nutrition and adequate supply of clean water. The Declaration of Alma-Ata set a goal for the year 2000 for all the people of the world to achieve a level of health such as to enable them to lead socially and economically productive lives. India, along with other countries, ratified the declaration.

India has a large public health care system. Primary health care is provided through a network of sub-centres, primary health care centres, community health centres and district hospitals. In rural areas, most primary health care is provided either by sub-centres or primary health care centres; whereas in urban areas it is provided via health posts and family welfare centres.

For the provision of health centres, the Indian Government has set the following targets: One sub-centre with one trained female and one trained male health worker per 5,000 persons in the plains and per 3,000 persons in hilly and tribal areas.

One Primary Health Centre (PHC) staffed by a medical officer and other paramedical staff per 30,000 persons in the plains and 20,000 persons in hilly, tribal and backward areas. Each PHC is to supervise six sub-centres.

One community health centre (CHC) or upgraded PHC with 30 beds and other basic facilities per 80,000-1,20,000 persons. The CHC is to operate as a referral centre for up to four PHCs.

In 1998, there were 1,37,006 sub-centres, 23,179 PHCs and 2,913 CHCs in India. There were 6,65,639 hospital beds or 6.9 hospital beds per 10,000 persons. Based on data collected by the National Family Health Survey-II 1998-99 (NFHS-II), in terms of population coverage, only 13 per cent of rural residents had access to a primary health centre, 33 per cent had access to a sub-centre, 9.6 per cent had access to a hospital and 28.3 per cent had access to a dispensary or clinic. One of the major determinants of the use of a health care facility, when it exists, is the distance to the location of the facility from the user's home. This is especially true for women and children in rural areas. Overall, 47.4 per cent villages had access to any health facility within their village and 38.9 per cent villages had access to any facility within less than five kilometres. According to the Fifteenth Human Development Report (1999), in India only 22 per cent of villages had a sub-centre within their village based on the population criteria. Coverage varies across Indian states. In Bihar, Orissa and Punjab, the proportion of villages with sub-centres was as low as 5-6 per cent; less than 30 per cent of villages had access to a primary health care centre or hospital in Bihar, Gujarat and Madhya Pradesh. There was better coverage quantitatively in Tamil Nadu with 50 per cent villages having access, and in Maharashtra and Haryana, between 30-36 per cent. Tamil Nadu, Kerala and Karnataka also had greater access to a hospital within five kilometres of the place of residence (Human Development Report India, 1999).

Apart from the number of health centres providing primary health care, the availability of primary health care also depends on the number of doctors, nurses and other medical personnel positioned in these centres. The public health system in India faces a critical problem of staff shortage, especially in rural areas, as medical personnel in general do not want to be located in rural and remote areas. As a result many posts in sub-centres and PHCs in rural areas remain vacant. For example, in 1996, as many as 4,281 of 29,699 doctors posts sanctioned remained unfilled in rural health institutions (Misra *et al.,* 2001). Thus, the existing extensive network of public health centres falls far short both in terms of population coverage and the guidelines set out by the government. As the poor are the main users of primary health care facilities, the rich preferring to use private clinics and hospitals, the absence of public primary health care services means that many people either forego any medical care altogether or use too little too late or choose to seek expensive and unregulated care in the private sector.

In India, the quality of health care services provided by the public health system is extremely low almost along all the criteria on which quality can be judged – infrastructure, availability of drugs and equipment, regular presence of qualified medical personnel and treatment of patients. Instead of being supportive and palliative of people's health, it will not be remiss to say that the health system itself poses a hazard to its intended beneficiaries, especially the poor, who are often as reluctant to use public health services as the rich.

Quality of health care services provided can be assessed along the following dimensions (which are by no means exhaustive): (1) an adequately equipped and easily accessible public health facility, (2) appropriate and timely clinical care, and (3) patient' satisfaction with health care received and the outcome of treatment. Ultimately, the real test of the quality of health care services is how they affect health outcomes, especially of the poor.

Bajpeyi and Goyal (2004) have extensively reviewed the quality of primary health care services in India along some criteria. At the least, a primary health care service centre should have the following in terms of infrastructure: the building in which it is housed to be in good condition; availability of electricity and running water; the presence of a telephone or some means of communication for situations where ambulatory and emergency care may be required.

One of the major lacunae in India's health system is lack of quality control. There is little public enforcement to ensure appropriate standards of care in clinical practices. This is as true of the public sector as of the private sector which is largely unregulated. The Medical Council of India, the main body overseeing standards of care, has no process in place whereby doctors are assessed, as to their competence with respect to current standards of care when they renew their registration. Given the lack of effective monitoring, there is little information to go by in terms of competence of medical personnel and actual practice in clinical settings, though there is some evidence of overuse of antibiotics and tranquilizers in public health care centres.

Delivery of public health care services in India is marked by pervasive absenteeism. According to one study, absenteeism among doctors was as high as 43 per cent and among other health workers, 39 per cent in government health care facilities across Indian states. A survey conducted by Banerjee (2003) in Udaipur in Rajasthan, found greater absenteeism in PHCs and CHCs than in sub-centres. This meant that for people seeking health care services, there was considerable uncertainty attached to a visit that is costly in terms of time and money, whether they would find it open and if open, finding someone there. Such uncertainty further attenuates people's incentives to make use of public health facilities. Under the family welfare programme, health or family planning workers are required to make regular visits to each household in their area of assignment to monitor women and children's health, provide family planning information and counsel and deliver selected services. Only 13 per cent of women in India, according to the NFHS-II, reported receiving a visit from a health or family planning worker in the last 12 months preceding the survey.

One notable failure of most of the rural health programmes is low community participation. Imposed from outside by the government functionaries and NGOs, these programmes could not garner community support. Western and westernized NGOs are incompatible with local culture, and needs and aspirations of people. Rarely local health practices and resources are taken cognizance of, or are the services of traditional practitioners acknowledged.

With increasing failure of western medicine, soaring coast of treatment and inaccessibility of medical staff led to the resurgence of traditional systems. Many of these traditional systems of treatment, like Ayurveda and herbal medicinal systems were compatible with socio-cultural beliefs and practices of the patients.

Traditional Health Care Services

Traditional medicine often refers to those healing practice that does not fall within the realm of modern medicine. These practices are considered to be historical and cultural, based on local beliefs, values and practices. Though there is wide diversity in tradition healing practices, they share many common characteristics, such as individualized treatment, treating the whole person, promoting self-care and self-healing and recognizing the spiritual nature of each individual.

Plurality of health care systems has always been accepted in India. A wide range of health and healing practices have been developed, practiced, improvised, and at times distorted in the long history. These parallel systems which range from highly developed medicinal system of Ayurveda to witchcraft have co-existed offering people a wide range of choices (Dalal, 2011). These traditional health care services can be broadly placed into two categories – folk and professional services (Kleinman, 1980). Folk practices are those which have evolved and thrived on popular beliefs about health and life in general. These comprise shamans, mystics, *tantriks*, diviners, priests, *ojhas*, *yogis*, *gurus*, *babas* and others. Though these healing practices are consistent with the cultural beliefs and have popular mass support, these are seen with skepticism by most of the government agencies and medical science. The second category labelled as traditional practices and recognized by the government as alternative medicinal systems are Ayurveda, Yunani system and homeopathy. Of course there are many others, such as herbal practitioners, naturopaths, acupuncturists, etc., who go through stipulated training and apprenticeship. These practitioners are frequented by patients and their families. Such a diversity of systems and their local variants constituted a rich tapestry of health care practices in India. They provided the whole range of services to cater to physical, mental, social and spiritual health of local communities. It may be noted that most of these practices and associated systems have evolved over a long history – some of these have been practiced for thousands of years, are time-tested and culturally-compatible (Dalal & Subha, 2005). These practices survived primarily on popular support and being integral to community life. WHO estimated that, "In many countries, 80 per cent or more of the population living in rural areas are cared for by traditional practitioners and birth attendants." (Bodekar, 2004).

There are a large number of folk health practitioners, ranging from faith healers to hydro-therapists. They can be found even in remote villages and towns. The statistics show that India, has about 3,80,000 practitioners of traditional medicines (1 per 2200 population). If we add to these figure 4,00,000 medical practitioners, India has one of the best patient-practitioner-ratio in the world. If these enormous resources are judiciously utilized by health policy-makers, India will have one of the best patient-practitioner ratios in the world. Integration of indigenous medicine with modern medicine can go a long way in meeting the health needs of the masses.

In reality, due to official apathy and dominance of modern medicine in health sector, traditional practices are in shambles. Only an insignificant portion of funds are allocated (1 to 2 per cent of the total health budget) to Ayurveda and other traditional medicine. As a result these services are weathering within the government sector. The worst victims of this official apathy are those rural poor who otherwise have no access to modern medicine.

Despite opposition from modern medicine, the popularity of alternative medicinal systems is rising worldwide. A study has shown that the use of alternative medicine had risen from 33.8 per cent in 1990 to 42.1 per cent in 1997 (Eisenberg, *et al.,* 1998). The report released by the *House of Lords*, UK (2000) suggested that the use of alternative medicine is high and rising. Studies assessing its prevalence in 13 countries concluded that about 31 per cent of cancer patients use some form of complementary and alternative medicine (Cassileth,1998). In developing nations where access to modern medicine is severely restricted by lack of resources and poverty, alternative remedies are quite popular. In Africa, traditional medicine is used for 80 per cent of primary health care, and in developing nations as a whole more than one-third of the population lack access to modern medicine (WHO, 2005).

A survey of US hospitals by Health Forum, a subsidiary of the American Hospital Association (2008) found that more than 37 per cent of responding hospitals indicated they offer one or more alternative medicine therapies, up from 26.5 per cent in 2005. In the United States, increasing numbers of medical colleges have started offering courses in alternative medicine. For example, in three separate research surveys that surveyed 729 schools (125 medical schools offering an MD degree, 25 medical schools offering a Doctor of *Osteopathic medicine* degree, and 585 schools offering a nursing degree), 60 per cent of the standard medical schools, 95 per cent of osteopathic medical schools and 84.8 per cent of the nursing schools teach some form of alternative medicine (Wetzel, Eisenberg & Kaptchuk, 1998). Resurgence of alternative medicine seems to be a worldwide phenomenon.

Background of the Integrated Approach

To understand the real challenge of integration of diverse systems, let us briefly review genesis of the issue. In 1938, largely as a result of the Freedom Struggle and emphasis on 'swadeshi', the National Planning Committee (NPC) set up by the Indian National Congress took a decision to absorb practitioners of Ayurveda and Yunani systems into the formal health set-up of independent India. In 1946, the Health Ministers' Conference adopted the NPC proposals and resolved to make appropriate financial allocations for: research, based on the application of scientific methods, in Ayurveda and Yunani; the establishment of colleges and schools for training in diploma/degree courses in indigenous systems:

(a) The establishment of postgraduate courses in Indian medicine,
(b) The absorption of *vaids* and *hakims* as doctors, health workers etc., and

(c) Inclusion of departments and practitioners of Indian medicine on national health committees.

As a result of the Conference resolutions, the government set up the Chopra Committee (1948) on the Indigenous Systems of Medicine to work out guidelines for the implementation of the above proposals. The Chopra Committee eventually came out in support of a synthesis of the Indian and Western systems through integrated teaching and research. It recommended that the curriculum be designed to strengthen and supplement one system with the other, with each making up for the other's deficiencies, while research should be concentrated on removing useless accretions to Ayurveda and making it intelligible to modern minds since a large portion of the texts were in Sanskrit. The ultimate objective of the research ought to be a synthesis of Indian and Western medicine which was suited to Indian conditions.

The Chopra Committee was followed by the Dave Committee which went into the issue of establishing standards in respect of education and regulation of practice in ISM. The Committee recommended an integrated course of teaching and some states in the Indian Union in fact started integrated colleges which taught both modern medicine and Ayurveda. In other states, however, pure Ayurveda colleges were also established. Indeed, the political and market forces were not favourable for any integrated approach. The medical practitioners who dominated health care services were not ready to dilute their education and practices to accommodate traditional practices.

As a consequence, the support for integrated medical colleges declined while pressure for pure Ayurvedic colleges increased. Ayurvedic practitioners and supporters of ayurveda generally pointed to the popularity of indigenous practitioners; the higher cost of integrated colleges due to the expensive equipment required teaching Western medicine; the tendency to spend too much time on allopathy; the availability of indigenous graduates for rural practice, and finally, the inherent incompatibility of the two systems. Eventually, the supporters of a pure system of education and training for Ayurveda, homeopathy and Yunani system gained political support in the country's political circles. This led to the formation of several independent Councils for looking after the research, development, training and regulatory aspects relating to ISM. However, it we look in terms of funding support, ISM always got ridiculously low funding out of the total health allocation. In the First Five Year Plan (1952-57) the total allocation for ISM was about one per cent of the total health budget; it increased marginally in subsequent plans, but came down to 1.3 per cent in the Seventh Plan (1985-90). The total allocation was raised from Rs. 35 crores last year to Rs. 100 crores in the year 2004, and this announcement drew applause from the starved ISM sector. It is appropriate to mention here that the total allocation for the Ministry of Health the same year was Rs. 4319 crores, and ISM got a mere 2.5 per cent of the whole budget. This is a clear indication of the marginalisation of the Indian systems of medicine in the public health care system (Banerji, 2004).

WHO which primarily relied on the medical model of health care blatantly promoted western medicine in developing countries, at least for the first two decades of its existence. In the Alma-Ata Conference (1977), to achieve the goal of 'Health for All' by 2000, it recommended that governments give high priority to the utilization of traditional medicine practitioners and traditional birth attendants and incorporate proven traditional remedies into national drug policies and regulations. Of course, most of the countries, including WHO, only paid lip service to this stated goal. The present resurgence of traditional medicines is outside the aegis of WHO and other international agencies, including national governments. It seems to be a logical consequence of the failure of modern medicine (D. Banerji, 2003).

To patronize and promote Ayurveda and other systems of indigenous medicine the Government of India, in 1995, established a separate Department for Indian Systems of Medicine and Homeopathy (ISM&H), which is now known as AYUSH (Ayurveda, Yoga, Unani, Siddha, Homeopathy). Among all the systems in AYUSH, presently Ayurveda holds a prominent position and a major share in the infrastructural facilities in terms of the number of hospitals, dispensaries, educational institutions and registered medical practitioners (Patvardhan, Gehlot, Singh & Rathore, 2011). The Central Council of Indian Medicine (CCIM), which was established through Indian Medicine Central Council Act of 1970, is the governing body that monitors the colleges in India offer a graduate level degree—"Ayurvedacharya" (Bachelor of ISM) every year. It is estimated that India has about 2,40,000 registered Ayurvedic practitioners, 12,000 Ayurvedic dispensaries, 1,452 hospitals and 100 postgraduate colleges. Besides, there are one million homeopathic practitioners.

As for research into ISM, the government first set up the Central Council for Research in Indian Medicine and Homeopathy in 1969. The Council guided and supervised research through its five technical advisory boards. This body, however, was replaced by CCIM in later period.

These alternative systems of medicine differ from biomedical medicine in many important ways. Alternative medicine (AM) greatly relies on healing powers of nature. It assumes that all of us have natural ability to heal ourselves. For example, an Ayurvedacharya will instead of using antibiotics to suppress the infection would medicate to improve immune system of the patient. It allows body's natural healing mechanism to take over. Two, alternative medicines are patient-centred rather than physician or profession-centred. They take into consideration patient's beliefs and personality into consideration in the treatment decision making. They treat patient as a person rather than as a body which medical treatment does. Three, AM generally resort to holistic treatment, taking into consideration, mental, social and moral conditions of the person. AM treats the whole person: not just her/his physical condition. Four, many of these AMs use natural substances, such as herbs, nutritional supplements, botanical plants, etc. for the treatment, not synthesized medicines or concentrates. Five, AMs more often deal with prevention and improvement of health, rather than merely on treatment of the diseases. It takes into consideration other factors, such as patient care, diet and anxieties while dealing with the patients. Lastly, AM practitioner involves family and community in the treatment procedure. Disease is considered to be a social event rather that an individual's pathology. Consequently, family and community are actively engaged in the treatment procedure.

Towards Developing an Integrated Model

There are two schools of thoughts in this regard. The first school views traditional systems as based on fundamentally different assumptions about human life, health and illness, which, in no way can reconcile with the theories of biomedicine. The traditional medicines attempt to restore the balance of mind-body-soul and treat patients holistically. The medical approach, on the contrary, treats a patient as a passive organism and focuses only on bodily aspects of the health problem. These fundamental differences in these two approaches are reflected in the differences in the formulation of the theories pertaining to causation of diseases, pharmacology and drug action, dietetics and nutrition, diagnostics, etc. (Shankar, 1992). Thus, those who subscribe to the first school consider western and traditional medicines irreconcilable and prefer them being practiced rather independently.

Many critiques of this school consider traditional systems as unscientific and of unpredicted efficacy. The skeptics of alternative practices argue that the symptomatic relief to an otherwise ineffective therapy can be attributed to placebo effect, or to the natural recovery from or the cyclical nature of an illness, or to the possibility that the person never originally had a true illness. However, studies show that mainstream medications may also show the placebo effect. An analysis of the 6 most widely prescribed antidepressants submitted to the *U.S. Food and Drug Administration* showed that approximately 80 per cent of the response to medication was duplicated in placebo control groups and improvement at the highest doses of medication was not different from improvement at the lowest doses (USFDAD, 2008). In fact, many of these alternative medicines are found to have a transformational experience that changed their worldview, relationship and self-concept; and identify the remedy with commitment to a social cause and personal growth.

The second school though acknowledges the differences in the two medicinal approaches; they see many possibilities of developing a unified health care delivery system. Their emphasis is on a creative synthesis between these two systems to develop a new Indian model of health care. The vast local resources of health care need to be mobilized into the crumbling public health services where different medicinal systems can work under one roof. There are many possibilities and we need to learn from the experiments done in many Asian countries.

Sri Lanka has the health care practices which is a good example of possible integration at the level of service delivery. There, all systems are allowed to practice freely but an enquiry is mandatory if there is any casualty of suspicious nature. This enquiry is conducted by a group of respectable local people. Because of this practice many folk practitioners refer serious cases to medical doctors, as cases of psychogenic illnesses are referred by medical practitioners to local healers. Such formal collaboration between modern and traditional medical sectors can grow to meet all health eventualities. Sri Lanka has very developed legislative and policy frameworks for the promotion and development of traditional medicine. It has a separate Ministry of Ayurveda for the last four decades, something which India did much later. Sri Lanka, with its meagre resources, has evolved one of the best health care systems in Asia and has achieved health targets almost on par with the western standards.

The health care system needs to be made more broad-based, so that it can handle all the facets of the problem, including public education about health and hygiene. Apart from providing curative services, rural health centres should have been the nucleus of all-round development. To achieve this dream, it is important that social workers, school teachers, religious leaders, and even faith healers are closely associated with the activities of the health centres. Indonesian health services have shown the way, where traditional healers are trained to refer serious cases to medical professionals, but these patients come back to the traditional healer for holy water, once they were cured (Sinha, 1990). This system, thus, not only relieves pressure on the medical practitioners, but also takes care of both curing and healing aspects of the disease.

A modest beginning in the direction of integration can be made at the level of Community Health Workers (CHWs). These health workers can be trained to be an important link between various schools of health care providers. The CHWs can be suitably trained to map and utilize local health resources. If the local healers who are respected and trusted by the villagers can be identified and trained in holistic health practices, they can provide the first level services. He/she may assist the Panchayats in meeting the basic health needs and act as a strong link between the Health Agencies and local people. In addition, there should be a massive effort in health education in the entire country, through school teachers, Panchayat members, youth clubs, Mahila Mandals and community development workers to help people inculcate a more rational and scientific understanding of both traditional medicine and public health issues. In this, national networks of voluntary organisations can play an important role.

While discussing the possibilities of integration of ISM at the level of primary health care we need to be wary of some new trends emerging in the global market. The market requirement of standardisation, commercialisation and pharmaceuticalisation of the medicine has substantially changing profile and practices of the ISM in the arena of health. There is an apparent paradox. While these processes have conferred a new legitimacy on traditional systems, their radical transformation has meant that even as their face-value has appreciated, their innate importance as systems of healing has declined. Indigenous medicine are in danger of falling prey to *pharmaceuticalisation, i.e.*, using the pharmacology of these systems to create new pharmaceuticals, or medicinal commodities, that could be sold independently of the original line of treatment (Bode, 2006). Such commodification of indigenous systems may give a false impression that its popularity is on increase, but in essence it could be allopathization of the Indian systems. Thus, while getting integrated within the primary health care, it is equally important that Indian systems of medicine preserve their humanistic-holistic character.

Clearly, integration of traditional medicines within the health care programmes does not imply that their inherent contradictions can be ignored or resolved. In fact, without taking cognizance of the differences any attempt at integration may be counterproductive. It is important that medical education and public awareness programmes take into account the limitations and strengths of different health systems. At times this is not an easy task when claims and counterclaims are made to promote one system over the other. There is, indeed, a lot to learn from the practical experience of patients and practitioners in the process of integrating diverse systems.

REFERENCES

American Hospital Association. (2008). Press release-09-15. *http: //www. aha.org/aha/press-release/2008/080915-pr-cam. html.* Retrieved on 2010-11-18.

Bajpeyi, N. and Goyal, S. (2004). *Primary health care in India: Coverage and quality*. Working paper no. 15, Earth Institute, Columbia University, New York.

Banerji, D. (2003). *Primary health care in India: An overview.* Guest Lecture at the National Seminar on 'Health for All' in the New Millennium, NIHFW, New Delhi, February 24-26.

Banerjee, M. (2004). *Whither indigenous medicine. http: //www. india-seminar. com/2004/489. html.*

Bode, M. (2006). Taking traditional knowledge to the market: The commoditization of Indian medicine. *Anthropology and Medicine*, 13 (2), 225-236.

Bodeker G.C. (1999). Traditional (*i.e.,* indigenous) and complementary medicine in the Commonwealth: new partnerships planned with the formal health sector. *Journal of Alternative Complementary Medicine,* 5, 97-101.

Bodeker, Gerard C. (2004). Traditional health systems and national policy. *http: //users.ox.ac.uk/~gree0179/*

Cassileth, B.R. (1998). *The Alternative Medicine Handbook: The Complete Reference Guide to Alternative and Complementary Therapies*. New York: WW Norton.

Chatterjee, M. (1993). Health for too many: India's experiments with truth. In J. Rohde, M. Chatterjee and D. Morley, (Eds.), *Reaching health for all*. New Delhi: Oxford University Press.

Chopra, R.N. (1948). *Report of the Committee on Indigenous Systems of Medicine.* New Delhi: Ministry of Health, Central Government.

CII (2010). *India Health Report*. New Delhi: The Confederation of Indian Industries.

Dalal, A.K. (2011). Folk Wisdom and Traditional Healing Practices: Some Lessons for Modern Psychotherapies. In M. Cornelisson, G. Misra & Verma, S. (eds.), *Foundations of Indian Psychology,* pp. 21-35. New Delhi: Pearson.

Dalal, A.K., and Subha, R. (2005). Social dimension of health and well-being: An overview of research trends. In A.K. Dalal & Subha Ray (Eds.), *Social dimensions of health.* Jaipur: Rawat.

Eisenberg, D.M.; Davis, R.B. Ettner, S.L., *et al.,* (November 1998). Trends in alternative medicine use in the United States, 1990–1997: Results of a follow-up national survey. *Journal of American Medical Association, 280* (18), 1569-75.

Human Development Report (1999).

Kleinman, A. (1980). *Patients and healers in the contexts of culture.* California: University of California Press.

Krishnakumar, A. (2004). An unhealthy trend. *Frontline,* 21 (24), 84-85.

McKinsey and Company Report (May, 2008). *Mapping the market for medical travel*. New Delhi: McKinsey & Company.

Misra, R.; Chatterjee, R. and Rao, S. (2001). *Changing the Indian health system: Current issues, future directions.* New Delhi: Indian Council for Research on International Economic Relations.

Nandy, A. and Visvanathan, S. (1990). Modern medicine and its non-modern critics. In F.A. Marglin and S. Marglin (Eds.), *Dominating Knowledge: Development, Culture and Resistance*. Oxford: Clarendon Press.

Planning Commission of India (1952). *First Five Year Plan (1952-1957).* New Delhi: Government of India.

Planning Commission of India (1992). *Fifth Five Year Plan (1992-97).* New Delhi: Government of India.

Planning Commission of India (2001). *Approach Paper to the Tenth Five Year Plan (2002-2007)*. New Delhi: Government of India.

Qadeer, I. (2001). Debt payment and devaluating elements of public health. *Economic and Political Weekly*, 37 (1), 12-16.

Shankar, D. (1992). Indigenous health services: The state of the art. In A. Mukhopadhyay (Ed.). *State of India's health*. New Delhi: Voluntary Health Association of India.

Sinha, D. (1990). Concept of psychological well-being: Western and Indian perspectives. *NIMHANS Journal*, 8, 1-11.

Vishwanathan, S. (April 3, 1998). A celebration of difference: Science and democracy in India. *Science*, 280, 42-43.

Wetzel, M.S.; Eisenberg, D.M. and Kaptchuk, T.J. (September 1998). Courses involving complementary and alternative medicine at US medical schools. *Journal of American Medical Association*, 280 (9), 784–7.

4

Mental Health Interventions at Community Level

Anuradha Sovani

Introduction

Communities are social groups with a collective identity or shared attitudes and experiences, whether social, cultural, political, occupational, or based on affiliation through geography, institutions, or communication channels. Most community based programmes, projects and interventions described in this chapter thus maximally utilize the quick reach to target audiences and populations that are possible in a smaller geographical region, and supplement this by creating audio-visual material for wider reach. Use of local media such as newspapers to catch the attention of the community is underlined. In the context of publications for the layman, a successful series of low cost pocket books by the author of this chapter has found favour with readers. (*Maanasrang*, Sovani, 2010).

What is the work setting of a psychologist? Many would answer this question by saying, 'the clinic' or professional office from which they operate. The tradition modality through which the psychologist works has long been that of the client approaching the professional at the work setting of the latter, seeking to find solutions to problems of daily living, occasionally arising out of stress, interpersonal conflict, and leading to maladjustment. Other answers to this question could be the school, where the psychologist may be appointed to resolve scholastic problems, as well as behavioural problems of students. Underachievement, learning disabilities, conductive disorder, and peer conflicts are often the work domain of these psychologists.

Psychologists may also attempt to resolve problems arising as a result of family conflict, marital discord, parent-child relationship issues, and thus consider the home as their domain for intervention. Alternatively, in the organizational setting, the workplace itself may become the work setting for the psychologist as they help resolve employer-employee conflicts, help in the selection and training of personnel, etc.

However, the rapidly emerging scenario around us shows more and more clearly that the community, the society, are in effect work settings for the psychologist. The setting need not come to the psychologist; rather, psychologists must make themselves available, useful, and even indispensable. The burden of this chapter is also to establish this claim. Most community based interventions take the form of either public health interventions or community development interventions. The effort here is to demonstrate the model of a social enterprise that encourages community based mental health interventions based on community needs assessment, and involves local community volunteers to ensure low service delivery costs and maximum community participation and ownership.

In a paper titled *Bridging Community Intervention and Mental Health Services Research,* Wells *et al.* (2004) discuss the potential of community intervention perspectives for increasing the relevance, reach, and public health impact of mental health services research. Participatory methods of community intervention are used to produce complementary functions, such as linking community-based case finding and referral with practice-based quality improvement, enhanced by community-based social support for treatment adherence. In the paper, the community intervention approach is seen as a major paradigm for affecting public health or addressing health disparities. Despite challenges in implementation and evaluation, the authors conclude that it represents a promising approach for extending the reach of mental health services interventions into diverse communities.

The traditional role of the psychologist has been that of a psychodiagnostician, a psychometrician and a psychotherapist. These roles become partially defunct in a community setting, since such sharp definitions may not be possible here. Their new burden of work, then in the social and community setting would include the following:

- Awareness building
- Preventive programmes
- Augmentation of strengths
- Sensitization
- De-stigmatization
- Rehabilitation

Awareness building: A large number of psychological problems often result from ignorance. If parents are unaware of the ills of pampering their child, the natural outcome is often behavioural problems which are then referred to the psychologist for intervention. Timely training in parenting can bypass this possibility. If couples were aware that better communication from the start of relationship would avoid many a quarrel later, they would surely have shared their thoughts often. Premarital counselling sessions and workshops can often help and ensure that many of these problems are avoided. Current trends in larger cities and metropolitan areas show an increase in workshops on premarital and marital counselling. Topics included in such workshops range from manner of choice of the partner, and which parameters to use during this selection, to sexual information and assertive communication. In the context of this chapter, it is the role of the psychologist to make these workshops and others like them, more acceptable, fun to attend and yet a rich learning experience. As a case in point, a simple Marathi book by the author (Sovani, 2010) on couple relationships seems to have appealed to readers.

Preventive programmes can thus be engineered around the probable frequency of a particular problem arising at a particular life stage, or as a result of some life circumstance, such as aging, retirement, etc. Wells *et al.* (2004) cited above state that few mental health studies have used community intervention strategies. Mental health preventive intervention research is largely limited to extensions of practice interventions to high-risk groups. Nevertheless, community interventions have been widely used to address other major public health problems and improve the management of chronic disease. For example, public campaigns have been used to reduce behavioural risk factors, increase early detection and intervention, and promote adherence with recommended treatments for heart disease, diabetes, and cancer including for stigmatized conditions like HIV infection. Hence, an attempt was made to identify youth who would do well to be armed with life skills even before they face life challenges. Project *Jidnyaasa* described below is a case in point.

At the same time, every individual has certain innate *strengths*, and these need to be *augmented* in order to prepare them for stressful times. Similarly, in competitive contexts such as sports, or examinations, it is these strengths which will stand a person in good stead, in order to maximize performance. Later in the chapter, examples from Sports psychology are cited to illustrate this domain of interventions.

Some of the following community based programmes help underline these three features of psychological intervention, before we go forward to the rest. Some *key features* of such programmes, however, need to be noted and recorded, in order to maximize success of these initiatives:

- Community stays engaged
- No fees charged or minimal fee
- Few or no sponsors
- Financially viable models
- Several deliverables, which constitute 'products' or positive outcomes
- Continuous documentation

The paragraphs that follow document some attempted programmes with adequate evidence base.

There is also an effort made to classify the interventions by the populations they serve, e.g. children, mentally ill, aging, etc.

Handling Examination Stress or Test Anxiety

Channel E-Ten was a programmes tarted by the Institute for Psychological Health around two decades ago. This was a period when new channels were abounding on national and regional television, and young people were excited at the prospect of any new channel. The programme is designed to tackle 'Exam tension', to use student jargon, and was dubbed "Channel E Ten" to stand for "channelize your exam tension." Annual feature workshops of one day duration are arranged, and schools and junior colleges are informed so that they can depute students to participate. Fee structure is uniformly low and students carry their own lunch so that they can take a tiffin break much like school or college. The day long programme content focuses largely on REBT based principles of handling anxiety arising from examinations, teaching students to identify irrational self-talk which would drive them to be more anxious and perform more poorly. Other than that, sessions focusing on study skills, creating study time tables, and good time management, psychological principles of massed vs. distributed practice with the latter yielding better results, etc. are shared with the participants.

A research data base has been generated by weaving research design into the programme, after obtaining consent and allowing anonymity and maintenance of confidentiality. The tool used for assessment has been the Friedben Test Anxiety Scale (FTAS), a 23 item scale by Friedman and Bendas Jacob (1997), validated in India, with Hindi and Marathi versions available. The factors are Social derogation, Cognitive obstruction and Tenseness. Findings based on the research studies, both Indian (Bhave, Sovani and Joshi, 2009) as well as cross-cultural (Bodas, Ollendick and Sovani, 2008) can be found in the research publications listed at the end of the chapter. Marathi writing for the layperson is done as well, and the book has been through several editions (Sovani, 2006).

Some interesting experiences arose out of the various repetitions of the Annual feature programme of Channel E-Ten. One year, a school referred their students to the programme with an expressed worry about their stress levels. Permission was thus pre-obtained from the school to code the students' response sheets numerically, maintain the master list with the principal researcher, and if any student scored alarmingly high on the FTAS, he or she could be identified by breaking the code and help offered. In the current scenario of student suicides reaching dizzying proportions, the value of such a practice becomes apparent.

Dealing with Adolescent Stresses and 'Growing Up'

Another key programme run by IPH, which was started in collaboration with Mumbai Police and Stree Mukti Sanghatana, is Project ***Jidnyaasa***, a Sanskrit, Hindi, Marathi word which means curiosity or the 'desire to know'. The programme started with the aim of offering Life skills training to children hailing from a low

SES background, often studying in Municipal schools. The three organizations that collaborated had common interests in the welfare of the girl child, in the fight against drugs of abuse as well as general well-being of adolescents who are often at high risk due to their life stage and an unhealthy social environment. Trainers from the lay community were trained in modules which included assertiveness; saying 'no' to drug use, sexuality, and academic and time management, among others, and follow up/refresher training was also conducted from time to time. Data of 10,000 has been collected and documented, and the deliverable of the project has been the manual of *Jidnyaasa* modules, which offers a user-friendly resource in order to access training material for adolescents. (*Jidnyaasa manual*, IPH, 2005)

Vocational and Career Choice

A feature programme conducted on the second weekend of December every year over the last nineteen years is ***VEDH***, again a Sanskrit based Marathi word meaning aim or target, and an acronym for Vocational Education, Direction and Harmony. The logo of this event combines all these elements, with an arrow hitting the target, and musical notes intertwined. The format for this programme centres on stage interviews of achievers in specific fields, as per the theme for that year. The focus of this informal interview is choices made, and struggles of the person being interviewed, hurdles faced and overcome by them, in order to give the audience a flavour of the 'human' side of the faculty. Almost three to four thousand students and their parents get to watch this stage interview live, and some get an opportunity to have their questions, which are written on chits and passed to the *dais*, read out and answered by the celebrity guest. Around two hundred achievers hailing from fields as diverse as science, music, acting, direction, research, social and commercial enterprise, and social service, have been the resource persons for this event so far. The audio-visual unit of IPH, *Avaahan*, has recorded VEDH events over the past several years on DVD, and have also compiled many of the VEDH anthems, a fresh song being created and sung by the 4000 strong student audience every year. As students gather at the covered open air venue for the event, the Managing Trustee and Director of IPH who manages the event leads the audience through the words, and ensures that they know them as well as the tune by the time the event formally begins. This helps set a note of unity and group spirit.

VEDH has proven its replicability since parallel Vedh programmes are being carried out in other areas of Maharashtra such as Aurangabad (four so far), Ahmednagar (five) and Nagpur (two), thereby generating thirty Vedh modules in all, each run over two days.

Career and vocational guidance is all about letting the child choose the field he or she enjoys, and would like to work in through life. Most of the time, with the emphasis in India on marks, grades and scholastic performance, parents are preoccupied with having a child who scores well, regardless of whether she or he is miserable in the process. Sternberg has made in interesting distinction between Intelligence, Cleverness and Wisdom, and parents need to realize that it is Wisdom that matters in the long run, and Cleverness that gets you through the blind alleys of life. To answer common questions parents ask about their child being 'clever', a simple Marathi book (Sovani, 2008c) was penned.

The above sections dealt largely with programmes designed keeping children and youth in mind. There is also a high need to address adults in their lives, teachers as well as parents, to ensure that needs evoked in children's minds after awareness building are met adequately. Some of the programmes and modules planned with this aim in mind are listed below.

Creating Teacher Mentors

Shikshak Prabodhini is an experiment in nurturing high school students to excel in their chosen fields with the help and support of their *teachers*; hence, the core concept is that of teachers as mentors. The objectives of this programme are to scientifically train a group of motivated secondary teachers, consciously and systematically inculcating in them the necessary skills of mentoring; to reach out to talented students in their respective schools, through these teachers; and to consciously nurture excellence in students, by providing specific inputs. Shikshak Probodhini modules have been run successfully for over two years in English and Marathi, and comprise of modules on self-development, rational thinking, communication skills, mentoring skills, event management skills, study skills, and concentration building. Both students and teachers have expressed satisfaction with this programme, and have volunteered to participate although it may mean contributing precious weekend and holiday time to the activity.

Parents too, express a need for guidance whether children are ill or well. Two group approaches described below help parents of very young children identify their strengths and weaknesses, and also assist parents of child with a specific problem. An example of the first kind of programme is *Little Beginnings*. For restless children as well as those diagnosed with ADHD and under medication for the same, *Naach re Mora* provided guidance. *Paalakshaalaa*, literally a 'school for parenting', provides parenting modules to serve all. Little Beginnings is a developmental observation group for children between ages of three and five years. Conducted over eight weeks, the programme has six sessions of two hours each with children, and two sessions at the beginning and end of the programme with parents. Each batch consists of twelve to fifteen participants. The sessions with children include:

• Physical Development	Gross & fine motor skills
• Intellectual development	Concept formation, problem solving
• Social development	Role plays, stories, singing
• Creative development	Sticking, Colouring, Cutting
• Emotional development	Emotional awareness, dealing with emotions
• Sensory development	Identifying different sensory stimuli

The initial session with parents focuses on developmental information about early childhood.

Wherein parents are briefed on issues related to parenting, and effective ways of communicating with the child. Parents are also given a personal data form of the child, in which they record information regarding the child. The last session is conducted individually with each parent, where every parent is given feedback about the development of child in all the areas earlier mentioned.

Inputs regarding sharpening the existing skills and inputs where the child is lagging behind are also given. If required the parents are directed to other professionals, such as occupational or speech therapists. Two popular Marathi books (Sovani, 2004, 2007) are dedicated to the role of parents in children's lives and the impact they have on the latter.

With regard to children with Attention Deficits, a similar set of modules was developed, although the programme has not been run with as much consistency over the years, and has remained need based. Parents are given inputs regarding the condition of attention deficit and hyperactivity or over activity. Findings based on parent ratings (Sovani, Thatte *et al.*, 1998) show that parent burnout causes overestimation of the difficulties encountered while parenting children with ADHD. Hoagwood *et al.*, (2001) report that until recently there has been no evidence to summarize, or critique, or review in the field of child and adolescent services. In fact, from a historical standpoint the concept of childhood mental illnesses did not arise until thelate 19th century. These illnesses were typically not seen as unique to children or distinguishable from adult mental illnesses until the early part of the 20th century. In the *Naach re Mora* modules (the title of the programme derives from a popular children's song in Maharashtra, which refers to the dancing peacock, the national bird. The title was an attempt to de-stigmatize by giving an attractive name to the child's dancing restlessness) state of the art pharmacological information is presented in a simple user-friendly manner, combined with information about other interventions such as SI (Sensory Integration), sensory stimulation using similar stimuli as are described in Little Beginnings above, etc.

Some community based mental health interventions are developed with special groups in mind. Some of the programmes and projects described below focus on sports people and mental fitness training (*Mission Excellence*), as well as help extended to the aging as well as those with chronic mental illness, in need of long-term psychosocial care.

Mental Fitness Training for Sportspersons

Mission Excellence is a programme that promotes sportsworthiness through psychological principles of Mental Fitness Training. The various methods used herein include methods of Mental Skills Training, Cognitive and Mental Rehearsal, Mental Imagery and Visualization, Cognitive-Behaviour Therapy and also Biofeedback, Progressive Muscle Relaxation and Meditation. The precursor for involvement in the group is individual counselling for sportspersons. Sports coaches and clubs are showing a keen interest in providing systematic training to their members. Inputs so far are yielding extremely good results and positive response from the participants.

Although this is a new, emerging field, some publications in books reviewing adolescent health and journals documenting good mental health practices are listed. (Sovani, 2002, 2008a)

Reaching out to the Aging

This effort comprises a variety of programmes such as *Vaanaprastha*, a Sanskrit word denoting the stage in life when the aging withdraw into a lifestyle of simple living and meditation in the forest; the word literally means 'living in the forest'. (Sovani, 1992) This programme, held close to the inception of the Institute in 1990, helped participants focus on emotional preparation for old age.

Other related efforts include Project Grey Skills, an initiative to help the experienced and wise elders to share knowledge and resources with the young, Project Silver Lining to psycho-educate family members about the Dementias, and also help empower caregivers. Other efforts are also made to reach out to the community, e.g. Through *Maitra*— a telephone helpline (Subramaniam, 2008) *Manovikas*, a set of pre-planned modules to explain mental illness concepts to the community, as well as a number of support groups targeting various conditions.

Maitra and *Manovikas* are concepts driven entirely by volunteers. *Maitra* is a telephone helpline entirely manned by volunteer resource persons, and boasts one of the best documentations of projects of its kind, with every call noted in detail, and the speakers remaining anonymous. Regular meetings are held with professional resource persons in the Institute to discuss difficult calls, and train the volunteers further.

Often as you interact with people in the community around you, you find that misconceptions regarding mental illness and mental health abound and there is a desire to set matters right. *Manovikas* grew out of such an initiative. FAQs regarding mental illness and health were collected, and committed volunteers were selected from the pool that frequented the Institute over the years. Careful volunteer selection has proven to be the backbone of many a community based programme, and here too it proved likewise. The volunteers then prepared scripts for role plays and enactments that could be conducted at street corners, in housing society, without any significant props or stage management. These scripts were vetted by mental health subject matter experts. The latter also wrote out correct answer to the FAQs, for the volunteers to master. The programmes were then run in the vicinity of Thane city and soon gained popularity. They began to receive invitations to perform at public functions, such as *Ganeshotsav*, the ten day festival of the Elephant God, and major deity in Maharashtra, Diwali, the festival of lights etc. Interestingly, the volunteers have by now even reached out to other stigmatized communities like prison inmates, bar girls, etc. who benefited from watching this programme.

Chronic Mental Illness

Although a number of support groups have been run for a number of conditions, ranging from parents of children with Autism spectrum disorders, people who stutter (*Atkepaar*), people with Epilepsy (*Uttejan*), the key interest area of the author has been chronic mental illness, specifically schizophrenia. Hence, although groups have also been created for resistant conditions like Obsessive Compulsive Disorder (*Perfect* group!); the main thrust of work reviewed hereafter is schizophrenia.

Schizophrenia is in a sense a disease of the young. Early onset is a key feature and hence a loss of often highly educated manpower with years of potential ahead, is a major result of the condition (Sovani, Thatte and Apte, 2004). Today, sustained remission has become a realistic goal for patients with schizophrenia; functional recovery without relapse allows the patient to work, sustain interpersonal relationships and lead more productive lives. Variables such as perceived social support and self-efficacy may influence their daily functioning.

Following early unpublished Doctoral work (Thatte, 1984; Sovani, 1990) and a UGC funded major research project (Deshpande, Thatte, Sovani *et al.*,1997), much of the work in the community setting has focused on answering some of the puzzling questions that schizophrenia challenges us with. Attempts to define the role of the professional in the effort to unravel the schizophrenia puzzle, led to the answers that we need to demystify the illness, to train caregivers to 'manage themselves', to help detect where exactly their needs lie, acknowledging that they may not be able to define their own needs clearly. Further, we need to train caregivers to manage the patient, to ensure that the caregivers' group bonds and creates a support system. (Sovani, 2008b).

The *Tridal* project at IPH is perhaps one of the most active and dynamic activities in the Institute, working towards creating a stress-free activity centre for people recovering from schizophrenia, dubbed the *Shubharthis* to reduce stigma associated with the label. (Sovani, 2009) The name Tridal denotes a three leaf structure, often granted holy status in Indian mythology, and in this instance standing for the family member, the professional and society, all of whom are committed to support the person with schizophrenia and help the recovery process. While pinpointing what was amiss, findings from the Doctoral work and MRP listed above were utilized and extended further, to develop Cognitive Remediation Therapy inputs, is a novel rehabilitation approach designed to improve neuro-cognitive abilities such as attention, memory and executive functioning. In fact, attention deficits were seen as the major culprit in lowering performance ability in people with schizophrenia and the interesting possibility of people with schizophrenia and those with epilepsy as being mutually helpful was explored. (Kadaba, 2005; Kadaba and Sovani, 2007)

Further, there was also a high need to cater to caregiver needs. Some research guided by the chapter author (Apte, 2005) explored the latter, and established on the basis of research evidence that psycho-education alone can help in reduction of stigma, caregivers with high burden will need on-going inputs related to problem solving, caregivers with high burnout need initial focus on handling their emotions and then future inputs work more effectively. Further, experience while conducting workshops showed that it is always helpful to start any intervention with the caregivers by addressing their emotional needs. People appreciate the inputs given later only if they get the feeling that their needs are "understood". Further research through a University of Mumbai funded project (Sovani, 2004-2005) explored the match vs. mismatch between patient needs and caregiver perceptions. While assessing the most efficacious means of retraining in various areas of cognition, an attempt was made to juxtapose, using a Greco-Latin square design, caregivers' intuitive wisdom with research findings of efficacy of different methods for different cognitive faculties. It was hypothesized that if there is a mismatch, caregiver and patient frustration will result, and that was what emerged leading to more inputs to caregiver support groups.

The chapter began with the new burden of work of the psychologist, and three domains not yet discussed are Sensitization, De-stigmatization and Rehabilitation. Much work is in progress in

Maharashtra, with path breaking films like 'Devrai' (the sacred grove) focusing on the experiences of people with schizophrenia, organizations like Schizophrenia Awareness Association (SAA) working to reduce ignorance about the condition, and creating public education modules to reach the as yet unreached. Attempts are currently on in order to scale up some of these interventions to Government mental health care settings such as regional mental hospitals, using the platform of UGC funded Centre for Excellence projects such as the Centre for Behavioural Research housed in the University of Mumbai.

The current on-going project of the above CBR of the UGC-UPE is an effort to offer Rehabilitation Technology Training (RTT) to professional caregivers in long stay inpatient settings. All too often, the latter are blissfully unaware of the implications of rehabilitation, and the additional benefits that patients can enjoy if pharmacotherapy is followed by rehabilitation efforts. The proposed project hopes to empower them with this knowledge, thus making them important stakeholders in the recovery process rather than mere bystanders and onlookers. This will ensure a marked reduction of the revolving door effect often seen in long stay institutions, and will render long stay patients more capable of surviving in the real world after discharge from the hospital setting. On a more global level, the World Health Organization too is helping to remedy the current situation with efforts such as the mhGAP action project. National bodies such as the UGC, ICMR, ICSSR, GOI Departments of Health and Family Welfare as well as Human Resources ministries, are offering aid to initiatives to help the marginalized and mentally ill.

Another 'dream project' is *Manas Parisar*, which is to come up on the Mumbai-Nasik Highway at Vashind on spread of two and a half acres of land. Residential programmes for Marital Counselling, Family Therapy with adolescents and may be reintegration learning for chronically mentally ill who have recovered is planned here. At the same time, one envisages people from creative art field coming for retreats when they could contribute to the happenings at that time with their skill and art, such as music, painting, drama, poetry etc. Hence, we could work on Disorder, Distress and Development—all could be worked on at the same time, in a residential set up.

The chapter ends on an effort at out of the box thinking, attempting to beat stigma with glory and grandeur and victory messages.

An IPH Experiment in de-stigmatization

The ***Dwij*** Puraskaar or the "born again" awards "Dwij" means 'reborn'. Annually, the "Dwij" awards are given to three people with chronic mental illness, specifically schizophrenia or Bipolar disorder, for beginning a new life, in spite of the illness and often with it. Two awards also go to two caregivers, the unsung heroes. Applications are invited from all-over the state, with forms to be filled by the person suffering from the illness, the caregiver and also the doctor or mental health professional under whose care the patient is. These applications are then screened by a panel of experts, and awards are finalized. The person receiving the award then appears on stage amid much fanfare and stands in a spotlight, in one of the most glamorous functions imaginable, before an audience strength of almost a thousand, and receives the coveted statuette at the hands of some well-known personality invited for this purpose, such as an actor, a singer, a writer, a scientist or an acclaimed social activist. There is a standing ovation at the end of the programme, triggered by the human stories that emerge on stage as the persons recovering from a chronic mental illness as well as the caregivers lay bare the heartrending graphs of their life story in a stage interview. Stigma has to slink away in the face of such courage and grit, as well as the willingness to admit to such an illness history and lay before the public an example of the will to survive and overcome all odds.

If psychology is to remain a living, productive discipline, we need to induct the fresh spirit of innovative mental health practices in the community, keep alive curiosity, a service orientation as well as the rigour of research and documentation. At the same time, we need to explore traditional sources of healing such a story telling, in the process of moving away from the western dominance over therapeutics into more indigenous modes, but that is substance of a whole different chapter! We need to create new generations of questing minds and keep adding to the existing fund of knowledge and skills.

Often, although one may be accused of "populist" thinking, it is necessary to motivate the young and involve them in a variety of activities linked with a mental health initiative, and carrying a mental health message. Listed in a box below are examples of some such activities, which can be conducted at low cost and with relatively low money and time investment, with large returns in terms of enthusiasm and interest generation.

REFERENCES

Apte, Savita (2005). *Stigma associated with schizophrenia, coping in caregivers and efficacy of targeted intervention.* Unpublished Doctoral thesis. University of Mumbai.

Bhave, Swati; Sovani, Anuradha; Joshi, Surekha (2008). Life Skill Education workshops with school students: some findings from Mumbai. Paper presented by AACCI at RGNYNID, Chennai, 2008.

Bodas, Jaee, Ollendick Thomas H. and Sovani Anuradha V. (2008). Test anxiety in Indian children: A cross-cultural perspective. *Anxiety, Stress & Coping*, 4, 387-404.

Deshpande, C.G. (PI); Thatte, S.S.; Sovani, A.V. and Kinkar, R. (1997). UGC Major Research project, '*Treatment resistant schizophrenia*', 1996-1999. Unpublished draft submitted.

Friedman, I. and Bendas-Jacob, O. (1997). Measuring perceived test anxiety in adolescents. *Educational and psychological measurement*, 57 (6), 1035-1046.

Hoagwood, K.; Burns, B.J.; Kiser, L.; Ringeisen, H. and Schoenwald, S.K. (2001). Evidence-Based Practice in Child and Adolescent Mental Health Services. *Psychiatric Services,* 52, 1179-1189.

Jidnyaasa modules, Institute for Psychological Health in-house publication, available for sale at IPH counter.

Kadaba, Shweta (2005). *Cognitive dysfunctions and correlates of visual and verbal processing in schizophrenia and brain damage.* Unpublished Doctoral thesis, University of Mumbai.

Sovani (2008). ICONS III, Symposium on rehabilitation. When more is better: The role of cognitive challenges, social support networks, and self-efficacy in schizophrenia rehabilitation. *International Conference on Schizophrenia*, Chennai.

Kadaba, Shwetha and Sovani, Anuradha (2007). Verbal learning difficulty in schizophrenia and epilepsy: implications for retraining. *Archives of Indian Psychiatry*, 9 (1), 49-52.

Sovani, A.V. (1990). *Positive, Negative and Mixed Symptom Schizophrenia – Effects of Interpersonal Interaction and Performance Contingent Verbal Feedback.* Unpublished Doctoral thesis, University of Mumbai.

Sovani, A. (1992). Vanaprastha: A community outreach programme for preparation for old age- Brief Communication. *Indian Journal of Social Psychiatry*, 8, (3-4), 66-68.

Sovani, A.; Thatte, S.; Amrapurkar, S.; Deshpande, S.; Gondhalekar, D. and Nadkarni, A. (1998). The ADD Puzzle and some Cognitive Behavioural solutions. *Asian Journal of Pediatric Practice*, 2 (2), 45-48.

Sovani, A. (2002). Content and process analysis of group interventions for mental health promotion. *Bombay Psychologist*, 18, (1), 66-71.

Sovani, Anuradha (2004). *Kovalee Maney, Saavarnaarey Haat*. (Marathi) Mumbai: Granthali (2000); 2nd ed. Pune: Unmesh Prakashan.

Sovani, A.S.; Thatte, S.S. and Apte, A. (2004). Social disadvantage as a sequel of schizophrenia, *Indian Psychological Review*, special issue on disability.

Sovani, Anuradha (2006). *Parikshecha Raakshas* (Marathi), Pune: Unmesh Prakashan.

Sovani (2007). *Aaaplee muley kaa 'bighadataat'?* (Marathi) Pune: Unmesh Prakashan.

Sovani, Anuradha (2008a). *Sport Psychology. In Handbook of Sports medicine for children and adolescents.* (ed.) Bhave, S.Y., Patel, D.R., and Greydanus, D.E. Jaypee Brothers medical publishers.

Sovani (2008b). ICONS III - Symposium on rehabilitation. *When more is better: The role of cognitive challenges, social support networks, and self-efficacy in schizophrenia rehabilitation.* Chennai.

Sovani, Anuradha (2008c). *Aapale Mool Hushaar Aahe Kaa*? (Marathi) Pune: Unmesh Prakashan.

Sovani, Anuradha (2009). "Shubharthis in India: De-stigmatising schizophrenia – a move towards inclusion" *Invited chapter in Disabilities: Insights From Across Fields and Around the World, 3 volume set.* Marshall, C.A. Kendall, E., Gover, R.M.S. & Banks, M. (Eds.). Westport, CT: Praeger Press, pp. 231-242.

Sovani, Anuradha (2010a). *Maanasrang series*. (Marathi) Pune: Unmesh Prakashan.

Sovani, Anuradha (2010b). *Naate Tujhe Maajhe.* (Marathi) Pune: Unmesh Prakashan.

Subramaniam, Sulabha (2008). *Of Human Bonds* (The Maitra story), IPH Publication.

Thatte, S.S. (1982). *Attentional deficits in psychiatric disorders with reference to arousal and pathology levels*. Unpublished Doctoral thesis. University of Mumbai.

Wells, K.; Miranda, J.; Bruce M.L.; Alegria, M. and Wallerstein, N. (2004). Bridging Community Intervention and Mental Health Services Research. *American Journal of Psychiatry,* 161, 955-963.

5

Integration of Traditional and Modern Systems for Care: The Story of *Dava* and *Dua*

Anuradha S. and *Milesh Hamlai*

Humans developed colonies and societies for support, affiliation and security. Even nomads moved around in groups. Thus began the co-dependence of individual and society. It has been the focus and a constant endeavour of social psychologist, sociologist and anthropologists, to study people and groups. We now understand that while the individual forms the group, the group in turn influences the individual (Baron, 2004). The group or the society that an individual belongs to, contributes in shaping the personality. Research in the field of social psychology has tried to study various aspects of the group that have implications on an individual's development and survival. Social psychology of health has tried to study the health implications of groups. By studying cultural aspects of health it has explored the aspects that influence an individual's overall health and health seeking behaviour. The immediate social situation and the interaction between person and situation variables may yield explanations to a variety of problems.

Worldwide interest in the area of social psychology of health has generated. Currently social psychologists have joined hands with health professionals worldwide in fighting with major health concerns such as cancer, HIV-AIDS and other significant mental health problems. The study of any disorder depends on a careful evaluation of the norms, beliefs and customs within the individual's cultural environment. Studies have found that community attitude and beliefs are the determining factors in the help-seeking behaviour and successful treatment of any health related problem. Therefore, role of the community in the prevention and care has now been widely acknowledged. Community intervention is regarded as the most appropriate basis for the development of health programmes in most of the countries.

In the mental health mission report published in 2003, the overall burden of mental health services was emphasized the most. Integration of existing activities of health care, capacity building and developing linkages amongst the various stakeholders were amongst the recommendations made by the report (Government of Gujarat, 2003). In this regard there were speculations whether community members could be integrated into the health care system to share the responsibility. The partnership between individuals of the community and the health care system has been tried and tested in many other endeavours within the healthcare system. The example of *anganwadi*[1] workers, community health workers and the *daimas*[2] in the maternal and child health projects is a tried and tested proof of the efficiency of the linkage between the community and the health care system (Udani, Chothani, Arora, & Kulkarni, 1980).

When and Where There are no Doctors

In countries like India where most of the expert services are provided at the urban locations, patients from rural areas are very often served by the primary health care providers. Communities very often turn towards their internal resources for help and support.

Traditional healing techniques have existed long before the advent of modern medicine. Herbs, home remedies and most importantly faith were used to cure physical health as well as mental health problems. In India and many other cultures, mental health problems have been attributed to supernatural phenomena. People very often believe that spirituality and religion impact their lives and well-being. Hence, they follow their cultural traditions in health and sickness.

Moreover, medical treatments in the rural areas are viewed as unaffordable and unsustainable in the long term. In a study conducted in West Bengal, 44 per cent families had sought the help of traditional practitioners. Most of the families expected treatments that were low cost and locally available (Pal, Das, Sengupta & Chaudhry, 2002). The results of the study emphasized on two major implications, affordability and accessibility.

In addition to being affordable and accessible, does spirituality and religious beliefs influence an individual's overall health? In a study conducted in Canada, religiousness was associated with less depression, mania and anxiety disorders. Faith has been found to be associated with increase in pain tolerance, lower levels of anxiety and better prognosis for depression. Faith was also positively linked with higher levels of personal growth, increase in self-esteem and healthy practices. In addition, some studies found that faith may decrease the chances of anti-social behaviour, substance abuse and high risk sexual behaviours.

Furthermore, it has been seen that people very often have greater faith in the faith healers than on medical practitioners. In spite of the presence of health services, people continue to follow the path of faith healing. In the study on epilepsy by Pal, Sharma, Prabhakar and Pathak (2008) they found that some families concurrently visited modern hospitals and occult healers seeking a cure for the disease. Approximately 7.5 per cent of the families admitted that they were going to faith healers. Similar findings were also reported by a study in Nigeria where 47.6 per cent used African traditional medicine alone, 24.1 per cent combined traditional medicine with spiritual healing, 20.4 per cent used spiritual healing alone and 7.5 per cent used other forms of alternative medicine (Danesi & Adetunji, 1994).

Hence, it would be unwise to ignore the influence that traditional practices have on people. As discussed earlier, people have faith in the traditional healers and practices. And hence, they frequently visit these places for any physical or mental health concerns. Often people require immediate and specific treatments that may be outside the scope of these traditional healing centres. In such situations, the condition deteriorates and leads to serious consequences. If these patients are directed to appropriate health facilities in time, the situation possibly can be brought under control. This gap may be bridged by integrating with these traditional healing centres. The idea is not to take over these traditional centres and turn them into medical centres but to make them referral points from where patients may be appropriately counselled. This could ensure timely follow up and continuous care. The faith healers or traditional healing practitioners may be trained for identification and referral of disorders (Nizamie, Akthar, Banerjee & Goyal, 2009). In the project conducted in Ranchi, the contribution of the traditional healers and voluntary participants from the community was found to be effective in identification of health problems and service delivery. Traditional healing practitioners and other voluntary health workers from the community can be effectively trained to identify mental illness in the community and persuade them to seek treatment. The delivery model should include intensive health awareness campaign, training of doctors and other health care providers, continuous followup for compliance and side-effects of drugs.

Integration of socio-cultural factors into the service delivery system may lead to effective community mental health interventions. Traditional healers as well as other community members like leaders may be integrated to create awareness about the causes, preventive measures, available resources etc. These members of the community can be regarded as vital agents in the process of developing positive mental health practices within the community.

Traditional healing centres can be found all over-India, in rural as well as in urban areas. These centres are bereft with individuals suffering from a variety of physical and psychological problems. While some people visit these places for religious reasons, others frequent them for their perceived healing powers. In 2002, Raguram and colleagues., compared outcomes of healing temples with that of clinical psychiatry in Tamil Nadu. They reported a 20 per cent reduction in the symptoms of schizophrenia. The clinical improvement was compared to that achieved by psychotropic drug treatments. The report stated that the temples were seen as supportive, non-threatening and reassuring settings by people.

At the same time these centres have also been blacklisted for illegal practices, human rights violations, unhygienic and unsafe locations. One such centre in Erwadi, Tamil Nadu was the site of a gruesome accident. Due to a fire that broke out in this shelter, 25 persons with mental health problems were charred to death. They could not escape as they were all chained. Following this incident, the Supreme Court of India gave a directive to all the state governments to ensure care for mentally challenged persons in all the States. All un-registered bodies such as these traditional healing centres were shut down. People who needed hospitalization were referred to State run facilities and those people who wandered and were homeless were sent to Government homes such as old age homes, state home for women etc.

The judicial intervention may have led to some positive consequences such as elimination of practices like beating and chaining. However, the legal system is also taking away community support. Centers like the Langar house Darga in Andhra Pradesh has stopped allowing people to stay overnight. This in turn has closed the doors for those people seeking a safe shelter with fewer stigmas. The criminalization of these places has left few alternatives for people who do not find a place in the already overflowing state run facilities.

Thus, there is a need to scientifically study the role of the healing centres and the traditional healers in community mental health interventions. In the following section, the illustration of the "Dava-Dua" project is presented. The origin of the project, the objectives and the outcome has been discussed in detail.

"Dava and Dua": A Case study

An ancient and popular Indian belief exists, that *Dava* (Medicine) and *Dua* (Prayers) together cure problems faster. Keeping the philosophical framework of this belief the idea of "Dava and Dua" was conceptualized to provide holistic mental health care to the people keeping their religious faith and belief intact. This project endeavours to bring together professionals and religious faith healers on a common platform for the care of the patients. This is an on-going project since 2005 in Gujarat.

All-over India, mentally ill patients are treated with traditional and religious rituals because generally people have more faith on religion and believe that mental and behavioural problems are caused due to the curse of God or some evil effect. Traditional healing centres are often found within religious set-ups such as temples and *dargahs*

The Dorgan (Dargah) of Mira Data is a famous historical place with strong religious significance. It is known across the nation for its unexplained ailments in the world of ghosts and djinns in regards to mental health problems. There are more than 500 Mujavars and around 1,500 families whose livelihood depends upon these rituals at this Dargah. Majority of the places provide one day care through rituals wherein at the Dargah of Mira Data the patients are retained for a period of 1 to 60 or more days for the rituals.

Characteristics of the Setting and Population under Study

The Dargah of Hazrat Mira Saiyed Ali Datar is situated 100 kms. away from Ahmedabad and is around 550 years old, well known for treating unexplained ailments related to the world of ghosts and Djinns (especially mental disorders). It is one of the biggest and most famous when it comes to patients' turnout. Some of the patients stay for months and even years due to various reasons. The Dargah has 74 rooms for the visitors to reside and they are allowed to stay for a period of 3 months. Over and above these rooms there are plenty of guest houses outside the Dargah for the visitors to reside. The Dargah is managed and maintained by these Mujavars who are the descendants of the Holy Saint Mira Saiyed Ali Datar and they all belong to Saiyed family. None other but only their male descendants can perform religious rituals in the Dargah.

The Dargah was formed as a Trust under the Bombay Trust Act in 1970. The Dargah Committee consists of 11 members out of which nine are Muslim Saiyed family heads and two Hindus. Only the Saiyed's have the right to become Chairman and every year the Chairman changes turn-wise. Their main occupation is to attend the pilgrims visiting the Dargah and perform rituals for them in turn charging them according to the pilgrim's capacity. Due to lack of education amongst the Mujavar community very few are literates and therefore a child from the age of 6-8 years starts performing rituals as per the instructions from their elders. Even those who are literates, due to lack of employment, get into the same business. Some do have side business of running guest houses and restaurants but those are few in number. Overall majority of these Mujavars come from a poor socio-economic background and their main livelihood is to perform religious rituals for the pilgrims visiting the Dargah.

Unava, the village where the Dargah is situated has a population of approximately 13,500[3], where this Muslim community is a minority. In the past it has a history of being a highly sensitive area in regards to religious clashes. As observed, the Dargah's surroundings are covered by the residences, guest houses and small restaurants of Mujavar families. The outskirt of Dargah is always crowded with beggars and a few wandering mentally ill patients. Prevalence of substance abuse such as tobacco in different forms is high amongst the Mujavar community. Children aged 6-7 years are seen consuming cigarettes and *gutkhas*.

The pilgrims who visit the Dargah are known as 'Savalis' visiting from various parts of the country (*majority from Gujarat, Maharashtra and Rajasthan*). Majority of the pilgrims come from a poor socio-economic background. They are either suggested by others who have visited the *Dargah* earlier or they know about the Dargah through other sources and visit the place seeking cure for their problems. These pilgrims are under high influence of these Mujavars and obediently follow everything that is directed by them. Once the trust and faith in Mujavar is built, it becomes blindestablished. Those who cannot afford these rooms and guest houses reside in the Dargah campus.

While patients with mental illness are seen more in the Dargah, patients with other health problems also visit the Dargah. Many such cases have been registered which have been referred to different hospitals and health care centres for availing treatment. Cases with heart problems, cancer, urology problems, skin problems and other issues are common. After the training and sensitization of Mujavars on mental health and its related issues many cases of mental illness were registered from the families of Mujavars who still avail treatment till date. Stigma prevails on a very high level against mental illness amongst these Mujavars.

Majority of mental health services are provided in urban centres by the government. There are four mental hospitals viz. Ahmedabad, Baroda, Bhuj and Jamnagar. Apart from these, there are other medical colleges providing psychiatry care but however they are limited in numbers and there is also an acute shortage of psychiatrists in the Government hospitals due to which many of the civil hospitals do not have mental health services. The private psychiatrists are also situated in the urban setups due to which accessibility and affordability becomes a big issue for people from lower socio-economic background which is at large.

The village of Unava has a PHC[4] with a Medical doctor to address general health issues. However it lacks facilities to address mental health issues. The nearest urban centre is Unjha 5 kms away from Unava with a cottage hospital which lacks a psychiatrist and psychotropic drugs, the second most and a bigger urban area is Mehsana situated 20 kms away from Unava where there are 3 private psychiatrists. A private psychiatrist from Mehsana visits the OPD of Dava & Dua programme also provides honorary services at Civil Hospital in Mehsana but the psychotropic drugs are not available at the hospital therefore they are prescribed from outside. The nearest full-fledged government mental health services are available at Ahmedabad which creates concerns of accessibility and is also time consuming.

This programme has not only been a boon for the pilgrims visiting the Dargah but also has started covering mentally ill patients from the local village and villages of the surrounding areas. Under the programme, diagnosis and medicines are provided free of cost. This has created greater faith in the government system and the programme has gained high popularity.

The "Dava & Dua" project was initiated after a pilot intervention. In the year of 2008 under PPP[5] module, Altruist[6] signed an MOU with the Hospital for Mental Health, Ahmedabad[7] who had received a grant from Gujarat Foundation for Mental Health and Allied Sciences to implement this mental health programme in the holy Shrine of Hazrat Mira Saiyad Ali Datar Dargah Unava, Unjha, Gujarat, India under supervision of Superintendent of Hospital for Mental Health, Ahmedabad. This project funded by Gujarat Foundation for Mental Health & Allied Sciences (GFMHAS) was initiated in 2008 at the Dargah of Mira Datar with an aim to achieve the following goals:

1. Prevention of violation of Human rights as per the Supreme Court Directives of 2004.
2. Provide medical treatment to the mentally ill visiting the Dargah.
3. Educate the traditional healers on issues related to Mental Health and sanitation/hygiene in the Dargah premises.
4. To establish linkages between the Health professionals and Faith Healers for continuity of care for the patients.

The experience from the pilot intervention in the programme (2005-2006), became the guiding stones for designing the final framework of the project and stating the key objectives. Hence, two main goals were formulated for the project for the duration of 2008-09.

To provide medical treatment to the patients visiting the Dargah for spiritual healing.

To create awareness on mental health at a religious place and amalgamate science and religion.

To achieve the above mentioned objectives, the following activities were carried out:

1. An OPD was started at the Dargah premise to provide medical treatment for the mentally ill visiting the Dargah.
2. Trainings for the traditional healers on different mental illnesses and identification of CMDs[8] and to refer the patients at the OPD for availing medical treatment were organized. They were also trained to monitor patients for regular intake of medicines till they stayed at the Dargah to perform their religious rituals.
3. Trainings and sensitization programmes for the traditional healers to prevent the disabilities and chronicity of mental illness.
4. Awareness programmes for the Mujavars on the Hon. Supreme Court Guidelines, Rights of the Patients and legal issues related to mental health as per the Mental Health Act, 1987.
5. Establish a linkage system between the Health Professionals and Mujavars for accessibility of mental health services. Mental health services to be provided by psychiatrists and physicians visiting the Dargah during the OPD hours. A back-up of mental health services by the HMH (Hospital for Mental Health) for admission of chronic patients.
   The local administration was involved and sensitized during the implementation of the programme for better support at PHC (Primary Health Centre), CHC (Community Health Centre) and Civil hospital, Mehsana level to provide care and treatment to the patients visiting the Dargah.
6. Establish a follow up system of the patients. After availing medical treatment the patients are referred back to the Mujavars. The clinical psychologist and the field workers then follow up the patients and their care-takers for counselling and create awareness amongst them on mental health in the presence of their Mujavars. This in turn sustains the medical treatment and improvement is seen amongst the patients. The field workers are in constant touch with the patients and once the patients are ready to leave the Dargah they are referred to the nearest government mental health services available in their area for continuity of care.

For the implementation of the above mentioned objectives planned strategies were employed. The following is a description of the strategies.

A triangular strategy was implemented in the first phase, the local administration and the Non-Government officials approached the Dargah Trustees to establish rapport with the Dargah Management.

As an initial phase of interactions through Focused Group Discussion (FGDs) and Key Informants Interview (KIIs) of the Mujavars, it was revealed that the Mujavars had a low and no understanding of mental illness and its symptoms, and their approach was based on time healing emotional disturbances. This more or less never worked in case of severe psychotic cases while patients languished at the Dargah for 10 years or more.

The Psychiatry OPD was opened after convincing the Dargah Management to provide scientific treatment to the patients within the premises of the Dargah (*Dargah Trust Office*). At the beginning, the OPD was run only twice a week. However, within 5 months it was so successful that the OPD services were extended to 6 days in a week and has been continued since then. Private Psychiatrists visited the Dargah from Monday to Saturday to attend the OPD. The role of the psychiatrists was to diagnose the mentally ill patients and provide them with free medication. These patients being referred by the Mujavars for medical interventions in the OPD were sent back to the Mujavars for continuation of their religious rituals. Thus this has become a tripartite programme (Fig. 5.1).

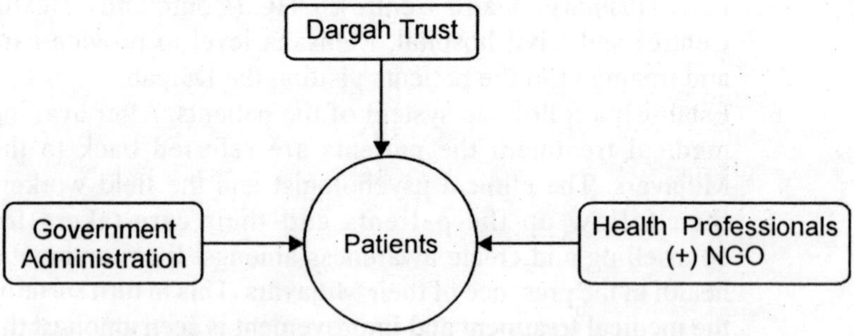

Fig. 5.1: Relationship among Government/Administration, health professional, Dargah trust, and the patients — a schematic representation.

Mujavar Community Mobilization Training (CMT): In the programme, community mobilization was one of the core strategies to build strong mental health awareness amongst the Mujavar community. It aimed to create knowledge based awareness on mental health. The network of health workers of the Altruist became the moving force at the grassroots level to which, the programmes success is highly attributable. Many Mujavars have displayed interest and have started undertaking "Dava & Dua" plus activities of advocating for other health services, sanitation and hygiene. During the programme implementation, the collective strength of the Mujavars was harnessed for sustaining the programme impact by making them an important link between the patient and the health professionals. Once the Mujavar referred a patient to the health professionals during the OPD, the patients were sent back to them. This gave a major thrust on their faith of not losing their client and slowly the Mujavars started bringing their family members who suffered from mental illness for medical treatment at the OPD.

Behaviour Change Communication (BCC): During the implementation BCC activities were planned. The BCC strategy was innovative and successfully used a mix of multi-mediums of posters, flip books, exhibitions, camps for promotion of mental health messages and targeting individuals, Mujavars and at community level audiences under specific mediums.

The direct implication of the BCC activities at the community and individual level was that mentally ill patients from the village started approaching OPD for medical treatment, the visitors of the Dargah started inquiring about the mental health services. Other community members became aware and started gaining knowledge about the positive and preventive mental health behaviours and also increasingly started practicing them.

Training had been a central theme for the "Dava and Dua" programme. Altruist has conducted need based general training on different types of mental illnesses, control of chronic cases, sanitation and hygiene, BCC and counselling and qualitative assessment techniques using the Appreciative Inquiry Approach, Audio Visuals, Demonstrations and learn-by-doing approaches. Under the programme the altruist organization employees were equipped with updated skills and knowledge provided by the Hospital for Mental Health, Ahmedabad. The implication of this successful strategy resulted in improved caregiver and care provider practices and protocols. It also strengthened the caregiver's decision-making skills for medical treatment for their mentally ill patients. The programme continued to use need based technical training on Mental health for BCC, Communication and counselling, Mujavar Community Mobilization and Leadership, and qualitative assessment techniques in regards to CMDs using the audio-visuals, demonstrations, and learn-by-doing approaches to promote positive mental health, improve sanitation and hygiene of the Dargah behaviours in the Dargah and community levels and to improve the knowledge, skills and practices of health care providers at the facility level.

During the programme implementation, updating of knowledge had been the main strategy to educate the Mujavars on mental illness and its symptoms.

Outcome

The programme covered population of approximately 1,782 mentally ill patients. Mental health services and referral services were mobilized during the programme duration. Currently, the project is provided continuous services and is in the process of including more interventions to the initial objectives of the project.

The number of cases attended by the mental health professionals within the Dargah premises shows the effect of the trainings conducted for the traditional healers. The Mujavars have also contributed in the project actively by referring patients to the mental health services. The overall number of patients seeking mental health services reflects the success of the project. The awareness created amongst the traditional healers has led to an increase in the efficiency of service delivery. In addition, the project result demonstrates increased use, coverage, quality and sustainability of the mental health services. Much appreciation has been shown to the project efforts and outcomes (NHRC, 2010). Similar outcomes were also reported in Gujarat under the mental health support programme. A Pune based NGO initiated a pilot project to study the role of traditional health practitioners and community health workers in the mental health services. Over 100 traditional health practitioners across five tribal areas were trained for identification and referral services in the area of mental health. As a result of this integration, 133 persons were identified with mental health problems and appropriate referrals were made to the district health centres (IIM, 2007).

With reference to the illustration of the "Dava & Dua" project, it may be concluded that the role of traditional healers as agents in the mental health service delivery system is crucial. The active and enthusiastic participation by the traditional healers sets an example of the community's innate strength for making the mental health services accessible, available and affordable.

In conclusion, faith is an integral part of the Indian culture. There is a need to study faith, faith healing and other traditional methods of healing systems used in the context of any culture. One has to recognize the inherent strength these systems hold in the well-being of its members. The essence of these systems varies from individual to individual and across cultures. While this project sets an example of a manner in which the traditional systems may be integrated with the modern systems, it also raises some social concerns. In the process of integration or amalgamation, are we trying to convert these places of religious and cultural significance into a pseudo-medical centre? Will the interference of medical professionals affect the accessibility of the common man into these places that are perceived as safe until now? These questions should not discourage us; in turn it should make us aware about the possible ramifications.

The continual presence of the "Dava & Dua" project within the Dargah premises and the continuous inflow of patients in the Dargah as well as the mental health services provided show that a harmonious relationship is possible to establish. The project does not interfere in the matter of traditional healing and the Dargah, this ensures the continuity in the ways of the traditional healing system. Thus, the amalgamation of the modern system and the traditional system can surely lead to efficient services not only in Gujarat but also in any culture.

REFERENCES

Baron (2004). *Introduction to Social Psychology*. Pearson India (Pvt) Ltd., New Delhi.

Danesi, M. A. & Adetunji, J. B. (1994). Use of alternative medicine by patients with epilepsy: A survey of 265 epileptic patients in a developing country. *Epilepsia*, Mar-Apr, 35, (2), 344-51.

Mental Health Care Pilots in Gujarat, Processes, Outcomes and Learning (2007), *Indian Institute of Management*, Ahmedabad.

Nizamie, S.H.; Akthar, S.; Banerjee, I.; Goyal, N. (2009). Health care delivery model in epilepsy to reduce treatment gap: World Health Organization study from a rural tribal population of India. *Epilepsy Research,* Apr, 84 (2-3), 146-52.

Pal, D.K.; Das, T.; Sengupta, S.; Chaudhury, G. (2002). Psychosocial, demographic, and treatment-seeking strategic behaviour, including faith healing practices, among patients with epilepsy in north-west India. *Epilepsia,* Aug; 43 (8), 904-11.

Pal, S.K.; Sharma, K.; Prabhakar, S. and Pathak, A. (2008). Psychosocial, demographic, and treatment-seeking strategic behaviour, including faith healing practices, among patients with epilepsy in north-west India. *Epilepsy & Behaviour*, Aug 13, (2), 323-32.

Raguram, R.; Venkateswaran, A.; Ramakrishna, J. and Weiss, M.G. (2002). Traditional community resources for mental health: A report of temple healing from India. *British Medical Journal*, 325, 38-40.

The Mission Report 2003 (2003). Priorities for mental health sector development in Gujarat. Department of Health and Family Welfare, Government of Gujarat.

Udani, R.H.; Chothani, S.; Arora, S. and Kulkarni, C.S. (1980). Evaluation of knowledge and efficiency of anganwadi workers, *Indian Journal of Pediatrics*. Vol. 47, No. 4, 289-292.

NOTES

1. Anganwadi workers: workers from the local community trained to work in the area of health; mainly reproductive and child health area.
2. Daimas: untrained nurses who assist in child birth.
3. As per the census 2001 figures.
4. Public Health Centre.
5. Public Private Partnership.
6. Altruist is an NGO working in the field of mental health with an experience of implementing mental health programmes, IEC, Trainings, public awareness and many such other activities.
7. The Hospital for Mental Health, Ahmedabad provides mental health services. It provides mental health care and services in the form of preventive and promotional services, curative services, mental health education and other services in the areas of mental health in the State of Gujarat.
8. Common Mental Disorders.

6

The Stress, Adaptation and Coping Pattern of Mothers with Children Having Cerebral Palsy

Urmi Nanda Biswas and *Mansi Shah*

Introduction

Parents and caregivers of children with chronic health conditions are known to run the risk of emotional distress and poor adjustment to the demands of caring for a child with special needs (Kersten *et al.*, 2001). Chronic illnesses and disability are highly demanding conditions requiring consistent care, as are the case with Cerebral Palsy and more severe degrees of intellectual disabilities. It has been observed that multiple stressors may contribute to this increased risk that include feelings of uncertainty over child's health outcome, daily difficulties associated with medical regimes, social isolation, role restrictions and financial strains (Kersten *et al.*, 2001; Brehaut *et al.*, 2004). Commonly known is the fact that caregivers of people with cancer and other chronic illnesses neglect their own physical well-being, but new evidence also suggests that they may also neglect their mental health. Caregivers of cancer patients have been reported to experience a clinically significant level of distress (Vanderwarkar, 2005). This distress and vulnerability to psychological disorders may have a bearing on the intervention for the person with disability as well as the caregivers themselves. In a study on the caregivers of children with cerebral palsy in Ontario, Canada, measures of caregiver psychological health showed greater reported distress, chronicity of distress, emotional problems and cognitive problems (Brehaut *et al.*, 2004). Such situations may place a higher demand on the caregivers to rely on their social support and family. Thus, the role of family and social support has increasing importance in supporting the caregivers of people with chronic disabilities.

Cerebral Palsy (CP)

"Cerebral" means brain. "Palsy" means a disorder of movement. CP refers to a group of non-progressive neuro-muscular problems of varying severity.

CP is damage to the brain, primarily to the part of the brain that controls motor functions. However other parts of the brain may also be affected and mental retardation could also be seen. An updated definition and classification of CP is given as follows:

CP describes a group of disorders of the development of movement & posture, causing activity limitations that are attributed to non-progressive disturbances that occurred in the developing foetal or infant brain. The motor disorders of cerebral palsy are often accompanied by disturbances of sensation, cognition, communication, perception and/or behaviour, and/or by seizure disorder (Gilham, 1987). Doctors classify cerebral palsy in two ways: by the affected limbs and by the nature of the movement disturbance.

By the affected limbs: the common types under this classification are Quadriplegia, Hemiplegia and Diplegia. By the nature of movement disturbances the group involves: Spastic Cerebral Palsy, Ataxic Cerebral Palsy, Athetoid Cerebral Palsy, Mixed Cerebral Palsy.

The present study includes children with Cerebral Palsy who are affected by limbs *i.e.,* diagnosed as Quadraplegia. When a child shows cerebral palsy in all four of their limbs—both arms and both legs, it is called Quadriplegia. Usually children with quadriplegia have trouble moving all the parts of their bodies, their face and trunk as well as their arms and legs, and may need a wheelchair to get around. Because of the problems related to controlling the muscles in their face and upper body, they also have trouble in talking and eating. The present research tries to understand the stress, adaptation and coping pattern of mothers of quadriplegic CP children from different socio-religious background in order to identify the role of various psychosocial and demographic parameters in their preferred coping strategies and adaptation pattern.

The Problem of Acceptance

The diagnosis of developmental disability in a child can trigger a range of emotional responses in parents and across family systems. For some, it will constitute a crisis that requires extraordinary psychological adjustment on a parent's part and contains elements of harm, loss, and weakness. For others, the birth of a disabled child will be viewed as an unfortunate event, yet one that has positive implications; it may provoke psychological growth in some family members or heightened overall family functioning. Indeed, this wide scope of behavioural and emotional responses, from largely positive to entirely negative, can result in most stress reactions in which potentially threatening or hurtful events are met by a range of possible subjective interpretations (Lazarus & Folkman, 1984).

Undoubtedly, it is difficult to accept the fact that a child is handicapped for life. This implies many things.

The mother may have to sacrifice fully or partially, her ambitions for a career.

The father, whatever the nature of his profession and opportunities available, may have to stay tied to a city or town where help is available for the child.

Physically, more efforts have to be put in to cope with the child. Lifestyles may require drastic changes to accommodate the child's needs.

Success may come slowly and in small measures, seemingly incommensurate with the efforts parents take.

Financially, it may take more to raise a handicapped child. And there is no guarantee that the child will someday earn his or her living.

A child with Cerebral Palsy has major adjustment problems, both with himself/herself, as also with family, teachers, caregivers and all those who happen to fall within his sphere of connectivity. If not handled properly, he becomes his own enemy first. Thereafter, it is only a downhill slide, not only in terms of physical deterioration but psychological as well.

In most cases of CP, the psychological disadvantage is just as major as the physical ones, with the two being very closely linked.

Lack of muscular control and coordination, in varying degrees, affects the gross and fine motor skills. In turn, they affect a child's movement and ability to handle things, even when the mind wills it otherwise. Physical impairments like inability to stand, sit, walk, talk, smile etc., as also a weakness of the facial muscles leading to drooling, and inability to speak and swallow are some of the initial manifestations of CP. It is the secondary and associated symptoms, like seizures and mental retardation, which are more difficult to cope with both by the affected child and his caregivers.

With physical impairments cause frustrations at the restriction of mobility, inability to do simple tasks, and at times even a distorted appearance. The feeling of hopelessness, helplessness, and resentment compounded by the grief and guilt of parents sends these children into a state of depression. The saddest part of it is that very often they touch rock bottom in their depressed state and harbour suicidal thoughts. But cognitive and physical impairment very often prevents them from acting on such thoughts. As such, their depression only grows, but is not seen by the family members and caregivers.

Feelings of acceptance, recognition and the desire to fit-in and be liked are as strong in children with CP as in normal children. But their feelings are not really understood, nor reciprocated by their peer group, generating a sense of alienation. With time, the needs of these children also change, as does the awareness about their physical limitations. The spate of questions that follow need to be answered, the pent up feelings given an avenue of expression, perspectives on problems need to be changed and seen as challenges rather than as punishment.

This is where the role of the parents and caregivers assumes great significance. Teenagers and young adults with CP need extra help to learn to live independently. Occupational skills, like learning to prepare a meal, handle money and use public transport are some of the ways to bring about this independence. Parents also need to shift their focus from their CP child, to other siblings for they run a higher risk of developing behavioural and emotional disturbances.

It is important for parents to take charge of them and build emotionally strong relationships at home, as also a strong support network. This will help them come up with creative strategies to cope with the challenges of raising a child with developmental disabilities.

Mothers play a pivotal role in many families and research and other studies have shown that they carry bulk of household chores and child care. Hautamaki (1997) has produced findings from a cross-

Nordic study in which she contrasted the situation of over 1000 mothers of children with down-syndrome with mother of non-disabled children. She found that the mothers of children with down-syndrome had increased care taking responsibility, had often amended their 'life project' goals, had more restricted leisure activities and different work patterns and when they did work they had high levels of sick leave. In her international study Mittler (1995) found that mothers typically remained the major care-givers throughout all region of the world.

The mother of a spastic child is in an unenviable position; more so in the patriarchal Indian society. Often, tacitly or openly, the mother is blamed for the handicap of the child. The care of the child is often left to the mother. The male relatives are "too busy" to spend time with the child. It is not uncommon for a mother to tend to the daily routine (washing, shaving, bathing) of her handicapped son who is in his thirties, because the male relatives choose not to be involved with these. The child grows to be excessively dependent on the mother and the relationship can get obsessive. It can get to be exhausting for the mother. On the flip side, the mother is likely to be the most reassuring figure in the child's life and her commitment can go a long way towards helping the child.

Little is known about the proportion of mothers of children with cerebral palsy (CP) who experience distress, particularly in terms of depressed and anxious moods (Barlow *et al.*, 2006). A study was conducted on the psychological well-being among mothers of children with cerebral palsy by addressing this issue by examining the level of maternal anxious and depressed moods. Results showed 29.8 per cent, 26 per cent and 11.7 per cent of mothers were at low, moderate, and high risk of clinically anxious mood compared with population female norms of 23 per cent, 13 per cent, and 3 per cent, respectively. A total of 22.1 per cent and 19.5 per cent of mothers were at low and moderate risk of clinically depressed mood compared with norms of 9 per cent and 4 per cent, respectively. Anxious and depressed moods were inversely associated with generalized self-efficacy and anxious mood was inversely associated with children's sleeping difficulties. In conclusion, levels of maternal psychological well-being are a cause for concern and warrant exploration of interventions that will reduce maternal distress, and increase self-efficacy.

Studies have suggested that parents of children with developmental disabilities, particularly mothers, experience greater stress and less psychological well-being than controls (Bradshaw &

Lawton, 1978; Breslau & Davis, 1986; Breslau, Staruch & Mortimer, 1982). Additionally some researchers have assessed the relationship of parental stress levels to relevant medical and social characteristics of the child and family. Chetwynd (1985) found higher stress levels in mothers of intellectually disabled children to be related to child temperament factors as well as socio-economic status.

Social class and maternal level of anxiety were found to be the best predictors of stress in mothers of seriously ill, hospitalized children (Wyckoff & Erickson 1987). Social support networks have also been investigated in families with developmentally disabled and chronically ill children (Kazak & Marvin, 1984; Kazak, Reber & Carter, 1988) and found to relate to level of stress. Thus, the role of social support in the life of mothers of CP children needs to be studied further as a stress buster.

Coping Strategies

Coping strategies refer to the specific efforts, both behavioural and psychological, that people employ to master, tolerate, reduce, or minimize stressful events. Two general coping strategies have been distinguished: problem-solving strategies are efforts to do something active to alleviate stressful circumstances, whereas emotion-focused coping strategies involve efforts to regulate the emotional consequences of stressful or potentially stressful events. Research indicates that people use both types of strategies to combat most stressful events (Folkman & Lazarus, 1980). The predominance of one type of strategy over another is determined, in part, by personal style (e.g., some people cope more actively than others) and also by the type of stressful event; for example, people typically employ problem-focused coping to deal with potential controllable problems such as work-related problems and family-related problems, whereas stressors perceived as less controllable, such as certain kinds of physical health problems, prompt more emotion-focused coping.

An additional distinction that is often made in the coping literature is between active and avoidant coping strategies. Active coping strategies are either behavioural or psychological responses designed to change the nature of the stressor itself or how one thinks about it, whereas avoidant coping strategies lead people into activities (such as alcohol use) or mental states (such as withdrawal) that keep them from directly addressing stressful events. Generally speaking, active coping strategies, whether behavioural or emotional, are thought to be better ways to deal with stressful events, and avoidant coping strategies appear to be a psychological risk factor or marker for adverse responses to stressful life events (Holahan & Moos, 1987).

Families use a variety of coping strategies that may influence family functioning. The work of Pearlin and Schooler (1978) and Folkman and Lazarus (Folkman & Lazarus, 1985; Folkman *et al.*, 1986; Lazarus & Folkrnan, 1980) indicate that coping is a major factor in the relation between stressful events and adaptation outcomes. This body of research is characterized by an interest in the different coping behaviours people employ in response to different life events. Family coping strategies can potentially strengthen or maintain family resources that serve to protect the family from the demands of stressful encounters (McCubbin *et al.,* 1980). The various types of strengths that families possess reflect the way in which families cope and grow (Dunst *et al.* 1988). Lazarus and Folkman (1985) have defined coping as "constantly changing cognitive and behavioural efforts to manage specific external and/or internal demands that are appraised as taxing or exceeding the resources of the person". According to this definition, coping includes any attempt or effort to manage stress, regardless of how well it works. Coping strategies involve efforts to alter the cause of the stress (problem-focused coping) and efforts to regulate emotional responses to the stressors (emotion-focused coping). For example, problem-focused forms of coping include active problem-solving and seeking social support as well as aggressive interpersonal efforts to alter the situation. In contrast, emotion-focused forms of coping include detaching from the situation, controlling one's feelings, wishing the problem would go away, and blaming oneself for the situation. According to Frey, Greenberg, and Fewell (1989), problem-solving is the preferred style of coping with disability-related problems. Research indicates that emotion-focused coping that involves wishful thinking, denial, or avoidance is positively related to reports of depressed moods (e.g., Aldwin & Revenson, 1987; Bolger, 1990; Cronkite & Moos, 1984; Folkman & Lazarus, 1986) and problem-focused coping is associated with reduced distress (Aldwin & Revenson, 1987; Folkman, Lazarus, Dunkel Schetter, DeLongis & Gruen, 1986). Promoting and building upon the range of existing family strengths and coping strategies that occur within the family has been suggested as a component of comprehensive support for families that include a member with a disability (Dunst *et al.,* 1994; Hanline & Daley, 1992; Turnbull & Turnbull, 1990). However, few studies provide an empirical basis to understand the coping strategies of families that help promote family strengths. Thus, it is important to understand the stress, adaptation and coping style of mothers of children with cerebral palsy as it would further help us know about their vulnerability to psychological disorders. Further, the kind of social support that these mothers as caregivers receive and how the kind of family system in turn extends a support are significant from the perspective of social health psychology. This will aid in understanding the stress and coping pattern of these mothers.

The objectives of the research were as follows:

- To study stress level and adaptation of mother of cerebral palsy children.
- To understand the preferred coping strategies that mothers of quadriplegic CP children use to handle their problems.
- To study the differences in coping pattern of mothers belonging to joint families from the coping patterns of mothers belonging to nuclear families.
- On the backdrop of the above review and the objective, the following hypotheses was conjectured:
  H1: There will be no significance difference in coping pattern of mothers having joint family or nuclear family.
  H2: There will be no significant difference among mothers from different religious backgrounds in their preferred coping strategies.

Method

Sample

Total sample comprised of 60 mother and child dyads. Inclusion criteria of mother of cerebral palsy children selected for the study was they should be living with their spouses. Included children who have already been detected with cerebral palsy along with mental retardation and below age 14. Total sample of 60 was divided according to two family types, 30 mothers were taken from joint family background which means they either stay with in-laws or with the parents and 30 from nuclear family.

The inclusion criteria of the sample for the study were that the mothers should be living with their spouses, the child's age should be between 3 and 16, and the child should be diagnosed as Quadraplegic Spastic and the child should be non-ambulatory.

The exclusion criteria of the study was that the mothers who were separated, divorced or not residing with spouse were not included and also the children with Hemiplegic and Diplegic Cerebral Palsy.

The final sample comprised of 60 mother and child dyads in all, where the minimum age of mother was 27 years, maximum age was 44 years and average age was 35.07 years. Mother's education ranged from education till SSC to Doctorates where on an average most mothers were graduates. Their occupation varied from being a homemaker to doing a business, however on an average most mothers were homemakers. They belonged to either Hindu or Islam religion and they had a single child or two children wherein sibling's age varied from 0 to 16 year. On an average they had a single child and if the child had a sibling then the mean age of the sibling was around 4 years.

Father's age, education and occupation varied from 30 to 46 years, HSC to Doctorates employed in government or private jobs to running their own business and their average age was 38.50 years. Monthly income of the family also varied but average income was Rs. 5000-10, 000. Out of the total sample of 60 mothers, 30 mothers belonged to joint family and 30 belonged to nuclear family thus number of family members living together ranged from 3 to 11. Child's age ranged from 5 years to 15 years, where mean age of the children was 9.35 years.

Tools

The measures used for studies are:

- Demographic details
- COPE questionnaire by Carver, Scheier and Weintraub (1989).
- Parental questionnaire (interview schedule)

Cope: The COPE is a multidimensional coping inventory developed by Carver *et al.* (1989). It incorporated 15 conceptually distinct scales which were developed on theoretical grounds or chosen on the basis of previous work which demonstrated their role in facilitating or impending adaptive coping in different context.

Test retest reliabilities for the dispositional version were obtained from two samples of subjects over six and eight week periods and ranged from 0.42 to 0.89 for different scales. This indicates that the coping tendencies measured by COPE are reasonably stable.

Explanation of some of the 15 dimensions used in cope scale:

Active Coping: Active coping over here means taking action and exerting efforts, to remove or lessen the distress that one would face.

Planning: In planning person would start thinking about how to confront the stressor, it is planning one's active coping efforts.

Seeking instrumental social support: In seeking instrumental social support person would try to cope by seeking information, assistance or advice about what to do. Here one would ask others in similar situation what they did or will take advice from others what to do.

Seeking emotional and social support: Here person would try to get sympathy or emotional support from someone, and would discuss their feelings and distress that they are going through.

Suppression of competing activities: In this particular coping mechanism one would start suppressing their attention to other activities in which one might engage, in order to concentrate more completely on dealing with stressor.

Turning to religion: In this coping technique there will be increase of engagement in religious and spiritual activities. Over here one would comparatively pray more than usual and would try to find comfort in their religion.

Positive reinterpretation and growth: Positive reinterpretation and growth means making the best of the situation by growing from it, or viewing it in a more favourable light.

Parental Questionnaire: Parental Questionnaire was developed by Bhargava (unpublished Ph.D. dissertation, Faculty of Human Development and Family Studies, M. S. University, Vadodara) and is also used in many researches. It consists of open ended questions measuring parental stress, adaptation and emotions of parents having disabled child.

Procedure

COPE and Parental questionnaire were first translated in Gujarati language and then were again translated back in English language to ensure its transliteral equivalence. After preparing questionnaire researcher contacted physiotherapist and orthopaedic surgeons of Ahmedabad city and identify ones who deal with CP children.

Background data of cerebral palsy children was collected which includes medical records, severity of problem etc., based on the information a sample was selected for inclusion in study. After the selection of sample mothers were contacted in children's clinic before or after the therapy session with permission from the clinician. The rapport was established and questionnaires were administered to mothers, who were willing. Completed questionnaires from 60 mothers were considered for the research.

Results and Discussion

Demographic details and two questionnaires were used by the researcher namely COPE and Parental Questionnaire for the study. Data available through parental questionnaire was subjected through qualitative analysis; specifically content analysis, whereas data analysis of COPE questionnaire and demographic detail was subjected through SPSS for *t* test and correlation.

Table 6.1: Initial Reaction

When you first came to know of your child's problem what was your reaction?				
	Joint		*Nuclear*	
	Frequency	*Percentage*	*Frequency*	*Percentage*
Disbelief	13	43.33	10	33.33
Bitterness	4	13.33	3	10
Guilt	7	23.33	5	16.67
Why me?	8	26.67	5	16.67
Self-blaming	17	56.67	13	43.33
Blaming spouse	0	0	0	0
Blaming god	10	33.33	4	13.33
Blaming fate	11	36.67	10	33.33
Should not have conceived	2	6.67	3	10
Could not understand problem	0	0	3	10
TOTAL	72		56	

Qualitative Analysis

Table 6.1 presents the initial reaction of mother when they came to know about their child's problem. The results indicated that 56.67 per cent of mothers from joint family and 43.33 per cent mothers from nuclear family blamed themselves as an initial reaction when they came to know about their child having Cerebral Palsy. Some of the mothers were also not able to believe that their child had a problem (43.33% joint family and 33.33% nuclear family). Even blaming of fate was seen a lot in mothers (36.67% joint family and 33.33% nuclear family). Some of the mothers had guilt feelings (23.33% joint family and 10% nuclear family) and some even blamed God (33.33% joint family and 13.33% nuclear family) when they came to know about their child's problem. Whereas none of the mothers from either family system blamed their spouse for the same (0% joint family and 0% nuclear family). This could be understood in light of the values and the belief system which are deeply rooted in the Indian culture.

Other reactions like 'bitterness' (13.33% joint family and 10% nuclear family), 'why me?' (26.67% joint family and 16.67% nuclear family), 'I should not have conceived' (6.67% joint family and 10% nuclear family) and 'I was not able to understand the problem (0% joint family and 10% nuclear family) were also prevalent among mothers having cerebral palsy child.

No major difference is seen in the initial reactions between mothers of joint family and nuclear family. The role of family system plays a major role in coping with the problem after the initial reaction. Self-blame and blaming the fate is higher among mothers as the fabric of the society is such where the mother's role and responsibilities are perceived to be more in child's health issues and upbringing (Table 6.2).

Table 6.2 describes how mothers tried to cope when they came to know that their child had problem. Most of the mothers went from one doctor to another doctor to understand the problem that their child had (43.33% joint family and 36.67% nuclear family), whereas some of them even started therapy (20% joint family and 10% nuclear family). Some of them gave explanations for their child's condition (6.67% joint family and 3.33% nuclear family) and some started using all their energy on child (13.33% joint family and 16.67% nuclear family).

Table 6.2: Cope

How did you try to cope?	*Joint*		*Nuclear*	
	Frequency	*Percentage*	*Frequency*	*Percentage*
Go from Dr to Dr to understand the problem?	13	43.33	11	36.67
Over a period of time started to feel that child does not have too much of problem	3	10	4	13.33
Gave explanations/reasons for child's condition	2	6.67	1	3.33
Used all your energy on child	4	13.33	5	16.67
Started looking something positive in it	0	0	1	3.33
Started therapy	6	20	3	10
Surfed net, read books to find out more	2	6.67	5	16.67
TOTAL	30		30	

Few of them even read books and surfed net to find out more about their child's problem (6.67% joint family and 16.67% nuclear family). This was higher in nuclear families compared to joint families as the accessibility to information from experienced family members is difficult. Some mothers over a period of time started feeling that their child does not have too much of problem (10% joint family, 13.33% nuclear family). Such a coping style may be expected from mothers who had problem accepting the child's condition and wanted to ease the burden of dealing with it.

Both, mothers belonging to joint family and that of nuclear family started coping in more or less similar way when they came to know about their child's problem. However, the idea of doctor's shop to understand the problem and giving explanations about child's condition, tends to be more among mothers belonging to joint family than nuclear family. This could be attributed to the causal beliefs of any illness that exists in a given family. So in order to seek confirmation, the idea of consulting several doctors and giving explanations seems to be viable for mothers from joint family.

The results also explain that mothers from nuclear families have limited social support due to which, apart from consulting several doctors, they read books or surf the net and give all the attention to the child.

Mothers were asked about different religious activities they adopt for the well-being of the child. Majority of mothers from joint family seek blessings for the child by means of making a vow (mannat), whereas, majority of mothers from nuclear family go to temple and light candles (diyas) regularly. Religious coping is strongly rooted in the Indian culture hence, mothers from both the families resort more frequently to religious coping styles. Mothers from joint family are more involved in religious practices which are recommended by the primary social support group.

When enquired what mothers feel about their child's progress, mothers from nuclear family reported that their child has made adequate progress more (73.33%) as compared to mothers from joint families (60%). As in joint family there are other members of family whose opinion also influences mother's belief and child's progress might even get compared with other cousins living with them, as a result less number of mothers from joint family believe that their child has made progress. Also, the mothers from nuclear families may feel that they are solely responsible for the child's progress, so increased belief in progress would keep the mothers motivated to further the child's progress.

Mothers were asked to report how they feel when child is not progressing consistently. Majority of mothers belonging to joint family feel worried (40%) when their child is not progressing consistently whereas majority of mothers from nuclear family (40%) get frustrated. Contrary to these, only 13.33 per cent of mothers from joint family get frustrated and only 26.67 per cent of mothers from nuclear family get worried. This kind of difference can be seen because of the differences in family structure. In joint family mothers will be having support of other family members as a result they might not get frustrated but vice a versa mothers from joint family worry more than mothers belonging to the nuclear family. Some of the mothers even get angry (20% joint family and 13.33% nuclear family) and some even feel depressed (23.33% joint family and 20% nuclear family) when their child is not progressing consistently. It was good to realize that, several mothers even treat it as challenge and start working more with the child (36.67% joint family and 30% nuclear family).

When mothers were asked how often they take their children for outing like taking to a park, social functions, to a friend's house etc., their reports indicated that 43.33 per cent of mothers from joint family and 40 per cent of mothers from nuclear family occasionally take their child for outings. This can be due to the reason that in a nuclear family no other member would be there to look after the child when the parents go out. There are few parents who rarely take their child out (26.67% joint family and 20% nuclear family), and they do so only when compelled. The social stigma associated to the illness may compel the parents to avoid outings or social gatherings, when they have to take their child out.

Quantitative Analysis

Table 6.3: Mean, Standard deviation and *t* ratio for the comparison of mean between mothers belonging to Hindu and Islam religion across the dimensions of COPE

	Hindu (N=35)		*Islam (N=25)*		*t*
Dimensions	*Mean*	*SD*	*Mean*	*SD*	
Active coping	12.2	1.34	11.36	1.38	2.35*
Planning	12.8	1.67	12.04	1.88	1.64
Seeking instrumental social support	13.74	1.33	13.56	1.89	0.43
Seeking emotional social support	9.89	1.92	10.6	2.02	-1.38
Suppression of social support	11.54	1.80	11.48	1.87	0.13
Turning to religion	12.34	2.64	12.92	2.58	-0.84
Positive reinterpretation and growth	12.2	1.762	11.6	1.44	1.39
Restraint coping	11.74	1.9	10.96	2.03	1.52
Acceptance	12.03	2.467	11.36	2.15	1.08
Focus on and venting of emotions	11.43	1.42	11.96	1.33	-1.46
Denial	6.91	1.579	7.52	1.85	-1.36
Mental disengagement	7.06	1.893	7.4	2.21	-0.64
Behavioural disengagement	7.26	1.738	7.44	1.7	-0.40
Alcohol/drugs use	4.51	0.853	5.04	1.20	-1.97*
Humour	4.86	1.033	4.8	1.19	.019

Note: $p < .05 =*$

A significant mean difference was found between mean scores of active coping and alcohol and drug abuse among mothers belonging to Hindu and Muslim religion. Looking at the means of both the groups, it shows that mean scores of mothers belonging to Hindu religion (12.20) is higher than the mean scores of mothers belonging to Islam religion (11.36) on active coping dimension. This shows that mothers belonging to Hindu religion do more of an active coping than mothers belonging to Islam religion.

Significant mean difference was also reported on the dimension of alcohol and drug use. Looking at the means of both the groups, it shows that mean scores of mother belonging to Islam religion (5.04) is higher than the mean scores of mothers belonging to Hindu religion (4.51) on the dimension of alcohol and drug use. This shows that mothers following Islamic religion use more drugs like sleeping pills and anti-depressant for coping than mothers belonging to Hindu religion.

The results suggest that coping pattern of mothers belonging to Hindu and Muslim groups differ on some of the dimensions of COPE. Hindu mothers resort to more of active coping, planning, suppression of social support, restraint coping and acceptance as compared to mothers belonging to the Muslim group. Whereas, mothers with Islamic beliefs resort more to turning to religion, focus on and venting of emotions, denial, mental disengagement and alcohol/drugs use as compared to Hindu mothers. Active coping has been conceptualized as taking action and exerting efforts, to remove or lessen the distress that one would face, thus it is higher among Hindu mothers than Islamic mothers. Islamic culture advocates close kinship ties which explains the positive coping styles. At the same time, because of this overinterfering nature of strong kinship network, they must be facing presence of strong social stigma which might be forcing Islamic mothers to indulge into alcohol/drug use (sleeping pills).

An independent sample *t* test was carried out to compare the mean scores on coping strategies used by mothers from joint and nuclear family background. Results report significant mean difference on focus on venting of emotions ($t = 2.6$; $p < .01$). Observing the means of both the groups, it shows that mean score of mothers belonging to joint family ($m = 12.1$, SD = 1.27) is higher than mean score of mothers belonging to nuclear family ($m = 11.2$, SD = 1.4). This implies that mothers from joint family use the coping skill of venting emotions more as compared to those from nuclear family. This is because in joint family mothers get social support because of which they are easily able to express their emotions and feelings to other family members and can communicate what they are going through. In joint family there will be always a family member who would be ready to lend an ear to the distress of mother whose child is physically and mentally challenged. Whereas in nuclear family nobody will be there to listen or understand the emotions of mother as a result of which, mothers of joint family use more of venting of emotions as coping style compared to mothers of nuclear family.

Coping pattern of mothers belonging to different family type differ on some of the dimensions of COPE scale. Mothers from joint family adapt more to coping patterns like planning, turning to religion, venting of emotions, behavioural disengagement and usage of alcohol and drugs and mothers of nuclear family adapt more to restraint coping. Whereas on other dimensions like active coping, seeking instrumental social support, seeking emotional social support, suppression of social support, positive reinterpretation and growth, acceptance, denial, mental disengagement and humour there is not much difference between mothers of joint family and nuclear family. Thus, the coping style of mothers from joint family lays strong emphasis on the role and strength of social support to aid the mothers who deal with their stress of raising a child with Cerebral Palsy.

Based on the content analysis done on Parental Questionnaire on Initial reactions, it was found that most of the people blame themselve or their fate when they came to know that their child is having cerebral palsy. On the basis of this finding researcher was curious to know whether there is difference in coping strategy used by mothers who blamed their fate and mothers who blamed themselves (see Table 6.4).

Table 6.4 : Comparison of mean scores on the dimensions of COPE between mothers who attributed to self and mothers who attributed to fate

	Self-blame N=24		*Blame fate N=19*		*t*
Dimensions	*Mean*	*SD*	*Mean*	*SD*	
Active coping	11.83	1.43	11.89	1.44	-0.13
Planning	12.58	1.64	12.16	2.36	0.69
Seeking instrumental social support	13.63	1.66	13.05	2.24	0.96
Seeking emotional social support	10.46	1.69	10.26	1.96	0.34
Suppression of social support	11.58	1.79	10.74	1.82	1.52
Turning to religion	12.92	2.35	11.42	2.47	2.02*
Positive reinterpretation and growth	11.96	1.57	12.11	1.41	-0.38
Restraint coping	11.33	2.20	10.79	2.20	0.80
Acceptance	11.83	2.03	12.79	2.27	-1.45
Focus on and venting of emotions	11.71	1.54	11.05	1.39	1.44
Denial	7.38	1.61	6.68	1.63	1.38
Mental disengagement	7.54	2.265	8.32	2.750	-1.01
Behavioural disengagement	7.13	1.569	8.26	1.881	-2.16*
Alcohol/drugs use	4.96	1.122	4.95	1.393	0.03
Humour	5.21	1.179	5.58	1.387	-0.95

Note: * = $p < .05$

The mean difference was found to be significant ($p < 0.05$) on dimension 'turning to religion'. Observing the mean of both the groups, it shows that mean scores of mother who blame themselves is higher than the mean scores of mother who blame their fate. This shows that mothers who blame themselve for the condition of their cerebral palsy child turn more towards religion than mothers to blame fate. This can be because mothers who blame themselve would incline more towards spirituality may be because of guilt feeling or attributing the causes to cosmic factors like "karma" and god's will. By resorting to religious coping, there is a hope to ease the burden and in turn strengthen the recovery beliefs.

Also, the mean difference was found to be significant on dimension 'behavioural disengagement'. Looking at the mean scores of both the group, it shows that mean scores of mothers who blamed their fate is higher than the mean scores of mothers who blamed themselves. This shows that mothers who blamed their fate use more of behavioural disengagement as coping technique compared to mothers who blamed themself for the condition of their cerebral palsy child. Giving up or withdrawing efforts from the attempt to attain the goal with which the stressor is interfering as a coping pattern may be higher among the mothers as a result of pain and anguish on learning about their child's condition.

Results suggest that the most dominant coping strategy is seeking instrumental social support and the least dominant coping strategy is alcohol and drug abuse. These results further highlight that mothers use active coping, planning, and turning to religion as other dominant strategies. Humour, alcohol drug use, mental and behavioural disengagement is preferred less as coping strategies to cope with the stress of being mothers of children suffering from chronic illness. The overall pattern suggests that, mother use more task oriented positive coping strategies as compared to avoidant or withdrawal based coping strategies.

To understand the relationship between correlation was carried out among some of the demographic variables (measured on continuous scale) and the preferred coping strategies used by mothers of CP children There was significant positive correlation between dimension planning and family income ($r = .30, p < .01$), which means higher the income of the family more planning can be seen. A significant negative correlation was reported between dimensions of suppression of social support and sibling's age ($r = -.28, p < .05$), which means more the age of the sibling less suppression of social support done by mothers. This could be because if parents suppress social support, sibling would also suffer.

A significant positive correlation was found out between the dimension of restraint coping and father and child's age ($r = .27$; $p < .05$). This means more the age of father, more the experience parents would be having in taking decisions for the child. This experience would have made them learn not to take hasty decision; as a result restraint in coping can be seen if father's age is more.

There is significant negative correlation between humour and mother's age ($r = -.32$; $p < .05$) and father's age ($r = -.30$; $p < .05$). This implies that the younger parents use humour as a coping skill more often. With growing age of parents, humour is less preferred as a coping strategy to handle the stress in their life.

Discussion

Any disease or illness will have an underlying cultural element forming the causal beliefs, perception about the illness and recovery beliefs. Reactions and attributions to the cause of illness will range from blaming Good *Karma* (fate) to self- blame. This further reflects the coping pattern and adaptation to the changing circumstances of the mothers with children having chronic disabilities. Fate and illness are closely associated in the cultural understanding of the cause of illness. Religious dependence as a coping pattern may be expected without bringing out striking differences between mothers belonging to either religion (e.g. Hindu or Muslim).

The results showed that there were some differences in coping pattern of mothers belonging to joint family and nuclear family. Mothers from joint family used the coping skill of venting emotions more as compared to those from nuclear family. This could be because in the joint family there are other family members like grandparents to whom mothers can easily express their emotions and feelings and can communicate what they are going through. Whereas, in nuclear family nobody will be there to listen or understand the emotions of mothers. Mirfin-Veitch and Bray (1997) showed that grandparents offer support that is both emotional and practical. It is to them that parents feel most comfortable to disclose their full range of emotions, and they also offer direct assistance to the family by shopping babysitting and helping through financial support. Thus, the significance of family as a primary support group clearly helps mothers cope better with the stress and adaptive demands imposed by the child.

Hasting (1997) and Hornby & Ashworth (1994) have reported that the child's grandparents are usually common source of support for the family, although many have difficulties in adapting to the situation and often attempt 'to deny the reality' of the disability or to reject the child.

Religious differences leading to differences in coping pattern among mothers was also observed in this study. Mothers belonging to Hindu religion adapt more to active coping whereas; mothers belonging to Islamic religion use more of drugs like sleeping pills and anti-depressant for coping.

Based on the content analyses done on parental questionnaire, it was found that most of the mothers blame themselve or their fate when they came to know that they are having a cerebral palsy child. The coping pattern of the mothers who blame themselve and who blame their fate also differs. It was found that mothers who blame themselve turned more towards the religion than mothers who blame on their fate. Mothers who blame their fate use more of behavioural disengagement as coping technique. Anxiety and being easily worried and depressed are the common emotional reactions of the mothers owing to the child's adequate progress. The research conducted by Barlow, Barlowa, Cullen-Powella & Cheshirea (2006) to study psychological well-being among mothers of children with cerebral palsy addressed this issue by examining the level of anxious and depressed moods in the mother of cerebral palsy children. Results indicated that anxious and depressed moods were inversely associated with generalized self-efficacy and anxious mood was inversely associated with children's sleeping difficulties. In conclusion, levels of maternal psychological well-being are a cause for concern and warrant exploration of interventions that will reduce maternal distress, and increase self-efficacy. Chetwynd (1985) found higher stress levels in mothers of intellectually disabled children to be related to child temperament factors as well as socio-economic status. Thus, the chronic disability of the child makes the mothers vulnerable to psychological disorders.

The results of correlation analysis among demographic variables and dimension of COPE scale showed that there is less of suppression of social support when number of children are more or when sibling's age is more. It was also seen that more of planning is done if family income is high. Higher the father's age, lesser is the use of humour as a coping skill. Increased attribution to fate for the negative consequences leads to higher degree of behavioural disengagement as a coping mechanism. Apart from these factors like the education level of the mother, awareness about seeking help and social support given to the mothers help them in adapting to the changing demands of the children with chronic disabilities.

The major findings of the study suggests that the preferred coping pattern of mothers of quadriplegic CP children is strongly influenced by their socio-religious and demographic background. Thus, promoting well-being amongst the caregivers of quadraplegic CP children can be designed successfully by integrating their socio-demographic religious characteristics into the intervention framework.

Implication: This study helps to understand stress and painful emotions experienced by mothers having a child with cerebral palsy and how family and social support can play an important role in their coping with the stress. The findings may help to plan intervention strategy for mothers of cerebral palsy children, to reduce their stress and support their children efficiently. This study will also help the professionals to understand what kind of professional help and support can be given to the mothers to enable them to cope with the stress effectively and take good care of their children.

REFERENCES

Aldwin, C.; Revenson, T. (1987). Does coping help? *Journal of Personality and Social Psychology,* 53, 337-348.

Barlow, J.H.; Barlowa, L.A.; Cullen-Powella & Cheshirea, A. (2006). Psychological well-being among mothers of children with cerebral palsy. Early Child Development and Care, 176 (3-4), 421-428.

Bachrach, F. & Miller, S. (1998). *Cerebral palsy: A guide for care*, The John Hopkins University Press.

Benzies, *et al.* (2011). Assessing the psychosocial well-being in mothers of children with disability: Evaluation of the parenting morale index and family impact of childhood disability scale. *Journal of Pediatric Psychology*, Volume 36 (5), pp. 506-516. Downloaded from // http: // jpepsy. cxfordjournals. org, accessed at 1: 30 p.m. (IST) on July 1, 2012.

Bolger, N. (1990). Coping as a Personality Process: A Prospective Study. *Journal of Personality and Social Psychology*, 59, 525-537.

Bradshaw, J. and Lawton, D. (1978). Tracing the cause of stress in families with handicapped children. *British Journal of Social Work*, 8, 181-192.

Brehaut, J.C.; Kohen, D.E.; Raina, P.; Walter, S.D.; Russell, D.J.; Swinton, M.; *et al.* (2004). The Health of Primary Caregivers of Children with Cerebral Palsy: How Does it Compare with that of Other Canadian Caregivers. *Pediatrics*, 114 (2), e182-e191. http: //dx. doi. org/10.1542/ peds. 114.2. e182. PMid: 15286255

Breslau, N. and Davis, G. (1986). Chronic stress and major depression. *Archives of General Psychiatry*, 43, 309-314.

Breslau, N.; Staruch, K.; Mortmer, E. (1982). Psychological distress in mothers of disabled children, *American Journal of Diseases of Childhood*, 136, 682-686.

Carver, C.S.; Scheier, M.F. and Weintraub, J.K. (1989). Assessing coping strategies: A theoretically based approach. *Journal of Personality and Social Psychology*, 56, 267-283.

Chetwynd, J. (1985). Factors contributing to stress on mothers caring for an intellectually handicapped child. *British Journal of Social Work*, 15, 295-304.

Dunst, C.J.; Trivette, C.M. and Deal, A.G. (1988). *Enabling and empowering families: Principles and guidelines for practice.* Cambridge, MA: Brookline.

Folkman, S., and Lazarus, R.S. (1980). An analysis of coping in a middle-aged community sample. *Journal of Health and Social Behaviour,* 21, 219-239.

Folkman, S. and Lazarus, R. (1985). If it changes it must be a process: Study of emotion and coping during 3 stages of a college examination. *Journal of Personality and Social Psychology,* 48 (1): 150-170.

Folkman, S.; Lazarus, R.S.; Dunkel-Schetter, C.; DeLongis, A. and Gruen, R.J. (1986). Dynamics of a stressful encounter: Cognitive appraisal, coping, and encounter outcomes. *Journal of Personality and Social Psychology*, 50, 992-1003.

Frey, K.S.; Greenberg, M.T. and Fewell, R.R. (1989). Stress and coping among parents of handicapped children: A multidimensional approach. *American Journal on Mental Retardation,* 94, 240-249.

Gerhardt *et al.* (2002), Comparing Parental Distress, Family Functioning and the Role of Social Support for Caregivers with or without a child with Juvenile Rheumatoid Arthritis. *Journal of Pediatric Psychology*, Vol. 28 (1), 2003, pp. 5-15. Downloaded from //http: //jpepsy. oxfordjournals. org, accessed at 1 p.m. (IST) on July 1, 2012.

Gilham, B. (1987). In *Handicapping conditions in children*; Croom Helm Publication, Beckenham, Kent, UK.

Hanline, M.F., and Daley, S.E. (1992). Family, coping strategies and strengths in Hispanic, African-American, and Caucasian families of young children. *Topics in Early Childhood Special Education*, 12, 351-366.

Hastings, R. (1997). Grandparents of children with disabilities: A review. *International Journal of Disability, Development and Education*, 44, 4,329-34.

Hautamaki, A. (1997). *Mothers—stress, stressors and strains: outcomes of a cross-Nordic study*, in B. Carpenter (ed.) Families in context: Emerging Trends in Family Support and Early Intervention. London: David Fulton.

Holahan, C.J. and Moos, R.H. (1987). Risk, resistance, and psychological distress: A longitudinal analysis with adults and children. *Journal of Abnormal Psychology*, 96, 3-13.

Hornby, G. and Ashworth, T. (1994). Grandparents' support for families who have children with disabilities. *Journal of Child Family Studies*, 3, 403-412.

Kazak, A. and Marvin, R. (1984). Differences, difficulties, and adaptation: Stress and social networks in Families with a handicapped child. *Family Relations*, 33, 67-77.

Kazak, A.; Reber, M. and Carter, A. (1988). Structural and qualitative aspects of social networks in families with young chronically ill children. *Journal of Pediatric Psychology*, 13, 171-182.

Kersten, P.; George, S.; Mclellan, L.; Smith, J.A.E.; Mullee, M.A. (2001). Needs of carers of severely disabled people: Are they identified and met adequately? *Health Soc Care Community*, 9 (4), 235-43. http: //dx. doi. org/10.1046/j. 1365-2524.2001.00297. x. PMid: 11560739

Manuel, J.; Naughton, M.; Balkrishnan, R.; Smith, B. and Koman, A. (2003), Stress and adaptation of mothers of children with Cerebral Palsy, *Journal of Pediatric Psychology,* Volume 28 (3), pp. 197-201. Downloaded from //http: //jpepsy. oxfordjournals. org, accessed at 1:10 p.m. (IST) on July 1, 2012.

Mc Cubbin. M.A. and Huang, S.T. T. (1989). Family strengths in the case of handicapped children: Targets for intervention. *Family Relations*, 38, 436-443.

Mirfin-Veitch, B. and Bray, A. (1997) Grandparents: Part of the family. In B.Carpenter (ed.) Families in Context: Emerging Trends in Family Support and Early Intervention (pp. 76-88). London: David Fulton.

Mittler, P. (1995). Rethinking Partnerships between Parents and Professionals. Children & Society, 9(3), 22-40.

Peaslin, L.I. and Schooler, C. (1978). The structure of coping. *Journal of Health and Social Behaviour*, 19, 2-21.

Ruswell, F. (2003). *British Journal of Special Education,* Vol. 30, No. 3, September 2003, pp. 144-149 (6).

Shu Li, Lin, (2000). Coping and Adaptation in Families of Children with

Cerebral Palsy. *Exceptional Children,* Vol. 66 (2). Downloaded from http: //www. freepatentsonline. com/article/ExceptionalChildren/ 59017864. html, Accessed at 2: 00 p.m. (IST) on August, 7, 2012.

Turnbull, A.P.; B. Turnbull, H.R. (1990). *Families, professionals, and exceptionality: A special partnership* (2nd edn.). Columbus, OH: Merrill.

www. unitedcerebralpalsy. com.

Vanderwerker L.C. (2005). Psychiatric Disorders and Mental Health Service Use Among Caregivers of Advanced Cancer Patients. *Journal of Clinical Oncology*, 23 (28), 6899-6907.

Wyckoff, P. and Erickson, M. (1987). Mediating factors of stress on mothers of seriously ill, hospitalized children. *Journal of Abnormal Child Psychology*, 9, 121-131.

7

Psychosocial Dynamics of HIV/AIDS: A Health Concern in India

Veena Panjwani

One of the major health concerns in the recent past has been pertaining to HIV/AIDS. Although the origin of HIV is relatively unknown, it is now a major reality for most of the countries in the world. HIV is now known to affect human beings from any race, religion, sex, age or ethnicity. It is one of the very few infections for which a vaccine is not available and it still remains the most researched area in medicine even today. There are very significant advances in terms of treatment available against HIV progression within the body, and methods of prevention of transmission from one person to another. Also, there has been identification of economic conditions leading to spread of HIV infection. However, more researches are required in the psychological and sociological factors of HIV transmission. There is a dearth of research in this area from a psychological perspective.

The Indian Government, way back in 1984 had rejected the possibility of spread of HIV within the country stating that it is a country of value, culture and high morals. But, it had to change its stand for the issue when there was report of fast spread of HIV in Tamil Nadu and in other states of India. The acceptance about the issue led to further formulation of national bodies to design and implement awareness programmes for prevention of HIV/AIDS. NACP-I was implemented during 1992-1999 with an objective to slow down the spread of HIV infections so as to reduce morbidity, mortality and impact of HIV epidemic in the country. To strengthen the management capacity, a National AIDS Control Board (NACB) was constituted and an autonomous National AIDS Control Organization (NACO) was set up to implement the project. The formation of National AIDS Control Organization was the first step to deal with the serious issue of HIV/AIDS transmission. With the passage of time, there was an increase in acceptance about the seriousness of the issue, a better awareness level, greater acceptance and recognition of threats associated with HIV because of the implementation of National AIDS Control Program-I (NACP-I).

The NACP-II was launched in 1999; it was implemented as a comprehensive programme for prevention and control of HIV/AIDS in India. The focus had shifted from raising awareness to changing behaviour, decentralization of programme at the state level (as evidenced by constitution of State AIDS Control Society at the state level) and greater involvement of NGOs. Several new NGOs were involved in the work which mainly was focused on identification of core population at risk of HIV and the bridge population through which HIV was spreading fast to the general population. The policy and strategic shift was reflected in two key objectives of NACP-II viz. to reduce the spread of HIV infection in India; and to increase India's capacity to respond to HIV/AIDS on a long-term basis.

To meet the above mentioned objectives of NACP-II, the policy initiatives taken were:

- Adoption of National AIDS Prevention and Control Policy (2002)
- National Blood Policy
- A strategy for Greater Involvement of People with HIV/AIDS (GIPA)
- Launching of National Rural Health Mission
- Launching of National Adolescence Education Programme
- Provision of Anti-Retroviral Therapy (ART)
- Setting of National Council on AIDS chaired by the Prime Minister.

Looking at the rich pool of data generated during NACP-II and learning from them, NACP-III was launched in 2007. The goal this time shifted from raising awareness and changing behaviour to halt and reverse the epidemic in India over the five years period

(2007-2012). To achieve this goal, the strategies adopted were preventing infection through saturation of coverage of high-risk groups with Targeted Interventions; providing greater support, care and treatment to a larger number of People Living with HIV/A!DS (PLHA); addressing human rights and fundamental rights of PLHA; strengthening the infrastructure systems and human resources in prevention, care, support, and treatment at the district, national and state levels; and strengthening the nationwide Strategic Information Management System to help track the epidemic (NACO, Annual Report, 2009-2010).

The core high-risk groups identified are Female Sex Workers (FSWs), Men who have Sex with Men (MSM), Transgender (TG), Injecting Drug Users (IDU), and also Bridge Populations (Migrants and Truckers). The trend in HIV transmission is hence identified as being driven majorly by unprotected sexual intercourse and sharing of drug injecting equipment (Fig. 7.1).

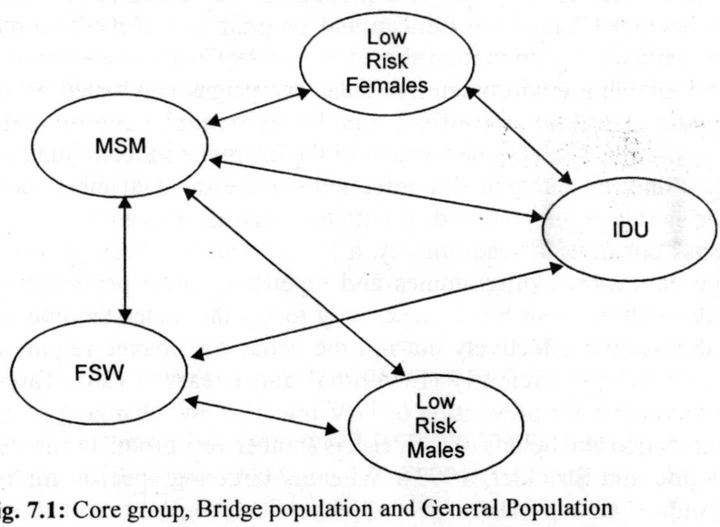

Fig. 7.1: Core group, Bridge population and General Population

The Core group here is reflected in MSM, FSW, and IDU population, the Bridge Population is the sexual and Needle share partners of the Core Group, whereas the sexual partners of these Bridge population are the individuals at risk in General Population. It is significant to identify here that the Core group does not exist in isolation from one another, and there can be sexual contacts between MSM, FSW and IDU.

It can be seen from Fig. 7.1 that the transmission of HIV beyond the HRG occurs through their sexual partners, who may also have sexual partners in the general population with low risk behaviour for HIV infection. For example, a partner of a MSM may have a wife or other sexual partner who is at risk of acquiring HIV from her higher risk partner, a similar example can be seen for a client of a sex worker or a partner of an injecting drug user. These individuals who are identified as partners of HRG are recognized as 'bridge population'. Hence, the most effective way recommended to achieve prevention of further transmission of HIV is to target the HRG and keep the HIV prevalence low in them. Therefore, the Targeted Interventions among HRG and Bridge Population is implemented through NACP-III.

The foremost component of Targeted Intervention is Behaviour Change Communication. It involves understanding and assessment of individual and group behaviours/practices which make an individual at risk for HIV, counselling through counsellors and creating enabling environment to reinforce safe practices. The strategies adopted for Behaviour Change are Educational programmes; Repetitive media presentation of information about the disease; Creating an empowering and enabling environment; Regular campaigns conducted on mass media; Outdoor activities; and Interpersonal communication. Counselling is mentioned as part of the interpersonal communication.

Since the threat of HIV infection is universal to all human beings, the strategies adopted to deal with the issue are also addressed to the mass population. Traditionally, a lot of focus has been provided to the educational programmes and repetitive media presentation of information about the disease, only to tap the understanding about the infection effectively but not the behaviour change required for prevention sufficiently (Leventhal and Cleary, 1980). Targeted intervention for prevention of HIV infection and changing peoples' perception and beliefs of their risk is another very promising approach (Kline and Strickler, 1993). Whereas targeting specific high-risk groups is an important aspect of prevention programmes, it allows to have focused content of programme addressing specific fears, concerns, behaviours, and misconceptions (Baum, Gatchel and Krantz, 1997).

The understanding of prevention leads to further exploration of preventive programmes for HIV/AIDS transmission in general population. Caplan (1970) provides with the possibility of classifying preventive programmes into three types, which grants with a clear goal and objective for each preventive measure taken at the policy level. The first type, Primary prevention, refers to the modification of behaviour, adoption of specific strategies, and learning skills to deal with the issue/disease before its onset; aimed at reduction of risk factors for development of a disease/disorder. For example, all the educational programmes and campaigns to promote 'safe-sex' practices among people to prevent HIV infection. Although it is the most effective way of dealing with any infection which pose a threat of mass infection; it is rather difficult to bring in a behaviour change of this level where people adopt a healthy behaviour in order to prevent oneself from dangers involved in the unhealthy, high risk health behaviours; simply because there is a lack of immediate benefits which could be measured in more noticeable way. The Secondary prevention model refers to early interventions adopted to arrest the progression of illness/infections within an individual, to prevent it from taking a severe form in less duration, for example, the early treatment for opportunistic infections in PLHA to prevent the fast progression of infection and deterioration of immunity within their body. Although it is a very practical approach, the issue lies in early identification of the infection/illness and timely availability of treatment to curb the progression. With more lack of understanding of the needs, and the ignorance on part of people at risk, this level is even more difficult to achieve, especially in a country like India. The Tertiary prevention refers to interventions for treatment of advanced stages of diseases/ disorders and rehabilitation of the patients. For example, provision of ART to PLHA with less than 250 CD4 cell count. Although it is less cost-effective and less beneficial in the longer run, it is relatively easier to accomplish because of the necessity felt by people in need and their readiness to comply with the norm (Fig. 7.2).

From Fig. 7.2, it is evident that the steps of Primary Prevention are of utmost importance for prevention of HIV transmission. If they are addressed properly then in totality it will be very cost-effective, as it does not require any extraordinary infrastructure setting up in terms of hospitals or health facilities; or recruitment of highly trained medical professionals. The steps of Primary Prevention only require satisfactory utilization of existing set ups and addressing appropriate target group for prevention of HIV transmission, for example, interaction with adolescent group in schools, or any community specific programmes through various NGOs or community based organizations.

Prevention of HIV Transmission

Primary Prevention	Secondary Prevention	Tertiary Prevention
Reduction of Risk factors, by means of: 1. Educational Programs 2. Awareness Campaigns 3. Counselling for Prevention of High Risk Behaviour 4. Skills training for Condom Use & other methods of safe sex practices	Early interventions to arrest the progression of infections 1. Timely testing & early identification of infection cases 2. Nutritional Counselling 3. Preventive Counselling 4. Early treatment against Opportunistic infections 5. Maintaining a healthy life style	Interventions for Treatment and Rehabilitation of PLHA 1. Provision of ART for PLHA 2. Adherence Counselling 3. Admittance to medical facility for better services and supervised care 4. Appropriate nutritional care

Fig. 7.2: Models for Prevention

Now, looking at the issue at hand from a different perspective is all the more important here. The need for change in behaviour, in particular, the High Risk Health Behaviour (HRHB) has been emphasized in all the programmes implemented for HIV prevention. The issue has been studied from different perspectives, viz., Physiological, Economic, and Sociological. For the purpose of this book, only sociological perspective on HIV/AIDS is presented here (Fig. 7.3).

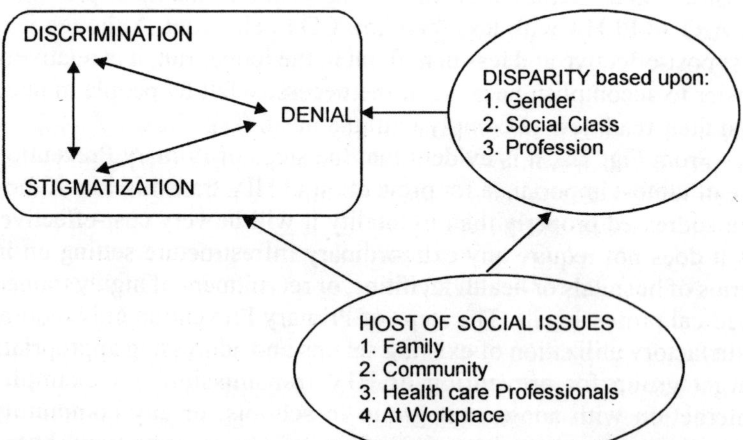

Fig. 7.3: Sociological Perspectives of HIV/AIDS

HIV is perceived as a condition of "Others". It is perceived as a concern of those people who are living on the margins of the society. A triangle of Discrimination, Stigmatization and Denial is a resultant of such a value affecting the lives of people in general in various settings viz. families, communities, workplace, schools, and health care settings. From Fig. 7.3, it can be seen that the triangle of DSD has a significant inter-mechanism. The sense of denial that one is not at the risk of HIV infection, it is the others, creates the classic distinction of self and others. This denial leads to further stigmatization and discrimination against HIV and HIV infected/affected people. There is a lot disparity within this practice of DSD pertaining to HIV infected people. There is a marked presence of discrimination against the marginalized group within the society (especially due to their work type and stigma associated with it, for e.g. FSW, MSM and IDUs). Another source for disparity is Gender, wherein the HIV positive males are shown support and sympathy from the family, which is not the scene in case of females who are HIV positive. The final source of disparity in practice of DSD is the social class. In India, practically there is a huge lack of resources for poor people. There is still a further burden created due to the poor care and inadequate services to marginalized people.

Virtually every Indian setting in which HIV infected people interact with other people provides a backdrop for DSD in contexts like Family, in Community, in Health care system, and at the workplace. A majority of people express the belief that infected people should terminate their life and it is at times believed to be a punishment from God.

A review of all the phases of NACP from a Psychological perspective leads to the conclusion that the emphasis has been on the awareness and prevention among the mass population. The strategies developed and the policies formed, mainly focus on the development of infrastructure and provision of services for the people at large, basically more generalized services have been offered. Furthermore, none of the policies were made addressing the psychological needs of individuals at risk. In addition, the NACP-III focuses on providing the highest priority in the intervention programmes to the sub-populations that have highest risk of exposure to HIV, viz. Sex Workers, MSM and IDU. But, the plans for these interventions are limited to provision of counselling to these HRG. The seeming lack of insight towards the real underlying issues may lead to failure of targeted counselling that is provided to these high risk groups at present. There is a great lack of understanding pertaining to the role of personality characteristics which are as equally important as the socio-economic characteristics are.

Personality Traits

Personality traits are underlying characteristics of an individual that are relatively stable over time, and explain regularities in people's behaviours. People react differently to the same situations, and these differences are caused by natural variations in personality traits. There are a small number of broad traits which account for the majority of people's personalities. Personality traits are approximately half of the time genetically determined and the remaining variance in personality traits is due to the way in which socialization has taken place. Personality traits like Risk Taking and Sensation Seeking are directly associated with the actions and risk for HIV infection.

Risk Taking

Risk taking is a personality trait, and peoples' attitudes to risk are predicted to be reasonably stable over time. A major difficulty is in the estimation of the values associated with things that are thought to be at risk. These represent social choices. Although the perception and assessment of risks are essentially phenomenologically based, the nature of risk is fundamentally interactive. Risks exist because things considered to have value are placed at risk, and as such the nature of risk concerns the interaction of people in their environment.

The risk assessment process can be seen as the attempt to predict future situational outcomes based upon the extrapolation from experience and the application of inductive logic. Certain behaviours are assessed to involve a high degree of risk in comparison with other equivalent behaviours, and also involve a high degree of actual risk as measured by the probability of death, injury, financial loss, etc.

Risk-taking theories based on Dispositional Traits examine individual differences between persons that might account for a propensity to take risks (Kaplan, 1980; Botvin, 1986; McCord, 1990; Petersen, Compas, Brooks-Gunn, Stemmler, Ey & Grant, 1993). Biological models of risk-taking examine genetic factors, neuroendocrine influences, and events (Irwin & Millstein, 1986;

Cloninger, 1987; Udry, 1988, 1990). Risk-taking is seen as a way of coping with normal developmental tasks such as exploration and achieving autonomy (Lavery, Siegel, Cousins & Rubovits, 1993; Millstein & Igra, 1995) and the difficulties people face in making decisions (Furby & Beyth-Marom, 1992). The Contemporary theorists stress the role of personality traits in differentiating between people who love taking risks and those who are risk averse. People adopt different approaches to perception of risk, which indicates their "risk orientation". There are three different risk taking types, namely "risk avoiders" (who avoid activities due to the risks involved), "risk reducers" (who participate in high risk activities in spite of the risks involved), and "risk optimizers" (who participate in high risk activities partly because of the risks involved) (Fig. 7.4).

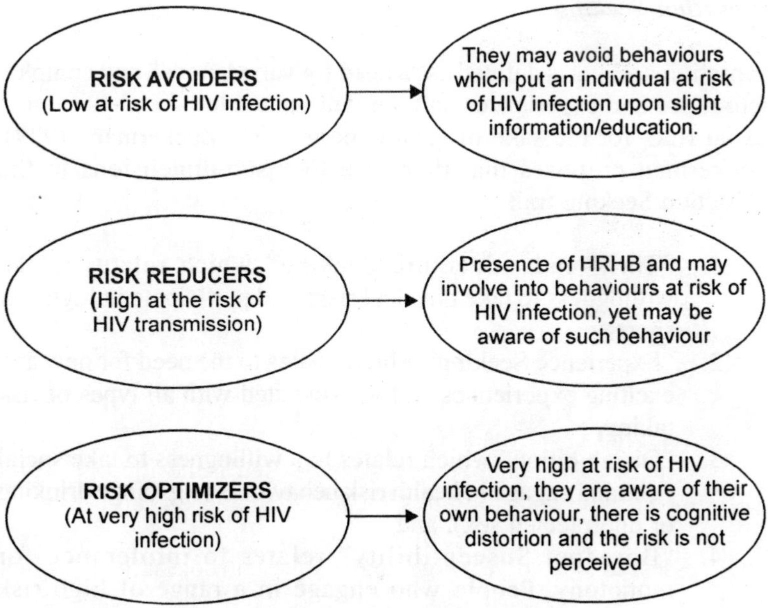

Fig. 7.4: Risk Orientation and its role in HIV prevention

The success of all the strategies implemented till date for HIV prevention can also be attributed to the Personality traits people have in general. The Risk Avoiders, who almost always avoid certain activities due to the risks involved, may grasp and execute behaviours needed for preventing oneself from HIV infection just by viewing educational programmes and mass media presentations about awareness of HIV/AIDS. Whereas, addressing, the Risk Reducers and Risk Optimizers, and bringing in a behaviour change from High Risk to low risk can be a herculean task for policy makers; especially when the personality traits are not taken into consideration of formation and implementation of various policies and programmes.

In general, involvement in high-risk activities has been positively associated with personality factors, such as social maladjustment, and with perceived benefit of risk (Lavery, Siegel, Cousins & Rubovits, 1993). Researchers reported that persons who were engaged in high-risk behaviours had higher scores on affiliation, desirability, dominance, exhibition, and self-esteem variables and they exhibited significantly higher sexual risk, smoking risk, driver and passenger risk and impulsiveness (Jackson, 1984; Moore & Rosenthal, 1993).

Sensation-Seeking

Sensation-seeking is defined as "a need for varied, novel, and complex sensations and experiences and the willingness to take physical and social risks for the sake of such experiences" (Zuckerman, 1979). Zuckerman proposes that there are four sub-dimensions to the Sensation Seeking trait:

1. "Thrill and Adventure Seeking" which relates to the willingness to take physical risks and participate in high risk sports,
2. "Experience Seeking" which relates to the need for new and exciting experiences and is associated with all types of risk taking,
3. "Disinhibition" which relates to a willingness to take social risks and engage in health risk behaviours (e.g. binge drinking or unprotected sex), and
4. "Boredom Susceptibility" relates to intolerance for monotony. People who engage in a range of high risk behaviours tend to be high Sensation Seekers as well. People take risks in order to have exciting, novel and intense new experiences (Fig. 7.5).

All the dimensions of Sensation Seeking are positively co-related with high risk health behaviour for HIV transmission. People high in Thrill and Adventure Seeking may engage into various activities which

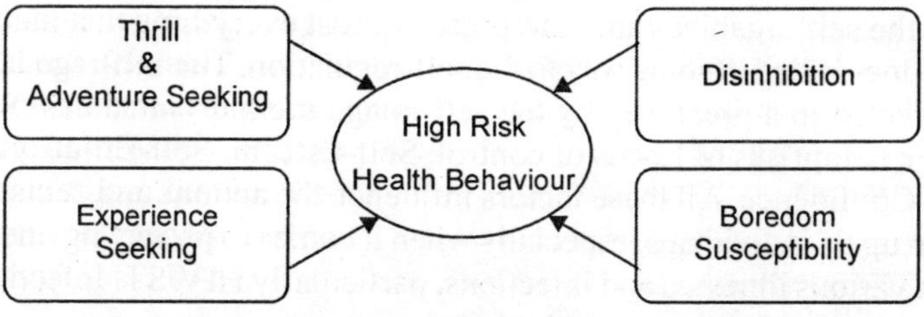

Fig. 7.5: Sensation Seeking Dimensions and their role in HIV prevention

may provide them with the sense of physical adventure. For example, it may involve engaging into sexual relationship with a total stranger in middle of a jungle or interior of a terrain. An individual high in Experience Seeking may engage in all reckless and uncontrolled sexual behaviours putting oneself at the risk of HIV. Furthermore, an individual high in Disinhibition may engage into unprotected sex or excessive drinking or any other drug abuse; all these are highly related with spread of HIV infection. Someone very high on Boredom Susceptibility would always try to avoid monotony, and hence may have multiple sexual partners, again putting oneself at the risk of HIV. In addition, all the dimensions of Sensation Seeking are interrelated and hence influence each other; posing a greater need for understanding HIV/AIDS prevention strategies from this perspective.

Smith, Ptacek, and Smoll (1992) assessed sensation-seeking as a moderator variable between sport-specific stress and athletes' injury vulnerability. Results showed that those low in sensation-seeking appeared to be at higher risk of injury following sport stress when compared to high sensation seekers. High sensation seekers had better coping skills for stress. Satinder and Black (1984) studied cannabis use and sensation-seeking orientation among college students. Cannabis users scored higher on all four sensation-seeking scales compared to non-users.

Apart from studying the personality characteristics, the understanding of the self becomes necessary here. Especially the mechanism involved for a functional self and decision making ability with reference to self-control aspect.

Mechanisms of Self

The mechanisms of self are important to understand in order to identify how the self organizes and interprets. Almost everything that the self is or does is tied in some way to the self-regulation. The self-regulation is affected in a great way by the self-image the individual has. Self-image comprises of Locus of control, Self-Esteem, Self-Efficacy and Self-Confidence. All these factors influence the actions and decisions taken up by individuals, especially when it comes to protecting oneself from various illnesses and infections, particularly HIV/STI infections, by having appropriate preventive behaviours.

Locus of Control

Locus of control refers to the extent to which individuals believe that they can control events that affect them (Rotter, 1962). Locus of control is the perception one has of the control he or she has over the events which occur in one's life. There is an internal/external dimension to this trait. Internal control refers "to the perception of positive and/or negative events as being a consequence of one's own actions and thereby under personal control; external control refers to the perception of positive and/or negative events as being unrelated to one's own behaviours in certain situations and therefore beyond personal control" (Rotter, Seeman & Liverant, 1962). Those with a low internal locus of control/external locus of control believe that powerful others, fate, or chance primarily determine the events.

Crisp and Barber (1995) reported that among adolescent drug users, those with an internal locus of control know they are taking risks, while those with an external locus of control believe they are invulnerable to risk, particularly for HIV.

Those with a high internal locus of control are more likely to assume that their efforts will be successful. They are more active in seeking information and knowledge concerning their situation. Further, individuals with external locus of control tend to attribute situational causes for their experiences and behaviours. Most often, they fail to take the onus for their behaviours and hence do not take an active participation in life. These individuals tend to live with the notion of victimized self and accept whatever comes in their way without challenging it. They fail to have a control over their life. Whereas, individuals with internal locus of control perceive their actions as guided by them only, most often take responsibility of their behaviours and are active in dealing with their life events (Levenson, & Weiner, 1970). Additional attributions could be to ability (an internal stable cause), effort (an internal unstable cause), task difficulty (an external stable cause) or luck (an external, unstable cause).

Now, comparing these two very different states of self, an individual with external locus of control may have a perception that s/he has nothing to do with engaging into self-protective behaviour. They are less likely to expect that their own efforts will result in success and are therefore less likely to work hard to achieve any goal, including better health status. For them, it is always the external cause which prevents them or puts them at risk of HIV infection or any other health risk. Most often, these individuals believe they are invulnerable to risk for HIV. And, here the immediate need is to bring in a change in their perception and belief system, which may seem a herculean task considering that they still have external locus of control. Hence, the foremost need is to identify the mechanism of individual self, in particular, bring in the internal locus of control, if a preventive behaviour is desired.

Maltby, Day and Macaskill (2007), link internal locus of control with improved physical health, mental health and quality of life in people undergoing conditions as diverse as HIV, migraines, diabetes, kidney disease and epilepsy.

Self-Esteem

Self-esteem is a stable sense of personal worth or worthiness (Morris Rosenberg, 1960). According to Nathaniel Branden (1969) self-esteem is the experience of being competent to cope with the basic challenges of life and being worthy of happiness. Implicit self-esteem refers to a person's disposition to evaluate oneself positively or negatively in a spontaneous, automatic, or unconscious manner. It contrasts with explicit self-esteem, which entails more conscious and reflective self-evaluation.

High self-esteem indicates feelings of worthiness and feeling right as a person, whereas, a low self-esteem indicates unwillingness for life and feeling wrong as a person. A middle self-esteem indicates a wavering self between the two previously mentioned states, feelings of being able at times and feelings of being useless at other time; which reinforces insecurity (Branden, 2001).

A person with low self-esteem may have behavioural patterns such as self-criticism, hypersensitivity to criticism, excessive will to please others, self-demand to do everything as expected by others (frustration when this self-demand is not fulfilled), exaggerations of magnitude of mistakes or offenses, inability for forgiveness, disappointment and dissatisfaction with almost everything, a general pessimism about life, future, and also oneself. It also indicates a general lack of will to live life with complete conviction. (Sedikides & Gregg, 2003, Crocker & Park, 2004).

At the same time, an individual with high self-esteem may display behaviours like having full trust in one's capacity to solve problems, asking for help when there is a need, trust on one's own judgment, and considering oneself equal in dignity to others, rather than inferior or superior (Mruk, 2006)

A comparison of these two levels of self-esteem indicates that an individual with high level of self-esteem will tend to engage in actions and behaviours for one's better health and life as compared to an individual with low self-esteem. The individual may avoid taking all the necessary steps for preventive measures against HIV/STIs just because s/he may not approve of her/his life completely. Individuals who have low self-esteem tend to have a disapproving sense for their life and are far more prone to depression and self-restrictive behaviour.

Self-Efficacy

Albert Bandura (1977) has defined self-efficacy as one's belief in one's ability to succeed in specific situations. It is also defined as the belief that one has the capabilities to execute the courses of actions required to manage prospective situations (Bandura, 1997). One's sense of self-efficacy can play a major role in how one approaches goals, tasks, and challenges.

Bandura's Social Cognitive Theory which emphasizes the role of Observational Learning and Social Experience in the development of Personality mainly focuses on development of sense of self-efficacy. It explains the cause of individual's actions and reactions in almost every situation as influenced by what s/he has observed in others. People invariably observe others in the surrounding, especially the significant others like parents and peers. The observations further get translated into imitation and people learn a lot of their cognitions and behaviours just by social observation. This theoretical approach proposes the idea that by changing how an individual learns the behaviours in the early stages of mental development could have a large impact on the mental processes in later stages of development.

Self-efficacy is developed from external experiences and self-perception and is influential in determining the outcome of many events. According to Bandura's theory, people with high self-efficacy that is, those who believe they can perform well are more likely to view difficult tasks as something to be mastered rather than something to be avoided.

People with high self-efficacy in a task are more likely to make more of an effort, and persist longer, than those with low efficacy. On the other hand, low self-efficacy provides an incentive to learn more about the subject. Low self-efficacy can lead people to believe that tasks are harder than they actually are. This often results in poor task planning, as well as increased stress. People with high self-efficacy are shown to be encouraged by obstacles to make a greater effort. Self-efficacy also affects how people respond to failure. People will be more inclined to take on a task if they believe they can succeed. People generally avoid tasks where their self-efficacy is low, but will engage in tasks where their self-efficacy is high. People with a self-efficacy significantly beyond their actual ability often overestimate their ability to complete tasks, which can lead to difficulties. On the other hand, people with a self-efficacy significantly lower than their ability are unlikely to grow and expand their skills (Bandura, 1986).

Health behaviours such as non-smoking, physical exercise, dieting, condom use, dental hygiene, seat belt use, breast self-examination etc. are dependent on one's level of perceived self-efficacy (Conner & Norman, 2005). Self-efficacy influences the effort one puts forth to change risk behaviour and the persistence to continue striving despite barriers and setbacks that may undermine motivation (Luszczynska & Schwarzer, 2005; Schwarzer, 2008).

An individual with low self-efficacy may not adapt to the protective behaviours required for preventing oneself from HIV infection, especially when s/he perceives it as beyond the actual ability. Although it can be changed, it requires a close attention on part of the professional working for adaption of protective behaviour by the individuals at high risk of HIV infection.

It is very important to understand the system of HIV transmission with reference to the mechanism of self. From Figure 7.6, it can be clearly seen that individuals who have low self-esteem, low self-efficacy and high external locus of control are maximally at risk of HIV infection because they fail to adopt appropriate behaviour for preventing oneself from infection. Also, their perception of risk is distorted. The viewing of various risk populations is important with this context. From various researches, it has been found that FSW, TG and MSM have low self-esteem, high external locus of control

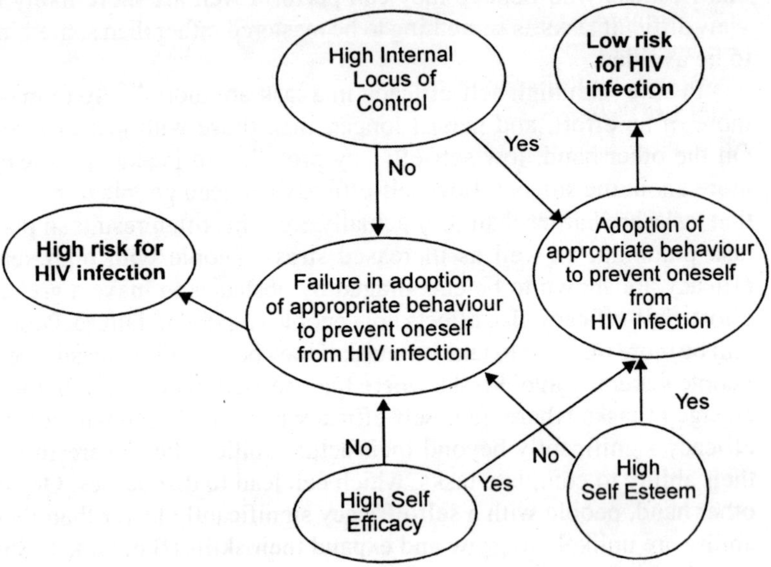

Fig. 7.6: Mechanism of Self and Risk of HIV Infection

and low sense of self-efficacy (Clements-Nolle, Marx, Guzman and D. Cohan, 2001; Lutnick, Davidson, Cloniger, Herlyn, and Breyer, 2006; Cobaugh, Wilson, Klausner, Harcourt, and Donovan, 2006). These researches create a very rich ground for proposing that more work is required with individualized care, community support and strength development for dealing with the high risk population for HIV transmission.

Self-Regulation: The Ultimate Aim

Self-Control as defined here is also known as impulse control or self-regulation. The term self-regulation is used to refer to the many processes individuals use to manage drives and emotions. Therefore, self-regulation also embodies the concept of willpower. Self-regulation is an extremely important executive function of the brain. Deficits in self-control/regulation are found in a large number of psychological disorders including ADHD, Antisocial Personality Disorder, Borderline Personality Disorder, addiction, eating disorders and impulse control disorders etc.

Self-regulation is identified as delay of short-term smaller benefits for a long-term bigger or more important benefit. Research by Roy Baumeister (2007) and colleagues has shown that people's ability to exert self-control depends on a strength-like resource that diminishes after use. After participants performed a task requiring self-control, they were less able to exert self-control, even in entirely different areas; this result was replicated in over a hundred experiments. Self-regulation is characterized as having three component parts:

- Establishing a goal,
- Engaging in actions that lead to obtaining this goal, and
- Monitoring progress towards the goal.

The goal of every counselling or psychotherapy session is to attain this self-control behaviour in order to become more functional and better adjusted within the society. This holds true for preventing oneself from risk of HIV transmission by adopting various means of self-regulation of behaviours which may put an individual at risk of HIV infection.

Baumeister and Heatherton (1996) have identified three causes for failure of self-control behaviour: presence of conflicting goals, failure to track one's own behaviour, and depletion of resources that permit self-control to operate.

The entire mechanism of self is instrumental in the establishment of self-regulatory mechanism. The constructs of self-esteem, self-efficacy and locus of control undergo a constant interplay to determine an effective self-control/self-regulatory action. This stands true for most of the behaviours, including health seeking behaviour and adapting to the necessary preventive measures against HIV infection.

The Self-Regulation for High Risk Health behaviour (both sexual behaviour and drug use) involves:

- Cognitive control (vs. Rationalization)
- Behavioural control (vs. Experimentation and Sensation seeking)
- Emotional control (vs. Experiencing Heightened affectivity).

Cognitive control (Mischel and Rodriguez, 1993; McCabe, Cunnington, and Brooks-Gunn, 2007) refers to the ability to inhibit automated responses in favour of desired behavioural responses. People involve in thinking and assessing the desirability of a behaviour for oneself and then adopt it, hence referred as cognitive control, for example, assessing the benefits of safe sex practices and condom use or avoidance of needle sharing in IDUs. It supplements the process of self-regulation. If individuals engage into providing different reasons and justifying the loss over self-control then it refers to rationalization, for example, reasons not to use condoms/reasons for having multiple sexual partners, etc. Rationalization of behaviours is a failure of self-regulation. Another level of control here involved is behavioural control (Richards and Gross, 2000). People may engage into appropriate behaviours and may avoid engaging into other behaviours which put them at risk of HIV, for example, regular and consistent use of condom. A failure in this mechanism is seen when there is experimentation in behaviour especially guided by sensation seeking, for example, multiple sexual partners or sharing of injecting drug needles. The final mechanism of self-regulation is that of emotional control (Calkins, 1994, 2007) which refers to the processes that serve to manage emotional arousal and support adaptive responses, for example, a control over emotional arousal in presence of a desired sexual partner. A failure in this mechanism would be experiencing heightened affectivity, wherein people may get easily aroused in a situation and perceive it positively even when it involves dangers of HIV infection.

Personality traits like Sensation Seeking (SS) behaviour and High Risk Health Behaviour (HRHB) often lead to failure of self-control behaviour and put an individual at the risk of various diseases, including HIV infection. Just because one thinks a certain behaviour is risky or beneficial, it is not necessarily reflective of his or her actual behaviour. For example, if several smokers were surveyed, it would be logical to assume that they could recite the risks of smoking, yet still smoke. One way to get to the participants' actual risk-taking behaviour is to set-up a simulated risk-taking scenario that will be more reflective of their decision-making processes in risk-taking behaviour. Both MSM and IDU are at high risk of HIV not only because of their behavioural practices but also due to their personality traits like SS and HRHB. All the awareness and education about the issues enable the individuals to take a conscious decision for self-regulation of HRHB; but more efficient service is required in terms of integrated psychotherapies to sustain that self-regulation.

Strengths Approach for Aiming Prevention

Before dealing with issues of the marginalized section of society which is highly at risk of HIV transmission, we need a shift in approach of dealing with these groups in general. To address the issue at hand, programmes are required to support the strengths of these diverse communities/groups. The question is 'Are these groups marginalized by the society at large?' The affirmation here would indicate the existing sets within the society which are completely self-biased and create a little scope for the marginalized section of our society to improvise in their condition. The traditional approach towards programmes and policies made for these marginalized groups (MSM/FSW/IDU/TG) reflect that they indicate and lead towards the possibilities of growth; for example, no schools for TG community, no recognition of a different gender in almost all the existing social structures.

The already existing set influences a great deal about what positive things a person can become, and it requires a reconsideration of values of society (Sanford, 1970) which are based on a narrow interpretation of human potential; which attributes very less opportunity of growth and success to the marginalized groups within India.

In order to come out from already existing sets, a shift in paradigm is required wherein a change in approach towards these groups is required. People must be permitted to live in an environment that affirms who they are, without any judgment passed by others in general. This one step designates development of self-esteem within people. Further, it is important to have a secure sense of one's own culture. It is important for strength building; especially for MSM and TG community. Another such step to build up the sense of strength within the community is to include them in the decision-making process for the development of policies and programmes. One obvious result of such a system for planning would be a fostering of a diversity of settings in which multiple lifestyles and goals are accepted as legitimate. There is need for not only a generalized service but more for Focalized Services in present scenario of HIV/AIDS: the need of the hour is to identify the cognitive processes of each high risk individual, and plan and implementation of an integrated psychotherapy for reduction of risk to HIV which is appropriate for the individual.

The targets of such prevention programme have competencies that are more important to understand and work with as compared to the weaknesses that have made them a target in the first place. It is required to have a greater understanding of the strengths existing within people, and that the deficits are less important than the strengths that are usually ignored. The expectations communicated to the persons should be that they are competent, adequate, perhaps different, but not deficient or maladjusted.

Lastly, the feedback from community is significant. It is aimed at finding the maximum benefits of a system/programme through continual analysis of what is not working and what is contributing less than the expected (Berck, 1976).

The Strengths approach enables to view the same issue from a different perspective and hence opens up new horizons of work with the community. The acknowledgment of understanding the salient features of each community or social group facilitates us with greater possibility of work with them with better results in short duration due to the cooperation given from the community members in the work (Fig. 7.7).

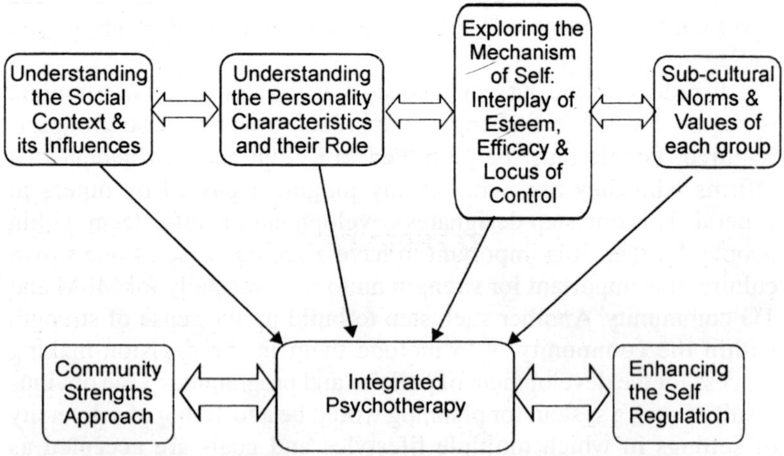

Fig. 7.7: The Proposed Action-Model for Prevention of HIV Transmission

The individualized and focalized services are required to bring a change in the behavioural mechanism of each individual at risk of HIV infection. After more than two decades of work by national level organizations, enough awareness is created among the high risk population for HIV. There are numerous loopholes in existing setup of counselling both in Targeted Interventions and in ICTC centres. The seriousness of the issue calls for a movement in this direction so that better psychological services could be provided to each and every person who is at the risk of HIV infection and comes for help or guidance. The understanding of the individual at risk from the perspectives of social-psychological-cultural, will facilitate the process of knowing why the individual is not able to prevent oneself from the risk and where the failures are taking place. Apart from this, a change in approach is required from traditional lack perspectives to strengths perspective in order to gain better results. Lastly, integrated psychotherapies should be adopted to bring change at the mechanism of self and also to deal with the personality characteristics of risk taking and sensation seeking behaviour. A successful intervention will be said to have taken place only when there is a better practice of self-regulation by the individual.

Major difficulty in the process would be hiring of trained professionals to go and work in the rural areas and other difficult interiors of India. As per the estimation based on HSS 2007, 57 per cent of the PLHA in India were living in rural areas (2007). National level policies should be made to appropriately train the suitable candidates for this work. Although, till now only counsellors have been appointed in the targeted intervention programmes, a recruitment of trained psychotherapists is a suggestible move.

REFERENCES

Alexander, C.S.; Kin, Y.J.; Ensminger, M.; Johnson, K.E.; Smith, B.J. and Dolan, L.J. (1990). A measure of risk taking for young adolescents: Reliability and validity assessments. *Journal of Youth and Adolescence*, 19 (6), 559-569.

American Psychiatric Association. (2000). *Diagnostic and statistical manual of mental disorders* (4th ed., text revision). Washington, DC.

Arnett, J. (1990). Contraceptive use, sensation seeking and adolescent egocentrism. *Journal of Youth and Adolescence*, 19, 171-180.

Bandura, A. (1994). *Self-efficacy.* John Wiley & Sons, Inc..

Bandura, A. (1989). Human agency in social cognitive theory. *American psychologist,* 44(9), 1175.

Bandura, A. (1989). Regulation of cognitive processes through perceived self-efficacy. *Developmental psychology,* 25(5), 729.

Baum, A.; Gatchel, R.J. and Krantz, D.S. An Introduction to Health Psychology. McGraw Hill, New York, 1997, 391-395.

Baumeister, R.F. and Vohs, K.D. (2007). *Handbook of Self-Regulation: Research, Theory, and Applications*. The Guilford Press, New York.

Baumeister, R.; Smart, L. and Boden, J. (1996). "Relation of threatened egotism to violence and aggression: The dark side of self-esteem". *Psychological Review*, 103, 5–33.

Baumeister, Roy F. (2001). "Violent Pride", in *Scientific American*, 284, No. 4, pp. 96-101; April 2001.

Baumeister, Roy F., *et al.,* (2003). "Does High Self-Esteem Cause Better Performance, Interpersonal Success, Happiness, or Healthier Lifestyles?", *Psychological Science in the Public Interest*, 4 (1), pages 1–44; May 2003. (ed. other researchers: Jennifer D. Campbell, Joachim I. Krueger and Kathleen D. Vohs)

Baumeister, Roy F., *et al.,* (2005). "Exploding the Self-Esteem Myth" *Scientific American*, January 2005. (ed. This study also involved Jennifer D. Campbell, Joachim I. Krueger and Kathleen D. Vohs)

Beyth-Marom, R.; Austin, L.; Fischhoff, B.; Palmgren, C. and Jacobs-Quadrel, M. (1993). Perceived consequences of risky behaviours: Adults and adolescents. *Developmental Psychology*, 29, 549-563.

Botvin, G.J. (1986). Substance abuse prevention research: Recent developments and future directions. *Journal of School Health*, 56, 369-374.

Branden, N. (1969). *The psychology of self-esteem*. New York: Bantam.

Branden, N. (2001). *The psychology of self-esteem: A revolutionary approach to self-understanding that launched a new era in modern psychology.* San Francisco: Jossey-Bass, 2001.

Bronfenbrenner, U. (1979). *The ecology of human development: Experiments by nature and design*. Cambridge, MA: Harvard University Press.

Clements-Nolle, K., Guzman, R., & Harris, S. G. (2008). Sex trade in a male-to-female transgender population: psychosocial correlates of inconsistent condom use. *Sexual health,* 5(1), 49-54.

Cloninger, C.R. (1987). Neurogenetic adaptive mechanisms in alcoholism. *Science*, 236, 410-416.

Cohan, D., Lutnick, A., Davidson, P., Cloniger, C, Herlyn, A., Breyer, J., Cobaugh, C, Wilson, D., & Klausner, J., (2006). Sex worker health: San Francisco style. *Sexually transmitted infections, 82(5),* 418-422.

Conner, M., & Norman, P. (2005). *Predicting health behaviour,* open university Press.

Cortez, F. C. P., Boer, D. P., & Baltieri, D. A. (2011). A Psychosocial Study of Male-to-Female Transgendered and Male Hustler Sex Workers in Sao Paulo, Brazil. *Archives of sexual behavior,* 40(6), 1223-1231.

Crisp, B.R., and Barber, J.G. (1995). The effect of locus of control on the association between risk perception and sexual risk-taking. *Personality and Individual Differences*, 19, 841-845.

Crocker, J. and Park, L.E. (2004). "The costly pursuit of self-esteem". *Psychological Bulletin*, 130 (3), 392–414.

Dalton, J.H., Elias, M.J., and Wandersman, A. (2001). *Community Psychology: Linking Individuals and Community*. Wadsworth Thomson Learning, Belmont.

De Santis, J. P. (2009). HIV infection risk factors among male-to-female transgender persons: a review of the literature. *Journal of the Association of Nurses in AIDS Care,* 20(5), 362-372.

Duerst, B.L.; Keller, M.L.; Mockrud, P. and Zimmerman, J. (1997). Consequences of sexual decisions: The perceptions of rural adolescents. *Issues in Comprehensive Pediatric Nursing*, 20, 51-65.

Furby, L., and Beyth-Marom, R. (1992). Risk-taking in Adolescence: A decision-making perspective. *Developmental Review*, 12, 1-44.

Gutierrez-Dona, B., Lippke, S., Renner, B., Kwon, S., & Schwarzer, R. (2009). Self-Efficacy and Planning Predict Dietary Behaviors in Costa Rican and South Korean Women: Two Moderated Mediation Analyses. *Applied Psychology: Health and Well-Being,* 1(1), 91-104.

Hecker, J.E. and Thorpe, G.L. (2005). *Introduction to Clinical Psychology: Science, Practice, and Ethics*. Pearson Education, Delhi.

Hill, S.E. and Buss, D.M. (2006). "The Evolution of Self-Esteem". In Michael Kernis, (Ed.), *Self Esteem: Issues and Answers: A Sourcebook of Current Perspectives*. Psychology Press: New York. 328-333.

Irwin, C.E. Jr., and Millstein, S.G. (1986). Risk-taking behaviours and biopsychosocial development during adolescence. In E. Susman, L.V. Feagans, and W. Roy (Eds.), *Emotion, cognition, health and development in children and adolescents: A two way street* (pp. 75-102). Hillsdale, NJ: Erlbaum.

Jackson, D.N. (1984). *The Jackson Personality Inventory Manual*. Port Huron, MI: Research Psychologists Press.

James, W. (1983). *The principles of psychology*. Cambridge, MA: Harvard University Press. (Original work published 1890).

Kaplan, H.B. (1980). *Deviant Behaviour in Defence of Self.* New York: Academic Press.

Kline, A., and Strickler, J. (1993). Perceptions of risk for AIDS among women in drug treatment. *Health Psychology,* 12 (4), 313-323.

Kohler, M.P. (1996). Risk-taking behaviour: A Cognitive Approach. *Psychological Reports*, 78, 489-490.

Koocher, G.P., Norcross, J.C., and Hill III, S.S. (1988). *Psychologists' Desk Reference*. Oxford University Press, New York, 1998.

Lahey, B., (2000). *Psychology*. Tata McGraw Hill Publishing Company Limited, New Delhi.

Lavery, B.; Siegel, A.W.; Cousins, J.H. and Rubovits, D.S. (1993). Adolescent risk-taking: An analysis of problem behaviours in problem children. *Journal of Experimental Child Psychology*, 55, 277-294.

Lazarus, L, Deering, K. N., Nabess, R., Gibson, K., Tyndall, M. W., & Shannon, K. (2012). Occupational stigma as a primary barrier to health care for street-based sex workers in Canada. *Culture, health & sexuality, 14(2),* 139-150.

Lerner, Barbara (1985). "Self-Esteem and Excellence: The Choice and the Paradox", *American Educator*, Winter 1985.

Levenson, H. (1973). Parental antecedents of internal, powrful others, and chance Locus of Control Orientations. *Developmental Psychology*, 9, 260-265.

Levenson, H. (1981). Differentiating among internality, powerful others, and chance. In H. Lefcourt (Ed.), Research with the Locus of Control Constuct (Vol. 1), New York: Academic Press, 15-63.

Leventhal, H. and Cleary, P.D. The smoking problem: A review of the research and theory in behavioural risk modification. *Psychological Bulletin,* 1980, 88, 370-405.

Lutnick, A., & Cohan, D. (2009). Criminalization, legalization or decriminalization of sex work: what female sex workers say in San Francisco, USA. *Reproductive health matters,* 17(34), 38-46.

Maltby, J., Macaskill, A., & Gillett, R. (2007). The cognitive nature of forgiveness: Using cognitive strategies of primary appraisal and coping to describe the process of forgiving. *Journal of clinical psychology, 63(6),* 555-566.

Maltby, J., Day, L., & Macaskill, A. (2007). *Personality, Individual Differences and Intelligence. Harlow: Pearson Prentice Hall.* ISBN 0-13-12976-0.

Maslow A.H. (1987). *Motivation and Personality* (3rd ed.). New York: Harper & Row.

McCord, J. (1990). Problem behaviours. In S.S. Feldman and G.R. Elliott (Eds.), *At the threshold: The developing adolescent* (pp. 414-443). Cambridge, MA: Harvard University Press.

McIntyre, A.; Saudargas, R.A. and Howard, R. (1991). Attribution of control and teenage pregnancy. *Journal of Applied Developmental Psychology*, 12, 55-61.

Mecca, Andrew M., *et al.* (1989). *The Social Importance of Self-esteem*, University of California Press.

Miller, P.H. (1989). Theories of adolescent development. In J. Worell and F. Danner (Eds.), *The adolescent as decision-maker*, pp. 13-46. San Diego, CA: Academic Press.

Millstein, S.G. and Igra, V. (1995). Theoretical models of adolescent risk-taking behaviour. In J.L. Wallander and L.J. Siegel (Eds.), *Adolescent health problems: Behavioural perspectives*, pp. 52-71. New York: Guilford Press.

Moore, S.M. and Rosenthal, D.A. (1992). Australian adolescents' perceptions of health-related risks. *Journal of Adolescent Research*, 7, 177-191.

Moore, S.M. and Rosenthal, D.A. (1993). Venturesomeness, impulsiveness, and risky behaviour among older adolescents. *Perceptual and Motor Skills*, 76, 98.

Moore, S.M.; Gullone, E. and Kostanski, M. (1997). An examination of adolescent risk-taking using a story completion task. *Journal of Adolescence*, 20, 369-379.

Mruk, C. (2006). *Self-Esteem research, theory, and practice: Toward a positive psychology of self-esteem* (3rd ed.). New York: Springer.

Norman, P., & Conner, M. (2005). Predicting and changing health behaviour: Future directions. *Predicting health behaviour,* 2, 324-371.

Parsons, J.T.; Siegel, A.W. and Cousins, J.H. (1997). Late adolescent risk-taking: Effects of perceived benefits and perceived risks on behavioural intentions and behavioural change. *Journal of Adolescence*, 20, 381-392.

Petersen, A.C.; Compas, B.E.; Brooks-Gunn, J.; Stemmler, M.; Ey, S. and Grant, K.E. (1993). Depression in adolescence. *American Psychologist*, 48, 155-168.

Rappaport, J. (1977). *Community Psychology: Values, Research, and Action*. Holt, Rinehart and Winston, New York.

Rodewalt, F. and Tragakis, M.W. (2003). "Self-esteem and self-regulation: Toward optimal studies of self-esteem". *Psychological Inquiry*, 14 (1), 66–70.

Rose, G., & Rosenberg, M. (1960). What College Students Think. *Princeton: Nostrand.*

Rotter, J.B. (1966). Generalized expectancies for internal versus external control of reinforcement. *Psychological Monographs*, 80 (1), Whole No. 609.

Rotter, J.B.; Seeman, M. and Liverant, S. (1962). Internal versus external control of reinforcement: A major variable in behaviour theory. In N.F. Washburne (Ed.), *Decisions, values, and groups*, Vol. 2, pp. 473-516. London: Pergamon.

Ruggiero, Vincent R. (2000). "Bad Attitude: Confronting the Views That Hinder Student's Learning", *American Educator*.

Satinder, K.P. and Black, A. (1984). Cannabis use and sensation-seeking orientation. *Journal of Psychology*, 116, 101-105.

Schwarzer, R., Boehmer, S., Luszczynska, A., Mohamed, N. E., & Knoll, N. (2005). Dispositional self-efficacy as a personal resource factor in coping after surgery. *Personality and Individual Differences,* 39(4), 807-818.

Sedikides, C. and Gregg, A.P. (2003). "Portraits of the self." In M.A. Hogg and J. Cooper (Eds.), *Sage Handbook of Social Psychology*, pp. 110-138. London: Sage Publications.

Siegel, A.W.; Cousins, J.H.; Rubovits, P.; Parsons, J.T.; Lavery, B. and Crowley, C.L. (1994). Adolescents' perceptions of the benefits and risks of their own risk taking. *Journal of Emotional and Behavioural Disorders*, 2, 89-98.

Sjoberg, M. D., Walch, S. E., & Stanny, C. J. (2006). Development and initial psychometric evaluation of the transgender adaptation and integration measure (TG AIM). *International journal of transgenderism,* 3(2), 35-45.

Smith, A.M.A. and Rosenthal, D.A. (1995). Adolescents' perceptions of their risk environment. *Journal of Adolescence*, 18, 229-245.

Smith, R.E.; Ptacek, J.T. and Smoll, F.L. (1992). Sensation seeking, stress, and adolescent injuries: A test of stress-buffering, risk-taking, and coping skills hypotheses. *Journal of Personality and Social Psychology*, 62, 1016-1024.

Solso, R.L. (2006). *Cognitive Psychology*. Pearson Education, Delhi.

Thuen, F. (1994). Injury-related behaviours and sensation seeking: An empirical study of a group of 14-year-old Norwegian school children. *Health Education Research*, 9, 465-472.

Twenge, Jean M. (2007). *Generation Me: Why Today's Young Americans are More Confident, Assertive, Entitled—and More Miserable Than Ever Before*. Free Press.

Udry, J.R. (1988). Biological predispositions and social control in adolescent sexual behaviour. *American Sociology Review*, 53, 709-722.

Udry, J.R. (1990). Biosocial models of adolescent problem behaviours. *Social Biology*, 37, 1-10.

Vanita, R. and Kidwai S. (2000). Same–Sex Love in India. Macmillan India Ltd., New Delhi.

Velicer, W. F., & Prochaska, J. O. (2008). Stage and Non-stage Theories of Behavior and Behavior Change: A Comment on Schwarzer. *Applied Psychology,* 57(1), 75-83.

Worell, J., and Danner, F. (1989). Adolescents in contemporary context. In J. Worell and F. Danner (Eds.), *The adolescent as decision-maker*, pp. 3-12. San Diego, CA: Academic Press.

Zuckerman, M. (1971). Dimensions in sensation seeking. *Journal of Consulting and Clinical Psychology*, 36, 45-62.

Zuckerman, M.; Eysenck, S. and Eysenck, H.I. (1978). Sensation-seeking in England and America: Cross-cultural, age, and sex comparisons. *Journal of Consulting and Clinical Psychology*, 46, 139-149.

8

Effect of Family Therapy on Depression among People Living with HIV/AIDs (PLWHA)

Kalpana Jain and *Monika Sharma*

Introduction

The Acquired Immuno-Deficiency Syndrome (AIDS) is a serious illness and a public health crisis that merits the concern of everyone (All & Fried, 1994). The global pandemic of HIV/AIDS has triggered responses of compassion, solidarity, and support. According to estimates from the UNAIDS/WHOAIDS Epidemic Update, 30.8 million adults and 2.5 million children were living with HIV at the end of 2006 (UNAIDS/WHO, 2007). Other responses, however, have associated the disease with stigma, ostracism, repression, and discrimination as many HIV infected individuals are rejected by their families, loved ones, and communities.

Depression is characterized by feelings of sadness, despair, melancholia and reduction of physical and mental drives. The World Health Organization defines depression as low mood, loss of interest or pleasure, feelings of guilt or low self-worth, disturbed sleep or appetite (either too much or too little), low energy, and poor concentration. Depressed persons may complain frequently of fatigue, being excessively tired upon waking up in the morning after an adequate amount of sleep. They may describe feeling of emptiness, isolation and alienation. They often complain of difficulty in concentrating.

The AIDS epidemic itself is an obvious source of psychological distress, and it is the foundation of the psychological epidemic. When living with HIV, people may face a dilemma in disclosing their HIV status to others, because it may lead to stigmatization and exclusion (UNAIDS, 2000). The HIV infection increases the risk of psychological ailments which are harmful to individuals, families and societies. HIV also evokes anxiety. HIV/AIDS is usually associated with high rates of psychiatric and emotional problems in addition to its social impact and much focus is given to the physical aspects of the disease, but mental health aspect is ignored from the general health assessment of the HIV positive (NARI, 2005).

HIV related stigma refers to unfavourable attitudes, beliefs, and policies directed toward people perceived to have HIV/AIDS as well as their loved ones, associates, social groups, and communities. HIV infection is a protracted and stigmatizing illness which can lead to the loss of both physical and cognitive functioning (Robertson *et al.*, 2006). With HIV/AIDS, the emotional trauma is compounded by a societal reaction that judges the HIV infected person very harshly. The prevalence of mental illnesses in HIV infected individuals is substantially higher than in the general population. Mej *et al.* (1994) found a greater prevalence of depression in the group of symptomatic HIV positive individuals when compared to the group of uninfected individuals.

Just as the virus depletes the human body of its natural defenses, it can also deplete families and communities of the assets and social structures necessary for successful prevention and provision of care and treatment for persons living with HIV/AIDS (Lyons, 1997). It is possible that good social support promotes psychological well-being which in turn promotes good health (Green, 1993).

Today, people with HIV/AIDS are regularly discriminated and rejected by their own loved ones, their social circles and communities when they need support the most. They may be forced out of their homes, lose their jobs, or be subjected to violent assault (Goffman, 1993). The disease is considered as a deserving punishment for immoral behaviour. Discrimination can become the hardest part of living with the HIV infection, creating a climate that is a private hell for those infected and affected. In many regions, people with HIV have been thrown out of their homes, rejected by families, turned away from jobs, and had their children expelled from schools. Stigma generally makes the disease more difficult to discuss and harder to deal with. It can spread infection through non-disclosure. Some people with HIV infection go for years without telling a soul (Sudha *et al.*, 2005).

AIDS stigma and discrimination have been seen all over the world, though it is found differently between countries, communities, religious groups and individuals. They are often seen in other forms of stigma and discrimination, such as racism etc. which can be associated with behaviours that are socially unacceptable such as prostitution or drug use.

Kendler *et al.* (1998) found that negative life events were significant factors for the development of a major depressive episode in HIV-positive women. They also found that presenting symptoms of illness were correlated with depression.

Family members who care for the patient are also close to HIV infected person and their attitude towards HIV infection may affect the psychological health of HIV infected and thus his/her immune system. Family members fulfil needs for social support in the face of economic hardship, social alienation, and difficulties accessing health care. Family members support can enhance compliance with medical care, reunion with family members, and abstinance from drug use. Chouhan and Bhati (1999) found that poor family environment and lack of emotional coherence in the family encourages HIV proneness among the patients. The social stigma that surrounds HIV may have adverse repercussions not only for the individual, but also for their family (Bor, 1993; Demi, 1997 and Snyder, 1999).

The goal of family therapy is to help family members improve communication, solve family problems and understand and handle special family situations (for example death, serious physical or mental illness). Family therapy can educate families about the illness and work out problems associated with care of the family member (Encyclopedia of Children's' Health, 2010). Therefore, it becomes important to understand the effectiveness of family therapy on depression among HIV infected persons.

Objectives

- To study the effect of HIV infection on Depression
- To study the effect of gender on Depression

- To study the interaction effect of HIV infection and gender on Depression
- To study the effect of Family Therapy on depression among HIV infected persons.

Methodology

Sample

Based on Purposive sampling technique, a sample of 120 respondents were selected from district hospitals of Udaipur. The respondents were divided into two categories: Subjects who were declared HIV infected through their blood test by doctors and subjects who were declared non-infected by the doctors. Thus, among these 120 respondents, 60 respondents (30 Males and 30 Females) were from HIV infected group and the rest 60 respondents (30 Males and 30 Females) were from non-infected group. For the second part of the research work, 12 HIV infected persons were randomly selected from this group of 60 infected subjects. Out of these 12 subjects, 6 were assigned to experimental group and 6 HIV infected persons were assigned to control group randomly. Family therapy was given to HIV infected persons in experimental group. To control group, no therapy was given. The age range of subjects was from 25-40 years.

Tools

IPAT Depression Scale developed by Krug, S.E. and Laughlin, J.E. (1976) was used to measure level of depression among HIV infected and non-infected male and female respondents. It contains 40 items.

Procedure

All adequate rapport was established with the client before the administration of the test. The test was administered individually on both HIV infected and non-infected males and females. Family therapy was provided to HIV infected individuals of experimental group. Family members who were close to the client or if any problematic relationship existed between the client and the family member, then they were included in the counselling sessions. Family members in these sessions were explained how they can help their family member to live positively with the disease and how much their behaviour can affect the client's mental and physical health. In the control group, no therapy was given to HIV infected individuals. Identity of respondents was kept confidential. Scoring was done with the help of the manual.

2×2 Factorial Analysis of Variance was used to find out the main and interaction effect of HIV infection and gender on the level of depression and Analysis of Covariance was used to find out the effect of family therapy on depression among HIV infected individuals (Table 8.1).

Results and Discussion

Table 8.1: Mean Values and Standard Deviation of Different Groups for Depression

HIV Status	*Male*	*Female*	
Infected	Mean = 35.77 SD = 4.11	Mean = 40.27 SD = 3.91	Mean = 38.02
Non-Infected	Mean = 28.47 SD = 3.97	Mean = 23.07 SD = 5.47	Mean = 25.77
Total	Mean = 32.12	Mean= 31.67	

Table 8.2: Analysis of Variance of Depression Scores among HIV Infected and Non-Infected Males and Females

Source of Variance	*SS*	*df*	*MS*	*F-value*
HIV Status	4501.88	1	4501.88	223.31*
Gender	6.08	1	6.08	0.30
HIV Status × Gender	735.08	1	735.08	36.46*
Error within group	2338.57	116	20.16	

* Significant at 0.01 level.

It can be seen from Table 8.2, that the effect of HIV infection on level of depression was significant at 0.01 level ($F = 223.31$, $df = 1/116$, $p > .01$). This shows that there was significant difference in depression scores of persons suffering from HIV infection and persons not having HIV infection. Table 8.2 shows that HIV infected persons had high depression scores (Mean = 38.02) in comparison to non-infected persons (Mean = 25.77). HIV infected persons were more depressed than non-infected persons because HIV is a virus that causes AIDS (Acquired Immuno Deficiency Syndrome) a health condition where a person is not capable of fighting with other diseases. Therefore, they may develop a feeling of hopelessness, fear, sadness and despair. HIV infected persons had more feelings of sadness, despair, emptiness, hopelessness, worthlessness, guilt, isolation and alienation. They had reduced physical and mental drives. They had feelings of irritability more and suffered from headaches, digestive disorders, insomnia, fear, or chronic pain than non-HIV infected persons. HIV infected individuals, their loved ones and even their caregivers are often subjected to rejection by their social circles and communities when they need support the most. They had more difficulty in concentration and feeling of worthlessness and guilt was also found to be more.

Table 8.2 shows that the F-ratio (F-ratio = 0.30, $df = 1/116$, $p > .01$) for gender (Male and Female) was found non-significant. It shows that Males and Females did not differ significantly on depression. In other words, gender had no effect on depression. Both Males and Females have equal level of depression. They were found to have equal feelings of sadness, despair, hope and mental and physical drive. They did not differ on physical symptoms like sleeplessness, fatigability, headache, multiple somatic complaints. They were found to be equal in symptoms like loss of appetite and feelings of worthlessness. They also had equal level of concentration, inner tension and interest.

Table 8.3: *t*-value between HIV Infected, Males and Females on Depression

HIV Status	*Male*	*Female*	*t-value*
Infected	Mean = 35.77 S.D. = 4.11	Mean = 40.27 S.D. = 3.92	4.43*
Non-Infected	Mean = 28.47 S.D. = 3.97	Mean = 23.07 S.D. = 5.47	4.30*
t-value	6.88*	13.77*	

*Significant at 0.01 level.

To study the interaction effect of infection and gender, further analysis was carried out and *t*-value was calculated. It indicates that independent variable namely HIV status and gender interacted significantly to bring variation in the level of depression. Table 8.3

shows that there was significant difference (t-value = 4.43, df = 58, $p < .01$) in the depression of HIV infected males (Mean = 38.02) and females (Mean = 40.27). It means that significant difference existed in the depression of HIV infected males and females. The depression level was high in HIV infected females than males. Women reported significantly more depressive symptoms than men. It may be because HIV infected women are more sensitive. They are discriminated against and treated badly; they have lower social support and lower sense of empowerment. Valverde and his colleagues (2007) found that HIV infected women reported significantly more depressive symptoms than HIV infected men. A women's role as a wife, worker, mother, and caretaker contribute to the levels of everyday stress. Women who are infected with HIV continue to face possible fear and rejection. Because of infection they may feel life to be full of struggles and stressful. HIV infected women were more depressed than HIV infected men. It may be that in most of the cases women get this infection from their partners. They suffer with this dreadful disease without being involved in wrong or illegal act. They may also feel more depressed because of dependency on males and on the society.

Table 8.3 also shows that there was significant difference (t- value = 4.30, df = 58, p <.01) in the depression level non-infected males (Mean = 28.47) and non-infected females (Mean = 23.07). It indicates that there was significant difference in the level of depression of non-infected male and female. Non-infected males had higher depression scores than females. It may be because now a days males have more responsibilities than women. They suffer problems in their jobs, they have all the financial responsibility of the family. Women in society are free to show their feelings and emotions, whereas, men are expected to suppress their feelings and not to show them in public. The role of men in society is often led by cultural roles that demand him to be tough and strong and to set emotions aside. They are supposed to be successful. They should be able to restrain their emotions. The idea of being a tough guy and staying in control of emotions, these cultural expectations can mask some of the true symptoms of depression, forcing men to express aggression and anger instead. This is one of the factors that may lead to depression among males.

Table 8.3 also shows that there was significant difference (t-value = 6.88, df = 58, p <.01) in the depression scores of HIV infected males (Mean = 35.77) and non-infected males (Mean = 28.47). The higher depression level among HIV infected persons may be because of their infection. HIV infected males showed symptoms of fatigue, insomnia, and weight loss. They had feeling of hopelessness, worthlessness and guilt etc. as their illness is associated with behaviours that are not acceptable socially, both as a product and producer of such behaviour. One of the reasons of depression among HIV infected males may be their worries about family members as in Indian society family members are dependent on males.

Table 8.3 also shows that there was significant difference (t-value = 13.77, df = 58, $p < .01$) in the depression of HIV infected females (Mean = 40.27) and non-infected females (23.67). It shows that there was significant difference in the level of depression of HIV infected and non-infected females. HIV infected females were more depressed than non-infected. It may be because HIV infection increases the risk of psychological ailments. The AIDS epidemic has often been associated with severe negative public reactions ranging from banning entry of HIV infected women to isolating an individual in the family. They look after the affairs of the family and children. They reported low level of social support. They also had difficulties in managing their illness and have fear because HIV/AIDS is associated with death. The feelings of guilt and rejection behaviour of society may cause them to have higher depression.

Table 8.4: Mean and S.D. Scores of Different Groups on Depression

Group	*Testing*	*Mean*	*S.D.*
Experimental Group N = 6	Pre-Test	40.83	4.67
	Post-test	31.17	4.49
Control Group N = 6	Pre-Test	40.17	5.93
	Post-Test	39.67	4.75

It is clear from Table 8.4 that mean pre-test scores of depression for experimental group and control group were 40.83 and 40.17 respectively. The mean post-test scores of depression were 31.17 and 39.67 for HIV infected persons of experimental group and control group respectively. It indicates that during pre-testing, the depression scores of all the subjects were high whereas, during post-testing the depression scores were reduced. To see the significance of difference analysis of covariance was done.

Table 8.5: ANOVA of Depression Scores during Pre- and Post-Testing

Source	*df*	*SS pre*	*SS post*	*MS pre*	*MS post*	*F ratio*
Among	1	1.33	216.75	1.33	216.75	F pre 0.04
Within	10	341.67	256.17	34.17	25.62	F post 8.46 *
Total	11	343	472.92			

* Significant at 0.05 level.

Table 8.5 shows that F ratio for the pre-test was insignificant, which indicates that experimenter was successful in getting random sample in HIV infected groups. It is reflected from the Table 8.5 that F ratio for post-test was significant at 0.05 level which indicates that there were significant differences in depression scores during post-testing.

Assuming the pre-assessment scores to be covariates, the Analysis of Covariance was carried out to determine the effects of the intervention over and above the other factors working on throughout the intervention. Generally, when it is difficult to equate the control and experimental variables at the start, ANCOVA allows making adjustments in final or terminal scores, thus allowing for differences in some initial variable.

Table 8.6: Analysis of Covariance of Depression Score

Source	*df*	*SS pre-post*	*SS post-pre*	*MS post-pre*	*SD post-pre*	*F post-pre*
Among	1	–17	244.29	244.29	6.39	71.42 *
Within	9	277.50	30.78	3.42		
Total	10	260.50	275.07			

*Significant at 0.01 level

It is clear from Table 8.6 that F post-pre ratio for depression was significant at 0.01 level. It indicates that the two means of depression which were dependent on intervention were significantly different after adjustment for initial differences in depression scores.

The adjusted mean difference between experimental group and control group was 9.04 ($p < 0.05$). It reflected that subjects of experimental group in which family members were also involved, were found to have less depression scores in comparison to control group. It implies that family counseling played an important role in reducing

Table 8.7: Adjusted Mean Difference and Significance of Depression Scores

Groups	*Adjusted Mean*	*Standard Error*	*Mean Differences Significant at*	
			0.05 level	0.01 level
Group I	30.90	3.69	8.34	11.99
Group II	39.94			

depression of HIV infected persons. HIV infected individuals of control group had more depression than experimental group in post testing. It implies that family counselling was effective in reducing depression in HIV infected individuals of experimental group. It indicates that family members played an important role in motivating HIV infected persons to live a healthy life. Family therapy might have reduced their tendency to take life in form of burden. Family members might have helped them to develop skills in managing their disease (Table 8.7).

Previous studies have also reported similar results. Lloyd, 1988; Powell-Cope and Brown (1992) observed that family members are also affected by social stigma and may experience rejection from friends, loss of jobs and harassment. Family members may display the same psychological symptoms as the infected person ranging from fear, anger, agitation and withdrawal to anxiety and depression (Beckett and Rutan, 1990). Family members of an HIV infected person also may face particular difficulties. When confronted with the knowledge of a person's illness or lifestyle, family members can become confused or angry. If these emotions can be addressed through therapy, family members can be helpful towards the (PLWHA).

The process and experiences of therapeutic interventions (family counselling) are mentioned below:

The counselling was done individually. In the first session, adequate rapport was established with subjects. Before the administration of psychological tests, it was explained to respondents that the purpose of interaction was research and their cooperation would be helpful to everyone. Each subject was assured that the details would be kept confidential. They were asked to fill the personal information sheet first. Then questionnaires for depression, death anxiety, life satisfaction, emotional competence, religious attitude were administered to the respondents. If they were not able to fill the questionnaire, it was filled by the researcher through interview technique. After the subjects had completed the questionnaires, they were collected. Subjects were thanked for their cooperation extended during collection of data. It was observed in this session that at the beginning the subjects were fearful, confused and anxious. They hesitated initially in giving their response and it took a lot of time to develop rapport. It was observed that education, caste, inhabitancy (rural, urban), knowledge of HIV and gender affected the time spent on establishment of rapport. Education, urban inhabitancy, exposure, knowledge of the infection to the client comparatively facilitated the establishment of rapport. It took a lot of effort to break the ice with the female clients.

In the second and third session, the problem was assessed determining how the family functioned and how family members interacted before the patient was diagnosed with HIV infection. In this session, significant members in the life of the client were involved like spouse, sister-in-law, father, mother, mother-in-law, sister, brother and cousin. It was observed that before HIV infection all family members were good to the client, they interacted with the client and used to do their routine work with the client but after the diagnosis of HIV infection their interaction with the client reduced significantly and their behaviour was not the same as before. It may be because they were also in a fearful situation but it created immense pressure and negative feelings in the client.

During counselling, rules were established for the session. Client and their family members were requested that one person at a time would speak. Equal opportunity was given to each person for their participation. Each member was allowed to speak without interruption The counsellor listened to what was being said, and also observed various features of the family relationships. The counsellor observed that there was communication gap among the family members. He noted the general atmosphere of the family; the closeness or distance among family members; how the family communicates, whether people listen to each other, are heard, and responded to; which feelings are expressed and whether they are recognized, acknowledged, and appropriately handled; how conflicts and problems are managed; whether decisions are made and acted upon. In these sessions, the counsellor found that atmosphere of four families was not appropriate where family members were not communicating sufficiently with each other. They were not blaming the client but were not talking enough with the client and it was one of the reasons which were giving stress to the client. Conflicts related to the HIV infection like the reason of getting HIV infection and how they should treat the client, were found among family members. Family members were made to discuss the impact of their behaviour on health and mental condition of the client. In one case, the client was a male and was infected but he and his wife were not talking to each other because of infection. In this family, the husband was infected and his wife was non-infected. Both were not ready to listen to each other. The male was dominating and he was less educated in comparison to his spouse. So, in the beginning individual sessions were taken by the counsellor then common sessions were organized for them where the husband and wife both blamed each other and released their negative emotions. The counsellor didn't interrupt them. After their catharsis, the counsellor explained them the importance of their releationship for each other and their children. If any of these aspects of family life is persistently or frequently dysfunctional, existing problems could be aggravated. Respondents were found more likely to seek support from family members than from friends. They need family members care when they are sick; this made an enormous difference both psychologically and physically on PLHA. (People Living with HIV/AIDS). The family support helped PLHA to develop a sense of responsibility and therefore changed their thoughts about HIV and their future.

The counsellor helped the patients as well as family members to understand the need for behaviour change and also provided psychological support for behaviour change. The counsellor raised the issue of HIV infection in the session with family members and clients. The counsellor discussed the anxiety and other negative emotions each one had in a facilitative and open atmosphere and explained that it was an infection like others and how they can handle it. The counsellor supported the client as well as family members for removal of their negative emotions. Thus, active listening, empathy and release of negative emotions helped to create an open atmosphere for interaction among family members. One of the client was a truck driver and was found in his report HIV infected. He did not want to disclose his status to his partner and his family members. He was afraid of losing custody of his children if his status became known. When he felt guilt and shame, the counsellor again assured the client that their talks would be kept confidential but he should disclose his status to his spouse for her safety and support and if he feels embarrassed or ashamed, then the counsellor would help the client. The counsellor, then discussed the client's status with his spouse in next session and also discussed about reasons of HIV infection. The counsellor explained the client's spouse about the client's mental stress which may affect his health and also explained that he needed psychological support.

In the following sessions, family members of clients who were close or had problematic relationship with the client were included in counselling. In this session, the counsellor examined the family members' beliefs and myths related to HIV infection. Clients and the family members were found to have less knowledge of HIV infection. By verbal communication with the client and their family members, the counsellor identified many myths about HIV infection. Before the family therapy sessions, most of the family members had myths about HIV infection. They were thinking that if they touch the infected person they might get infection or if they talk, drink or eat anything with the infected person they might get infection easily so they tried to keep distance from the infected person and this developed negative feelings in the client. Knowledge about HIV infection and its prevention was imparted to the client and family members to reduce their anxiety. Myths about this infection were also discussed and clarified. Care was taken regarding the cultural compatibility between therapists and patients, as it was important in creating an atmosphere of trust in which sensitive issues such as family support were addressed. Counsellor addressed the issues of risk reduction for family members who are not (or not yet) HIV infected. Counsellor also assisted the family members in developing the appropriate skills to sustain the behaviour change. The counsellor talked with the family members about the client's stressful mental condition after the diagnosis of HIV infection. They were also explained that in this situation he/she needed proper support otherwise family members' behaviour can affect the health of the client.

One of the clients whose HIV antibody test was positive had stopped talking with anyone after getting her test report. Her husband was non-infected. In the third session, she cried and shared her feelings with the counsellor that how she got the virus. The counsellor did not interrupt her because after a long time she showed her feelings and that was very important for her emotional health. In this session, role play technique was also used with rigid family members. The client was living in a joint family in which her sister-in-law and her mother-in-law were rude to her before getting infection so when she got infection she was scared of those family members. In this case, the counsellor talked to these family members yet they were not trying to understand the client's mental condition but after 2-3 meetings they started behaving in a better way with the client. In this case, the client's husband was cooperative and he had no negative attitude towards his wife. Though he was not much educated but he was giving emotional support to his wife.

In next sessions, as a result of counselling given to the client, it reduced the amount of fear related to their disease. Two of the clients were pregnant so counsellor convinced them for Hospital delivery and also discussed about how they could reduce the risk of HIV infection in their baby. In this session, one of the family members or client's spouse was involved in the counselling and their behaviour was observed and checked if any behaviour was seen which can affect the client's health. In this condition, they were given counselling again.

In last few sessions, follow-up was devised to find how the solutions were working, and family members were invited to come with the client. In these sessions family members were included for observation of their behaviour with the client.

In the last session, clients were asked to fill the questionnaires again and it was found by scoring that client's symptoms like fear, anxiety isolation, anger and grief related to their illness were reduced. They have accepted their infection and started living their life positively. They did not feel guilt as before and were not thinking about death. It may be because family members' behaviour has changed and they have started showing care for the client and were giving psychological support to them. Counselling skills might have helped them to increase their self-confidence. They did not feel they were ignored by family members, peers and other persons. They also learned that they should not consider themselves as disabled when faced with unexpected situations. They did not feel that their family members do not love them because they were HIV infected. Family members might have helped them to improve positive thinking and gave family support; they were able to reduce depression through their love and care. Counselling of family members might have changed their negative attitude towards HIV infection and also made them aware of their roles and responsibilities towards infected family member. The clients feeling of guilt reduced significantly post-therapy. Family counselling decreased family members' misconceptions about

HIV/AIDS and might have helped them to understand the emotions and behaviour of HIV infected persons.

It clearly showed that family counselling is important to provide social support to HIV positive individuals which help them to maintain their health. Social support is helpful for an individual to come out of trauma of an incurable infection especially in a culture where family and society's values are considered important.

This finding is also supported by other studies. Serovich (2005) found that HIV-positive men were less likely to be depressed if they received support from their families. In another such study, HIV-positive men who received social support from their families were less likely to engage in risky sexual behaviours than were men who did not (Kimberly, 1999). Green (1993) also observed that social support is an important factor in helping people to adapt psychologically to living with HIV infection. Kalichman (2003) found that this type of support promotes a sense of emotional well-being. Although some people with HIV/AIDS have strong family support systems, many do not (Martin, 1998). The India government should develop programmes that improve family and social support to the infected ones. Another study on the effect of family support on the psychological well-being of heterosexual couples with at least one HIV seropositive partner, showed an association between a general lack of family support with psychological distress (Kennedy, 1995).

Conclusion

Thus, it is clear from the study that depression of HIV infected persons was higher than non-infected individuals. Depression was more among infected females than infected males. Family members if given counselling can be helpful to the infected person in overcoming depression and trauma of the disease.

REFERENCES

Anita C. All and Juliet H. Fried (1994). Psychosocial Issues Surrounding HIV Infection that affect Rehabilitation. *The Journal of Rehabilitation*, Vol. 60. retrieved from http: //www. questia. com/

Beckett, A. and Rutan, J. (1990). Treating persons with ARC and AIDS in group psychotherapy. *International Group Psychotherapy*, 40, 19-29.

Bor, R.; Miller, R. and Goldman, E. (1993). HIV/AIDS and the Family: A Review of Research in the First Decade. *Journal of Family Therapy,* 15: 187-204.

Chouhan, V.L. and Bhati, H. (1999). *A Comparative Study of Certain Personality Variables of Sexually Acquired Patients*. Ph.D. Thesis, Department of Psychology, College of Social Sciences, M.L. S.U., Udaipur, Raj. (India), 1-72.

Demi, A. (1997). Effects of Resources and Stressors on Burden and Depression of Family Members Who Provide Care to an HIV Infected Woman. *Journal of Family Psychology*, 11 (1): 35-48.

Elliott, A. (1998). Anxiety and HIV Infection. *STEP Perspect*, 98: 11-14.

Green, G. (1993). Social support and HIV. *AIDS Care,* 5: 87–104.

Goffman, E. (1993). Stigma Notes on the Management of Spoiled Identity. Retrieved from http: //hab. hrsa. gov/publications.

Encyclopedia of Childeren's Health (2010). *Family Therapy*. Retrieved from http: //www. healthochildren. com

Kalichman, S.C.; DiMarco, M.; Austin, J.; Luke, W. and DiFonzo, K. (2003). Stress, social support and HIVstatus disclosure to family and friends among HIV-positive men and women. *Journal of Behavioural Medicine*, 26 (4): 315–32.

Kendler, K.S.; Gardner, C.O. and Prescott, C.A. (1998). A population-based twin study of self-esteem and gender. *Psychological Medicine*, 28: 1403-1409.

Kennedy, C.A.; Skurnick, J.H.; Foley, M. and Louria, D.B. (1997). Gender differences in HIV-related psychological distress in heterosexual couples. *AIDS Care,* 7 (11): 33–38.

Kimberly, J.A. and Serovich, J.M. (1999). The role of family and friend social support in reducing risk behaviours among HIV-positive Gay men. *AIDS care,* 11: 537–46.

Lloyd, G. (1988). HIV infection, AIDS and family disruption. In: A. Fleming, M. Carballo, D. FitzSimons, M. Bailey and J. Mann (eds), *The Global Impact of AIDS.* New York: A.R. Liss.

Lyons, M. (1997). The impact of HIV and AIDS on children, families and communities: Risks and realities of childhood during the HIV epidemic. *HIV and Development Programmes*, 1-10.

Mej, M.; Satz, P.; Janssen, R.; Zaudig, M., Starace, F. and D'Elia, L. (1994). WHO Neuropsychiatric AIDS study, cross-sectional phase II. Neuropsychological and Neurological Findings. *Arch Gen Psychiatry*, 51: 51-58.

Martin, P.J. (1998). End of life care in HIV/AIDS. UCSF HIV Inside Knowledge Base. Retrieved from http: //hivsiteuscf. edu/insite

NARI (2005). *The third phase of HIV pandemic social consequences of HIV/AIDS*. Pune, India, 471-484.

Powell-Cope, G. and Brown, M. (1992). Going public as an AIDS family caregiver. *Social Science and Medicine,* 34, 571-580.

Robertson, K.; Parsons, T.D.; Horst, C. and Hall, C. (2006). Thoughts of Death and Suicidal Ideation in Non-psychiatric Human Immunodeficiency Virus Seropositive Individuals. *Death Studies,* 30: 455-469.

Serovich, J.M.; Esbensen, A.J. and Mason, T.L. (2005). HIV disclosure by men who have sex with men to immediate family over time. *AIDS Patient Care STDS.*

Snyder, M.; Omoto, A.M. and Crain, A.L. (1999). Punished for their good deeds. *American Behavioural Scientist,* 42: 1171-1181.

Sudha, R.T.; Vijay, D.T. and Lakshmi, V. (2005). Awareness, attitudes, and beliefs of the general public towards HIV/AIDS in Hyderabad, a capital city from South India, *Indian Journal of Medical Sciences,* 59: 307-316, [cited 2010 Feb 10] Retrieved from: http: //www. indianjmedsci. org/text. asp?2005/59/7/307/16506

UNAIDS (2000). *Opening up the HIV/AIDS epidemic: guidance on encouraging beneficial disclosure, ethical partner counselling and appropriate use of HIV case reporting*. Geneva, Joint United Nations Programme on HIV/AIDS.

UNAIDS/WHO (2007). *UNAIDS/WHO AIDS Epidemic*. UNAIDS/WHO.

Valverde, E. E; Purcell, D.W.; Waldrop-Valverde, D.; Malow, R.; Knowlton, A.R.; Gómez, C.A.; Farrell, N. and Latka, M.H. (2007). Correlates of depression among HIV-positive women and men who inject drugs. *J Acquir Immune Defic Syndr*, 46: 96-100.

World Health Organization, (2008). *HIV/AIDS and mental health*. Executive Board, 124th Session, Provisional agenda item 4.3.

9

'SAKSHAM'—An Innovative Approach to Counselling for HIV/AIDS Patients and Caregivers

Chelani, U. and *Gunthey, R.*

Opportunities to do better make life easy. Along with personal motivation, all of us feel the need of a congenial atmosphere. There are various ways of approach and one sure method to solve problems like depression or severe mental imbalance is seeking the help of a Counsellor. Counselling concentrates on making the patient capable by accepting the problem. Counselling is a principled relationship characterized by the application of one or more psychological theories and a recognized set of communication skills modified by experience, intuition and other interpersonal factors, to clients' intimate concerns, problem, or aspirations.

HIV counselling is a confidential dialogue between a client and a counsellor aimed at enabling the client to cope with stress and take personal decisions related to HIV/AIDS. It concentrates specifically on emotional and social issues related to possible or actual infection with HIV and AIDS. With the consent of the client, counselling can be extended to spouses, sex partners, and relatives. HIV counselling process includes the evaluation of preventive behaviour and evaluation of coping mechanisms when the client is confronted with a positive result. HIV/AIDS is a life-threatening, lifelong illness. Its diagnosis has many implications—psychological, social, and physical. Preventive counselling and behaviour change can prevent transmission of HIV and improve the quality of life. Its aims are facilitating decisions to undergo HIV test. It aims to provide psychological, social, and emotional support to people who have been infected with the virus and preventing transmission of HIV by providing information about risk-behaviour such as unsafe sex or needle sharing. Other aims are to motivate people to take good care of their health, to assist them to develop personal skills necessary for behaviour change, adopt, and negotiate safe sexual practices and lastly, to ensur effective use of treatment programmes by establishing treatment goals and ensure regular follow up (NACO, 2006).

When the HIV enters our body, it weakens the natural defenses and makes the body vulnerable to a collection of potentially deadly diseases and infections called AIDS. Currently, there is no cure for HIV disease. AIDS is a hard disease to get; it does not spread by casual contact. The HIV can be dormant for years. Although HIV infection and its progression to AIDS is generally a slow process, HIV can develop at an extremely variable rate; it can take less than 5 years or as long as 15 years to progress to AIDS. The Centre for Disease Control (CDC) defines AIDS as one of more than 20 diseases occurring in an individual with no known cause of decreased resistance to the disease. The basic difference between AIDS and HIV is that the human immunodeficiency virus or HIV, which weakens the body's natural defenses making the person more susceptible to infection, causes AIDS. HIV infected people have absolutely no symptoms for several months or even years after they are infected with HIV. Some people have mild, temporary illness early in the infection, consisting of fatigue, fever and swollen glands. Later the person has repeated bows viral and fungal infections. AIDS occurs when an HIV infected person becomes ill with AIDS-defining conditions such as Kaposi's sarcoma (a rare form of cancer) (Moore, 2008).

Vulnerabilities in Rajasthan

In the context of HIV in India, Rajasthan with an official sero prevalence of 0.5 per cent can be described as a highly vulnerable, high-priority state. There are strong indications that Rajasthan is indeed a highly vulnerable state. These include:

- HIV already exists in the state, especially among vulnerable sub-populations.
- Given the large population of Rajasthan (56.4 million), even a small increase in HIV would translate into a large number of cases.
- Emerging Rajasthan data indicates HIV and AIDS is equally a rural as an urban epidemic.
- Rajasthan has thousands of people annually immigrating to higher prevalence states such as Maharashtra, Gujarat, etc., Migration though looks like temporary phenomena, has become a generation trap for significant percentage the migrant people.
- Rajasthan accounts for 19 per cent of all mines in India, employing over 5,00,000 workers, many of them inmigrants. An estimated 25,000 trucks travel daily through Rajasthan on National Highway 8 alone.
- Rajasthan is the site for many religious fairs and festivals, and attracts 25 per cent of total Indian tourism (both domestic and foreign).
- Proximity to international border and interstate borders, illiteracy and low percentage of awareness especially in rural and tribal areas, recurrent droughts, and high poverty are also some of the important factors.

Capacity building is an ongoing process through which individuals, groups, organizations and societies enhance their ability to identify and meet development challenges. The UN Development Programme (UNDP) has defined "capacity" as "the ability of individuals, institutions and societies to perform functions, solve problems, and set and achieve objectives in a sustainable manner." The terms "capacity building" or "capacity development" describes the task of establishing human and institutional capacity. Capacity building is the main foundation for the development work of the organization whether they are private business enterprises or government ministries. Capacity building is not the sole preserve of any specific organization. It is applicable to any organization irrespective of its nature of work or the structure. To be effective in their role, these organizations often need support in their own progress and development. This organizational development not only focuses on the organization's system and physical assets, but on its people, its culture and its ability to plan for future. At the other end of the capacity-building spectrum, the process can be defined not just as something relating to organizations or institutions, but to individuals and communities. In this context, capacity building can involve strengthening people's understanding of their own needs, entitlements and rights. Building their understanding and knowledge in these areas and enabling them to organize themselves to respond to this understanding, is a definition of capacity-building as a far broader approach to development. From the very essence of the definition, it would be clear that capacity-building is not something that happens overnight. It is not a quick fix. To be meaningful in the long-term, capacity-building is best done as a part of a process, rather than as an end in itself, carried out in partnership and not as a pre-condition or as something, which is imposed.

The issue of HIV was well taken by the Tata Institute of Social Sciences Mumbai under the Banner SAKSHAM with funding from Global Fund scheme from Bill and Melinda Gates Foundation.

Saksham comes from an Indian word that means "Capable" or "Self-reliant". Saksham is part of GFATM (Global Fund to Fight AIDS, Tuberculosis, and Malaria) Round-7, HIV/AIDS programme in India that aims to strengthen human and institutional capacities of the national health system to better meet the goals of the National AIDS Control Programme. Saksham is a unique partnership between 40 academic institutions spread over 25 states of India. It works closely with the National AIDS Control Organization, State AIDS Control Societies, and Non-Government Organization, representatives of Positive People's Networks and corporate agencies to enhance the overall quality of HIV/AIDS counselling and counselling training programmes in India.

Saksham aims to fulfil one of GFATM Round 7's objectives: *i.e.* "To enhance the institutional capacities of key counsellor training institutes and conduct capacity building programmes for counsellors." (http://www.tissgfatmr7.com/homepage/index.php)

Scope of Saksham

The HIV/AIDS scenario in India is complex, with intense focal epidemic among sub-groups (IDU's, sex workers, truckers, men who have sex with men) in some states and a lower prevalence in other states. Although the overall prevalence would mean an increase in large number of people living with HIV in real terms. NACO (National AIDS Control Organization) envisions an India where every person living with HIV has access to quality care and is treated with dignity. The NACP-III vision is to halt and reverse the epidemic in India over the next 5 years by integrating programmes for prevention, care, support, and treatment. Counselling has a very critical and pivotal role to play in prevention, treatment, care and support in the context of HIV/AIDS. During NACP-III, NACO plans to extend ICTC, PPTCT and ART services up to the sub-district level. Thus, there is a pressing need for large number of good quality and skilled counsellors throughout India.

Saksham is committed to responding to the needs of the national programme about HIV/AIDS counselling training through:

- Enhancement of quality of trainers.
- Improvement of the quality of training infrastructure and training systems.
- Support and supervision of training institutions and counsellors.

SAKSHAM programme is a successful key to open the door of awareness regarding HIV/AIDS in urban, rural, and remote areas of Rajasthan through counsellors. Capacity building programme contributes to the community and society through training of HIV counsellors. Master trainers who were raw hands are now the resource persons, as they are valuable contributors in the field of training programmes for HIV counsellors. A unique and successful combination between academic institute and corporate sector prepare the ground for such training programmes. Interaction with Rajasthan State Aids Control Society (RSACS) encouraged the Saksham programme to achieve the given targets within the time limits. Trainings like Supportive Supervision, M&E, Field visits, Refresher courses, one day Target Intervention Training of the Trainers (TI TOT) etc, all these are working as backbone of training programmes. Saksham programme is a bridge between RSACS and Academic institute as well as between ICTC, PPTCT, ART, CCC and RSACS. A well-set virtual library and infrastructure is an asset to the University, as it will help the students in other research works also. This programme not only gives the financial support but also the opportunity to learn new things to the youngsters. Last but not the least, the conversion of the autonomous body *i.e.*, the Universities into highly trained and technical units by introduction of e-monitoring system has enabled controlling all procedural affairs through it. It has proved convenient as well, time saving too as exchange of information can be done within few minutes. It is not only beneficial now but in future also, marvellous results could be yielded by using it elsewhere.

At Jai Narain Vyas University, Jodhpur (Rajasthan - India) a group of Master Trainers (MT) was selected after an interaction with the senior staff members of Psychology Department, and they were trained at Tata Institute of Social Sciences on the topics like – Epidemiology of HIV, Pre-Post test counselling, family counselling, MSM counselling, ART Adherence, Youth Counselling, grief bereavement, nutrition and diet, etc. Timely training programmes have been conducted for MTs and by MTs. MTs in turn have been conducting certain district level induction as well as refresher training programmes in accordance to the NACO module. MTs are using various innovative training methodologies like role-plays, brainstorming, discussions, games, films & drama, etc. Panel discussion with counsellors is also done to solve their problems related to counselling. This project is not only training the counsellors but also creating awareness among the students. 30 Master Trainers, about 330 Counsellors (11 batches of 30 counsellors in each batch) have so far been trained. Different induction as well as refresher trainings (ICTC, PPTCT, STI, ANM, TI) are being conducted by Jodhpur Saksham team. Till date, 9 ICTC induction as well as refresher trainings, 1 PPTCT, 1 STI, 1 TI and 2 staff nurses' trainings have been successfully and enthusiastically organized not only by the staff members but also by the MTs as well. Within a year of the start of this project, encouraging results are reported in relation to Capacity Building Programme for Human Resources. Apart from these certain, other awareness programmes are also conducted by MTs in rural areas for creating awareness about practicing safe sex, blood transfusion, etc.

Another milestone to this era is the introduction of the concept of Supportive Supervision (SS) for trained counsellors. Supportive supervision encourages open, two-way communication, and building team approaches that facilitate problem solving. It focuses on monitoring performance towards goals, and using data for decision-making, and depends upon regular follow-up with staff to ensure that new tasks are being implemented correctly. Now the MTs are also working as SS for quality improvement, which provides additional information on the concepts, principles, and approach. MT will be visiting once in a three months to provide support and supervision to the counsellors.

Pre-test Counselling

HIV counselling is often given in connection with a voluntary HIV test. Such counselling helps to prepare the client for the HIV test, explains the implications of knowing that one is or is not infected with HIV, and facilitates discussion about ways to cope with knowing one's HIV status. It also involves a discussion of sexuality, relationships, possible sex- and drug-related risk behaviours, and how to prevent infection. It helps correct myths and misinformation around the subject of AIDS. Whenever resources permit, pre-test counselling should be made available to those who desire it. People who do not want or do not have access to pre-test counselling should not be prevented from taking a voluntary HIV test, however; in contrast, informed consent is *always* required before an HIV test where the individual's name will be linked to the result. To allay anxieties while awaiting the test result, some individuals may seek support not only from their own families but also from a knowledgeable community worker.

The client has to be explained as to how to assess the risk and this could be done in following manner: Client should be informed about the risk of factors like multiple sex partners, non-consensual sex and S.T.I.'s, health seeking behaviour for him/herself or partner. Also, give information about sexual activities, safer sex, and I.D.U.'s the clients. To reduce the above-mentioned risks following points are to be kept in mind (NACO, 2006):

- Choosing complete sexual abstinence.
- Not having penetrative sex.
- Deciding to limit oneself to masturbation.
- Use of condom in all sexual activities.
- Avoiding casual or unplanned sexual activities.
- Partners should be faithful to each other.
- Reducing the number of partners.
- Avoid sharing sex toys.
- Avoiding substance abuse, this may lower inhibitions and encourage unsafe sexual practices.

- Avoiding unnecessary blood transfusion and if needed obtain HIV tested blood from registered blood bank.
- Using and insisting on disposable needles on all occasions.
- Universal safety precautions on all occasions.
- Preventing parent to child transmission during pregnancy.

Post-test Counselling

Post-test counselling helps the client understand and cope with the HIV test result. Here, the counsellor prepares the client for the result, gives the result and then provides the client with any further information required, if necessary referring the person to other services. The two usually discuss ways to reduce the risk of infection or transmission. HIV test results should always be given with counselling. The form of post-test counselling will depend on what the test result is. Where it is positive, the counsellor needs to tell the client clearly, and as gently and humanly as possible, providing emotional support and discussing with the client on how best to cope, including information on relevant referral services. Ongoing counselling will help clients accept their HIV status, and take a positive attitude to their lives. Through ongoing counselling, the infected person may choose to invite a trusted family member to share confidentiality and participate in the counselling enabling the family to start practicing family level counselling.

Counselling is also important when providing an HIV negative result. While the client is likely to feel relieved, the counsellor must also emphasize and clarify a few important issues like Window Period and repeat testing, safe behaviour to stay positive. It is important that counsellors be aware of any potential risks of exposure their clients incurred within the window period and encourage to repeat test.

Counselling for Negative Result

- Discuss the meaning of a negative result.
- Feelings produced because of report.
- Window Period.
- Sexually Transmitted Infections (STI's) and Reproductive Tract Infections (RTI's).
- Discussing family planning methods.

Counselling for Positive Result

- Ensuring that the person understands what a positive test result means.
- Discussing how they feel about being infected.
- Providing support to help the person with these feelings.
- Discussing their plans for the immediate future or disclosure.

Issues to be dealt either in Post-Test or in Ongoing:

- Partner, disclosure, counselling and testing.
- Sexual health issues.
- Nutrition/Diet.
- Regular medical check-ups.
- CD4 count test.
- Access to health care services or ART.
- PPTCT counselling or reproductive health issues.
- Family support, discrimination, and stigma.
- Violence.

Case Study

Following is an example of preparing a client who was continuously denying to undergo HIV testing:

A boy of 2nd year of engineering college donated blood in an NSS camp. Two months later, blood bank reported him HIV positive. At initial stages, he denied any blood transmission, drug induction and any sexual relations with anyone. The boy was not prepared for HIV testing–

Following is the narration of Pre-test counselling session between counsellor and the client :

Counsellor after establishing rapport with the client –

Counsellor – There is a doubt that your blood may be HIV infected, do you know What HIV is?

Client – No, not much. However, I know that it is a life threatening disease, which has no cure.

Counsellor – You are wrong. At initial stages if it is diagnosed, then treatment is available.

Client – Is it so!

Counsellor – Yes, the evidences are there and still the researches are going on and I hope that in near future this disease will be completely cured.

Client – Why are you informing me all this?

Counsellor – You know there are some chances that you might be infected by HIV infection but I cannot say anything just now.

Client – But I am sure that I did not do anything wrong or the blood transmitted to me. How can I have the infection?

Counsellor – What I am saying is that it is only a doubt, so there is no harm in getting it tested.

Client – But when I am confident that infection is not in me then why should I go for testing.

Counsellor – I do agree with you. However, if it is there and not tested now then it will be beyond of treatment after some days. So better get it tested now. This testing will not only save your future but the future of your fiancée and other family members.

Client – Did you observe any symptom of HIV in me?

Counsellor – No, not at all. However, if the virus is there then it will immune your body resistance. I myself also was tested for some doubts and this is my report. See it is HIV negative. This type of testing results you may also have.

Client – Why you went for testing my dear? In fun!

Counsellor – No, No. Actually, I was sitting with a group of drug users and was offered to have an experience of injecting drugs. I refused strongly. But the peer pressure compelled me to have an experience of that. I did it. After a few days, I had fever like you and narrated actual happening to my doctor. He asked me to get HIV testing. I did it. I was also in dilemma that I used injected drug only once then why should I go for testing. Nevertheless, my doctor counselled me that there is no harm in being tested.

Client – Are there any chances to get the infection in one time?

Counsellor – It is 1/100. That means once in 100 times.
Client – If it is so then I am ready to get myself tested for this infection.
Counsellor – Why you asked 'if it is so'?
Client – Once I went to a neighborhood woman who approached me for sexual relation, believe me it was only once in my life. As you said that chances are 1/100, I am sure that I have escaped. Now I have prepared myself for testing.

(Chelani U., 2010)

Counselling for Children

In many places, children are increasingly affected by the epidemic. Apart from those themselves infected with HIV, they include children where one or both of the parents are either living with HIV or AIDS or have died of AIDS. These children have special counselling needs, such as the emotional trauma of seeing their parents being ill or die, discrimination by other children and adults, and emotional worries about their own continuing illness. Older children may need counselling related to sexual issues, and on the avoidance of risk behaviour.

Counselling for Pregnant Women

Counselling can benefit pregnant women—or women wanting to become pregnant—who are either HIV-positive or unaware of their HIV status. It facilitates their making informed decisions about whether to become pregnant if HIV-infected; whether to take a test before pregnancy; and, if pregnant, whether to terminate the pregnancy, where abortion is legally available. For those already pregnant, counselling can also discuss the use of zidovudine (ZDV, also known as AZT), where available, to reduce the risk of transmitting HIV to the unborn child, and breastfeeding and other infant feeding options (see UNAIDS Technical Update on mother-to-child transmission). Where possible, and when the woman agrees, it is advantageous to involve her male partner in the counselling sessions. Ideally, women should have counselling available to them before they become pregnant.

Couple Counselling

Counselling is sometimes provided to a pair of sex partners, who agree to attend sessions together. It can help resolve misunderstandings between the two people—such as worries when one of them is tested HIV-positive—that can lead in some cases to violence, particularly against women. Couple counselling can also be given to a client and his or her sex partner or spouse, before or after an HIV test. It is also provided as part of premarital counselling. The issues of blood safety and legal issues are addresssed here.

Family Counselling

Family counselling can be defined as a systematic effort to produce beneficial changes in a family unit by introducing changes in the patterns of interaction between members of the family (NACO, 2006). Its aim is the establishment of more satisfying ways of living for the entire family and for individual member. Family counselling involves all the family members in resolving problematic relationships (emotional or sexual) and facilitates communication between them. Therefore, family therapy enables each member to accept his or her position in the changed scenario, facilitating the process of solving the crisis. It attempts to alter situation – specific maladaptive patterns and interaction within the family as a whole and its goal is to develop positive feelings and adjustment among the family members.

The counsellor forms an integral part of family counselling as they facilitate identification and definition of the problem. He involves all concerned family members and significant others in the therapeutic process. He is the facilitator and provides support to the family.

In family counselling the major issues to be considered are—

- Uncertainty of prognosis (parents and children)
- Confidentiality of HIV status or disclosure (to whom)
- Explanation for the children
- Coping with the multiple losses
- Planning for the future (NACO, 2006)

In family counselling, each member of the family is interviewed separately to obtain epidemiological information (including sexual practices). Both partners should be present together for one counselling session per unit. Counselling should focus on how to purchase, store and use condoms. Male and female genital models should be used to educate couples about HIV transmission, contraception, and conception. Sessions should also include role-plays to build self-esteem and confidence and discussions on social, financial, and legal issues associated with infection of HIV. Although practicing safer sex is the goal of the counselling, non-judgmental support rather than persuasion should be offered. Counselling should be conducted on an average every six months in which couples should be encouraged to ask questions and describe any problem, which they face, related to safer sex practices. (Padian *et al.*, 1998)

Process

The initial contact with the counsellor may be initiated by the family members or through referrals. A good rapport has to be built-up in the first interview. Family functioning evaluation should adopt an existential approach. The focus should remain on current issues in the clients and their families. Less emphasis should be laid on diagnosis of HIV/AIDS. Certain ground rules should be established. The counsellor should avoid being trapped in situations wherein confidential information is given by anyone of the family members. The counsellor should also not be prejudiced by information given by anyone family member about the other. The counsellor should shift his focus from the individual to the family and restructure the family system. He should discourage and prevent the "blame game" among the family members as far as possible. (NACO, 2006)

Pradhan *et al.* (2006) reported the socio-economic impact of HIV and AIDS in India. It was observed that the family is the main source of care and support for PLHAs. While families provide care and support, they may also perpetuate stigma and discrimination against infected individuals. Women are more likely to be badly treated than men or children. Daughters-in-laws are treated much worse than the sons are and there is no place in the family for them if the son dies (Bharat, 2001). HIV/AIDS-related stigma and discrimination in communities is commonly visible in the form of blame, scapegoat, difficult in procuring a place of stay, teasing and name-calling. Communities often shun or gossip about those perceived to have HIV or AIDS. In more extreme cases, it could take the form of violence. HIV/AIDS-related Stigma and Discrimination is known to extend to families, neighbours and friends of PLHA. This 'secondary' stigmatization and discrimination has played an important role in creating and reinforcing social isolation of those affected by the epidemic, such as the children and partners of PLHA.

A woman who was infected with HIV expressed her view as follows which reveals her catharsis :

> "My mother-in-law has kept everything separate for me—my glass, my plate. They never discriminate like this with their son. They used to eat together with him. For me, its do this or do not touch that and even if I use a bucket to bathe, they yell – 'wash it, wash it'. They really harass me. I wish nobody acts into my situation and I wish nobody does this to anybody. However, what can I do? My parents and brother also do not want me back."
>
> — *HIV-positive woman aged 23, India*

Family and marital counselling can be defined as a systematic effort to produce beneficial changes in a martial or family unit by introducing changes in the patterns of interaction between members of the family/partners. Its aim is the establishment of more satisfying ways of living for the entire family and for individual members. Marital or couples therapy involves both the partners in resolving problematic (emotional or sexual) transactional patterns and facilitates communication between couples. Family therapy enables each member to accept his or her position in the changed scenario, facilitating the process of solving the crisis. It attempts to alter situation – specific maladaptive patterns/ interactions among family members and to improve interactions within the family as a whole and the goal is to develop positive feelings and adjustment among the family members.

Case Study

Meena, a lady of 34 years, whose husband was a migrant, got to know that she was HIV positive and got this disease from her husband. She was in dilemma as to what to do now, as she was pregnant. She cried a lot but got no solution. Finally, she approached a counsellor who counselled her and made her believe that it was not certain that her child would also get HIV or would be HIV positive. The counsellor told her in detail about the nevrapin dose and the precautions to be taken at the time of delivery. In the end, the counsellor was able to create a ray of hope in the woman. The woman got convinced after several follow-up sessions and then she decided to discuss it with her family. After discussing and convincing her family members, she decided to plan for the baby. Counselling proved very beneficial and it changed her prejudices and of the family as well.

(Chelani, U., 2010)

HIV positive individuals often grapple with many simultaneous emotions including fear, grief, depression, denial, anger and anxiety. For anyone diagnosed as HIV positive, it does not mean the end of life, it just means that they have to start living positively. Positive living or living positively with HIV/AIDS is a term used to describe leading normal, non-risky life while following preventive and supportive measures to live, though infected with HIV. Another aspect of positive living is to prevent the spread of HIV from an infected person to a non-infected one.

Various dimensions of positive living are outlined which are essential in the development and provision of HIV/AIDS comprehensive care system. Hope is considered a potent factor in positive living, it helps PLHA to live positively rather than wait to die. However, women live longer because they are attached with their children. Persons with HIV need assistance to realize a sense of purpose and meaning, work energetically whether through job rehabilitation, assistance redefining self-worth or finding a flexible job.

To meet the physical, emotional, social and economic needs of PLHA, the following dimensions should govern positive living:

- Hope
- Openness or disclosure
- Accepting one's status
- Respect human right
- Strong sense of purpose
- Accessibility and availability
- Balance and healthy nutrition
- Equity
- Spirituality

Positive living can be promoted among people with HIV/AIDS by asking them to take care of themselves. Research evidence shows that people believe that HIV/AIDS people who abstain from sex can live longer than those who do not. HIV positive people should take care of the following:

- Keep a positive outlook in life, have plans, projects and dreams.
- They should not stop loving life.
- Maintain an active social life.
- Pay special attention to basic rules of good hygiene.
- Get enough sleep.
- Avoid stress.
- Eat a balanced diet.
- Stay in close touch with your doctor and HIV advisor/counsellor.
- Never agonize on HIV status.
- Have peace of mind and avoid stress.
- Exercise properly.

Above-mentioned points shed light on some practices that can promote positive living.

The following is an excerpt of interview which was taken by the author with President of PLHA (People Living with HIV/AIDS) Association, Jodhpur (Rajasthan) –

> "You are talking about rehabilitation for PLHAs, do you know it is too difficult to maintain or remain in job after disclosing the status of HIV? Widows and children are the major victims of this disease because they have to fight with not only the family members but society too. Do you know that within 2-3 years, we have been thrown out of six houses? As soon as the landlords came to know about our status they immediately got rid of us.
>
> Though we are invited by the relatives to attend the marriage but unfortunately not responsible work is given to us like serving of food, water etc. We are always told that 'you take rest as you are not well'. I myself experience that if I offer a glass of water to someone in a function he tries to throw the

water without my notice, in my opinion; society should be educated for the difference between HIV/AIDS. The knowledge between these differences will reduce our problem to some extent."

Impact of Families and Communities

The pandemic of HIV/AIDS has spread to all regions of the globe and infected over forty million victims worldwide that are currently living with this fatal disease. Tragically, the people infected with HIV/ AIDS are not the only ones whose lives are forever altered by this debilitating virus, family members, neighbours and friends of HIV/ AIDS victims are strongly connected to the individual struggling to manage the virus on a day to day basis. Although those infected are fighting this disease and doing everything they can to overcome the illness, there are still powerful issues like :

Disclosure: Disclosure of HIV status to family and partners has always been a great issue as there are many factors involved like – the manner in which they were infected, whether they were infected by a partner or whether they have infected a partner or partners. Counselling and education helps a lot to resolve these difficult decisions. As this lead to the increase in support from their families, and perhaps, ultimately, for them to understand what medical aid they require. For a HIV positive person, family acts as a 'front line' of their emotional support.

In order to prevent the onward transmission of the virus, counselling with HIV positive and family includes discussion of safer sex and methods of safe injecting. They are made to understand that they have an obligation, both moral and legal to prevent transmitting the virus to another person.

Stigma and discrimination: With the recognition of HIV and AIDS as a communicable disease social responses of fear, denial, stigma and discrimination have accompanied the epidemic. It has also shown itself capable of triggering responses of compassion, solidarity and support. From early on in the AIDS epidemic, a series of powerful images were used that reinforced and legitimized stigmatization as HIV/AIDS was considered as a punishment for immoral behaviour, as a crime in relation to innocent and guilty victims, as a war in relation to a virus that need to be fought etc. Together with the widespread belief that HIV/AIDS are shameful, these images represent 'ready-made' but inaccurate explanations that provide a powerful basis for both stigma and discrimination. These stereotypes also enable some people to deny that they personally are likely to be infected or affected. To come out of this, the counselling approach offers real hope in the persons to fight against AIDS. Counselling helps the patients and their family members to cope up with their emotional stresses resulting from AIDS. The counsellor is able to facilitate, initiate and maintain the interactive process when shows feelings of spontaneity warmth, tolerance, respect and sincerity.

Decrease in the level of depression: An HIV infected person, who suffers physically and choledogically, is unable do cope with the environmental challenges effectively. Such patients' self-esteem fades quickly as they develop guilt feelings and blame themselves for having contracted the disease. Moreover, this self-blame leads to depression, anxiety, self-anger and pessimistic outlook towards life (Lefton, 1997). Sometimes, the person is not responsible for the disease but he or she is blamed for such traumatic experience which results in acute depression and greater anxiety. Depression is a clinical syndrome, encompassing emotional, motivational, cognitive, somatic and behavioural symptoms. In addition, the feelings associated with a depressed mood includes disappointment, helplessness and hopelessness (Comer, 1995). Therefore, for this counselling plays key role as it brings a voluntary change in both the clients and the family members. The client alone is responsible for the decisions he makes but the counsellor assists in the critical moments with his warmth and understanding relationship. Then with all this, the support led by the family makes things even easier. So, in this friendly and warm atmosphere the client may without any hesitation or fear of criticism of ridicule, be able to do a little self-exploration and self-examination leading to self-understanding. Through this process, the client slowly and steadily progress towards self-realization. Therefore, counselling is essential because it can help in preventing the spread of HIV and it reduces the psychological and psychosocial stresses of AIDS patients.

Betterment in the condition of women: The impact of HIV/AIDS on women is particularly acute. Women are often economically, culturally and socially disadvantaged and lack equal access to treatment, financial support and education. They are mistakenly perceived as the main transmitters of sexually transmitted diseases

(STDs). HIV positive women are treated very differently from men. Men are likely to be excused for their behaviour that resulted in their infection, whereas women are not.

Family is considered as the primary caregiver to sick members. There is clear evidence of the importance of the role that the family plays in providing support and care for people living with HIV/AIDS. Moreover, all this has been possible only because of the counselling provided to the society (family members, friends etc).

There are certain other issues worth discussing like how counselling leads to awareness, not only among the clients but also the family members as well. In addition, this leads to the increase in regularity of treatment and intake of clients at rehabilitation centre. It also leads to the increase in follow-up counselling. The factor of 'Hope' among the family members is increased, as they have understood that it is just like any other life-threatening disease (T.B., Cancer and Malaria).

For all this, the credit goes to counselling as because of it the mindset of society can be changed and people are able to discuss about this matter freely and frankly. Counselling to PLWHA and their family members has enhanced personal development, resolved the conflicts and developed necessary social skills for proper social adjustment in order to meet new challenges of modern life.

REFERENCES

AIDS InfoNet, http://www.thebody.com/index.html downloaded on 25th November, 2011.

Bharat, S.; Aggleton, P. and Tyrer, P. (2001). *India: HIV and AIDS-related Discrimination, Stigmatisation and Denial*. Geneva: UNAIDS.

Bor, R. and Elford J. (1998). *The Family and HIV Today*, New York, Redwood Books, Trowbridge, Wiltshire.

Capacity Building guide (2011). City University London, http: //uk.oneworld.net/guides/capacitybuilding

Chelani, U. (2010). *HIV counselling – Positive thinking,* Unpublished Research work, Jodhpur, Dept. of Psychology, Jai Narain Vyas University.

Comer, R.I. (1995). *Abnormal Psychology*, New York: Freeman and Company.

Lefton, I.A. (1997). *Psychology* (6th ed). Neetham Heights, MA: Allyn and Becon

Moore, L.H.; Parkes, C.M. (2008). *Speaking of Dying: A Practical Guide to Using Counselling Skills in Palliative Care*, Jessica Kingsley: New York.

National AIDS Control Organisation NACO. (2006). Ministry of Health and Family Welfare, Government of India.

Padian, N.S.; Van der Straten, A.; Vemon K.A.; Knight, Gomez C.A. (1998). *Managing HIV among serodiscordant heterosexual couples, serostatus, stigma and sex, AIDS care*, Oct 10 (5): 533-48.

Pradhan, B., Sundar, R. and Singh, S. (2006). *Socio-economic impact of HIV and AIDS in India*, National AIDS Control Organization (NACO), Ministry of Health and Family Welfare, New Delhi, Government of India.

TATA Institute of Social Sciences (2010). Mumbai http://www.tiss.edu/TopMenuBar/about-tiss/history downloaded on 16th December, 2010.

Vulnerabilities in Rajasthan (2006). www.aidsalliance. in, downloaded on 16th December, 2010.

10

Domestic Violence against Women and its Health Implications

Urmi Nanda Biswas

Domestic violence is the most serious violation of all basic rights that a woman suffers in her own home at the hands of her family. It is pervasive in all existing categories of class, culture, religion, and as well as caste. Moreover, it has been consistently observed to have an inherent gender bias to it, with most accounts of such violence being perpetrated by a male figure upon a female in a relationship. In this sense, domestic violence can be viewed as being at the core of the patriarchal orientation of societies as they subjugate women as well as assume authority over their lives. Other accounts cite cases about violence incurred upon children by adults within a household, besides rare instances of cases in which males too are victims in the hands of female.

The phenomenon of domestic violence is not one of isolated events; it increases in frequency with passing time and the victim's growing helplessness. In this sense, it breeds in a pathological environment that prepares the ground for such a vicious cycle. Domestic violence has serious deterring consequences upon the health and well-being of the victim as well as the overall productivity and health of a nation.

Definition of Violence

Violence is an act of aggression usually in interpersonal interaction or relations. It may also include aggression of individual women against themselves, such as suicide, self-mutilation, negligence of ailments, sex determination tests, food denial, and so on (Karlekar, 1998). Indian scholars in woman and gender studies have emphasized the dynamics of power and powerlessness involved in a violent act. It is a coercive mechanism "to assert one's will over another to prove or to feel a sense of power" (Litke, 1992, 174). Going further, Govind Kelkar situates violence against women "in the socio-economic and political content of power relations." She feels the view that it is "an act of illegal criminal use of force" is inadequate and should include "exploitation, discrimination upholding of unequal economic and social structures, the creation of an atmosphere of terror, threat or reprisal and forms of religio-cultural and political violence" (Kelkar, 1991). As the focus is on the household, the term "domestic violence" is preferred to that of "family violence", the former focusing on the physical unit of the home rather than the more amorphous content of the family, even though the underlying worldview may be that of the larger familial or kin group.

This chapter reviews and discusses different forms of domestic violence against girl children and women and the prevalence of each one of those at the national level. Various factors, working as antecedents, consequences, moderators, or mediators to sustain domestic violence in the society, will be delineated here, inclusive of the demographic, psychosocial, and health correlates of domestic violence.

Types of Domestic Violence against Girl Children and Women

Violence against the girl child in India assumes many forms, ranging from physical and sexual abuse to deliberate health and nutritional neglect. India has a high rate of infant mortality overall, but the rate is higher for infant girls than for infant boys. Even worse, after one year of age, the infant mortality rate for the female child is one and half times that of the male child (Singh and Kapur, 2002).

Current Status of the Girl Child

India's experience is crucial in understanding the current increase in the proportion of males vs. females in populations across Asia. According to the UNICEF report (Guilmoto, 2007), the following reasons are important why India needs urgent monitoring of current sex-ratio trends. First, rising sex ratios in India have been recorded since the early 1980s, and have since continued increasing with no sign, so far, of reversing course. The impact of this early rise is already visible among the adult population of several Indian districts. Second, even if sex-ratio values in India is still beneath those of China, its potential contribution to the 'masculinization' of Asia (and consequently the world population) is particularly formidable in view of India's demographic weight (see, Guilmoto, 2007). The Indian scenario of female discrimination in terms of female feticide, infanticide, sexual violence, and female mortality as evident from sex-ratio, child population, and mortality from 2001 census of India and National Family and Health Survey rounds is extremely complex. The complexity, which is a result of India's socio-economic diversity, interplay of cultural, economic and social factors, fabricated with recent policy initiatives, also offers ways to better understand the heterogeneous situation and mechanisms at work across contexts and to inform the policy debate on female feticide.

The declining sex ratio, which has dropped to alarming levels, especially in the north-western states according to Census 2001 reports, can be understood as an offshoot of the proliferation and abuse of advanced technologies coupled with social factors contributing to the low status of women such as dowry, concerns with family name and looking up to the son as a breadwinner in the middle and higher socio-economic households. Despite the existence of the Prenatal Diagnostic Techniques Act, there is a dire need to strengthen this law since the number of convictions is despairingly low as compared to the burden posed by this crime. An additional dimension that emerges from this analysis springs from socio-economic differentials. Urban India has higher sex ratio than rural India. Further analysis also points to the positive linkage between abnormal sex ratio and better socio-economic status and literacy. This contradicts the common sense assumption of sex selection being an archaic practice common only among the uneducated. Moreover, it is necessary to gear efforts against the cultural, economic and religious roots of this social malady by woman empowerment and intensive Information, Education and Communication campaigns (Garg & Nath, 2008). Data suggests that there is more female feticide among urban, educated, higher SES category. Moreover, it is important to understand the active role played by elite households in gender discrimination

(Census of India, 2001, 2011; Bhat and Zavier, 2007; Retherford, and Roy, 2003). Data from NFHS-2 on abortions, sex-ratios at birth, son preference and the use of ultrasound and amniocentesis during pregnancy present compelling evidence of the extensive use of sex-selective abortions particularly in most prosperous area of Gujarat, Haryana and Punjab, Rajasthan and Delhi. This declining sex-ratio could result in a demographic and social disaster. Recent efforts of government against the practice are not likely to be successful without changes in the societal conditions that foster son preference (Arnold, Kishor & Roy, 2002; Jha, Kumar, Vasa, Dhingre, Thiruchalavam & Moineddin, 2006). When we wonder, whether the pregnant women's attitude and awareness plays a role in this sex-selective abortion and low sex-ratio, findings of research supports a very high percentage of pregnant women which are ignorant about the consequences of low birth-ratio, and gender imbalance in society (Srivasava and Durge, 2010).

In an extensive review article on characteristics of sex ratio imbalance in India and future scenarios, Guilmoto (2007) discusses the increasingly threatening scenario of male migrations from the country, significant changes in Indian Family structure, late marriages, and increased risk of gender based violence, rising demand for sex-work and the development of trafficking networks.

The important Human Development Indicators (HDI) are presented in Table 10.1 which shows the dismal status of the girl child in India. The sharp decline in female sex ratios over the years

Table 10.1: Important Human Development Index (HDI) of girl child

Indicators	*Males*	*Females*	*People*
Population (0-6)	8,19,11,041	7,59,52,104	15,78,63,145
Sex ratio (0-6)	—	—	927/1,000
IMR (April 2006) (infant mortality rate)	—	—	58
MMR (mother mortality rate)	—	407	—
Child mortality rate (0-4) (2000)	18.6%	20.6%	19.5%
Anemia (15-19)	—	56%	—
Literacy rate	75.26	53.67	64.84

Source : Working Group on Development of Children for the Eleventh Five Year Plan (2007-2012), Report, Ministry of Women and Child Development, India (2007).

suggests that female feticide and infanticide might be primarily responsible for this phenomenon followed by general neglect of the girl child. The sex ratio has been dwindling even in states like Haryana, Punjab, Uttar Pradesh, and Gujarat, which are supposed to be economically prosperous.

Female Feticide

Female feticide has become popular with the spread of amniocentesis, a medical technique evolved to discover birth defects, a part of which establishes the sex of the foetus. Introduced in 1974 at a leading government-run hospital in New-Delhi, the new technology was quickly appropriated by medical entrepreneurs. In spite of a series of government circulars from 1977 onward banning the tests, the privatization and commercialization of the technology was well underway within a few years of its introduction. It is still very much used on the sly across the country and is instrumental in female feticide. Unfortunately, as it is banned, punishable, and illegal, the reported cases of female feticide are the tip of the iceberg, the actual problem being a thousand times more pernicious.

The data available from reported cases of female feticide under Sections 315 and 316 IPC across states shows a consistent increase over the years until 2006, with a decreasing trend after that. In 2006, there were 125 reported cases of female feticide, coming down to 96 cases in 2007 and 73 cases in 2008. Among the states, Punjab has the highest number (24/73, or 33%) of feticide in 2008. Punjab and Rajasthan are two northern states which explain more than 40 per cent of the feticide over the years. Maharashtra and Madhya Pradesh also show a higher trend of female feticide (Table 10.2).

Table 10.2: Number of female feticides in India (2001-2008)

States/UTs	2001	2002	2003	2004	2005	2006	2007	2008
India	55	84	57	86	86	125	96	73

Note: Figures are from 2001 to 2008 under Sections 315 and 316 IPC.
Source: Ministry of Health and Family Welfare (10443) and (ON74).

Crimes against Girl Children

The data compiled by India's Ministry of Human Resource Development for crime against girl children categorizes crime under the sections such as rape of girls below age sixteen, infanticide, feticide, procuring a minor, selling girls for prostitution, and buying girls for prostitution. Although the available data is quite old, still the numbers are alarming. In 2000, there were 3,115 cases of rape, 104 cases of infanticide, 90 cases of female feticide, 147 cases of procuring a minor, 15 cases of selling of girls for prostitution, and 53 cases of buying girls for prostitution. Madhya Pradesh, Maharashtra, and Uttar Pradesh report the highest number of rape cases. Maharashtra and Madhya Pradesh also report highest number of infanticide, feticide, and procuring a minor. However, Gujarat state reports highest number of (43/53, or 80%) of girls bought for prostitution.

Table 10.3: Incidence of crimes committed against girl children in India (2000).

States/UTs	*Rape (below 16 years)*	*Infanticide*	*Feticide*	*Procuration of minor*	*Selling of girls for prostitution*	*Buying of girls for prostitution*
India	3,132	104	91	147	15	53

Source: Ministry of Human Resource Development, India.

Female Infanticide

A far more pernicious manifestation of an ideology that devalues girl children is the recent resurgence of female infanticide. It is the deliberate act of killing a female child within one year of its birth, either directly, by using poisonous organic or inorganic chemicals, or indirectly, by deliberately neglecting to feed the infant. It is reported that female infanticide has existed in India since 1789 in several districts of Rajasthan; along the western shores in Gujarat - Surat and Kutch; and among a clan of Rajputs in eastern part of Uttar Pradesh. In 1870, the British government in India outlawed infanticide (see Kashmir, 1994), but over a century later, there are alarming reports of baby girls murdered in areas where the custom did not previously exist. Barbara Miller (1981), based on historical records, noted that "female infanticide in 19th Century India was practiced primarily in the higher social groups of the north, though this point is debatable." (55). Miller related this practice to the control and distribution of property and variations in the tradition of dowry. Further, fieldwork and analysis of census data led her to conclude that there was distinct sex preference in the north, related to inheritance patterns as well as sex-related work roles. Social sanction and legitimization of infanticide are surely important in communities where the poor fear dowry and the rich fear a fragmentation of property (Karlekar, 1998).

Poverty, alcoholism among men, ignorance of family planning, and the cost of dowry are the possible causes of this practice, and there is scattered evidence to suggest that it is more prevalent in other parts of India than is readily acknowledged. At the same time, while instances of infanticide are indicative of negative attitude toward girls, a certain caution needs to be exercised before extrapolating on the likely spread of this social malaise. It is useful to keep in mind Chunkath and Athreya's (1997) observation that birth order determines the fate of a girl child. The findings from household data where female infanticides had occurred in 1995 showed that "the first female infant is in a majority of cases not a victim of female infanticide, the second girl child would often escape it and the third girl is invariably the victim."

Facts on Female Infanticide

According to a recent report by the United Nations Children's Fund (UNICEF), up to fifty million girls and women are missing from India's population as a result of systematic gender discrimination. In most countries in the world, there are approximately 105 female births for every 100 males, but in India, there are less than 93 women for every 100 men in the population.

The United Nations says an estimated two thousand unborn girls are illegally aborted every day in India. (India Development Gateway, http://www. indg. in/social-sector/social-awareness/stop-female-infanticide/stop-female-infanticide). The reported cases (under IPC 315) of female infanticide as available in the records of the Ministry of Health and Family Welfare of India show that the trend has been consistently increasing after 2005. The reported cases have gone up from 108 in 2005 to 140 in 2008. Speaking state-wise, Uttar Pradesh and Madhya Pradesh together account for more than 50 per cent of the female infanticide. Tamil Nadu also follows in terms of higher number of female Infanticide.

Table 10.4: Number of female infanticide in India (1999-2008)

States/UTs	1999	2000	2001	2002	2003	2004	2005	2006	2007	2008
India	87	104	133	115	103	102	108	126	134	140

Note: Figures are for 2001 to 2007 under Section 315 IPC.
Source: Ministry of Health and Family Welfare, India (10443) and (ON74).

In India, marriage continuous to be universally regarded as essential for a girl, irrespective of class, caste, religion, and ethnicity. Concern over the conduct of the sexually vulnerable girl is an important cause of early marriage. The National Family Health Survey (NFHS) of 1998-99 (NFHS-II) showed that, despite the steady rise in the age of first marriage, almost universally marriage is early in India, and 30 per cent of women in the age group of fifteen to nineteen were married. Another 4 per cent are married but "gauna" (sending the bride to bridegroom's place after attaining maturity) has not been performed. As official age for marriage is eighteen for girls, it is possible that a large percentage of these marriages were of underage girls. Among women age twenty to twenty-four, almost 25 per cent were married before fifteen and half were married before eighteen. The mean age of marriage is about two and half years lower in rural areas than in urban areas. Illiteracy, poverty, cultural norms, and an anxiety based on the desire to marry off girls as soon as possible are factors that are often cited for child marriage (Joshi, 2000).

Violence against Women

The World Health Organization (WHO) (2007) reports that the proportion of women who have experienced physical or sexual violence or both by an intimate partner ranges from 15 to 71 per cent, with the majority between 29 and 62 per cent. Violence against women can be of different types and of different magnitudes (measured in terms of its effect on victim's physical, mental, and emotional health). According to National Family Health Survey (NFHS-III) of 2005-06, domestic violence against women is defined as an act involving physical and sexual violence for all women by anyone person in the family or spousal physical, sexual or emotional violence for ever-married women or combination of both. Table 10.5 shows the data available from the Ministry of Health and Family Welfare (2005-06), for violence against women in the age group of fifteen to nineteen who have experienced physical violence since age fifteen. The data states that 85.3 per cent of currently or once-married women reported the current husband as the perpetrator, whereas never-married women identified the father (26.6%), mother/stepmother (57.1%), or sister/brother (36.3%) as the main perpetrator. Table 10.5 also presents distribution of married women who have ever suffered emotional, physical, and sexual violence by their husband in last twelve months. The data reveals that emotional, physical, and sexual violence gradually reduced along with advancing age, the violence being highest in the younger age group, that is, fifteen to nineteen years of age. In rural area, the physical and sexual violence happens more often as compared to emotional violence, whereas emotional violence shows a higher trend in urban areas. With respect to the employment status, women employed for cash are subjected to more violence that is emotional as against women who are not employed or employed not for cash. However, women employed not for cash experience more physical or sexual violence as compared to other two groups. Compared to women with children, childless women are subjected to more emotional, physical, and sexual violence by their husband. Interestingly, it seems that the higher the number of children, the less violence is meted out to the mother. Divorced/deserted and separated women reported being subjected to more emotional violence as compared to married women, whereas married women experience much more physical and sexual violence.

The 2005-06 National Family Health Survey data on preference of men for sons and daughters in different age groups reveal that men in the age group of forty to forty-nine (oldest) want more sons and at least one son as compared to their younger age groups. Age has an inverse relationship with reported preference for sons. Men from rural background prefer more sons as compared to daughters. Education also has an inverse relationship with want of sons, the more educated men show lower percentage of preference for sons. Religion-wise, Muslim men significantly differ from men in other religion in their desire and preference for a son, followed by Hindus, with Sikhs being the lowest. However, across all demographically

Table 10.5: Among Women Age 15-49 who have Experienced Physical Violence Since Age 15, Percentage who Report Specific Persons who Committed Violence, according to Respondent's Marital Status in India (2005-2006)

Person	*Marital status*			*Total*
	Ever married	*Married, gauna not performed*	*Never married*	
Current husband	85.3	-4.9	NA	77
Former husband	7.3	0	NA	6.6
Current boyfriend	0	0	0.1	0
Former boyfriend	0	-4.9	0.5	0.1
Father/step-father	4.4	-29.5	26.6	6.6
Mother/step-mother	8.9	-64.3	57.1	13.7
Sister/brother	4.7	-19.6	36.3	7.8
Daughter/son	0.1	0	0.5	0.1
Other relative	1.4	-3.4	3	1.5
Mother-in-law	1.9	0	NA	1.7
Father-in-law	0.6	0	NA	0.6
Other in-law	1.5	0	NA	1.3
Teacher	1.7	-16.3	14.9	3
Employer/someone at work	0	0	0.1	0
Police/soldier	0	0	0.1	0
Other	0.2	0	0.8	0.3
Number of women	25,337	85	2,656	28,078

Source: National Family Health Survey (2005-06).

categorized groups, men show consistently more preference and want for a son as compared to daughters.

Domestic Violence and Health

Domestic violence has harmful physical and psychological health correlates. Some of the health related correlates are as follows.

Nutritional Deficits

Ackerson and Subramanian (2008), analysed the NFHS data and reported anaemia and low weight among the women who reported physical domestic violence and victimization. Results indicated associations of multiple incidents of domestic violence with anaemia, and underweight in women and children. Possible mechanisms for this relation include the withholding of food as a form of abuse and stress-mediated influences of domestic violence and nutritional outcomes. Pandey, Singh, and Yadav (2009) examined the effect of domestic violence on the health of married women of reproductive age group in India. The study used NFHS-III micro-level data (from national and state level), where body mass index, poor nutrition levels, and anaemia were measured as health outcomes, and physical, emotional, and sexual forms of domestic violence as predictors of health. The study reports that domestic violence has negative impact on the overall women's health and nutritional status.

Psycho-somatic Problems

Subramanian, Leland, Malavika, and Rosalind (2007), in their research based on a nationally representative sample, suggest that women who experience domestic violence either recently or in the past were at greater risk of being asthmatics as compared to those who did not report any abuse. In households where women reported to have experienced domestic violence, asthma risk was higher for all individuals in those households. The study reports a consistent association between being exposed to and having experienced domestic violence and asthma prevalence. Ackerson, Kawachi, Barbeau, and Subramaniam (2007) investigated the relation between domestic violence and tobacco use among adults in India. The study found out that women who reported being abused more than one year ago and those who reported being abused in the past year were more likely to smoke and chew tobacco than women who have never experienced domestic violence. Compared to individuals who lived in homes where no abuse was reported, those who lived in homes where a woman reported experiencing domestic violence were more likely to smoke and chew tobacco. Domestic violence is associated with higher odds of smoking and chewing tobacco in India. Stress induced mechanisms, partially captured through violence and social circumstances may be a critical explanatory link in furthering our understanding of the social disparities in asthma.

Sexual and Reproductive Health

There is increasing recognition of the global scope of domestic violence and the potential reproductive health consequences of violence. Koenig *et al.* (2006) examined the association between domestic violence and the subsequent adoption of modern contraception in northern India. A significant negative association was found between a husband's reporting of using physical domestic violence against his wife and the couple's adoption of a modern method of contraception. The results highlight the need to address the issue of support for women experiencing such violence within existing family planning services and to sensitize service providers to specific needs of women experiencing such violence. Stephenson and colleagues (2008) examined the relationship between male-to-female physical domestic violence and unwanted pregnancy among women in three culturally and economically diverse area of India (four states). The study reports that women who experience physical violence from their husbands are significantly less likely to adopt contraception and more likely to experience an unwanted pregnancy. Results demonstrate a clear relationship between a women's experience of physical violence from her husband and her ability to achieve her fertility intentions.

Stephenson, Koenig, and Ahmed (2006) studied 36,642 couples from northern India for the association between men's reports of physical and sexual violence they had perpetrated against their wives and wives reports of gynaecologic symptoms. The study reported that 34 per cent of women, whose husbands reported engaging in physical and sexual violence, testified at least one symptom of gynaecologic, morbidity, compared to the women whose husbands reported no violence. Plausible mechanisms through which domestic violence may influence gynaecologic morbidity include physical trauma, psychological stress on transmission of STIs. Stephenson (2007), in his research, highlights the possible link between domestic violence and prevalence of HIV in India. Findings report evidence that strongly suggests that women at risk of violence may not have the autonomy to insist on safe sexual practices, thus lending themselves more vulnerable to risk of contracting STIs and HIV.

The findings of the above-mentioned research indicate that reducing domestic violence is important not only from a moral and intrinsic perspective but also because of the instrumental health benefits likely to accrue.

Psychosocial Correlates of Domestic Violence

Demographic Correlates

The prevalence of physical domestic violence/violence against women by husbands is staggeringly high across the Indian subcontinent. Although gender-based power inequality seems to be the underlying reason of women's vulnerability, relatively little is known about risk and protective factors.

Demographic and social characteristics of the victim (women): Almost two out of five currently or once-married women in India are subject to spousal violence. A study done on women attending OPDs in the Urban Health Centre in Ludhiana, Punjab reveals that 53.3 per cent of the total women interviewed reported occurrence of domestic violence. It was found to be significantly higher in those women who were working (68.4%) compared to homemakers. In women whose husbands were alcoholic, 87.5 per cent had experienced violence. Emotional abuse occurred in 40.6 per cent of the cases, followed by economical abuse (37.0%) and physical violence (Chaudhary, Girdhar, and Seni, 2009). Krishnan *et al.* (2010), identifying the risk and protective factors which affects physical violence (among women in southern India,) reported that in lower socio-economic status groups, women's employment status, and their perceptions of their husbands' employment stability is associated with physical violence. Women who were newly employed have 80 per cent more risk of facing violence, whereas women whose husband are facing difficulty in their employment are 1.7 times more susceptible to violence. Thus, a change in spousal employment status is also linked to violence that is more physical.

Tichy, Becker, and Sisco (2009) examining the effect of social values and status on perception of domestic violence reported that women of higher status were found to be less likely to acknowledge abuse as a societal problem. These women accurately identified abuse events and sought help to report abuse. Women who had more realistic conceptions of abuse were more likely to seek help but also more likely to experience more severe psychological distress. In a population-based study surveying both women and men from three of the four states of eastern India, Babu and Kar (2009) reported that the prevalence of physical, psychological, sexual, and other types of violence among women of eastern India were 16,52,25, and 56 per cent respectively.

Men reported higher prevalence of all forms of violence apart from sexual violence. The socio-economic characteristics of women, which have significant association with the occurrence of domestic violence, are urban residence, older age, lower education, and lower family income. The study reports higher incidences of domestic violence in eastern India as compared to national statistics. On the whole, domestic correlates of violence against women comprises of more economic parameters rather than anything else.

Demographic and psychosocial characteristics of perpetrators (husbands): Hollander (2006) based on results of his survey reports that men with at least seven years of education were significantly less likely to engage in violence against their wives than those with none. The possibility of violence also was reduced for men whose households had the greatest amount of assets and was elevated among those for whom economic pressure demanded borrowing money to cover medical expenses.

Verma and Collumbien (2003), exploring the link between male sexual health sexual risk behaviours, and domestic violence in a poor slum in Mumbai used community-based data and considered the perspective of both perpetrators and victims of abuse. The study demonstrates that poor sexual health among men is an important risk marker for perpetrating abuse against women. The strength of association is increased by the fact that the severity of abuse suffered by women shows a clear increasing trend with the reported prevalence of the husband's sexual problems. Both sexual risk behaviour and feelings of sexual inadequacy are linked to violence. Pandey, Dutt, and Banerjee (2009), in a cross-sectional study in a representative sample of 751 women living in slums, studied individual factors related to domestic violence. The study concluded that adverse socio-economic conditions create low self-esteem and insecurity among men, who find expression in aberrant behaviours, and violence is used as a compensatory behaviour. Babu and Kar (2010), examining the factors associated with victimization and perpetration of domestic violence in eastern India, identified age, education, occupation, marital duration, and husbands' alcoholism as significant predictors. A higher level of family income was found to be highly protective against the risk of violence. Together the findings suggest that interventions to reduce domestic violence should go beyond the victim centric approach and address partner and relationship issues for greater impact.

Community Environment

Research studying community-level influences on domestic violence in Uttar Pradesh, North India (Koenig, Ahmed, Stephenson, Jejeebhoy, & Campbell, 2006) reports that recent physical and sexual domestic violence was associated with the individual level variables of childlessness, economic pressure, and intergenerational transmission of violence. A community environment of violent crime was associated with elevated risks of both physical and sexual violence. Community-level norms concerning wife beating were significantly related only to physical violence. Higher socio-economic status was found to be protective against physical but not sexual violence (Koening *et al.*, 2006). Solomon *et al.* (2009) examined the prevalence of physical and sexual violence among 1,974 married women from forty low-economic communities from Chennai (southern India). The study reports a 99 and 75 per cent lifetime prevalence of physical abuse and forced sex, respectively, whereas 65 per cent of the women experienced more than five episodes of physical abuse in the three months preceding the survey. These findings exceed prior Indian reports, suggesting women in slums may be at increased risk for HIV and other sexually transmitted infection.

Response to Domestic Violence

India is still struggling and finding out effective ways to fight with domestic violence. Although often condoned by culture, this systemic violence enforces gender inequality by curtailing a woman's freedom and right to self-determination. While formulating policies that seek to combat domestic violence in the Indian setting, it must be borne in mind that outside marriage, there are extremely limited options available to most rural Indian women. Rao argues that while marriage for Indian women is never a matter of choice but is almost entirely driven by social norms and the preferences of parents, the burden of any adversity in the marriage market or within a marriage after it has been arranged is almost exclusively borne by the wife or bride (Rao, 1998). One of the ways suggested by many scholars is to educate and empower women to fight domestic violence. Sen (1999) focuses on the role played by education and social networks in enhancing choices of women in responding to domestic violence in Calcutta, India. The study identified factors responsible for the resolution of domestic violence are employment and empowerment.

However, Rocca and colleagues (2009, as cited in Krishnan *et al.*, 2010) examined the relationship between factors that are often considered to be social and economic resources for women and recent occurrence of domestic violence. Efforts to help women empower themselves through vocational training, employment opportunities, and social groups need to consider the potential unintended consequences for these women, such as an increased risk of domestic violence. In spite of these type of reports, the authors strongly feel that solutions to domestic violence will have to be found within the family or community setting. Women can acquire courage and a sense of independence when they are educated and have opportunities for sustained livelihood. The education of girl children has gained momentum in India's national educational policies in the recent years. Even free education for girls is being provided by all government institutions in many states (e.g., Gujarat) to encourage and facilitate poor and rural families to get their daughters educated.

Another strategy that has been adopted by the Government of India is the empowerment of women. The advancement of women's interests has been incorporated into national policy since the Fifth Five Year Plan (1974-78) (WCD, 2001). The Self-Help Group (SHG) model was introduced as a core strategy to achieve empowerment in the Ninth Plan (1997-2002) with the objective being to "organize women into Self Help Groups and then mark the beginning of the major process of empowering women" (Planning Commission 1997). This strategy was continued in the Tenth Plan (2002-07), with the government committed to encourage SHG model to act as the agents of social change, development and empowerment of women. In India SHGs are groups of ten to twenty women initiated by the development agency (such as NGO, state development department, or bilateral and multilateral agency) for a purposeful development intervention. The SHGs have become very successful by promoting the concept of micro-finance, self-employment, and income generation for various groups of women in rural and suburban areas.

A third and most powerful measure to fight domestic violence is the intervention made by government and non-government action implemented through non-government organizations (NGOs) and community-based organizations (CBOs). Talking about response to domestic violence through government and non-government action,

Poonacha and Pandey (2000) suggest participatory and interactive strategies seem to help in extending organizational outreach. The sustainable and effective programmes act as catalysts of social change and make the local communities self-reliant in handling and addressing the issues of domestic violence within the framework of acceptable social norms.

Gujarat is one of the few states with a skewed sex ratio and rampant female foeticide. Even the remote villages in the state have got the facility for sex determination. Alarm bells started ringing when the Census 2001 data was released. It revealed a drastic fall in the sex ratio, especially the child sex ratio. Whereas the overall sex ratio dropped from 934 to 920 per 1000 males, the child sex ratio fell shockingly from 928 to 883 in Gujarat. Mehsana, which is one of the most prosperous districts of the state, had the lowest child sex ratio of 798. This came as a rude shock for one of the most developed states of India. The sex ratio in Gujarat has shown a steady rise in the period between 2002 and 2008, says the annual registration survey conducted by the Registrar General of the Government of India. The ratio has gone up to 898 per 1000 in 2008 from 844 per 1000 in 2002 (www.census-2011.co.in/census 2011 India population. mht posted on 27th April, www.developmentchannel.org/sex ratio.st.mht). Even data of girl child ratio from 0-6 yrs year-wise showing increase in girl child ratio after save the girl child campaign in 2005.

Year	2005	2006	2007	2008	2009	2010
No. of Girl child	844	865	893	900	905	910

Above data of urban Vadodara as per the data available from Vadodara Mahanagar Sewa Sadan Nagrik Suvidha Kendra (Vadodara Municipality, 2011) almost from 844 in 2005 to 910 in 2010 shows significant increase in girl child ratio shows less female feticide during the years of campaign.

However, Tribal and rural areas have performed well in both these categories in comparison to developed districts. In order to tackle the issue of increasing female foeticide and infanticide, the state government had come up with various campaigns such as 'Beti Bachao' and 'Beti Vadhavo', which played a very important role in improving the female population. The government also spread awareness through paintings, hoardings, bill boards etc. across the state on the dangers of having an unbalance sex ratio. The Government's latest initiative, which has been implemented in 2010, includes setting up of district-level cells, compulsory registration of ultrasound machines, stricter implementation of the relevant Preconception and Prenatal Diagnostic Techniques (Prohibition of Sex Selection) Act (called P&PDT Act), and surprise checking of maternity homes and private clinics (*www. unicefindia.com/*media centre/Gujarat launches save the girl child campaign to arrest declining sex ratio.mht). In addition, a series of activities were organized to create awareness among the different stakeholders and community at large.

A skewed sex ratio that the 2011 Census threw up in the case of Madhya Pradesh, particularly among its elite social strata, has prompted the state government to implement a three-pronged strategy to remedy the grave socio-demographic issue. Following Gujarat experience, government of Madhya Pradesh has launched "Beti Bachao Abhiyan" (Save the Girl Child Campaign). The endeavour comes after the present trend portended a situation where more than 28 million boys in the state would be forced to remain single by 2050. This is because of female foeticide and infanticide, which is originated by the deep-rooted gender bias. The more progressive districts which boast high literacy rates, and sound economic growth have alarmingly low on the sex ratio in 2011 census. For example, it has gone down from 932 girls for every 1000 boys in 2001 to 912 girls in 1000 boys in 2011 in Indore district (Trivedi, 2011; Soni, 2011).

Amazingly however; whether it is in Orissa or in Madhya Pradesh, in the backward tribal districts, the sex-ratio continues to be encouraging all through, having more number of female births compared to male births.

Madhya Pradesh government has also launched a scheme to provide incentives and pensions to the couples having only girl child, which aims at changing the pro-son mindset and help parents overcome the fear about their possible plight in the old age. This measure may reduce the insecurities which lead to female foeticide and infanticide (Soni, 2011).

These social health campaigns in Gujarat and Madhya Pradesh may be illustrative for other states to adopt systemic strategies to abolish the social evil of female foeticide, infanticide and other types of violence against women, which have got long term serious implications for nation's health.

REFERENCES

Ackerson, L.; I. Kawachi, E. Barbeau, and S.V. Subramanian. (2007). Exposure to domestic violence associated with adult smoking in India: A population based study. *Tobacco Control* 16 (6): 378-383.

Arnold, F.; Kishor, M. and Roy, T.K. (2002). Sex-selective abortions in India. *Population and Development Review*, 28 (4), 759-785.

Babu, B.V. and S.K. Kar (2010). Domestic violence in eastern India: Factors associated with victimization and perpetration. *Public Health,* 124 (3): 136-148.

Bhat, P.N. Mari and Zavier, F.A. J. (2007). Factors influencing the use of prenatal diagnostic techniques and sex ratio at birth in India. In I. Attane, and C.Z. Guilmoto (Eds.) *Watering the Neighbours Garden. The Growing Female Deficit in Asia.* CICRED, Paris, 135-164.

Chaudhary, A.; Girdhar, S. and Soni, R. (2009). Epidemiological correlates of domestic violence in married women in urban areas of Ludhiana, Punjab, India. *Internet Journal of Health*, 9 (1), 9-9.

Chukanth, S.R. and Athreya, V.B. (1997). Female infanticide in Tamil Nadu: Some evidence. *Economic and Political Weekly*, 32 (17), WS-22-29.

Ackerson, L.K. and Subramaniam, S.V. (2009). Domestic violence and chronic malnutrition among women and children in India. *American Journal of Epidemiology* 170 (2), 267-268.

Garg, S. and Nath, A. (2008). Female feticide in India Issues and concerns. *Journal of Post Graduate Medicine*, 54 (4), 276-279.

Guilmoto, C.Z. (2007). *Characteristics of sex-ratio imbalance in India and future scenarios*. Paper presented at 4th Asia Pacific Conference Reproductive and Sexual Health and Rights, held by UNICEF at Hyderabad, India, from October 29th-31st.

Hollander, D. (2006). Domestic violence in India is linked to individual and community factors. *International Family Planning Perspectives*, 32 (1), 52-53.

India: New law decrees one year prison and fine for wife abuse. 2003. *Women's International Network News*, 29 (3), 35-37.

Jha, P.; Kumar, R.; Vasa, P.; Dhingra, N.; Thiruchelvam, D.; Moineddin, R. (2006). Low female-to-male sex ratio of children born in India: National survey of 1·1 million households. *Lancet*, 367: 211-18.

Joshi, U. (2000). Child marriage Causes and prevention. *Social Welfare*, 46 (10), 18-19.

Karlekar, M. (1998). *Women and Economic Reform in India: A case Study from the Health Sector*. Issue 26, Occasional Paper, Centre for Women's Development Studies, New Delhi.

Kelkar, G. (1991). *Violence against women in India: Perspectives and strategies*. Asian Institute of Technology, Bangkok.

Koenig, M.A.; Ahmed, S.; Stephenson, R.; Jejeebhoy, S.; and Campbell, J. (2006). Individual and contextual determinants of domestic violence in north India. *American Journal of Public Health* 96 (1): 132-138.

Krishnan, S.; Rocca, C.H.; Hubbard, A.E.; Subbiah, K.; Edmeades, J.; Padian, N.S. (2010). Do changes in spousal employment status lead to domestic violence? Insights from a prospective study in Bangalore, India. *Social Science & Medicine,* 70 (1): 136-143.

Miller, B.D. (1981). *The Endangered Sex Neglect of Female Children in Rural North India*. Oxford Press, New York.

Pandey, G. K.; Dutt, D. and Banerjee, B. (2009). Partner and relationship factors in domestic violence: Perspectives of women from a slum in Calcutta, India. *Journal of Interpersonal Violence*, 24 (7), 1175-1191.

Pandey, M.K.; Singh, P. and Yadav, R.A. (2009). *Domestic Violence and Women's Health in India: Evidence from Health Survey*. Working Paper No. 13, Australia South Asia Research Center (ASARC).

Planning Commission (1997). *Ninth Five Year Plan (1997–2002)*. New Delhi.

Planning Commission (2002). *Tenth Five Year Plan (2002-2007)*. Planning commission nic.in /plans/planned/five year/Accessed August 21, 2012.

Poonacha, V. and Pandey, D. (2000). Responses to domestic violence: Government and non-government action in Karnataka and Gujarat. *Economic and Political Weekly,* February12.

Retherford, R.D. and Roy. T.K. (2003). *Factors Affecting Sex-selective Abortions in India and 17Major States.* National Family Health Survey Subject Report No. 21, Mumbai-International Institute of Population Science.

Sen, P. (1999). Enhancing Women's Choices in Responding to Domestic Violence in Calcutta: A comparison of employment and education. *European Journal of Development Research*, 11 (2): 65-76.

Singh, K., and D. Kapur. (2001). Law, violence and the girl child. *Health and Human Rights*, 5 (2): 9-29.

Solomon, S.; Subbaraman, R.; Srikrishnan, A.; Johnson, S.; Vasudevan, C.; Anand, S.; Ganesh, S. and Celentano, D. (2009). Domestic violence and forced sex among the urban poor in south India. *Violence Against Women*, 15 (7), 753-773.

Soni, P.S. (2011). Save the Girl Child Campaign launched in Madhya Pradesh. In categories, *Madhya Pradesh: News and Views* (on 10.7.2011). Retrieved from www.worldhealthtimes.com on August 12, 2012.

Srivasava, A. and Durge, P.M. (2010). Female feticide in India: A social evil. *Journal of Obstetrics and Gynecology*, 60 (6), 503-506.

Stephenson, R.; Koenig, M.A.; and Ahmed, S. (2006). Domestic Violence and Symptoms of Gynecologic Morbidity Among Women in North India. *International Family Planning Perspectives*, 32 (4), 201-208.

Stephenson, R. (2007). Human immunodeficiency virus and domestic violence the sleeping giants of Indian health? *Indian Journal of Medical Sciences,* 61 (5), 251-252.

Stephenson, R.; Koenig, M.; Acharya, R. and Roy, T. (2008). Domestic violence, contraceptive use, and unwanted pregnancy in rural India. *Studies in Family Planning*, 39 (3), 177-186.

Subramanian, S.V., Leland, K.A., Malavika, A.S. and Rosalind, J.W. (2007). Domestic violence is associated with adult and childhood asthma prevalence in India. *International Journal of Epidemiology*, 36 (3), 568-569.

Tichy, L.; J. Becker and M. Sisco. (2009). The downside of patriarchal benevolence: Ambivalence in addressing domestic violence and socio-economic considerations for women of Tamil Nadu, India. *Family Violence*, 24 (8): 547-558.

Trivedi, S. (5th October, 2011). Madhya Pradesh launched 'Save the Girl Child'. Business Standard, New Delhi. Retrieved from www.businessstandard.com on August 12, 2012

Verma, R.K. and Collumbien, M. (2003). Wife beating and the link with poor sexual health and risk behaviour among men in urban slums in India. *Journal of Comparative Family Studies*, 34 (1), 61-74.

www.census of India.com/India at a glance sex ratio.mht.downloaded on 16th June, 2011

www.census-2011.co.in/census2011 India population.mht posted on 27th April, 2011 and downloaded on 16th June, 2011.

www.developmentchannel.org/sex ratio.st.mht.published on Tuesday on 22nd June, 2010 downloaded on 16th june, 2011.

www.unicefindia.com/media centre/Gujarat launches save the girl child campaign to arrest declining sex ratio.mht downloaded on 16th June, 2011.

11

Psychosocial Adaptation of Destitute Women

Nivedita Das and *Fakir Mohan Sahoo*

Destitution is an economic, social and political phenomenon. While coming to the economic aspects of destitution, destitution is a twofold kind of deprivation in the 'space' of income or monetary poverty. It involves, first, the absence of any control over assets and, second, the loss of access to income from one's own labour. These economic definitions refer to a process of loss, one which deprives a person of control over assets and income. Destitution is being conceived of here as an individual phenomenon because, by the time a person becomes a destitute, he/she is usually an individuated remnant of a collapsed household. As per the social aspects of destitution, it has already become evident that destitution is not simply to be measured in the monetary domain, it is also the loss of entitlements which are not price-mediated, (e.g., the loss of access to 'common' property and public goods and services), the disappearance of political legitimacy and citizenship (*i.e.* the violation of political rights). It means the collapse of moral units above the level of the individual, the draining away of social support. Rather than being passively socially excluded they may be actively socially expelled. The process of expulsion may involve forcible physical exclusion from the space of a moral unit like a caste or a village. Social responses to destitution are contradictory. It initiates social expulsion, practices notions of justice involving 'stigma' which permit harsh oppressive treatment.

It gives a customary license to harass, to abuse, thieve from, or be violent towards, push to impure space and not to come to the aid of destitute people.

Destitute people search for new kinds of common property resources, to which they may gain access in order to stay, have food and sleep. By and large, organized civil society is also responsible for this neglect. There are nothing more than *ad hoc* links between destitute people and other kinds of oppressed people or those who for other reasons are unable to earn wages covering their daily maintenance. In general, aid and development agencies do not see destitution as a development problem which they can address. One kind of NGO response is to rehabilitate individual destitute people or to provide facilities to which they may turn. Destitution is an extreme condition of income poverty; destitute people have been socially expelled; most destitute people are extremely deprived in capability dimensions of poverty too. So there is also a high probability that those deprived in all dimensions will be destitute. Unlike "poverty" or "food insecurity", "destitution" is an undefined term in the development literature. Although the word is often used, with the colloquial meaning of severe poverty and dependence on the goodwill of others, there is no accepted technical definition, nor does a standardized set of tools exist for analysing and quantifying destitution. Destitution is popularly understood as a state of poverty so severe that the individual concerned is dependent for their survival on the goodwill of others, including charity from the public or welfare support from the state or non-governmental agencies. Common categories of destitute people include beggars, people with disabilities without family support, and victims of natural disasters such as a drought-triggered famine. In the cultural context of Britain, destitution as a label attaches mainly to the homeless – people who sleep on the streets and sell the *Big Issue* magazine outside supermarkets. Common to these images is the idea that the destitute have nothing – no work, no savings, no possessions, but also no home to go to, no family or friends to turn to (*i.e.,* very few material assets), but no social assets either. The Oxford English Dictionary (OED) lists four definitions of "destitution", including: 'The condition of being destitute of resources; want of the necessaries of life'. The American Heritage Dictionary of the English Language defines destitution as 'complete poverty'. Interestingly, another OED definition is 'the action of deserting or forsaking' which suggests social marginalization and the individualization of destitution as a human experience. This is echoed in the definition of "destitute" as 'forsaken, left friendless or helpless, forlorn'. Other OED definitions of "destitute" include: 'One who is destitute, without friends, resources, or the means of subsistence', and 'bereft of power to do something', which together capture the sense of destitution as economic, social and political powerlessness. In his book, *An Inquiry into Well-being and Destitution*, the Cambridge economist Partha Dasgupta defines destitution as 'an extreme condition of ill-being' or 'extreme commodity deprivation', which results in a failure to meet a 'basic minimum living standard' or 'basic physiological needs'. The understanding of "destitution" has several salient features. Destitution is characterized as primarily a crisis of livelihoods, in which households and communities lack sufficient access to the key productive resources and the opportunities they need to construct viable livelihoods. As a result, they become dependent on assistance, either from within the community or from outside organizations, including the government and NGOs.

Destitute Women

The plight of destitute women has remained a matter of concern to the society for a long time. Our society has a significantly large number of socially disowned women such as widows, abandoned divorcees, victims of deceit and cheating and those young girls who after becoming victims of rape are discarded/rejected by their own families. Cases of single mothers pushed out of their houses into the street are numerous. Female children, teenagers and older women who flee their home for fear of severe battering, sexual abuse and mental torture are also on the increase. Attempts to resist the atrocities generally end up in desertion of such women. Destitution, the term, is a by-product of many social evils and faulty systems. Women learn to suffer silently and bear the injustice perpetrated on them as they are expected to make other members in the family happy by sacrificing their own needs. Male dominance in all matters including finances and the male violence manifested in different ways in the different stages of a woman's life are the causes of destitution. A woman sees the father and brother as the provider and protector when she is a child and then the dependency gets transferred to the husband and in her old age she relies on her son for her financial, emotional and social needs. The ruthless customs of patriarchal society and the male arrogance leave women with no other option but to seek outside help and leave their own home for their own safety. The causes of destitution can be traced to poor education, poor living conditions, strained family relationships especially oppression, violence, sexual abuse, subordination and devaluation of women.

Violence against women within the family is a global phenomenon. However, its ramifications are more complex and its intensity much greater in India. The most pathetic aspect of such atrocities is domestic violence. There are two equally strong viewpoints about the causes of destitution. The first view is that it is the cruelty against women in various forms such as sexual abuse, neglect, battering, divorce and male chauvinism that is responsible for destitution. The other argument is that it is the deviant personality of the women concerned that makes them destitute.

However, there is no single cause that lucidly explains "destitution". There are several theories which explain the social problem of destitution. Value-conflict theorists define destitution simply as conditions that are incompatible with group values. In the feminist perspective, destitution is understood in the context of heterosexist patriarchal oppression. It is also argued that it is the emotional immaturity, maladjustment and other deviant behaviours of some women that make them destitute. But it has been observed that violence against women is the main cause of women being forced to leave their houses.

Forms of Domestic Violence

The various forms of violence are physical violence and psychological violence.

Physical violence includes the following forms:

(i) Female foeticide and female infanticide;
(ii) Incest, rape within marriage, abusing of women in the household;
(iii) Physical torture like slapping, punching, grabbing, and killing;
(iv) Neglect of women's health problems.

Psychological violence includes the following forms:

(i) Curbing the freedom to associate with the natal family, neighbours, and friends;
(ii) Curtailment of right to self-expression;
(iii) Promiscuity of the husband;
(iv) Accusing the women in the household of unchaste behaviour;
(v) Irresponsible behaviour and alcoholism of the husband;
(vi) Humiliating and victimizing women;
(vii) Fleecing women and their parents of their money and assets by compulsion and threat.

A woman in the home has multiple roles to perform: of mother, cook, tailor, laundry person, nurse, housekeeper and so on. To perform excellently in all the roles is a strenuous task that affects her health adversely. India ranks as a medium-risk country in terms of women's overall health and reproductive health. India has a reproductive risk index of 39.5, a figure worked out on the basis of several factors including the number of births, abortions, pregnancies, anaemia and other illnesses and maternal deaths, per woman.

The steady decline in the sex ratio noted for over a century in India from 972 females for 1000 males in the population in 1901 to 927 females in 1991 and the prevalence of female foeticide in at least 10 States of India are critical indicators of violence against women. Female foeticide and female infanticide are basically socio-cultural problems and not just a law and order problem. In the year 1991, UNICEF reported that 40-50 million women are missing from the Indian population due to female foeticide. The National Family Health Survey of 2000 (NFHS-II) reports about the inequality and violence pervading in our country. Sixty-eight per cent of the women under the survey reported that they needed permission from husbands or in-laws to go to the market and 76 per cent had to seek consent of their husbands before they could visit friends or relatives. Only 60 per cent could use money the way they wished. In addition, one in every five women experienced domestic violence from the age of 15 onwards. Very often, women used to suffer violence on them in silence for the fear of adverse repercussions. The National Crime Report of 1991 reveals that in every 33 minutes a woman is abused by her husband. CSR (Centre for Social Research) annually receives nearly 800 cases of domestic violence in its six Crisis Intervention Centers (CICs) located in different parts of Delhi.

Violence Against Women in India

Violence against women is partly a result of gender relations that assumes men to be superior to women. Given the subordinate status of women, much of gender violence is considered normal and enjoys social sanction. Manifestations of violence include physical aggression, such as blows of varying intensity, burns, attempted hanging, sexual abuse and rape, psychological violence through insults, humiliation, coersion, blackmail, economic or emotional threats, and control over speech and actions. In extreme, but not unknown cases, death is the result. These expressions of violence take place in a man-woman relationship within the family, state and society. Usually, domestic aggression towards women and girls, due to various reasons remain hidden. Cultural and social factors are interlinked with the development and propagation of violent behaviour. With different processes of socialization that men and women undergo, men take up stereotyped gender roles of domination and control, whereas women take up that of submission, dependence and respect for authority. A female child grows up with a constant sense of being weak and in need of protection, whether physical social or economic. This helplessness has led to her exploitation at almost every stage of life. The family socializes its members to accept hierarchical relations expressed in unequal division of labour between the sexes and power over the allocation of resources. The family and its operational unit is where the child is exposed to gender differences since birth, and in recent times even before birth, in the form of sex-determination tests leading to foeticide and female infanticide. The home, which is supposed to be the most secure place, is where women are most exposed to violence. Violence against women has been clearly defined as a form of discrimination in numerous documents. The World Human Rights Conference in Vienna, first recognized gender-based violence as a human rights violation in 1993. In the same year, *United Nations* declaration, 1993, defined *violence against women* as "any act of gender-based violence that results in, or is likely to result in, physical, sexual or psychological harm or suffering to a woman, including threats of such acts, coercion or arbitrary deprivations of liberty, whether occurring in public or private life".

Radhika Coomaraswamy identifies different kinds of violence against women, in the United Nation's special report, 1995, on *Violence Against Women*. They can be categorized as:

(a) Physical, sexual and psychological violence occurring in the family, including battering, sexual abuse of female children in the household, dowry related violence, marital rape, female genital mutilation and other traditional practices harmful to women, non-spousal violence and violence related to exploitation.
(b) Physical sexual and psychological violence occurring within the general community, including rape, sexual abuse, sexual harassment and intimidation at work, in educational institutions and elsewhere, trafficking in women and forced prostitution.
(c) Physical, sexual and psychological violence perpetrated or condoned by the state, wherever it occurs.

Women are vulnerable to various forms of violent treatment for several reasons, all based on gender. They are:

1. Because of being female, a woman is subject to rape, female circumcision/genital mutilation, female infanticide and sex related crimes. This reason relates to society's construction of female sexuality and its role in social hierarchy.
2. Because of her relationship to a man, a woman is vulnerable to domestic violence, dowry murder, *Sati.* This reason relates to society's concept of a woman as a property and dependent on the male protectors like father, husband, son, etc.
3. Because of the social group which she belongs to, in times of war and riots. In case of ethnic, caste, or class violence, a woman may be raped and brutalized as a means of humiliating the community to which she belongs. This also relates to male perception of female sexuality and women as the property of men.

Combining these types of abuse with the concept of hierarchical gender relations, a useful way to view gender violence is by identifying contexts where the violence towards women occurs. Essentially, violence happens in three contexts — the family, the community and the state and unfortunately at each point key social institutions fulfils critical and interactive functions in defining legitimating and maintaining the violence. The family socializes its members to accept hierarchical relations between the sexes and power over the allocation of resources. The community (*i.e.,* social, economic, religious, and cultural institutions) provides the mechanisms for perpetuating male control over women's sexuality, mobility and labour. The state legitimizes the proprietary rights of men over women, providing a legal basis to the family and the community to perpetuate these relations. The state does this through the enactment of discriminatory application of the law.

Gender violence can be divided into four major categories:

1. Overt physical abuse (battering sexual assault, at home and in the workplace).
2. Psychological abuse (confinement, forced marriage).
3. Deprivation of resources for physical and psychological well-being (health/nutrition, education, means of livelihood).
4. Commoditization of women (trafficking, prostitution).

There are two basic forms of violence—structural and direct. *Structural violence* arises from the dominant political, economic and social systems. Structural violence is the basis of direct violence, because it influences the socialization which causes individuals to accept or inflict suffering, according to the social function they fulfil. *Open or direct violence* is exercised through aggression, arms or physical force. The Fourth Conference of Women, 1995 has defined violence against women as a physical act of aggression of one individual or group against another or others. Violence against women is any act of gender-based violence which results in, physical, sexual or arbitrary deprivation of liberty in public or private life and violation of human rights of women in situations of armed conflicts. (Conference on Women, Beijing, 1995 Country Report). *Violence* is an act carried out with the intention or perceived intention of physically hurting another person. *Gender Violence* is defined as "any act involving use of force or coercion with the intent of perpetuating or promoting hierarchical gender relations". Adding gender dimension to that definition amplifies it to include violent acts perpetrated on women because they are women. Understanding the phenomenon of gender violence requires an analysis of the patterns of violence directed towards women and the underlying mechanisms that permit the emergence and perpetuation of these patterns.

Destitute Women in Odisha

In Odisha there are 37 short stay homes run by the State Social Welfare Board, which comes under the Women and Child Development Department and there are around 1100 (reported for the year 2008-2009) beneficiaries residing in these homes only. Similarly, there are equal number of other rescue homes and *swadhar* homes run by different organizations in the different districts of Orissa.

In these rescue homes and short stay homes the destitute women are engaged in learning skills to be able to self-sufficient like stitching, embroidery, incense stick making. Their families generally don't take them back without legal intervention. As it is these women are in a very vulnerable state yet they adjust in a new situation which becomes their home until their case is resolved. Adjusting with the emotional turmoil and to a new environment with unknown people is not an easy task for these battered women.

Psychosocial Adaptation

Sociological data and demographic features are available on destitute women both in global and national context but no bold serious attempt has been undertaken to understand the dynamic process of adaptation of these women. Whatever scanty attempt has been made is made in clinical terms only.

Now we are entering into a climate where a group of psychologists are attempting to explain behaviour in terms of virtues and strengths. Positive psychology takes interest in positive subjective experiences, positive traits, and the adaptation processes used by individuals when life seems meaningless. It also answers how people manage to improve the quality of life and live with dignity despite all hurdles in life. Thus, psychology needs to develop such atmosphere that fosters the strengths of these destitute women and helps in their psychosocial adaptation. Certain terms like psychosocial adaptation, happiness, and well-being are being used interchangeably.

Psychosocial adaptation is defined as the process of putting oneself in harmony with the changing circumstances of life so as to enhance one's sense of well-being and long-term survivorship. Psychosocial adaptation is achieved through the processes of assimilation (incorporating new information into existing structures) and accommodation (changing existing structures to accommodate new information), involving the psychological (e.g., changes in perception, attitude, behaviour, and motivation) and social (e.g., change in one's social environment) domains. Outcome indicators of effective psychosocial adaptation include the maintenance of good physical health, life satisfaction, good mental health, positive life-and-death attitudes, high meaning and purpose in life, and a stable personality.

Facilitators of Adaptation

Talking about good mental health, positive attitudes, meaning and purpose of life forces us to look into the newly evolved and widely acknowledged branch of psychology called positive psychology. While the circumstantial evidence and societal variables have been identified by social activist, sociologists and political scientists, behavioural scientists have mostly focused on the variables relevant for empowerment process. Behavioural scientists in general and psychologists in particular have examined the role of pertinent psycho-social variables. Although a number of variables have been delineated, psychologists have focused on the empowerment process in terms of women's personality and self-concept variables (Bandura, 1997). The pertinent literature has shown that the positive self-concept of women and certain specific personality variables such as dominance and achievement orientation have contributed significantly towards successful adaptation of women. These variables have been considered important in combination with political and social empowerment stressed by sociologists and political scientists. In recent years, a new look movement in psychology has highlighted the importance of positive elements in human behaviour. The growth of positive psychology in recent decades has reoriented research efforts in the direction of virtues and character strength in human beings (Seligman, 2002). While a multiple number of constructs have been floated in the context of positive psychology, a brief description about its prominent constructs serves a useful purpose.

Self-efficacy. The construct of self-efficacy has been well articulated by Bandura (1997) within the theoretical framework of social learning. Self-efficacy refers to the extent of belief that an individual can execute a function competently. According to Bandura, the generalized personal self-efficacy denotes a general level of self-confidence, whereas, a domain specific self-efficacy such as self-efficacy in work habits indicates the belief system pertaining to work domain. Similarly, collective efficacy is a shared belief system of the group and it is a stable predictor of successful social change. All these variables are measurable and it is possible to examine specific predictions on the basis of efficacy variables.

The other advantage with the concept of self-efficacy is its process-like nature. It may be indicated that many of the personality variables are trait-like concepts, which are not easily changed. On the contrary, self-efficacy is a state-like concept. Bandura has provided a developmental framework to explain the source and growth of self-efficacy. Accordingly, it is possible to devise mechanism for enhancement of self-efficacy in destitute women once the existing levels of their self-efficacy are measured.

In the event of stressful life transitions of these destitute women, general beliefs of efficacy may serve either as a personal resource or vulnerability factor. People with a high sense of perceived efficacy interpret demanding situations and difficulties as challenges than as threats. As high perceived efficacy enables individuals to face stressful situations with confidence and they attribute their own effort to positive events and judge negative events as caused by external circumstances. A generalized belief in one's efficacy serves as a resource factor that helps in handling distressing situations. In case of stressful transitional adaptation of these women, self-efficacy can function as a personal resource protecting against negative emotions and health impairment.

Self-efficacy, it has been observed, enhances human achievement and personal well-being. Efficacy can be developed by five main sources of influence. They are mastery experience, intelligent structuring of initial experiences, vicarious experiences provided by role models, social persuasion and positive interpretation of physical and psychological arousal. The most effective way to create a strong sense of efficacy in these women is through mastery experience which in their context translates into proper vocational training and work experience. If these women are trained and are allowed to venture out to be able to financially and professionally independent they will acquire an enhanced self-efficacy. The second way of strengthening efficacious belief is through intelligent structuring of initial experiences. If their task of learning new skills and earning a livelihood is broken into simple and achievable targets and are arranged intelligently, success can be expected from them which can be maintained for a long time. The third source involves the vicarious experiences and emphasizes the importance of role models which can help in shaping the efficacy of these women. But the role model has to be somebody who they can identify with. The role model can have a strong impact when these women can perceive a similarity of their conditions and status with that of the role model. They will be strongly motivated to imitate them when there is similarity. They will accept the role model as a source of information and inspiration. The fourth way of strengthening self-efficacy beliefs is by social persuasion. The caregivers stationed at the organizations where these women take shelter can persuade them by using the persuasive message "You can do it" with a strong force of conviction. And in addition to that these women need to be placed in well-structured situations where they can be successful in many ways and situations where there are chances of failure should be avoided. The fifth source of influence is physiological and psychological arousal. As normally people rely on their physiological and emotional cues to assess their capability these women can be trained to interpret physiological arousals and the corresponding emotions in a positive way.

Optimism. Optimism refers to "the conviction that the future holds desirable outcomes irrespective of one's personal ability to control those outcomes". It is also defined as a "mood or attitude associated with an expectation about the social or material future, one which the evaluator regards as socially desirable, to his/her own advantage or for his/her pleasure". Optimism as a behavioural construct is intimately related to many of the domains of human functioning. Studies have shown that optimism is prospectively associated with important physical and mental health outcomes, including lower levels of postpartum depression, lower levels of physical symptoms and successful completion of an alcohol aftercare treatment programme.

The construct of learned optimism is popularized by Seligman (1990). He proposed the ABCDE model for optimism. According to Seligman, a phenomenon starts with an activating event or antecedent (A). This event generates some belief (B) which in turn leads to a consequence (C). If the consequence is negative, disputation (D) method can be adopted. Disputation is a remediation method which restructures the negative faulty thought and helps in adopting activity or which is known as energization (E). Thus, these destitute women can be trained in optimism. For example, if a woman is tortured and violated by the men it may lead her to believe that all men out there are cruel and don't respect the dignity of a women. Thus she may avoid meeting any male person for other requirements like legal problems or vocational training and for selling and buying of their products. Her withdrawing may complicate matters more and will not help in making her self-reliant. Her faulty thought which is stopping her from meeting any male member of the society can be modified or dispelled by disputation. After restructuring her thought she can be energized to meet other men and take appropriate help instead of remaining in a self-created shell.

Hope. The construct of hope offers another scope of understanding women's adaptation. Hope is considered to be "the very heart and centre of a human being. It is the best resource of man, always there on the inside, making everything possible when he is in action, or waiting to be illuminated when he is ill." Hope has been defined as the fundamental knowledge that a difficult situation can be worked out and that goals can be reached. Imagining and wishing are not possible for the hopeless. Hopelessness prevents one from imagining beyond the present. Hope and hopelessness reflect a person's estimate of the probability of his achieving certain goals. The individual determines the probability relative to past successes and failures with similar goals. If there is an expectation of success in meeting goals through one's plans of action, hope exists. If failure is predicted, hopelessness exists. Thus, hope and hopelessness are described as opposite expectations and self-efficacy as a fundamental component of self-esteem and a major element in determining whether one feels hopeful or hopeless.

According to Snyder, hope consists of three elements and that can be illustrated in a diagram as mentioned in his book *Handbook of Hope* (Pg 10).

A ————————→ B

The Person (A) perceives himself or herself as capable of producing a route or pathway to desired goal (B). All the three elements are necessary for people to maintain a hopeful position in life. To hope, we need to have a goal, we need to believe we can attain the goal and we need to see a pathway leading to the goal. Human actions are goal directed and hope flourishes under probabilities of intermediate goal attainment. These women can be trained to set goals and view themselves as capable of generating workable routes to their goals. In this process of pathways thinking the thoughts of being able to generate, at least one and often more, usable route to a desired goal is important. The goals must be attainable and the hope theory can be used to help in understanding the adjustment process of these women. Adjustment or coping is the ability to effectively respond to a stressor so as to reduce psychological (and physical) pain. In hope theory stressor is the element that interferes with one's normal on-going goal of being happy. When confronted with a stressor one must find alternative paths to attain the goal and be mobilized to use those paths. In the case of destitute women, hope is crucial for their psychological health. Hopeful thoughts help in developing the ability to establish clear goals and imagine workable pathways and motivate one to work toward goals. These positive expectations will also yield higher confidence, and high hope people perceive that their hopeful thinking will protect them against future stressors (Snyder, 2000). In addition, higher hope seems to moderate the relationship between unforeseen stressors and successful coping. Unlike people with low levels of hope who tend to get stressed about the future, people with high levels of hope are able to think effectively about the future, being fully aware of the fact that they will need to face major life stressors.

Resilience: Resilience refers to a class of phenomena characterized by good outcomes in spite of serious threats to adaptation or development. Research on resilience aims to understand the processes that account for these good outcomes. Resilience is an inferential and contextual construct that requires two major kinds of judgments (Masten, 2001). The first judgment addresses the threat side of the inference. Individuals are not considered resilient, if there has never been a significant threat to their development; there must be current or past hazards judged to have the potential to derail normative development. The second judgment involved in an inference about resilience is the criteria by which the quality of adaptation or developmental outcome is assessed or evaluated as "good" or "ok". There is little debate about whether such criteria exist, but much controversy remains about who should define resilience and by what standards. This is a highly complex issue that is only beginning to be addressed empirically.

The capacity to minimize and prevent the negative effects of adverse circumstances is an attribute which can go a long way in the psychological well-being of destitute women. Resilience is not about responding to a setback. For these women to be truly resilient they have to accept and face the reality. To build resiliency, it is also important to make meaning of terrible times. For example, if a woman is ill-treated she has to accept the fact that she truly is not being treated well by others. Then she has to make meaning of the situation and make decisions that will create significant changes in her life. The other building block of resilience is the ability to make do with whatever is at hand, to improvise a solution to a problem without proper or obvious tools or materials. For example, the women can learn to make use of the facilities available for them at the rescue homes and try to learn to be financially independent instead of hoping for some instant solution to their financial needs. Resilience is a way of facing and understanding the world for these women. These women can be trained to face reality, make meaning of hardship instead of crying out in despair. Training programmes for resilience for these women can involve risk focused strategy, asset focused strategy and process focused strategy. In risk focused strategy, the aim should be to reduce the exposure to hazardous or stressful experiences. In asset focused strategy, the aim should be to increase the assets or quality of resources which can strengthen the social or financial capital of the women. For example establishing counselling centres, vocational training with marketing facilities can be asset building strategies for these women. Process focused strategies that aim to influence processes that will change women's life can be designed. These programmes will help to prevent or reduce problems by promoting good adaptation.

The health-promoting roles of these constructs cannot be denied in the context of psychosocial adaptation of destitute women. Behavioural intervention programmes can be designed to facilitate the adaptation process of these women which in turn can help in including them in the mainstream. The growth of this major yet unnoticed section of the society can contribute in a large way to the overall growth of the society.

Conclusion

For application of behavioural intervention programmes, the initial (existing) levels of these parameters are to be assessed. There are effective methods of measuring these constructs. A brief discussion about the measures will throw a light on their usefulness in this context. The *Measure of Generalized Self-efficacy* is based on Albert Bandura's construct of self-efficacy and is developed by a group of researchers in Free University of Berlin (Wegner, M., Schwarzer, R. & Jerusalem, M., 1993). The scale presents ten statements and respondents are asked to indicate their level of agreement on a four point scale where "1" is indicative of least agreement and "4" is indicative of maximum agreement. All the items are keyed in positive direction. The sum of ratings across all 12 items indicates self-efficacy score of an individual. The measure has been extensively used in cross-cultural research. *Work related Self-efficacy* is a domain specific measure of self-efficacy. The scale presents a number of odds. Respondents are asked to indicate their level of confidence that they can execute a work despite such obstructions.

The Measure of Optimism is developed and validated by Seligman (1992). The scale is based on the proposition that an optimistic individual explains positive events in terms of internal, stable and global factors whereas negative events are explained in terms of external unstable and specific factors. The scale presents 48 hypothetical events out of which 24 are positive events and 24 events are negative. Each event is followed by two hypothetical causal explanations. An equal number of causal events are indicative of internal, global and stable factors. Respondents are asked to imagine the events happening to them. They are also asked to choose one of the two alternative causal explanations that appear appropriate for them. In this process, it is possible to compute the score of an individual with respect to internality, globality and stability. With the help of a scoring key the optimistic explanation score of an individual can be computed.

The Connor-Davidson Resilience Scale was developed to estimate levels of resilience. The scale has 25 items to which the participant has to respond on a 5 point scale (0-4). The sum of scores across items is indicative of an individual's resiliency.

The Scale of Hopefulness is a standardized questionnaire to measure an individual's hopefulness. Sahoo and Das (2008) have developed and validated the scale to suit our cultural setting. Some of the positively keyed items are derived from Snyder's scale. The scale is in the likert format. Respondents are asked to indicate their agreement and disagreement on a 5 point scale. Items are keyed both in the positive and negative direction. The sum of scores represents the magnitude of hopelessness. The scale has been pilot tested and its psychometric property is of satisfactory level.

As indicated earlier, effective methods of measurement of the positive psychological constructs exist and some steps have already been taken for their cultural adaptation. With availability of these resources, it is possible to make use of intervention to improve the psychosocial adaptation of destitute women. Since all these concepts are state-like constructs, appropriate learning and development can be arranged. However, prior to undertaking interventions for a wide variety of population, it is appropriate to include a relatively small test-sample for this purpose. Accordingly the application of the multi-construct intervention is intended for a representative sample of destitute women in the state of Odisha of Indian Union.

REFERENCES

Bandura, A. (1997), *Self-efficacy*, New York: Freeman.

Connor, K. M and Davidson, J.R.T. (2003), Development of a new resilience scale. *Depression and Anxiety*, 18, 76-82.

Dasgupta, P. (1993), *An inquiry into well-being and destitution.* New York: Oxford University Press.

Jerusalem, M. and Mittag, W. (1995). Self-efficacy in stressful life transitions. In Bandura, A. (Ed) *Self-efficacy in changing societies,* pp. 177-201. New York: Cambridge University Press.

Peterson, C. (2000). The future of optimism. *American Psychologist*, 55 (1), 44-55.

Masten, A.S. (2001). Ordinary magic, *American Psychologist*, 56 (3), 227-238.

Sahoo, F.M. and Das, N. (2008). *Scale of Hopefulness*, Unpublished Report, Xavier Institute of Management, Bhubaneswar, India.

Schwarzer, R. and Fuchs, R. (1995). Changing risk behaviours and adopting health behaviours: The role of self-efficacy beliefs. In Bandura, A. (Ed.)

Self-efficacy in changing societies, pp. 259-288, New York: Cambridge University Press.

Seligman, M.E.P. (1992), *Learned Optimism,* New York: Pocket Books.

Snyder, C.R. (2000), *Handbook of Hope*, London: Academic Press.

Snyder, C.R. (2003), *The Psychology of Hope: You Can get There from Here*, New York: The Free Press.

Stanley, M.A. and Maddux, J.E. (1986). Cognitive processes in health enhancement: Investigation of a combined protection motivation and self-efficacy model. *Basic and Applied Psychology*, 7 (2), 101-113.

Wegner, M.; Schwarzer, R. and Jerusalem, M. (1993). *Measurement of perceived self-efficacy*, Berlin: Free University.

12

A Study of the Mental Health, Subjective Well-being and Emotional Stability of Female Commercial Sex Workers in Vadodara City

Priyanka Behrani and *Nitu Singh Bhadouria*

Commercial sex work is a growing industry. According to an analysis of data from the National Survey of Sexual Attitudes and Lifestyles (Ward, Mercer, Wellings, 2005), the proportion of men who reported paying women for sex more than doubled from 2.0 to 4.2 per cent between 1990 and 2000. In India, people living with HIV are estimated 24 lakh in the age group of 19-30 yrs in the year 2009. The primary drivers of HIV epidemic in India are unprotected paid sex/commercial female sex work. It is estimated that there are 12.6 lakh female sex workers in India (annual report NACO, 2009-10) and six Indian states have been categorized as high prevalence states because HIV prevalence in these states exceeds 5 per cent among the high-risk individuals and one per cent among the women attending antenatal clinics. In these six states, HIV is estimated to be transmitted through heterosexual contact. Around the world, the number of people living with HIV continues to rise despite the fact that effective prevention strategies exist. India has the largest number and is linked to sex work in four states of Andhra Pradesh, Karnataka, Maharashtra, and Tamil Nadu, and through injecting drug use in the other two states of Manipur and Nagaland.

Commercial Sex work is the provision of sexual services for money or its equivalent. Sex workers may be male, female, or transgendered, and the boundaries of sex work are vague, ranging from erotic displays without physical contact with the client, through to high risk unprotected sexual intercourse with numerous clients. Individuals may occasionally and opportunistically exact a fee or gift for a sexual favoor without perceiving themselves to be sex workers, or they may engage more or less full time in the explicitly commercial provision of sex services. This variability results in a spectrum of implications for public health and health service provision; yet sex work is typically stigmatized and often criminalized.

Commercial sex work is a growing industry. According to an analysis of data from the National Survey of Sexual Attitudes and Lifestyles by (Ward, Mercer, and Wellings, 2005), the proportion of men who reported paying women for sex more than doubled from 2.0 to 4.2 per cent between 1990 and 2000. Commercial sex work is considered controversial, which appears to have been always subject to regulation by law or custom. The nature of legal and social control over sex-worker activities has varied over time and between countries. Because sex work is quasi-legal, and lies outside the usual social norms it renders these individuals vulnerable to occupational health hazards as a result the medical, legal and welfare needs of sex workers are not properly addressed.

Public health action has often been driven by the narrow focus of limiting HIV-AIDS rather than by general considerations of the health and well-being of the workers themselves. Very few published reports give weight to sex workers' own views of these important themes. Much of the literature about sex work reveals the prejudice of the writer, hence unbiased data to support or refute the claims made are hard to find. As a marginalized professional group, CSW exhibit poor health parameters, either due to the exposure to greater health risks or due to poor appropriate medical care facilities.

There are four main categories of health risks faced by workers in the commercial sex industry. These relate to the acquisition of sexually transmitted infections (STI), harm through violence from clients, factors associated with the substance abuse and mental health.

The pathways that lead people into commercial sex work are also varied. At one end of the spectrum are those who work autonomously, undertake sex work by choice and are well organized with respect to their sexual health and accessing services (Clark,

Squires, 2005). These workers may have entered sex work for a specific reason (e.g. to fund higher education costs, pay debts or to cover family expenses), may be intermittent or opportunistic in their involvement in sex work (Pyett, Haste, Snow, 1993) and succeed in exiting the industry at a time of their choice. Others make a career decision to work in the sex industry and may enjoy a high level of job satisfaction and independence. In contrast, are those who are driven into commercial sex work through drug addiction or coercion, and have little autonomy (Zimmerman, 2003). These workers, including women sold for the purposes of trafficking, are highly vulnerable and have little prospect of leaving the industry unassisted (Hester, Westmarland, 2004). Between these extremes lie the majority, who work in the industry due to varying degrees of economic necessity and choice (Clark, Squires, 2005).

Research on commercial sex work is hampered by several methodological challenges. First, the study populations are usually small and unrepresentative due to problems in gaining access to sex workers and establishing trust. As a result, researchers rely on individuals who attend sexual health clinics voluntarily, who may be poorly representative of the local CSW population, particularly the more vulnerable groups. Second, there is likely to be reporting bias in response to questionnaires or structured interviews on topics such as condom use and drug habits (Wilsom 1999, Zenilman, Weisman and Rompalo, 1995). Third, the heterogeneity of CSW with respect to adherence to safer sex, drug misuse and local factors such as pimping and policing means that generalizability of results may be limited. Finally, CSW represent an unstable population both temporally and geographically, which means prospective studies are difficult to conduct without the loss of significant numbers of subjects, which itself may bias results.

Mental Health

There is a strong relationship between mental ill-health and risk-taking behaviours (drug use or sexual practices) among CSW (Kelly, Murphy, Baker, 1993). Several studies have reported higher levels of psychological distress levels in CSW, than a non-CSW control group, even after adjusting for confounding factors such as age, previous rape and substance use. (Paone, Cooper, Alperen, Shi, Desjulais, 1999).

What remains unclear is the relative contribution to the distress of working as a sex worker versus pre-existing psychological trauma as a result of drug use, previous childhood abuse, domestic violence or imprisonment. (Vanwesenbeeck, 2005) partly addressed this issue in an assessment of 'burnout' among 96 CSW in Holland, using measures of emotional exhaustion, depersonalization and personal competence in comparison with a group of female nurses. Increases in the first two were attributed to factors such as coercion, violence, negative social reactions, lack of control with clients and inadequate support from managers. Personal competence was positively associated with having a professional attitude towards sex work and with support from colleagues and managers. It was concluded that the conditions under which sex work are conducted have a greater influence on the worker's psychological well-being than the nature of the work itself.

On-going review made very clear that number of studies done with CSW's is related to their physical health and contracting HIV and STI. (Nolle, Marx, Guzman, Katz, 2001; Fung, Nickerman, Watts, Jani, Gandhi, 2007). Most of the studies emphasis on the prevention from contracting infections hence the focus of the intervention is on physical health. Very few studies emphasized on the mental health of CSW (Martin, Romans, Herbison, Potter, 2000; Ilan, Belmaker, 2002).

Most of the intervention do not focus on the mental health of the CSWs, it is more narrowed down to the physical and reproductive health. Commercial sex work presents specific mental health concerns.

There are three major pathways that link stressful life events to ill-health: one is physiological changes as a mediator between origin and outcome, in particular, changes of immune parameters, and endocrine and cardiovascular reactivity and health compromising behaviours. People under stress might want to relieve their tension by consuming more tobacco, illicit drugs, alcohol, and so on. They feel too absorbed by their stress to monitor their diets and to maintain other preventive behaviours. Adherence to routine self-care might suffer during a stress episode. A third pathway pertains to all kinds of negative affect often associated with experiencing stress. Constant rumination, worrying, anxiety, pessimism, depression, and anger are health compromising in the long run. Studies have shown that optimism is related to good health, whereas depression can be a precursor of sickness (Carver, 2001).

Subjective well-being: Subjective well-being can be simply defined as the individual's current evaluation of his/her happiness. Such an evaluation is often expressed in affective terms, when ask about subjective well-being participants will often say, "I feel good" (Schwartz and Strack, 1999). Subjective well-being is thus, at least in part, a proxy for a global affective evaluation. Happiness has been associated with positive outcomes such as, increased sociability (Diener, *et al.,*1994), creativity (Hirt, E.R., Melton, R.J. McDonald, H.E. and Harackkiewicz, J.M., 1996), increased health and marital satisfaction.

SWB consists of two distinctive components: an affective part, which refers to both the presence of positive affect (PA), and the absence of negative affect (NA), and a cognitive part. The affective part is a hedonic evaluation guided by emotions and feelings, while the cognitive part is an information-based appraisal of one's life for which people judge the extent to which their life so far measures up to their expectations and resembles their envisioned 'ideal' life (Diener, 1999). Psychologists have deeply studied the influence of personality on SWB, and found it to be the strongest and most dependable factor underlying differences in SWB between persons. In a famous study (Tellegen *et al.,* 1988).

Emotional stability: Emotional stability is one of the effective's determinants of the personality patterns. The concept of stable emotional behaviour at any level is that which reflects the fruits of the normal emotional development. An individual who is able to keep his emotions stable and under control even in extreme situations, might still be emotionally stunned or be childish in his behaviour sometimes.

According to Smitson (1994) emotional stability is the process in which the personality is continuously striving for greater sense of emotional health, both intra-physically and intra-personally. It has been emphasized that the emotionally stable individual has the capacity to withstand delay in satisfaction of needs, ability to tolerate a reasonable amount of frustration, belief in long-term planning and is capable of delaying or revising his expectations in terms of demands of the situations. However, stability does not mean merely the capacity for such attitudes and functions, but also the ability to enjoy them fully. A number of characteristics like the capability of responding in gradation, ability to delay responses, especially negative emotions, freedom from unreasonable fears and the ability to commit mistakes without feeling disgraced etc. are found in an emotionally stable individual.

Method

Objectives of the Study

To assess the mental health of FCSW in Vadodara city.
To assess their subjective well-being.
To assess their emotional stability.

Tools

1. **Subjective well-being inventory By Nagpal, R. and Sell, H. (1992).** The inventory is designed to measure the feelings of well-being and ill-being being experienced by an individual in various day to day life concerns. There are total 40 items measuring 11 different dimensions plus three inferred dimensions by combing scores, which are explained below:
   (a) *General well-being positive effect:* This dimension reflect feelings of well-being arising out of an overall perception of life as functioning smoothly and joyfully.
   (b) *Expectation achievement congruence:* This dimension refers to feeling of well-being generated by achieving success and the standard of living as per one's expectation or what may be called satisfaction.
   (c) *Confidence in coping:* This dimension is related to perceived personality strength, the ability to master critical or unexpected situations. It reflects what sometimes called positive mental health in an ecological sense i.e. The ability to change face adversities without breakdown.
   (d) *Transcendence:* This dimension refers to life experiences that are ordinary day to day material and rational experience. It reflects the feeling of subjective well-being derived from values of a spiritual quality.
   (e) *Family group support:* This dimension refers to positive feelings derived from the perception of the wider family as supportive, cohesive and emotionally attached.

(f) *Social support:* This dimension refers to perceived social environment beyond the family as supportive in general and in times of crisis.

(g) *Primary group concern:* This dimension refers to the positive and the negative about the primary family.

(h) *Inadequate mental mastery:* This dimension refers to a sense of insufficient control over, or inability to deal effectively with certain aspects of everyday life that capable of disturbing the mental equilibrium.

(i) *Perceived ill-health:* This dimension refers to worry and problems related to health and physical fitness.

(j) *Deficiency in social contacts:* This dimension refers to the worrying about being disliked and the feelings of missing friends.

(k) *General well-being–negative effect:* This dimension refers to generally depressed outlook on life.

(l) *Overall positive:* This dimension refers to an inferred dimension from the first 7 positive dimensions of well-being.

(m) *Overall negative:* This dimension is an inferred dimension from the last 4 negative dimensions of well-being.

(n) *Total:* This dimension is an inferred dimension from the total scores on all the dimensions put together.

2. **Mental Health Inventory (Srivastava and Jagdish):** Mental health here refers to person's ability to make positive self-evaluation, to perceive the reality, to integrate the personality, autonomy, group oriented attitudes and environmental mastery. The scale has 56 items and six dimensions of mental health. The reliability coefficients ranged from .71 to .75 for different dimensions.
   Dimensions are explained below:

   (i) *Positive self-evaluation:* It includes self-confidence, self-acceptance, self-identity, feeling of being worth while, realization of one's potentialities, etc.

   (ii) *Perception of the reality:* It is related to perception free from need distortion, absence of excessive fantasy and broad outlook on the world.

   (iii) *Integration of the personality:* It indicates balances of psychic forces in the individual and includes the ability to understand and to share other people's emotions, the ability to concentrate at work and interest in several activities.

(iv) *Autonomy*: It includes stable set of internal standards for one's action, dependence for own development upon own potentialities rather than dependence on other people.

(v) *Group oriented attitudes:* It is associated with the ability to get along with others, work with others and the ability to find recreation.

(vi) *Environmental mastery:* It includes efficiency in meeting situational requirements, the ability to work and play, the ability to take responsibilities and capacity for adjustment.

3. **Emotional Stability Questionnaire: Vohra (1995):** Emotional Stability here refers to dynamic integration and emotional maturity as opposed to uncontrolled, disorganized, general emotionality. The test is designed to measuring the general adult population. The test had 60 items each of the question has three choices, of which the subject had to choose one. The split half reliability of the scale is .87 and test retest reliability is .78.
4. **Semi structured Questionnaire:** It consisted of 10 questions for in-depth interview. This was constructed keeping in mind the objectives of the study.

Procedure

The permission from the NGO was sought to conduct the study. The participants were identified and taken the consent to be the part of research and as per limitation of getting the data only those female CSW were taken who were registered and visited for the counselling sessions at an NGO working in the area of sexual health.

For the convenience of the researcher the questionnaire and semi-structured interview was translated to local language and contextualized and back translated to make the participants more comfortable.

The data was collected by one to one interview followed by the three inventories.

Sample

Table 12.1

		Total
Age	19-55	50
Education	Illiterate-post graduation	
Experience	1-21 years	

The sample taken for the study included 50 female sex workers residing in different parts of the Vadodara city.

Table 12.2

Experience	*No. of respondents*	*Age*	*No. of respondents*	*education*	*No. of respondents*
1-2 yrs	13	19-25	19	Illiterate	18
3-13 yrs	25	26-35	20	School edu.	26
14-21 yrs	12	36-55	11	University edu.	06
Total	50		50		50

Results

The results were obtained through quantitative data on the three inventories namely mental health inventory, Emotional Stability Questionnaire, Subjective well-being inventory and qualitative data that was obtained through semi-structured in-depth interview.

Table 12.3: Group means on mental health inventory

Dimensions	*Group means*	*State of mental health*
Positive self-evaluation	27.68	Poor
Perception of reality	20.34	Poor
Integration of personality	30.02	Poor
Autonomy	16.26	Poor
Group oriented attitudes	25.04	Very poor
Environmental competence	23.50	Poor

Results on mental health inventory clearly indicate the poor status of CSWs on 5 dimensions *i.e.*, positive self-evaluation, perception of reality, integration of personality, autonomy and environmental competence and very poor on dimension of group oriented attitude.

In order to see if there was difference on the mental health in terms of the age, education and years of experience in the profession T- test was conducted, which indicated that irrespective of age group, experience and education, the sample does not differ significantly.

Table 12.4: Group means of subjective well-being

Dimensions	*Group means*	*Interpretation*
General well-being positive effect	6.22	Ill-being
Expectation achievement congruence	6.18	Difficulties
Confidence in coping	7.36	Difficulties
Transcendence	6.56	Difficulties
Family group support	7.76	Difficulties
Social support	6.56	Difficulties
Primary group concern	5.44	Well-being
Inadequate mental mastery	13.16	Difficulties
Perceived ill-health	12.94	Difficulties
Deficiency in social contacts	6.94	Difficulties
General well-being – negative effect	6.04	Ill-being
Overall positive	39.64	Difficulties
Overall negative	84.16	Difficulties

The result indicates difficulties in the 8 areas of subjective well-being, they are Expectation achievement congruence, Confidence in coping, Transcendence, Family group support, Social support, Inadequate mental mastery, Perceived ill-health, Deficiency in social contacts, Overall positive and overall negative. Ill-being is seen in the two areas they are overall general positive and general negative dimension and well-being in 1 area that is Primary group concern.

A *t*-test was conducted to see if there was difference on the dimension of subjective well-being in terms of the age, Education and years of experience in the profession. Which reflected clearly that irrespective of age group, experience and education the sample does not differ significantly except for a dimension 7 *i.e.*, primary group concern of subjective well-being when compared with the education the values were 3.376 at 0.043 level and dimension one *i.e.*, general well-being positive effect 3.363 at 0.043 level.

When compared with the years of experience except for dimension of subjective well-being that is of overall negative effect on 5.609 at .007 levels.

A very interesting finding of the study is the average emotional stability of the group.

Table 12.5: Group means of emotional stability

Dimension	*Mean*	*Interpretation*
Emotional stability	67.86	Average

For comparison with age groups, years of experience in the profession and level of education on emotional stability *t*-test was conducted. No significant difference was found.

General Discussion

The objective of the study was to assess the mental health status, subjective well-being and emotional stability of FSW of Vadodara city because little is known about it. The result show poor mental health status of the group taken for study on all the dimensions—positive self-evaluation, perception of reality, integration of personality, group oriented attitudes autonomy, and environmental competence. This is consistent with the results of a study showing the heavy burden of mental health problems found among sex workers (Alegria *et al.,* 1994; el-Bassel *et al.,* 1997; Farley & Barkan, 1998; Gilchrist *et al.,* 2005; Roxburgh *et al.,* 2006). The poor status on positive self-evaluation indicate that they did not show self-confidence and realization of one's potentialities and difficulties in self-identity. The results are validated with the interview when they reported mixed feelings of anger, sadness and helplessness. Most of them said, "who would like to willingly come to this profession". Few of them who were willing to give the interview initially but could not finish it and left the interview in between, when they were asked, "How you came to this business?" some of them said if "I do not do this then what do I do".

On the items of group oriented attitudes which is associated with the ability to get along with others, work with others and the ability to find recreation, showed very poor status. This was very clearly indicated in the responses in interview when most of them confessed that they were afraid of disclosing their identity. Even if their partner/spouse knows about their profession, they don't wish others to know regarding it, as they consider this field to be immoral. They have continuous fear of dejection/rejection from the society so they themselves keep distance from people.

The scores of subjective well-being show difficulties and ill-being in most but overall general positive and general negative dimension show ill-being. This indicates that overall general positive effect reflect feelings of well-being arising out of an overall perception of life as functioning smoothly and joyfully are not experienced by most of them and that was supported in the interview when they reported.

Most of them experience stress/worries about their future and they express it by saying, "what will happen in future" and "I do not know I will have to continue for how long?..."

Most of them were worried of getting the HIV infection. If their children were younger than they worried that what will happen to their children in future if she will die, or something happens to them.

If their children are mature enough then they hardly have faith that they will support them in their old age. They even expressed this fear through saying, "I get myself tested every 2-3 months, if something happens to me who will take care of my children. "

On Expectation achievement congruence, dimension, which refers to feeling of well-being generated by achieving success and the standard of living as per one's expectation or what may be called satisfaction showed ill-being. Which implies though they are in the profession of commercial sex work but that does not give sense of fulfilment as they are into it because of some need and because of their own sweet will some of them who were not married expressed the will to do so but had the worries who will marry them. The women who had grown up children had worries that who will marry their children and she was not sure if her daughter-in-law will allow her to stay with their family or not?

The well-being in the area of primary group concern indicates that they are happy about their primary family and are contributing to the care and well-being of the family. This is also validated by the interview when most of the subjects reported that they were not worried about themselves but at least they are able to manage the expenses of the family.

On the dimension of emotional stability the group means indicate average; this finding implies that in spite of the profession the commercial sex workers are into, still they are able to handle their emotions. The interview reflects that most of the CSWs were upset/ uneasy or uncomfortable while sharing about their past life and the present life and showed mixed feelings of anger, sadness and helplessness but they have accepted the fact and so the feeling that their jobs help the family and gives them the sense of fulfilment. Most of them reported they feel very helpless, they tried to earn through other methods now this is the only way". This can be attributed to experience in the field for so many years and months so they have accepted the situation. As most of them clearly said, "Who would like to come into this profession by itself madam but it is the need that makes me do so." They do not let emotional needs obscure realities of a situation.

The results on the *t*-test show that irrespective of the age, years of experience, and the education there is no difference on mental health, subjective well-being and emotional stability of the sample considered for the study. This was also validated by the interview when most of them showed similar kind of insecurities, aggression and worries experienced by sex workers of different age groups and education. So it can be inferred that the age, education and years of experience does not make any difference with respect to above variables, it is the kind of profession that attributes to the similarity in their status.

The present study has some limitation; women outside the NGO network were not included. The FSWs who participated in this study may not be representative of all FSWs as they were recruited through FSW facilitators suggesting a bias towards those who are better connected with their peers, and hence the results should be interpreted within this limitation. The number of participant seems to be relatively small because of non-availability of the sample and refusal of participation for research so the sample size was 50.

In conclusion this research has intervention implications for practitioners, policy makers and social workers. Sex work is a major health problem worldwide. It exist in our society too and FSW suffer from poor mental health status and negative general well-being. The measures to address this should include interventions to improve the well-being and mental health apart from physical health.

Acknowledgments

We thank all the sex workers who participated in this study, a special thanks to all the support that was extended from my colleagues from Department of Psychology, The MS University of Baroda.

REFERENCES:

Alegria, M.; Vera, M.; Freeman Jr. D. H.; Robles, R.; Santos, M.C.; and Rivera, C.L. (1994). HIV infection, risk behaviours, and depressive symptoms among Puerto Rican sex workers. *American Journal of Public Health*, 84 (12), 2000-2002.

Annual report 2009-2010, Deparment of AIDS control, Ministry of Health and Family Welfare.

Bassel, N.; Schilling, R.; Irwin, K.L. *et al.* (1997). Sex trading and psychological distress among women recruited from the streets of Harlem. *Journal of Public Health*, 87, 66-70.

Carver, C.S. (2001). Depression, hopelessness, optimism and health. In N.J. Smelser and P.B. Baltes (Eds.), *The International Encyclopedia of The Social and Behavioural Sciences*, (Vol. 5, pp. 3516-3522). Oxford: England.

Chaudakov, B.; Ilan, K.; and Belmaker, R. (2002). The motivation and mental health of sex workers. *Journal of Sex and Marital Therapy,* 28, 305-315.

Clark, M. and Squires, S. (2005). Worlds forever apart? Using vulnerable adult protection policies to deliver better health and social services to street prostitutes. *Journal of Adult Protection,* 7, 24-31.

Diener, E. (1994). Assessing Subjective Well-Being: Progress and Opportunities. *Social Indicators Research*, 31 (2), 103-157.

Diener, E.; Eunkook, M.; Suh, R.; Lucas and Smith, S. (1999). 'Subjective Well-Being: Three Decades of Progress. *Psychological Bulletin*, 125 (2), 276-302.

Harcourt, C. and Donovan, B. The many faces of sex work (2005). *Sexually transmitted infection;* 81: 201-6

Hester, M. and Westmarland, N. Research Study 279 (2004). *Tackling Street Prostitution: Towards a Holistic Approach*. London: Home Office.

Jha, P.; Nagelkereke, NJD. and Ngugi, E., *et al.* (2001). Reducing HIV transmission in developing countries. *Science*; 292: 224–5.

Khanna, N.; Nadkarni, V.; Bhutani, L.; Brown, T.; Chan, R.; Mugrditchian, D. *et al.,* eds. (1998). *Sexually transmitted diseases in Asia and the Pacific.* Armidale, NSW, Venereology Publishing: East-West Center, Thai Red Cross.

Kelly, J.; Murphy, D. and Baker, G. (1993). Factors Associated with Severity of Depression and High Risk Sexual Behaviour Among Persons Diagnosed with HIV Infection. *Health Psychology*, 12, 215-219.

National AIDS Control Organisation: An overview of the spread and prevalence of HIV/AIDS in India. [http://www.nacoonline.org/factsnfigures/Indianscenario.pdf

Joint United Nations Programme on HIV/AIDS (UNAIDS): Report on the global AIDS epidemic: 4th global report. Geneva: UNAIDS, 2004.

Paone, D.; Cooper, H.; Alperen, J.; Shi, Q. and Jarlais, D. (1999). HIV Risk Behaviours of Current Sex Workers Attending Syringe Exchange: The Experiences of Women in Five US Cities. *AIDS Care: Psychological and Socio-Medical Aspects of AIDS/HIV,* 11: 269-280.

Pyett, P.; Haste, B. and Snow, J. (1993). Who works in the sex industry? A Profile of Female. Prostitutes In Victoria Australian and New Zealand *Journal of Public Health*, 20: 431-433.

Schwarz, N. and Strack (1999). Reports of Subjective Well-Being: Judgmental Processes and their Methodological Implications. In: Kahneman, D. Diener, E. & Norbert Schwarz (eds.) *Well-Being: The Foundations of Hedonic Psychology*. New York: Russell Sage Foundation, 61-84.

Sompura, R., *et al.* (2001). *The concept of happiness and construction of norms –The subjective well-being inventory,* 2001. An unpublished field work from The Department of Psychology, The M.S. University of Baroda.

Tellegen, A.; Lykken, D.; Thomas, J.; Wilcox, K.; Segal, N. and Stephen, R. (1988). 'Personality Similarity in Twins Reared Apart and Together. *Journal of Personality and Social Psychology,* 54 (6), 1031-1039.

Thangjam S. (2011). Emotional stability, *Self Esteem and Subjective Well-Being of Young Adults of Single Parent Family.* An Unpublished Dissertation from the Department of Psychology, The M.S. University of Baroda.

Vanwesenbeeck, I. (2005). Burnout among female indoor sex workers. *Archives of Sex Behaviours*, 34: 627-639.

Ward, H.; Mercer, H. and Wellings, K. *et al.* (2005). Who pays for sex? An analysis of the increasing prevalence of female commercial sex contacts among men in Britain. *Sexually Transmitted Infection*, 81: 467-471.

Wilson J. (1999). Outreach programmes for female commercial sex workers. *International Journal of STD AIDS*, 10: 697-698.

Zenilman, JW.; Weisman, CS.; Rompalo, AM.; *et al.* (1995). Condom use to prevent incident of STDs: the validity of self-reported condom use. *Sexually Transmitted Infection* 22: 15-2.

Zimmerman C. (2003). The Health Risks and Consequences of Trafficking in Women and Children: Findings from a European Study. London School of Hygiene and Tropical Medicine. http://www.ishtm.ac.uk (9 march,2006, last day accessed).

13

Social Well-Being: An Indian Perspective

Renu Sharma

Introduction

The term "well-being" as used in present-day literature is an extremely vague notion (Seedhouse, 1995). While psychologists believe well-being is constructed out of three components: (1) life-satisfaction, (2) positive affect, and (3) low negative affect, Krishna Mohan (2001) concludes that judgments of well-being are irreducibly subjective and that the meaning and content of the term can only be referred in the context of its use. Myers and Diener (1995) define high subjective well-being as frequent positive affect, infrequent negative affect and a global sense of satisfaction with life.

Compass of well-being in current positive psychology movement includes several attributes such as empathy, love, wisdom, gratitude, resilience and authenticity (Snyder & Lopez, 1999). Diener and Biswas-Diener (2008) have added spiritual aspects in well-being. The contours of well-being are thus contextual and ever expanding to the demand of the research. For our purpose, however, Krishna Mohan's (2001) operational definition of well-being is adequate. The well-being includes: (1) the broader meaning of what constitutes happiness, (2) what people think and feel about themselves *i.e.*, the cognitive and affective conclusions they reach when they evaluate their existence, (3) individual's entire condition *i.e.*, psychological, social, and spiritual aspects of one's existence, and (4) context and relativity

- relative to the situation as well as to the values of the particular culture one belongs to, for example the traditional "Indian-ness" of avoiding extreme and maintaining equilibrium, of having good health and practicing self-control, self-realization and dissolution of the self.

Personal wellness and social well-being are interdependent entities. The social well-being as a positive state associated with optimal functioning within one's social network and community incorporates social integration, social contribution, social coherence, social actualization and social acceptance (Dalal & Misra, 2011). It may be noted that social well-being is largely an extension of personal well-being and therefore author has used the term of well-being for both. For the purpose of this chapter social "health" and social "well-being" are equated. There are important distinctions between mental health and mental well-being, as the latter refers to the positive aspects of mental health. But, in the case of social health and social well-being no such distinctions are seen in literature (Larson, 2003).

Indian Culture and Social Well-Being

Culture serves as a major force shaping the way people conceptualize the self, the society and the feeling of well-being. For example, Indian culture, being socially oriented views well-being in a way different than Western culture which is individually oriented. Indian culture emphasizes relatedness, morality, self-constraint, harmony, sensitivity to others, and subjective well-being for the Indians is construed around fulfilling one's obligations (*dharma*) through righteous deeds (*karma)*.

Indian culture is indeed a complex one. Indian cultural traditions can be traced back at least five thousand years. Immigrations, invasions, colonial rule and modernization have brought with them streams of alien influences, only parts of which were assimilated into the primordial. Sinha and Kumar (2004) describe Indian culture as characterized by three major themes: cosmic collectivism, hierarchical order, and spiritual orientation. Spirituality is considered as an important cultural construct and is built into the Indian psyche (Roland, 1988), although animal impulses and material strivings are very much a part of life.

Indians are collectivists, but they also have a well-protected secret self that contains highly individualistic thoughts, feelings and fantasies (Roland, 1988) as well as a striving to serve self-interests and achieve individual distinctions. Expressed differently, the Indians possess both an 'independent' as well as an 'interdependent self' (Markus & Kitayama, 1998). The 'independent self' is associated with a desire to pursue individualistic goals whereas the 'interdependent self' is always concerned with fulfilling the expectations of others. The 'other' is highly evident in the consciousness of the 'interdependent self' and this leads to a preoccupation with fulfilling the obligations of significant others (Higgins, 1987). They have strong hierarchical orientation, and yet have reverence for persons with high integrity, altruism and superior human qualities (Roland, 1988). They thus look for personal well-being for the ultimate life-goal of *moksha* through social well-being by way of conducting *nishkama karma* within the limits of *dharma* and for the purpose of *loksangrha.*

The equivalent word for culture in India is *sanskriti*. In broad terms *sanskriti* expects Indians to work within the ambit of *dharma*. The behaviour is guided by the embedded belief system in certain unique philosophical concepts such as *dharma, purushartha*, theory of *karma* and *samaskara*, concept of *rin*, and its religion and spirituality. Nucleus of Indian culture is the spirit of sacrifice in which, because all is known as the one Self, each gives himself for the good of others. Indian culture places highest priority of life as self-realization. But, to reach that he has to first conduct his duties as prescribed through *varnashrma*, and his social obligations of *loksangrha*. The social well-being is thus a core cultural aspect. Its emphasis is depicted in the whole of ancient literature.

This chapter systematically delineates core elements of the traditional Indian cultural views on social well-being and then briefly discusses relevance of theses traditions in today's society. It is to be noted that despite its intuitive simplicity, well-being is in fact a complex construct. Because meanings and concepts are molded by culture (Bruner, 1990), and the fact that Indian culture is embedded in its religion and rich spiritual philosophy, besides its caste based social system, the idea of social well-being in India can be explored only through its unique cultural concepts.

Vedas are the oldest ancient literature of Hindus. Naturally, their essence is deep-rooted in the belief system of Hindus. *Vedic* scriptures recognize the importance of the individual and social aspects of life. In the personal category, a person is essentially an individual: one thinks for oneself; one's actions are mainly directed towards one's personal welfare; and one seeks to advance one's personal well-being. It is natural to be self-seeking but life still remains unfulfiled. In the second category, a person is compelled by social urges to make life more meaningful and complete. The individual finds one's fulfilment by being a part of society.

Vedic religion has classified a system for the advancement of these two essential requirements of life. To serve the social needs of a person to the greatest possible extent, classification of society into four groups or *varnas* came into being. For the fulfilment of individual goals life span was divided into the four stages, called *ashrams*, each of 25 years and of specified goals. *Vedic* scriptures have thus devised a way of life where the progress of the individual and the society is inter-linked.

Purusharthas represent core value system of India. The principles known as *dharma, artha, kama, and moksha* are, in essence, the methods adopted for bringing together values that are personal and social. *Purusha* means human being and *artha* means object or objective. *Purusharthas* thus means objectives of man. It also means *purusha* (spirit) and *artha* (for the sake of), meaning "that which is pursued for the sake of the spirit." The pursuit of *purushartha* is then what a man should strive to achieve, and it gives human activities their basic meaning and purpose. They form the objective of very existence of individual self.

Apart from *purusharthas*, *varnashram dharma* and related constructs such as *karma*, *rin*, *swabhava* and *swadharma* are the key psychological themes. A brief discussion of these themes in specific context of their relevance to well-being is presented in following sections. Social system in Indian literature still remains a peerless example of cultivating love, peace and cooperation in every domain of human life. The universal mottos of *'Sarve bhavantu sukhinah'* (may all beings be happy), *'Sarveshama avirodhena, brahmkarma samarabhe'* (performing noble duties without any conflict with anyone), *'Vasudhaiva kutumbakam'* (treating the entire world as a family), are deeply embedded in people's psyche.

Purushrathas

Purusharthas are the canonical four ends or aims of human life. *Purushartha* means aim or goal of human life. Every individual in a society is expected to achieve four objectives and seek fulfilment in his life before departing from here. The concept of *purusharthas* clearly establishes the fact that Hinduism does not advocate a life of self negation and hardship, but a life of balance, achievement and fulfilment. The four *purusharthas* are:

Dharma is the noblest of all human goals and forms the foundation for the pursuit of other three goals. The *Sanskrit* term "*dharma*" signifies the *underlying* order in *nature*. Human life and behaviour considered to be in accordance with that order. Ethically, it means 'right way of living' or 'proper conduct,' especially in a religious sense. *Dharma* is a central concept in religions and philosophies originating in India. This means that, ends like *artha* and *kama* should be acquired through righteousness, honesty and straightforwardness. In all stages of a man's life either as a student or as a householder, as a forest dweller or an ascetic, *dharma* has to be accepted as paramount. Swami Krishnanandji (1970) argues that *dharma* is the harmonizer of things. It is that which prevents us from having extreme views. There are people who take extreme views either on the side of *moksha* or on the side of *artha* and *kama*. Therefore, most of the *dharmashastras* lay down the duties of people during the different stages of life and the duties of the different *varnas*. *Dharma* is the over-riding umbrella under which one has to live. The *Vedas* advise to follow the scriptures and walk the right path. *Dharmam cara. Dharmat na pramaditavyam* – do not deviate from right conduct. *Dharma* is thus a moral code that creates a social system, where all can live in peace and harmony. Obligations of *dharma* make a man socially responsible.

Artha means wealth. Hinduism recognizes the importance of material wealth for the overall happiness and well-being of an individual. A householder requires wealth, because he has to perform many duties to uphold *dharma* and ensure the welfare and progress of his family and society. A person may have the intention to uphold the *dharma*, but if he has no money he would not be able to perform his duties and fulfil his *dharma*. Hinduism therefore rightly places material wealth as the second most important objective in human life.

Artha recognizes the physical or material needs, which are not contrary to spiritual life. The material well-being is considered as a legitimate social need. It is greed and attachment to wealth that is hurdle to higher *purushratha*, not the wealth by itself. The *artha* needs to be earned through means that are not contrary to *dharma*. Through adequate division of resources and wealth, a man can contribute immensely to the society. In fact, it will be nearly impossible for a common man to have a sense of well-being without pursuing *artha*.

Kama is ordinarily termed as physical and emotional pleasure, fulfilment of biological and physical needs. Desires must be acknowledged and reasonably fulfilled with mindfulness so as to move towards freedom from them, by not adding it to a continuous cycle of fulfilling and escalating. *Artha* and *Kama* are important goals for the growth and progress of society but their fulfilment needs to be in accordance of *dharma*. Both these desires are to be fulfiled in *grahsthashram*.

Moksha, etymologically, means to get 'rid of' or 'release.' It is also understood as liberation. In Bhagavad-Gita, *moksa* is mentioned as the supreme tranquility and the highest bliss. It is the highest end of life, attainable only by the individual himself, with the help and guidance of *dharma*. *Moksa* as the last end signifies that its attainment is impossible without first fulfilling the obligations of the other three. It is a state of non-action. It is the stage where man's cravings cease and along with that ceases the need for attainment and fulfilment. It is realization and living of the truth, namely *aham brahma asmi* and *tat tvam asi*. In other words, it is waking up of human consciousness at the highest level of reality *i.e.*, *paramarthik satta*. The liberated person may work for the good of humanity without moral obligation. But he has no duties to perform.

To follow anyone particular *purushartha* exclusively would be to negate it as a *purushartha*. For example, *kama* without the mediation of the other three *purusharthas* would not be humane desire. Or, *moksha* without regard for the other three *purusharthas* would not be selfless. In the absence of mutual control *artha* becomes materialistic quest, *kama* becomes lust, *dharma* becomes legalistic and ritualistic and *moksha* becomes a kind of escape.

From the perspective of *purushartha*, the social obligations under *dharma* and *artha* need to be fulfilled, before attempting final life goal – *moksha*. Or in other words, the need for social well-being takes precedence over individual well-being.

Varna System

The human personality is an admixture of various potentials – the physical body, the *pranas*, the mind and the intellect, the spirit – are all there in every individual, but none is fully developed in persons. Some may have perfect body, while others may be intellectually smart. Each person thus has potential to excel in some areas of work. The early Indian society noted these individual differences and devised a social system taking advantage of individual strengths. Samkhya philosophy illustrates an example of using strengths of two imperfect individuals through the work of *purusha* and *prakriti* jointly. *Purusha* is supposed to be like a lame man who can see; *prakriti* is supposed to be like a blind person who can walk. The two are individually imperfect; but, suppose the one who can see but has no legs sits upon the shoulders of the person who cannot see but has legs, then there is an appearance of a complete person. This is how the ancient *varna* system was supposed to be evolved. No man is complete, and therefore necessity was felt in the interest of the welfare of society to bring together the various partialities into a wholeness. Imperfect individuals, complementing each other formed a perfect social structure. The dependence of each individual on others provided social solidarity. The very idea of formation of *varna* system was, thus, to create a society that can actualize the both – the personal and the social well-being.

The *Varna* scheme is a multi-dimensional, omnibus scheme of social organization. According to Sri Aurobindo (2007, p. 166), it is "at once spiritual, psychic, ethical and economic order." There were four *varnas*: *Brahmin, Ksatriya, Vaisya* and *Sudra*. Brahmin was defined as *brahman nayati iti brahmin*. People who preached spiritual teachings to the society and lived spiritual lives were called *Brahmins*. *Ksatriya* was defined as *kseeyate traayate iti ksatriya*. These were the people who protected the society against external attacks and maintained internal order. *Vaisya* was defined as *visati iti vaisya*. Businessmen, traders and farmers fell under this category. *Sudras* were the people engaged in services. Carpenters, blacksmiths, goldsmiths, cobblers, porters etc. fell under this category. This system ensured that the religious, political, financial and physical powers were all separated into four different social classes. Due to this fair separation of political and intellectual powers, ancient Indian society could not turn itself into a theocratic or autocratic society (Jain, 2011).

Philosophically, the *varna* may be thought of as attributes of *gunas* of *prakriti* – *sattva, rajas,* and *tamas*. These three properties of *prakriti* are the basis of personality typology. *Sattva*, *rajas* and *tamas* cover the whole range of human race. Combination of theses *gunas* will give different characteristics to individuals. According to Bhagvat Gita (4.13), *varna* is conferred on the basis of the intrinsic nature of an individual, which is a combination of three *gunas* (qualities), namely, *sattva, rajas*, and *tamas*. In this way, the system of *varnas* placed individuals in positions that best suited their *gunas*, and the system of *ashrams* maintained the focus of society on life duties and goals.

In the early years of *varna* system, there was no hierarchy of *varna*. Mahabharat says that there is no superior *varna* and people were divided into *varnas* according to their aptitude. According to Hitopades, whole mankind is one family. The *varnas* were merely designated to persons based on their aptitude, quality, mental state and characteristic. Although birth or parentage may have played an important role in the later times, the original system seems to be based on aptitude and potential of a person rather than on birth alone. The system of *varna* insisted that the law of social life should not be cold and cruel competition, but harmony and co-operation. Society should not be a field of rivalry among individuals. The *varnas* were not allowed to compete with one another. *Varna* divisions were based on individual temperament, which were not immutable.

Ashram System

Ashrams are an outstanding feature of the social organization in ancient India. While it is necessary to organize individuals into a society because of the partiality of endowments of different individuals, it is at the same time necessary to see that the individuals themselves are disciplined and perfected to the extent possible under the circumstances available. This perfection of the individuality is attempted through what is known as the *ashram* system. They are stages of life through which one has to pass. The life-span of the individual has been graded into four stages. After the first stage, the next one is undertaken, until all the stages are completed.

The *vedic* ideal of a life-span of a hundred years is envisaged in the four *ashrams*. The *veda mantra*, *Jivem sharadah shatam*, is a prayer for a life of a hundred years. It is for this reason that each of the four stages of life is expected to cover about twenty five years. The four stages (*ashrams*) are *Brahmacharya* - celibacy, *Grahsth* - family life, *Vanprasth* - forestration and *Sannyas* - renunciation.

Brahmacharya Ashram: The early years of one's life are meant to be a preparation for adulthood. The first twenty-five years are taken as the stage of *Brahmacharya*, when a gradual but complete education of the individual is ensured by the parents and the *guru*. A growing child is educated effectively in the early years to develop his inborn and dormant abilities and talent. In the ancient days the pupil used to stay in *guru*'s *ashram* (school). The life at *gurukul* was away from the worldly material atmosphere ruled by strict discipline, to enable the student to become mentally and physically strong.

In the *ashram*—the house of the *guru*, there was no *varna* discrimination. All the children lived together with the children of the *guru* himself on absolute equality, irrespective of the rank or caste of their parents. Disciples received training necessary for the successful passage of next stages of life. They learnt to be respectful and sensitive towards other *varna*-fellows and thus prepared for harmonious community life in *grahsthashram*. A sort of ground is paved at the very outset, in the beginning itself, for the contribution that this disciple has to make later on when he becomes an adult, a unit of human society, as a *Brahmana*, *Kshatriya*, *Vaishya* or *Shudra*. This had a bearing on social well-being. By disciplining himself the student is not only prepared for a matured role in the society, but also got equipped for the *yama-niyama* practice that is essential for *yoga* to be pursued in later life of *vanaprasthashram* and *sanyashram*.

Grahsth Ashram: At the end of the *brahmacharyashram*, the youth is prepared to enter the next stage in the forward journey of *grahasth ashram*. One then becomes the householder after undergoing a marriage ceremony. This is the beginning of a family. The householder must have a means of livelihood as the upkeep of the family becomes his responsibility. The person must work according to his *varna* for earning. In addition, there is the need for love, understanding and affection towards all the members of the family for a cordial relationship. Neighbours and friends are also important. When an attitude of friendship prevails in a society, it ensures the well-being, harmony and happiness of all.

Vanprasth Ashram: *Vanprasth* is the third stage in life when a person takes leave of family responsibilities to live in the forest or in quietitude to practice a religious discipline. The person entering this stage was expected to renounce the comforts of a settled home life and retire from the world. He was expected to give up all physical and worldly desires. Duty of a person is to serve human beings. For him all human beings are his family. His purpose is to contribute to the peace and happiness of human beings by dispelling ignorance and enabling the individual to awaken the divinity that lies within him. A self-imposed discipline of harshness and meditation are the requirements of the *vanprasthashram*. The purpose of the *vanprasth* life is social work, religious practices and spiritual enlightenment.

Sannyas Ashram: The *vanprasthashram* culminates in the *sannyasashram*. *Sannyas* means complete renunciation of all worldly attachments. The person is withdrawn from the sources of pleasure and sorrow. The mind is then saturated with holiness and spiritual knowledge. The focus in *sanyasashram* is on Higher Self and the person is not bound by social obligations. The person is engrossed in spiritual practices with sole objective of *moksha*.

By adhering to the four *ashrams* an individual goes forward in life as prescribed by the *vedas* on a ladder similar to the Maslow's needs of hierarchy, the highest need of self-realization being targeted in last *ashram* – the *sanyasashram*. *Ashram* model attempts to fulfil all human psychological needs in a life span in progressive manner. It nurtures potential of the self and of the society. It makes social well-being as precondition to personal well-being.

Karma-Yoga

The doctrine of *karma yoga* forms the core of the Indian philosophy of work. The relationship between humankind and work has been elaborated in India through the Bhagavad Gita. The Gita, which is part of the epic Mahabharat explains the philosophy of right action or *karma-yoga* using the situation of Arjuna, a warrior on the battle field who finds himself helpless when he is called to action. Bhagavadgita's gospel of *karma yoga* hinges upon two factors (Krishnanand, n d): In the universal setup of things everybody has to participate in some way or the other according to their proclivity, due to the predominance of the *gunas* of *prakriti* in one's nature; and this participation should be based on the nature of one's consciousness of one's unity with the cosmos – *dharma* based on *buddhi, karma* based on *jnana,* in a state of equilibrium, or poised attitude of the mind.

Karma-yoga leads to salvation through action. Work is the central and defining characteristic of life. Attachment with the result leads to stress, competition and aggression. According to Bhagvad Gita an individual should follow *niskamakarma* (desire-less action). *Niskamakarma* is not renunciation of action but the renunciation of expectations. It is because 'no one under any circumstances can remain even for moment, without undertaking acting; everyone is compelled to act, by the modes born of nature' (BG 3: 5). A *niskamakarma-yogi* performs all the actions but without being attached to its fruit (*phala*). Krishna says that 'he, who controls his senses through the mind and engages himself in the path of action, with the organs of action and sense, without being attached, is superior' (BG 3: 7). One thing that is remarkable in the concept of *niskamakarma*, is that at this level, one is completely free from all self-interests and self-satisfaction (Ojha, 2011). He performs action only as a duty for the well-being of the others (*lokasangraha*). As Bhagvad Gita says, 'It was by action alone, that Janaka and others attained perfection. Thou should perform selfless action, also for the good of the world' (BG 3: 20). Thus, an individual being self-realized or self-conscious creates a kind of intentional relation to society as whole. He, being in the state of *lokasangraha*, can construct the interactional processes by which human beings in society sustain and create shared meanings (Ojha, 2011). In this regard Bhagvad Gita says, 'Whatsoever an ideal person does, he is followed by others, as well. Whatever standard he sets, the world follows the same' (BG 3: 21).

Belief in *Rin*

The concept of "service" has its roots in the ancient Hindu tradition of the five-fold debt system. According to the Taittiriya Sanhita (6.3. 10.5), a child is born with three *rins* (debts) to be repaid in his lifetime: *deva rin* (debt to deity) to be repaid by performing various religious acts and worships (*puja*); *rishi rin* to be paid by studying and acquiring knowledge, more importantly by evolving further knowledge; and *pitri rin* to be repaid by procreation as well as performing rituals in remembrance of the ancestors.

Another ancient Hindu scripture, Shatpath Brahman (1.7. 2.1-6), added two more debts. According to this scripture: (1) a person is indebted to humanity at large (*nri rin* or *manushya-rin*) which can be repaid by treating others with respect and helping them, and (2) a person is indebted to plants, animals and nature (*bhuta rin*). These debts are repaid by performing the five great sacrificial fires (*panchamahayadnya*) in the stage of the householder. The concept of five debts generates awareness of one's duties and responsibilities, provides moral and ethical direction to life, encourages family values, and helps a harmonized society (Shraddhanand, n d).

Swabhav and *Swadharma*

In the classical Indian worldview, there is an underlying concept of *swabhava* and *swadharma*. *Swabhava* depends on the prominence of one of the three *gunas* called *sattva* or the element of knowledge, *rajas* or the principle of activity, which on the affective side is the cause of all painful experiences, and *tamas* or the principle of passivity that clouds intellect thereby producing ignorance.

Social well-being is possible only under "conducive environment." People will generally need a "facilitative" society in which they can express *gunas* in positive light. Conducive environment is the one that not only provides opportunity to a person to express his *gunas* positively, and work according to his nature (*swabhava*) but also according to *swadharma (varna)*. Basically, *swadharma* and *swabhava* go hand in hand. Promoting vocation as per the *swabhava* and *swadharma* will be a happy situation for both - to the individual and to the society. Within this perspective, *rajasic* will realize the *nishkama karma* and *tamasic* will attain deep *bhakti yoga,* whereas *sattvic* will strive for knowledge (*gyana*). Self is to be realized while living in material world through the instrument of pure mind. Logically, it follows that mind is pure when it is in harmony with *swabhava* and *swadharma*. Nobody can be expected to be happy out of one's nature.

Relevance of Ancient Systems in Contemporary India

***Ashram System*:** The basic premise of *ashram* system was that people go through several developmental or life stages and these stages could be defined by socially relevant roles and responsibilities. Identifying and supporting theses roles would lead to a satisfying passage of life cycle. In a contemporary research, the same theme is played by almost all the developmental psychologists. Neugarten (1976) says that "the individual passes through a socially regulated cycle from birth to death as inexorably as he passes through the biological cycle: a succession of socially delineated age-statuses, each with recognized rights, duties, and obligations." Further, Neugarten's work suggests that all societies are age-grated, with a system of expectations about age-appropriate behaviour.

Immediate parallel of *ashram* system can be categorization in the Levinson's (1978) development model wherein each era has its distinctive and unifying character of learning. Each transition between eras requires a change in the character of one's life. Levinson argues that the life-cycle comprises a sequence of four eras, each lasting for approximately twenty-five years. The eras and main developmental periods he identifies are: (1) Childhood and adolescence: birth to age-twenty (early childhood transition by age three); (2) Early adulthood: age seventeen to forty-five; (3) Middle adulthood: age forty to sixty-five; and (4) Late adulthood: age sixty onwards.

Levinson (1978) views midlife as a period where one needs to redress the dominance of attachment to the external world: to find a better balance between the needs of the self and the needs of society—a greater integration of separateness and attachment: "Greater individuation allows him to be more separate from the world, to be more independent and self-generating. But it also gives him the confidence and understanding to have more intense attachments in the world and to feel more fully a part of it" (p. 195). This is nearly how *vanprsthashram* is referred in ancient Indian literature. *Ashram* system does not elaborate on how human development occurs at four stages of life, but it rather provides what one should do during these phases and provides facilitative environment for the successful passage. It may be noted that Indian culture being collectivist, the *ashram* system is designed more from the society's perspective rather than mere individual development. Among personality theories, Erickson also accords equal emphasis to the roles of society and to the persons themselves with respect to development and organization of personality.

Goals of *brahmacharyashrma* was to prioritize not only academic learning, but also social, emotional, and ethical competencies under strict discipline of *guru*. In today's context, Cohen (2006) asserts that social, emotional, ethical, and academic education is a human right that all students are entitled to, and argues that ignoring this amounts to a social injustice. The *ashram* system also recognized the role of community in the development of individuals and devoted one full stage of *vanprasthasharm* for an individual to contribute towards the well-being of the society. During the era of *ashrams*, people in the last phase (*sannyas*) would retire from active social life. They would reflect, meditate and work for *moksha*. This is an inward journey. The research in gerontology suggests the human development in last lag of life is universally same, as was thought in *ashram* system. As elders grow older, both body transcendence (focusing on psychological strengths) and ego transcendence (orienting toward a larger, more distant future) increase. In a study of elderly women, those in their eighties and nineties stated with greater certainty than those in their sixties that they "accept the changes brought about by aging", "have moved beyond fear of death", "have a clearer sense of the meaning of life" and "have found new, positive spiritual gifts to explore" (Brown & Lowis, 2003).

Drawing on her own experience of aging, her observations of her husband's final years, and the work of others on the positive potential of the years shortly before death, Joan Erikson speculated that success in attaining gerotranscendence is apparent in heightened inner calm and contentment and additional time spent in quiet reflection (Erikson, 1998; Tornstam & Tornqvist, 2000). Although interviews with people in their ninth and tenth decades reveal that many (but not all) experience this peaceful, contemplative state, more research is needed to confirm the existence of a distinct, transcendent late-life stage. Spirituality and faith may advance to a higher level in late adulthood—away from prescribed beliefs toward a more reflective approach that emphasizes links to others, that is at ease with mystery and uncertainty, and that accepts one's own belief system as one of many possible worldviews (Fowler, 1981; McFadden, 1996). Western world does not have concept of *moksha*, yet looking at the growth in spirituality at late adulthood in their culture, it may be said that psychosocial path towards the end is nearly same.

Varna, Swabhava and Swadharma: From a social perspective, the *varnas* were classifications based on personal dispositions that, as a whole, created a balanced society in which everyone played a productive role. Though the caste system exists today, it is no more for the selection of profession or trade. *Varna* system has relevance only if viewed in the context of its original purpose. Stephen Knapp (n d) argues that the traditional *vedic* system conferred one's occupational class by recognizing one's natural talents, interests, tendencies, and abilities. He likens it with the "modern system of having high school counsellors adjust a student's academic courses by discussing with the students their academic performance conjunction with the results of their aptitude tests. Thus, such counsellors see what occupational direction is best suited for the students so they can achieve a fitting career that is of interest to them and helps them be a contributor to society at the same time.' Knapp justifies the four basic divisions of society and calls them "natural classifications and found everywhere, in every society, call it what you want."

Modern management practices, like *varna*, lay emphasis on the ability, aptitude and personality make up for the selection of professionals. The basic premise of *varna* system was distribution of job according to *swabhava* or personality type—*sattva, rajas* or *tamas*. This was done to have fair distribution of work, and better outcome. Current research confirms the basic assumptions of awarding work based on *swabhava* and competence in *varna* system. Meta-analyses by several researchers have shown repeatedly that personality measures can predict job performance fairly well (e.g., Barrick & Mount, 1991; Hough, 1992; Salgado, 1997; Tett, Jackson, & Rothstein, 1991; Sharma, 1999). A work suiting to own *swabhava*, will result in job satisfaction and thus life satisfaction. Since a job is a significant part of one's life, the relationship between job satisfaction and life satisfaction makes sense—one's job experiences spill over into one's life. Judge and Hulin (1993) found support for the hypothesis that the relationship between job satisfaction and subjective well-being is reciprocally causal. They summarized the implications of their findings by stating: "to spend the majority of one's waking hours at a dissatisfying job appears to have a significant influence on the overall experienced well-being in one's life. Conversely, spending an equal amount of time at a satisfying and perhaps challenging and motivating job has a strong positive influence on one's subjective well-being" (Judge & Hulin, 1993, p. 414).

One of the advantages of *varna* system was absence of role conflict and role confusion resulting in better work performance. Once the profession is allocated based on *swabhava*, it becomes one's *swadharma* to accomplish it. According to Kahn, Wolfe, Quinn and Snoek (1964) role conflict, on the one hand, occurs when a person experiences incompatible job demands. Role ambiguity, on the other hand, occurs when an individual has inadequate knowledge or information about how to perform a job. Both of these role perceptions have detrimental, negative consequences for the individual. First, they trigger emotional turmoil, such as stress, tension and dissatisfaction (Jackson & Schuler, 1985; Kahn *et al.,* 1964). These emotions can lead to anger and aggression (Fox & Spector, 1999). Finally, they can even have severe negative impact on job effectiveness and performance (Abramis, 1994; Jackson & Schuler, 1985; Tubre & Collins, 2000). In the period of *varna* system the jobs were not so complex, yet the idea of awarding work according to *swabhava* and competence without role conflict or ambiguity was a well thought out plan.

***Karma-Yoga*:** The doctrine of *karma* theory is practical and relevant in today's competitive world more than it was in Mahabharat times. The theory provides an operational basis for constructive achievement. It emphasizes detachment and equanimous attitude towards success and failure, and inculcating virtues like sacrifice, dedication, belief and greater good of the people as the motive for action. The tenets of *nishkama karmayoga* can serve as guidelines and codes for the managers of the business, if they are striving towards achieving long-lasting success and happiness. *Karma-yoga* has three dimensions viz., duty-orientation, detachment to rewards (*nishkam karma)*, and equanimity. Since *karma-yoga* talks of an absence of desire for rewards, it is in conflict with the dimension of aspiration. Mulla and Krishnan (2009), on a study on 75 executives, found that belief in Indian philosophy enhanced duty orientation, and absence of desire for rewards enhanced life satisfaction.

Practice in *karma-yoga* has been found to have positive effect on moral dimensions. Mulla and Krishnan (2006, 2007) validate *karma yoga* against three dimensions of moral development, viz., moral sensitivity, moral motivation, and moral character. Thus, *karma yoga* shows good potential as an alternative model for moral development in the Indian context. *Karma-yoga* as duty-orientation and detachment to rewards presupposes an altruistic motive in which the individual is more concerned about being of service to others rather than benefiting one's own person. Effective Indian managers place a high value on the idea of 'doing good for the society', and leading a simple life, and involvement in social activity (Dayal, 1999). "Self-sacrifice" and "Giving model of motivation", the two of the seven 'unique Indian' sub-dimensions of transformational leadership identified by Singh and Krishnan (2005) seem to be related with *karma-yoga*.

A commonly expressed doubt about *karma-yoga* is - how can we put in efforts without expecting any reward in return for our efforts? Using a modified list of Rokeach's instrumental values, Mulla and Krishanan (2011) investigated Indian students see any difference between the values "ambitious" and "hardworking." It was assumed that ambitious people would expect rewards. They noted that for individuals who are high on *karma yoga*, "hardworking" was more important than being "ambitious".

***Rin*:** Conceptually, *rin* can be considered equivalent to gratitude at operational level and is expected to be strongly related to well-being. An existing body of research supports an association between gratitude and an overall sense of well-being. Research has suggested that feelings of gratitude may be beneficial to subjective emotional well-being (Emmons & McCullough, 2003). In a sample of 389 adults, Wood *et al.* (2008) concluded in their research that gratitude has a unique relationship with life satisfaction. Research by Tseng (2008) and Froh *et al.* (2009) also confirms an association between gratitude and well-being. A sense of *rin* or gratitude towards the *guru*, parents, nature and Higher Self should therefore have positive effect on life satisfaction and general well-being. In the period of *ashrams*, the nature was in its best form, yet the seers could foresee future possibilities and included nature in the list of whom we should feel gratitude to. In the current context, research findings in health, medicine and psychology also appear to be supportive of the proposition that nature has some inherently positive effects on physical and psychological well-being for humans. Wilson's (1984) *biophilia hypothesis* predicts that people's psychological health is associated with their relationship to nature.

***Purusharthas*:** Research has shown that there are three routes to happiness: positive emotion and pleasure, engagement, and meaning (Seligman, 2002). While positive emotion, pleasure and engagement is found in *artha*, and *kama*, meaning can be inferred through *dharma* and *moksha*.

Interestingly, pleasure seems to be the least consequential pathway to a happy, satisfied life (Peterson *et al.,* 2005). Research has demonstrated that engagement and meaning (work with *dharma* and *moksha*) are the most important and lasting forms of well-being. Research in positive psychology reveals that recognizing, honouring, and developing our strengths is the most important way to instill a true sense of engagement (Lopez & Snyder, 2003; Peterson & Seligman, 2004). Finding a sense of meaning or purpose in life is essential element that contributes to our feelings of well-being and happiness. Positive psychology suggests that developing such a sense rests on our ability to use our strengths and virtues in the service of something much larger than ourselves (Seligman *et al.,* 2005). Whether our focus is on *artha, dharma, kama* or *moksha,* these larger domains are all socially and emotionally grounded. Altruistic actions are necessarily social, emotional, and ethical, as well as cognitive endeavours. They are also deeply tied to our long-term social well-being.

Final Remarks

The chapter is evolved around well-being rather than on health alone because well-being is broader concept that integrates mental health and physical health resulting in more holistic approaches to disease prevention and health promotion (Dunn, 1973). Well-being is a valid population outcome measure beyond morbidity, mortality, and economic status that tells us how people perceive their life is going from their own perspective (Diener & Seligman, 2004; Diener, 2009; Frey & Stutzer, 2002). Results from cross-sectional, longitudinal and experimental studies (Diener & Seligman, 2004; Lyubomirsky, King, & Diener, 2005) find that well-being is associated with self-perceived health, longevity, healthy behaviours, mental and physical illness, social connectedness, productivity, and factors in the physical and social environment.

To sum up, social well-being is the inherent content of Indian social system – a continuum of ancient culture. It is this reason that binds over a billion people speaking different languages, and divided as different castes, socio-economic classes and socio-philosophical followings. Despite scientific thought and modernity, most Indians continue to be culturally conservative and collectivist. Family and society continue to override personal preferences. To the outside world, the core of Indian culture revolves around the principle of *'vasudhaiva kutumbakam'* treating the entire world as our own family, which reflects universality of serene love, altruism, sharing of responsibilities and caring for all beings – a true picture of social well-being. There is however a need to research on some current aspects of Indian culture that are detrimental to social well-being. First among them is corruption which has now become a part of culture. The other is disrespect to the law. The first reflects moral degradation of society, and other the failure of governance. In the current socio-political system these two anomalies are detrimental to overall well-being and may have far reaching consequences.

REFERENCES

Abramis, D.J. (1994). Work role ambiguity, job satisfaction, and job performance: Meta-analyses and review. *Psychological Reports*, 75, 1411-1433.

Aurobindo, S. (2007). *The human cycle*. Delhi: Butler Press.

Barrick, M.R. and Mount, M.K. (1991). The big five personality dimensions and job performance: A meta-analysis. *Personnel Psychology*, 44, 1-26.

Bhagavad-Gita. (1986). Translation and commentary by Swami Prabhupada. Mumbai: Bhaktivedanta Book Trust.

Brown, C. and Lowis, M. (2003). Psychosocial development in the elderly: An investigation into Erikson's ninth stage. *Journal of Aging Studies,* 17, 4, 415-426.

Bruner, J. (1990). *Acts of meaning*. Cambridge, MA: Harvard University Press.

Cohen, J. (2006). Social, emotional, ethical, and academic education: Creating a climate for learning, participation in democracy, and well-being. *Harvard Educational Review*, 76, 2, 201-237. Retrieved from http://www.schoolclimate.org/climate/documents/policy/cohen-HE-Paper-7-06. pdf

Dalal, A.K. and Misra, G. (2011). Advances in psychology of health and well-being. In G. Misra (Ed), *Handbook of Psychology in India,* New Delhi: Oxford University Press.

Dayal, I. (1999). *Can organizations develop leaders? A study of effective leaders.* New Delhi: Mittal Publications.

Diener, E. and Biswas-Diener, R. (2008). *Happiness: Unlocking the mysteries of psychological wealth.* New York: Wiley-Blackwell.

Diener, E. and Seligman, M.E. (2004). Beyond money: Toward an economy of well-being. *Psychological Science in the Public Interest,* 5, 1, 1-31.

Diener, E. (2009). *Assessing well-being: The collected works of Ed Diener*. New York: Springer.

Dunn, H.L. (1973). *High level wellness*. Arlington: R.W. Beatty.

Emmons, R.A. and McCullough, M.E. (2003). Counting blessings versus burdens: An experimental investigation of gratitude and subjective well-being in daily life. *Journal of Personality and Social Psychology*, 84, 377–389.

Erikson, E.H. (1998). *The life-cycle completed. Extended version with new chapters on the ninth stage* by Joan M. Erikson. New York: Norton.

Fowler, J.W. (1981). *Stages of faith*. New York: Harper & Row.

Fox, S. and Spector, P.E. (1999). A model of work frustration-aggression. *Journal of Organizational Behaviour*, 20, 6, 915-931.

Frey, B.S. and Stutzer, A. (2002). *Happiness and economics*. Princeton, N. J: Princeton University Press.

Froh, J.J.; Yurkewicz, C. and Kashdan, T.B. (2009). Gratitude and subjective well-being in early adolescence: Examining gender differences. *Journal of Adolescence*, 32, 633–650.

Higgins, E.T. (1987). Self discrepancy: A theory relating self and affect. *Psychological Review,* 94, 319-340.

Hough, L.M. (1992). The "Big Five" personality variables-construct confusion: Description versus prediction. *Human Performance*, 5, 139-155.

Jain, P.K. (2011). *The caste system of Hindu society*. Retrieved from *http: / /www. huffingtonpost. com/pankaj-jain-phd/varna-and-caste-system-of_b_877981. html*

Jackson, S.E. and Schuler, R.S. (1985). A meta-analyses and conceptual critique of research on role ambiguity and role conflict in work settings. *Organizational Behaviour and Human Decision Processes*, 36, 16-78.

Judge, T.A. and Hulin, C.L. (1993). Job satisfaction as a reflection of disposition: A multiple source causal analysis. *Organizational Behaviour and Human Decision Processes,* 56, 388-421.

Kahn, R.L.; Wolfe, D.M.; Quinn, R.P.; and Snoek, J.D. (1964). *Organizational stress: Studies in role conflict and ambiguity*. Florida: Krieger Publishing Company.

Knapp, S. (n d). *Vedic literature says caste by birth is unjust*. Retrieved from *http://www. stephen-knapp.com/vedic_literature_says_caste_by_birth_is_unjust. htm*

Krishnananda, S. (1970). *The Path to freedom: Mastering the art of total perception*.

Rishikesh: Divine Life Society. Retrieved from *http://www.swami-krishnananda.org/freedom/freedom_05.html*

Krishnananda, S. (n d). *A study of the Bhagavadgita*. Retrieved from http:// *www.swami-krishnananda.org/gital/bhagavadgita_05a.html*

Larson, J.S. (2003). The measurement of social well-being. *Social Indicators Research,* 28, 285-296.

Levinson, D. (1978). *The seasons of a man's life*. New York: Knopf.

Lopez, S.J. and Snyder, C.R. (2003). *Positive psychological assessment: A handbook of models and measures*. Washington, DC: American Psychological Association.

Lyubomirsky, S.; King, L. and Diener, E. (2005). The benefits of frequent positive affect: Does happiness lead to success? *Psychological Bulletin,* 131, 6, 803-855.

Markus, H.R. and Kitayama, S. (1998). The cultural psychology of personality. *Journal of Cross-Cultural Psychology*, 29, 63–87.

McFadden, S.H. (1996). Religion, spirituality, and aging. In J.E. Birren and K.W. Schaie (Eds.), *Handbook of the Psychology of Aging* (4th ed., pp. 162-177). San Diego: Academic Press.

Mohan, K. (2001). Spirituality and well-being: An overview. In M. Cornelissen (Ed). *Consciousness and its transformation*. Pondicherry: SAICE.

Mulla, Z.R. and Krishnan, V.R. (2006). Karma-yoga: A conceptualization and validation of the Indian philosophy of work. *Journal of Indian Psychology*, 24 (1/2), 26–43.

Mulla, Z.R. and Krishnan, V.R. (2007). Karma-yoga: Construct validation using value systems and emotional intelligence. *South Asian Journal of Management*, 14 (4), 116–36.

Mulla, Z.R. and Krishnan, V.R. (2009). Do Karma-yogis make better leaders? Exploring the relationship between the leader's karma-yoga and transformational leadership. *Journal of Human Values,* 15, 2, 167-183.

Mulla, Z.R. and Krishnan, V.R. (2011). Is karma-yoga possible? Can we be hardworking without being ambitious? *Great Lakes Herald,* 5, 2, 46-55.

Myers, D. G. and Diener, E.D. (1995). Who is happy? *Psychological Science*, 6, 10-19.

Neugarten, B. (1976). Adaptation and the life cycle. *Counselling Psychologist*, 6, 16-20.

Ojha, A.K. (2011). Indian culture is actually extremely diverse. *Dialogue*. Retrieved from http: //www.asthabharti.org/Dia_July%2011/aru. htm.

Peterson, C. and Seligman, M. (eds.). (2004). *Character strengths and virtues: A handbook and classification*. New York: Oxford University Press.

Peterson, C.; Park, N. and Seligman, M.E. (2005). Orientation to happiness and life satisfaction: The full life versus the empty life. *Journal of Happiness Studies*, 6, 1, 25-41.

Roland, A. (1988). *In Search of self in India and Japan: Towards a cross-cultural psychology.* Princeton, NJ: Princeton University Press.

Salgado, J.F. (1997). The five factor model of personality and job performance in the European community. *Journal of Applied Psychology*, 82, 30-43.

Seedhouse, D. (1995). Well-being: Health promotions red herring. *Health Promotion International*, 10, 61-67.

Seligman, M.E. P. (2002). *Authentic happiness*. New York: Free Press.

Seligman, M.E. P.; Steen, T.A.; Park, N. and Peterson, C. (2005). Positive psychology progress: Empirical validation of interventions. *American Psychologist*, 60, 410–421.

Shraddhanand Swami (n d). *Duties and responsibilities: The Hindu social framework*. Retrieved from http://www.shraddhananda.com/Duties_and_Responsibilities_The_Hindu_Social_Framework.html

Sharma, R. (1999). Self-concept and job satisfaction in *sattva, rajas* and *tamas*personalities. *Journal of Indian Psychology*, 17, 2, 9-17.

Singh, N. and Krishnan, V.R. (2005). Towards understanding

transformational leadership in India: A grounded theory approach. *Vision: The Journal of Business Perspective*, 9 (2), 5–17.

Sinha, J.B. P. and Kumar, R. (2004). Methodology for understanding Indian culture. *The Copenhagen Journal of Asian Studies*, 89-104. Retrieved from http: //ej.lib.cbs.dk/index.php/cjas/article/download/27/26

Snyder, C. and Lopez, S. (1999). *Handbook of Positive Psychology*. New York: Oxford University Press.

Tseng, W.C. (2008). Resilience in life events, interpersonal strength, and mental health among college students: An examination of mediation and moderation effects. *Bulletin of Educational Psychology*, 40, 239-259.

Tett, R.P.; Jackson, D.N. and Rothstein, M. (1991). Personality measures as predictors of job performance: A meta-analytic review. *Personnel Psychology*, 44, 703-742.

Tornstam, L. and Tornqvist, M. (2000). Nursing staff's interpretations of "Gerotranscendental Behaviour" in the elderly. *Journal of Aging and Identity,* 5, 1, 15-29.

Tubre, T.C. and Collins, J.M. (2000). Jackson and Schuler (1985) revisited: A meta-analyses of the relationship between role ambiguity, role conflict, and job performance. *Journal of Management*, 26, 1, 155-169.

Wilson, E.O. (1984). *Biophilia*. New York: Harvard University Press.

Wood, A.M.; Joseph, S. and Maltby, J. (2008). Gratitude uniquely predicts satisfaction with life: Incremental validity above the domains and facets of the five factor model. *Personality and Individual Differences*, 45, 49-54.

14

Culture, Social Process and Suicide: A Qualitative Enquiry

Sunil K. Verma, Swati A. Sachdeva and *Binu Sundas*

Suicide is the outcome of a complex interplay of etiological factors which are psychological, biological, and social in origin (Mann *et al.*, 2005). Suicide, widely considered as the most tragic way of ending one's life, poses a major challenge to civil society.

The increasing suicide rate around the globe has drawn the attention of social scientists, policy makers and mental health professionals towards dynamics of suicidal behaviour. Suicide constitutes a major public health problem across the world. The United Nations has estimated that between 500,000 to 1.12 million deaths happen owing to suicide each year worldwide. According to World Health Organization, estimates in the year 2000, approximately 1 million people die by committing suicide and 10-20 times more people have been reported attempted suicide worldwide. In most countries, suicide is now one of the leading causes of death among people aged 15-34 years (Kumar & Mandal, 2010).

The national suicide rate is 10.5 per lakh persons, however in Sikkim, in the last decade, the suicide rate was higher than the national rate. Data shows that in year 2000, a total of 84 suicide cases were recorded but in year 2001 it was 94; in 2002 it was 78; in 2003 it was 105; in 2004 it was 98; in 2005 it was 109; in 2006 it was 145; in 2007 it was 124; in 2008 it was 287 and in the year 2009 a total of 241 cases were recorded. The data of 2008 and 2009 shows that Sikkim has the highest suicide rate in India.

Between 2000-2007, a total of 835 suicide cases were recorded out of which 63.47 per cent were males and 36.52 per cent were females. The age range was, 4.30 per cent suicide was committed by people who were less than 15 years old, 36.15 per cent by people who were between 15-29 years, 28.6 per cent by people who were between 30-44 years, 17.87 per cent by people who were between 45-59 years and 13.07 per cent by people who were above 60 years. Overall 650 cases, 82.92 per cent suicides were committed by the youth and middle aged person. In the context of Education, out of 835 cases 33.35 per cent are uneducated, 29.9 per cent suicide victims are those who have studied up to the primary level, 18.81 per cent up to the Middle school, 11.36 per cent up to matric level, 4.49 up to Intermediate level, 0.95 per cent have done Diploma, 1.06 per cent are undergraduates. So out of 835 cases 93 per cent suicide victims are people who have studied below the metric level. In context of profession, it shows that out of 835 cases, 25.63 per cent suicide victims are farmers and most of them are male, 13.7 per cent are self-employed and 10.46 per cent are males. Whereas, 12.99 per cent are housewives, 12.6 per cent suicides takes place due to unemployment, 9.50 per cent suicide victims are student, 8.79 per cent are from private sector and 3 per cent from government sector. Out of 835 suicide cases, cause for 25.51 per cent of suicide is insanity, 17.93 per cent family problem, 6.25 per cent due to prolonged illness, 3.6 per cent due to drug abuse/alcoholism and 1.32 per cent due to love affairs. 10.22 per cent cases had other than the above mentioned causes whereas causes for the 29.72 per cent cases were not known. Social Science researches on suicide indicate toward two major causes of suicide— Psychological and Social. With regards to psychological causes, the major causes are: psychological disorder, mood disorder, alcohol abuse and chronic disorder. In terms of social causes, religiosity, social support, family care, unemployment, low socio-economic condition, marital status, and gender play the most pivotal role.

There are two approaches to study suicide. One approach is retrospective analysis which is a psychological autopsy in which clinicians and researchers piece together information from the person's past (Jacobs & Klien, 1993). Relatives, friends, or therapists may remember past statements, conversations, and behaviour that shed light on a suicide. Another approach is retrospective information, where information is provided by the suicide notes that some victims leave behind. However, these sources of information may not always be available as less than one-quarter of all suicide victims are found to have been in therapy (Fleer & Pasewark, 1982), and less than one-third leave notes prior to committing suicide (Black, 1993; Leenaars, 1992, 1989).

Psychological Perspective of Suicide

Many psychodynamic theorists believe that suicide results from depression and from anger at others, which is redirected towards oneself. This theory was first stated by Wilhelm Stekel (1910), when he proclaimed that "no one kills himself who has not wanted to kill another or at least wished the death of another" (Shneidman, 1979). Freud (1922) identified instinct as drives that were innate, universal and constantly felt. There are two types: life instinct (Eros) and death instinct (Thanatos). In extreme emotional distress the death instinct dominates and becomes powerful over life instinct and this extreme emotional distress is known as depression i.e., self-accusation and feeling of worthlessness. This feeling of depression refers to a real or imagined behaviour of another person, i.e., domination of death instinct is manifested in the form of aggression and sadism. In the theory of Freud, depression and suicidal act result from withdrawal from society and represent hostile impulse directed towards others (Shalini Marwaha, 2005).

According to Futterman (1961), these two instincts are not separate and cannot really function independently of each other, but that they always exist in variable amounts. Menninger (1938) in his work, extended the concept of death instinct and generated a hypothesis that three elements exist in constantly shifting patterns in all self-destructive behaviour—the wish to kill, the wish to be killed, and the wish to die. In support of Freud's view, researchers have found a relationship between childhood and later suicidal behaviours (Paykel, 1991). One study of 200 family histories found that suicide attempters were much more likely to have lost a parent during their childhood than were non-suicidal control subjects (Adam, Bouckoms, & Streiner, 1982). Common forms of loss were death of the father and divorce or separation of the parents, especially during either the early years of life or late adolescence. Shneidman (1993) suggests that the key to suicide is "psychache", a feeling of psychological pain, tension, and suffering that makes life intolerable. Suicide attempts may also be preceded by shifts in patterns of thinking. Individuals may become preoccupied with their problems, loss of perspective, and see suicide as the only effective solution to their difficulties (Shneidman, 1993). They develop a sense of hopelessness – a pessimistic belief that their present conditions, circumstances, problems or moods will not change (Klingman & Hochdorf, 1993).

Hopelessness theory states that "the expectation that highly desired outcomes will not occur or that highly aversive outcomes will occur and that there is nothing one can do to change this situation." (Abramson, Metalsky, & Alloy, 1989). Thus a kind of "hopelessness depression" sets in when it seems that there is no prospect to get either what one really wants or to avoid what one really doesn't want. As part of this theory, negative events can serve as "occasion setters" for people to become hopeless, and there is a "cognitive vulnerability" depressive thinking that accompanies the stress of such negative life events. The self-discrepancy theory (Higgins, 1987) draws on three different concepts of the self: the actual self, as one sees oneself; the ought self, which is the self one thinks one ought to be; and the ideal self; which is the self one would most like to be. Though there are three self concepts, the theory states that "individuals are motivated to achieve a state in which there is a consistency between the self-concept and these self-evaluative standards." Those who possess discrepancies between their actual and ideal selves are relatively more prone to developing depression while those who possess discrepancies between their actual and ought selves are relatively more prone to developing anxiety. Simply put, this theory has shown a strong correlation between negative evaluation of the self and suicidality. The Escape theory (Baumeister, 1990) states that "Self-destructive behaviours can be explained in terms of motivation to escape from aversive self-awareness and negative effect." An acute negative experience, calamity, or stressor can point out the large discrepancy that exists between what one wants or expects and what actually occurs and where what are often "unrealistically high expectations or standards" can be abruptly dashed. Then, "when setbacks or discrepancies occur, individuals can either attribute it to external factors and absolve themselves of responsibility, or blame themselves and take on responsibility for the failure." Negative emotions, such as depression, anxiety, and anger, can arise from the resulting aversive, negative self-awareness.

Suicidal behaviour is most likely when a person sees his or her situation as intolerable or hopeless. According to Cassem, suicide can stem from a hateful, even murderous impulse, or from an irrepressible need to escape one's own overpowering suffering.

Finally, it can be seen that Psychologists viewed suicide, as an intensely personal act of self-destruction and highlighted the role of the psychopathic states like depression and feeling of hopelessness and helplessness in explaining suicides. It emphasizes and examines the individual and the conflicts within a particular mind leading to self-destructive behaviour. Psychologists emphasize on unbearable and unendurable pain as a cause of suicide but they did not explain the source of these unbearable and unendurable pain.

Sociological Perspective of Suicide

Contrary to psychological approach, sociologists consider not only the individual causes of suicide but also rates of suicides that are treated as social facts and need to be comprehended with social facts preceding it. The rate of suicide in a society/group remain more or less constant over a period of time reflecting the nature of individual's integration with the group. The variations in the suicidal rates are explained through gender, age, rural-urban, race, religion, occupational status and marital status.

Durkheim considered that the propensity of an individual to commit suicide was related to two basic concepts—(1) Levels of social integration, and (2) Levels of social regulation. By 'social integration', Durkheim meant the way in which people come to see and feel themselves to be part of a society or a particular group. An integrated individual feels secure because he/she feels wanted and/or needed by others. Without this sense of belonging, Durkheim argued, people feel "lost" and "worthless" from the normal activities of the society into which they were born.

By "social regulation", Durkheim meant the ways in which social groups/societies attempt to control their members' range of behaviour. Durkheim believed that people who were integrated strongly into social groups, and whose desires and aspirations were regulated by social norms were less likely to commit suicide. He identified four types of suicide, in accordance with the relative presence or absence of integration and regulation. First, *Egoistic suicide* (lack of social integration) occurs among men and women who are less integrated with social groups and emphasize more on individual identity. Such individuals have no social support needed to handle the stress. Second, *Altruistic suicide* (over-integration) was a result of too much integration of individual with group and individual having no independent identity from the group. Examples of such "altruistic" suicide include the Indian custom of '*sati*' where widows burn themselves to death and Japanese seppuku or *hara-kiri*. Third "*Anomic*" suicide is found in the social milieu where social regulations are weak and a state of "normlessness" exists. As Nisbet (1965) notes: "Anomic suicide is caused by the sudden dislocation of normative systems – the breakdown of values by which one may have lived for a lifetime." In this respect, anomic forms of suicide become a possibility when an individual becomes uncertain about the world in which he/she lives. Fourth type of suicide is *Fatalistic suicide* (Over-regulation): this form of suicide was seen by Durkheim to be the opposite of anomic suicide and was seen to occur amongst social groups that suffered from oppressive social discipline and regulation.

There are a number of different studies on suicide as Halbwachs (1930) identified a concept of "social isolation". Individuals who were socially isolated, in some way, suffered from a form of under regulation/lack of social integration and this made them more susceptible to suicidal forms of behaviour. Sainsbury (1956) found that there was a relationship between the two, insofar as the districts with the highest recorded levels of suicide also had the highest levels of social isolation and social mobility.

Gibbs and Martin (1964) argued that, since Durkheim gave no clear definition of social integration, it was not possible to operationalize this idea. As an alternative, they proposed using the idea of "status integration", in order to measure the extent to which an individual's different social statuses overlapped. According to Gibbs and Martin (1964), the greater the level of social support he is able to get from his other statuses in life (father, employee and so forth), the less likely he is to actually commit suicide.

Bilton (1996) notes: "Suicide is very much the product of meaningful categorisation by officials investigating agencies and it cannot be assumed that these officials share the same meanings on which they base their interpretations.

Hence, two main implications are evident: (1) Suicide rates and suicide statistics are not necessarily "facts" in the way that Durkheim assumed; (2) On the contrary, like all official statistics, the determination of suicide involves a social process of interpretation by numerous social actors. In this respect, we have no real way of determining either the reliability or validity of suicide statistics.

According to Douglas (1967), we must understand the social act of suicide; we must understand how it is socially defined by significant social actors (the police, the medical profession, investigators and so forth). We must attempt to understand the meanings that suicidal individuals "construct" for their actions. For Douglas, the person who intends to commit suicide can attempt to convey to others the meaning of their act (through the use of "suicide notes", the way in which they construct their death and so forth). The researcher, therefore, needs to get as close as possible to the world which he or she is attempting to study and the "most appropriate" methods of investigation involve such things as participant observation (of the people involved in the social construction process), in-depth interviews, personal documents, and case studies of individual deaths.

According to Freud (1936), when death instinct dominates over life instinct, then the feeling of extreme depression and mood disorder emerges. Instinct and depression are not self-inbuilt but emerge due to negative changes in structural conditions wherein the individual lives. Durkheim emphasized on constructive process of suicide though he ignored the process. So, to comprehend the suicide among cultivators, we have to understand the structural conditions of the society.

The predominant perspectives in the comprehension of suicides are *psychological – social psychological* and sociological. The conception and causes of suicides vary with these perspectives. Literature on suicide indicates that most of the studies on suicide were conducted in Western countries and in urban areas and very few studies were conducted in developing countries

In India, in the last decades, major emphasis was on the study on suicide of farmers. States like Andhra Pradesh, Karnataka, Maharashtra, and Punjab revealed that debt, crop failure, economic hardship were the leading causes of suicide among cultivators. Besides this, domestic discord, alcohol and drug abuse were also found to be contributing to suicides. (Shiva and Jafri, 1998; Deshpande, 2002; Assadi 1998; Revathi, 1998; Vasavi, 1999; Dash *et al.*, 1998). Surveys conducted in Punjab attributed suicides among cultivators to crop failure and high intensity of indebtedness among cultivators

'*Movement against State Repression*' (MASR), (1998); Iyer and Manick, (2000); Kumar, (1998). Mohanty (2005), tried to comprehend the phenomenon of suicides among cultivators in Maharashtra. He found that the rate of suicide among small sizes of landholders is more as they devote more than 60 per cent of their total land for Cotton cultivation. Even though different sizes of landholders are cultivating high yielding varieties of crops that require more capital, differential consequences are observed on the basis of landholdings. Most of the small sizes of landholders fail to recover the production cost and thus fail to repay the borrowed loan either from formal or informal agencies or both. However, larger size of landholders experienced more intensity of family quarrels, business failures, degradation of social status and power that seems to have contributed to suicides among rich peasants. Sharma & Mohankumar (2006) further supports these findings on the basis of their study in Kerala. Jodhka (2006) observed that drought leads to differential consequences on the basis of the size of landholdings. It affected more intensively the small cultivators and resulted in downward social mobility in terms of landholdings leading to loss of status in rural life. Narasimha & Suri (2006) found supportive evidence to the earlier studies from their study in Andhra Pradesh. Mishra (2006) compared the normal cultivators with the suicide victim cultivators and found that indebtedness in proportion to the asset what the suicide victims owned is very high than the normal cultivators. In addition to this, the suicide victims' households have larger size of family with more women and non-workers. Sridhar (2006) observed that the suicides are concomitantly related to the shift in cropping pattern from traditional rain fed cereal crops to commercial crops in the recent past in Andhra Pradesh. Sanjay (2006) in his study "Suicide among cultivators in Sangroor" found that the shift of family values individualism towards collectivism and luxurious lifestyle of youth was cause of suicide.

However, these above-mentioned studies have given a scant attention to the following issues: firstly, the integration of the individual with institutions like family, economic and cultural needs to be comprehended more systematically. Secondly, the use of loans and its recovery process by formal and informal lending agencies also needs to be understood that affects the family and the individual in terms of social isolation, feelings of degradation of status, disintegration of joint household and drop-out of the children from schools. Thirdly, the occupational diversification of the family and the urban support system to the rural kin also needs to be looked at in order to comprehend this phenomenon more holistically in a comparative framework. An interdisciplinary attempt is made to realize the impact of the indebtedness on status order i.e., its effect on status, honour and prestige. If the status order goes down, then its relation with feelings of helplessness, hopelessness, isolation, worthless life, reduces social interaction and its relation with suicide.

After going through the literature on the recent trend of Indian studies, it can be observed that researchers have given much emphasis on suicide of farmers because recently in India the suicide of farmers has become a big problem for the society. So the major studies trend shows that, debt, crop failure and economic hardships are the leading causes of the suicide. Besides this domestic discard, alcohol and drug abuse are also the causes of suicide. Generally, the recent suicide studies in India emphasizes on poverty and situational factor as well as social factor as a cause of suicide. NCRB data shows that the low education, illness and family problems are the major causes of suicide. But the general perception about Sikkim is that there is no problem regarding poverty and education. However, employment was not a problem till recent times but today it has become one of the pressing problems in Sikkim. The state is pressed with the major problem of drug abuse/alcoholism. However, data reveals that out of all the suicide victims, only 3.6 per cent are due to drugs. Beside this, 90 per cent of the victims are below matric education and 25 per cent are farmers. Except this, 12.6 per cent are due to the problem of unemployment. If we see the literacy rate of Sikkim, it is very high but the enrolment in senior secondary and higher education is very low (Annual Reports, 2007-08 & 2004-05). In terms of the agricultural sector in Sikkim, it is the largest employer in the state. More than half of the population is engaged in agricultural practices. But its contribution to the State's GDP is gradually declining since 1999-2000 (Statistical Profile of Sikkim, 2007). Unemployment problem is worst in Sikkim. During the period 1993-2000, the rate of unemployment in the state had increased from 0.80 per cent to 3.1 per cent. In the urban areas of the state, unemployment had increased from 2.90 per cent to 8.40 per cent where as in rural areas it increased from 5.1 per cent to 17.5 per cent. Unemployment in the state increased among youth (15-29 years) and overall suicide victims (36%) are from this group (Sikkim Development Report, 2008).

Therefore, there is a need to explore the role of demographic factors on suicide. In Sikkim, most of the suicide victims are youth. Modernization, urbanization and changing lifestyle and values (individualism/collectivism) play an important role in suicide. On the basis of these facts, the objectives of the study are:

- To study the suicide pattern in Sikkim and to explore the unknown causes and other factors of suicide.
- To identify the influencing factors of suicide.
- To understand the psycho-social processes of suicide.

Method

The objective of the study is to study the pattern of suicide and examine the role of social and psychological factors. The study also seeks to examine the role of demographic variable in guiding the behaviour of individual. For this purpose the study is conducted in two phases.

Phase I

In phase I, for understanding the pattern of suicide in the last 10 years (2001-2009) secondary data provided by the Sikkim Crime Bureau was analyzed. After analyzing the secondary data and identifying the trends in the suicide pattern, the IInd phase of study was conducted.

Phase II

In Phase II, field study was undertaken to identify the role of psycho-social factor as mediator in suicidal behaviour. For this, Psychological autopsy was used as a method and interviews were also conducted with close members (Family/Friends) of the suicide victim.

Sample Criteria

Two basic criteria were followed for the sample selection

- Persons closest to the suicide victim (family/friend).
- People who lived with suicide victims for at least the last

15 days and members who continuously lived with the suicide victim.

There was no gender preference and, both males and females are taken as respondents in this study. Purposive and snowball sampling method was adopted for collecting the data. Assuming that the phenomological information is descriptive of an experience can be the best description from the individual (Geertz, 1973) narrative as the tool of inquiry was chosen. For maintaining the confidentiality of participants, each of them have been given a pseudo name.

Sample: In the first stage, total 25 people (from the suicide victim's family) were interviewed. After that, out of 25 respondents 7 respondents were interviewed as theoretical sampling.

Brief Introduction of Suicide Victims and Participants of Theoretical Sampling

1. Savita, 20 years old, separated, belonging to Kalimpong. Savita migrated from Kalimpong (to Gangtok), she left her father's home due to the financial crisis. Her mother had left her father long time back for her boyfriend and her father had become a drunkard. He is not financially well-off and works as a wood cutter.
   Respondent: Her friend who was working with her for the past 1 year.
2. Ramesh is 39 year old, SSC passed, separated, male who worked as a medical representative. But after some time he left the job and took to drinking.
   Respondent: His elder brother.
3. Jiwan 14 year old boy, studying in class 12th from Todong school. Besides studies he was actively involved in a music band group and was also very good in singing and dancing. Very extrovert by nature and liked by everyone.
   Respondent: His mother and sister.
4. Mohan 27 year old. Graduate from Scottish College in Kolkata. He had an elder sister who was married. His father and mother were government employees. In June 2009, his mother passed away. He also worked on Muster Roll in the Accounts department. He resided away from his family and was staying with his grandfather in his house.

Respondent: His Father.

5. Shyam was a 23 year old taxi driver. He studied till class V. He had a love marriage and his wife had a daughter from her previous marriage. After two years of marriage he got involved in an extra marital affair and started indulging in domestic violence. On the night of his suicide he had fought with his wife.
   Respondent: His wife.
6. Nisha, was a 26 year old lady and educated up to class seventh. She was married to a taxi driver and her husband rarely came home and did not give her any money for livelihood. Her husband had an extramarital affair. She was dependent on her brother and brother-in-law and used to live with them. But her sister-in-law was not supportive and they pressurized her to leave their home.
   Respondent: Brother in law.
7. Sonam 25 years old. Working as home guard in Sikkim Police, depressed after not getting a permanent job and was contemplating suicide for quite some time.
   Respondent: Sister.

Tool of Inquiry-Narrative Approach

Scholars in humanities and social sciences have debated on the nature and significance of narrative in literature, popular media, and personal documentary such as diaries and letters, oral stories of various kinds as well as the academic discipline itself. Most scholars point out the ubiquity of narrative in western societies and concur that all forms of narrative share the fundamental interest in experience, the interest in constructing and communicating meaning.

Within contemporary psychology, Bruner (1990) calls it "narrative mode of knowing" which gives privilege to the particular lived experiences rather than logical positivist constructs about variables and classes. It is an effort to approach the understanding of lives in the context rather than through a prefigured and narrowing lens. This means that it is not inherent in an act or experience, but is constructed through social discourses, it is generated by the linkages the participants make between aspects of life they have lived, and by the explicit linkages the researcher makes between their understanding and interpretation. This empathic stand orients the researcher to other people's experience and meaning making. It is communicated through narrative which in Geertz's (1973) suggestion is a way of thinking which involves looking over someone else's shoulder and observing the text they are reading and writing.

Narrative approach also forces the researcher to supersede dichotomies. People are extrovert or introvert, field dependent or field independent. Dichotomous thinking eliminates the inner contradiction that is intrinsic to human personality. Because people are composed of dialectic of opposites, the self inherent is dialogical self.

Narratives provide insight into people's thoughts, feelings, and words as they deal with issues of loss, sometimes failing and sometimes succeeding. Stories can heal as they endow experience with meaning. Harvey (1996) poignantly states, "Without the pain that comes with significant loss, there can be no story. Without the story telling, there can be no meaning. Without meaning, there can be no healing". Since suicide and their psycho-social process is to be understood retrospectively within the participants, narratives were considered to be an apt tool of inquiry, giving ample space to participants for reflecting back and forth in making sense of their experiences.

Research Location and Interviewing Setting

To study the phenomena, sample was taken from different areas in Sikkim, but majority of the respondents belonged to the surrounding areas of the capital, Gangtok like Tadong, Sayari, 6th mile, Intel, Diesel Power House, and Namnang.

Interview Setting

Ten narratives were taken for the study, some of which were conducted within the premise of the above-mentioned location. Consent was taken from the participants to pen down their interview, but before doing so, the researcher indulged in rapport formation and informal interactions with the participant so as to develop a sense of familiarity with them and making them comfortable about their participation in the study. It was during the informal sessions of interaction, that the researcher tried to locate those individuals whom they felt appropriate to be interviewed. Some opening questions were also framed during these informal sessions.

Interview Protocol

There was no fixed interview protocol for all the respondents. Order and nature of questions varied according to the respondents and their life experiences. In this free floating interview, the inquiry centred on eliciting the following information:

- Each participant was interviewed for more than an hour, depending on the flow.
- Who was the suicide victim and what his/her relation with the victim was.
- Family background and economic position of suicide victims.
- What were the Personality characteristics and the daily routine of the suicide victim.
- What were the changes (behavioural) they perceived in the suicide victim in the last one month.
- What were the incidences going on since last three months?
- If any medical help was sought or not?

The interviews were mostly conducted at his/her room/home of the victim. Receptivity and ease of the participant for giving the interview at that point of time was assured before initiating it. As it often happens, despite the consent, often the participants didn't seem relaxed enough so that the interview could be conducted. The situation was handled gently without making the participant feel unfit or blocked in any sense, eventually turning it into an informal chat.

Data Analysis and Theoretical Sampling

The first round of narratives was transcribed in order to code and to filter out the emerging codes and categories. Grounded theory involves three levels of coding. First level coding is a close objective analysis of the data, often line-by-line for obtaining the narrative data. Selected words, phrases, and other single units (termed as *in vivo* codes) of meaning are labelled as codes. This is the most basic and least abstract of the coding process. The three basic steps for coding are as: *Line by line coding* where the data is fractured for taking each line (sometimes words, phrases) with its uniqueness. The researcher tried labelling each line, treating it as an independent indicator. This was done for all the collected interviews.

Soon after line-by-line coding progressed through several transcripts, second level coding which is *focused coding* began, which is an aggregation of first level codes into categories. As preliminary categories emerged, the researchers developed a codebook that included a list of emerging categories, preliminary descriptions of these categories, inclusion and exclusion criteria of these categories, and exemplars of text. A text unit is a part of the narrative text that represents "a meaningful point of fact, story or idea expressed by the participant" (Grant Proposal, 2003, p. 61). Each category was operationally defined through the emerging codes from the transcripts.

Out of ten participants, six who presented the most relevant and richest data, considering both the quantity and quality of the textual units, were selected as the sample for the study. The two main analytic activities for the study were content analysis and constant comparison method to develop the theory.

The constant comparison method is an iterative process, a back and forth process of evaluating all sources of data (e.g. transcripts, memos, literature research, expert consults) (Schreiber, 2001). Ongoing category and theoretical development occurred through intensive analysis of twelve data rich transcripts. Adequate evidence was found from the data to saturate categories and support the emerging theoretical framework.

Once categories began to form, relationships between the categories were considered. This was third level coding, also called *theoretical coding*, which increased in abstractness (involving relationships between categories) and generated the theory extracted from and grounded in the data. However, even at the second level coding or the development of categories, theoretical coding took place in order to generate valid categories. Theoretical coding denoted a theoretical or hypothesis driven thought processing in analyzing and coding the data. The goal was to develop the abstractness and breadth of the informants' realities and meanings. Crucial to effective theoretical coding and theoretical sampling was ongoing, memoing and review of memoing. Memoing, the process of making conceptual notes about the coding process, including questions, comments, and suggestions for further data collection and analysis, was conducted through the data collection and analysis phase (Schreiber, 2001). Often substantive coding (first level and some second level coding) occurred concurrently with theoretical coding (third level and some second level coding). This was part of the constant comparison and iterative processes of grounded theory.

Also, at the third level of coding the level of abstractness was more open to formulating the core category (Schreiber, 2001). Several techniques were used to facilitate the analysis. Theoretical sampling was used to refine the developing categories by exploring the indicators of defined categories till it was completely saturated leaving no further inclusion of any new indicator. Theoretical sampling included several second interviews with the selected participants. Credibility of the analysis was ensured by ongoing immersion in the data on consultation with experts in the field whereas dependability was assured by extensive memoing, theoretical and methodological discussion, and the detailed audit trail.

Results

The results of the study are presented in two sections. The first section deals with the demographic analysis of last 10 years data for identifying the pattern of suicide along with demographic variable as provided by Sikkim Crime Bureau. The second section consists of qualitative data and its analysis in identifying social and cultural factors of suicide and its processes.

Section A

There is a particular major trend of suicide in Sikkim along with the demographic variable and the cause of suicides. There are some disparities in data provided by NCBR Sikkim with regard to the data pertaining to the professional categorization of the suicide victims. The categorization has been done only for 783 and the rest from the 835 are not accounted for. The Major trends are:

Table 14.1 shows that in 2000-2007, the total number of suicide that were committed was 835. Out of 835 cases, 84 (10.5%) suicide cases were recorded in 2000, 94 (11.25%) in 2001, 78 (9.34%) in 2002, 105 (12.5%) in 2003, 98 (11.73%) in 2004, 109 (13.05%) in 2005, 145 (17.36%) in 2006 and 122 (14.6%) in 2007. From the Table 14.2, we can infer that the number of suicides committed in Sikkim since 2004 has gradually increased.

According to NCBR, **Sikkim (2010),** the gender ratio of the individuals committing suicide is as follows. Out of the 835 suicide cases recorded till 2007, 530 are male and 305 are female. There is a large number of males committing suicide in Sikkim than their female counterparts.

Table 14.1: Annually suicide rate

Year	*No. of Studies*	*% of Suicide*
2000	84	10.50
2001	94	11.25
2002	78	9.34
2003	105	12.50
2004	98	11.73
2005	109	13.05
2006	145	17.36
2007	122	14.60
Total	**835**	**100.00**

Source: NCBR Sikkim, 2010.

Table 14.2: Gender ratio of suicide victims

Total	*Male*	*Female*
835	530	305

Source: NCBR Sikkim, 2010.

Table 14.2 shows that gender ratio of committed suicide during 2000-2007. Out of the 835 suicide cases recorded till 2007, 530 are male and 305 are female. There is a large number of males committing suicide in Sikkim than their female counterparts.

Table 14.3: After 2002 Suicide and Age Range

Age Range	*Male*	*Female*	*Total*	*%*
Below 15	15	13	28	4.30
15-29	156 (24)	79 (12.15)	235	36.15
30-44	124 (19.7)	62 (9.32)	186	28.6
45-59	73	43	116	17.87
60 & above	50	35	85	13.07
Total			**650**	

Source: NCBR Sikkim, 2010.

Table 14.3 shows that after 2002, the total number of suicide cases were 650. 4.30 per cent of suicide cases took place up to 15 years group, 36.15 per cent from 15-29 years, 28.6 per cent from 30-44 years, 17.87 per cent from 45-59 years and 13.07 per cent among those who are above 60 years of age. Over all 82.62 per cent suicide, cases occurred among the youth and middle aged individuals.

Table 14.4 illustrates the profession of the suicide victims. It is found that 25.63 per cent suicide victims were farmers and 18.65 per cent of them were males. 13.7 per cent were self employed and 10.46 per cent were males. Whereas 12.99 per cent were house wives, 12.6 per cent suicides took place due to unemployment, 9.50 per cent suicide victims were students, 8.79 per cent from private sector and 3 per cent from government sector.

Table 14.4: Profession of Suicide victims

Profession	*Male*	*Female*	*Total*	*Percentage*
House wife	0	108	108	12.99
Government Service	19	6	25	3.00
Private service	62	11	73	8.79
Public Sector Undertaking	1	1	2	0.24
Student	51	28	79	9.50
Unemployment	78	27	105	12.6
Self Employment (Businessman)	12	2	14	1.68
Farming	155	58	213	25.63
Self Employment (Others)	87	27	114	13.7
Retired	1	0	1	0.12
Others	27	22	49	5.89
Total			**783**	

Source: NCBR Sikkim, 2010.

Table 14.5: Educational Profile of Suicide victims

Education	*Male*	*Female*	*Total*	*%*
Uneducated	172	110	282	33.57
Primary	159	84	243	29.9
Middle	96	63	159	18.81
Matric	56	40	96	11.36
Intermediate	34	4	38	4.49
Diploma	6	2	8	0.95
Undergraduate	7	2	9	1.06
Postgraduate			835	

Source: NCBR Sikkim, 2010.

Table 14.5 shows the educational profile of suicide victims. Out of 835 cases, 33.35 per cent were uneducated, 29.9 per cent suicide victims were only educated up to the primary level, 18.81 per cent had studied up to Middle school, 11.36 per cent up to matric level, 4.49 per cent up to Intermediate level, 0.95 per cent had done some Diploma courses and 1.06 per cent were undergraduates. 93 per cent of the victims were individuals who were educated up to or below the matric level.

Table 14.6: Causes of Suicide in Sikkim

Causes	*Male*	*Female*	*Total*	*Percentage*
Bankruptcy	8	1	9	1.08
Illicit Relation	—	—	—	—
Non-settlement of Marriage	—	1	1	0.12
Not Having children	—	1	1	0.12
AIDS	—	1	1	0.12
Insanity	128	84	212	25.51
Prolonged Illness	37	15	52	6.25
Death from depression	4	1	5	0.60
Divorce	1	—	1	0.12
Drug abuse/Alcoholism	29	1	30	3.6
Failure in Exam.	5	2	7	0.84
Fail in Social reputation	2	4	6	0.72
Family problem	79	70	149	17.93
Love affairs	6	5	11	1.32
Physical Abuse	2	1	3	0.36
Poverty	3	—	3	0.36
Unemployment	8	—	8	0.96
Causes Unknown	169	70	239	29.72
Other Causes	42	43	85	10.22
Total			**823**	

Source: NCBR Sikkim, 2010.

Table 14.6 shows, that out of 823 suicide cases, insanity was the cause for 25.51 per cent cases, family problems was the cause for 17.93 per cent cases, prolonged illness for 6.25 per cent, drug abuse/ alcoholism for 3.6 per cent and 1.32 per cent were due to love affairs. The causes for 10.22 per cent were other than the ones mentioned above and the factors responsible for 29.72 per cent cases were not known.

Section B

Results from the Qualitative Analysis of Primary Data

After analyzing the narratives, following are the major indicators which guide the suicide behaviour separately or with interaction of another variables. The Meaning of indicator according to context is given below.

Table 14.7: Indicators and their definitions

Category	Indicators	Operational definition
Structural level	Employment Status	It is defined in terms of whether individual is employed or not, or what kind of job they have. Nature of job they are associated with.
	Modernization	Refers to the pattern of behaviour and values based on rational, logical, and scientific against the traditional customs, ritual, and values.
	Life style	Pattern of everyday habits associated with substance abuse (drug, alcohol) and spending free time with friend or outside the home.
	Childrearing Practices	The pattern of child rearing practices where family members giving more freedom and autonomy to the children
	Disturbed Relationship	Defined in terms of unfruitful and unpleasant relationship with family member and friends (with husband/wife, peer group, and male/female friends).
	Societal values	Societal values defined in terms of Individualism Priority for self and own family wife, son-daughter, etc. concern. Collectivism refers to priority given to all family (brother-sister, mother-father, uncle aunty, etc.) member living in the household than the individual; Bi-gamy, Extramarital affair etc.
	Generational conflict	Defined in terms of differences in terms of opinion, values and attitude.
Personal level	High Aspiration	Individual has high aspiration and desire in terms of materialistic orientation and leisure.
	High expectations	Individual has high expectation toward/from society family member, peer group and relative in terms of physical, emotional and economic support.
	Substance Abuse	Individuals are in the habit of taking drug, alcohol etc.
	Autonomy	Refers to a person's ability to think and act independently and take decisions regarding oneself and others without pressure.
	Freedom	The power or right to act, speak, think and live freely.
	Pre-emotional maturity	Defined in terms of emotional maturity before time. For example individual begins to understand the aspects of physical intimacy (sex, love and hate) before the age of 14 years.

(*Contd.*)

Table 14.7 (*Contd.*)

Category	*Indicators*	*Operational definition*
Subjective experience	Isolation	Defined in terms of cut-off, detachment or isolation from the main stream society/family/ peer group. Individuals experience being isolated from society.
	Loneliness	Occurs when a person has fewer interpersonal relationships than desired or when these relationships are not as satisfying as desired. It covers two streams emotional (absence of intimate attachment) and social (lack of friendship and network).
	Depression	Is a mental set or state of mind, where individuals have a state of sadness, gloom, pessimistic ideation with loss of pleasures in normally enjoyable activity, great unhappiness and hopelessness.
	Dependency for Survival	Individuals experience that they are dependent on other person for livelihood.
Negative Subjective experiences	Meaninglessness	Defined in terms of people having no meaning, direction or purpose in their life.
	Worthlessness	It is a negative mindset where individuals experience that they are useless, do not have real value and good quality.
	Self-Esteem	Defined in terms of positive and negative evaluation about own self.
	Guilt	"Feeling of responsibility or remorse for some offense, crime, wrong, etc., whether real or imagined." Or its feeling of having done something wrong.
	Shame	A painful emotion or feeling caused by a strong sense of guilt, embarrassment, unworthiness, or disgrace from one's awareness that one has done something wrong or foolish.
Mediating Variable	Low Future Orientation	It is a state of hopelessness where individual perceives future negatively.
	Justified Suicide Behaviour	Defined in terms of individuals showing positive behaviour before attempting suicide in terms of pro-social helping behaviour and fulfiling his/her responsibility.
	Internal Attribution	It is a process of evaluation where individual attributes own self for any cause.

Result and Interpretation

Suicidal behaviour is not always the symptom or result of psychiatric disorder but is also due to tiredness of life dependent on external circumstances. An essential distinction between suicidal tendencies are expression of different situations of life crisis.

Table 14.2 shows the suicide pattern of Sikkim *i.e.* in last ten years, 63.47 per cent suicide victims were male and 36.35 per cent were female. In terms of age and suicide, Table 14.3 shows that 36.15 per cent suicide victims belonged to 15-29 age group, 28.6 per cent belonged to 30-44 age group, 17.65 belonged to 45-59 age group and 13.07 per cent belonged to above 60 years. However, 4 per cent suicide victims were below 15 years. In context of education, Table 14.5 shows that 33.57 per cent suicide victims were illiterate, 60.07 per cent below high school, 4.49 per cent Intermediate and1.06 per cent graduate. In context of employment, Table 14.4 shows that 25.63 per cent suicide victims were farmers, 13.7 per cent were self-employed, 12.99 per cent were housewives, 12.6 per cent suicides victims were unemployed, 9.50 per cent suicide victims were students, 8.79 per cent were working in the private sector and 3 per cent were working in the government sector. In context of causes of suicide, Table 14.6 shows that 25.51 per cent suicide is caused due to Insanity, 17.93 per cent due to family problems, 6.25 per cent due to prolonged illness, 3.6 per cent due to drug abuse/alcoholism, and 1.32 per cent due to love affairs. Whereas 10.22 per cent cases account for other causes than those mentioned and the causes for 29.72 per cent was not known.

Table 14.7 shows that suicide instigating factors in terms of personal level factor structural level factor, subjective experiences and mediating factors in suicide. In personal factor, high aspiration, high expectations, substance abuse, autonomy and freedom can be witnessed; and in structural level variable, employment status, modernization, lifestyle, childrearing practices, societal values, disturbed relationship and generational conflict are illustrated. However in context of subjective experiences individual have feeling of isolation, loneliness, depression, and dependency for survival whereas in negative subjective experience individual had feeling of meaninglessness, worthlessness, self-esteem, guilt, shame and low future orientation. In context of mediating variables, internal attribution, justified suicidal behaviour and low level of education work as the mediating variable in suicide.

Figure 14.1 reveals that individual lived within a psychological comfort zone where individual lived with own fantasy, values, life-style, and what he needed in his life. Basically comfort zone is type of mental conditioning and behavioural state that cause a person to create and operate in mental boundaries; such behaviours create an

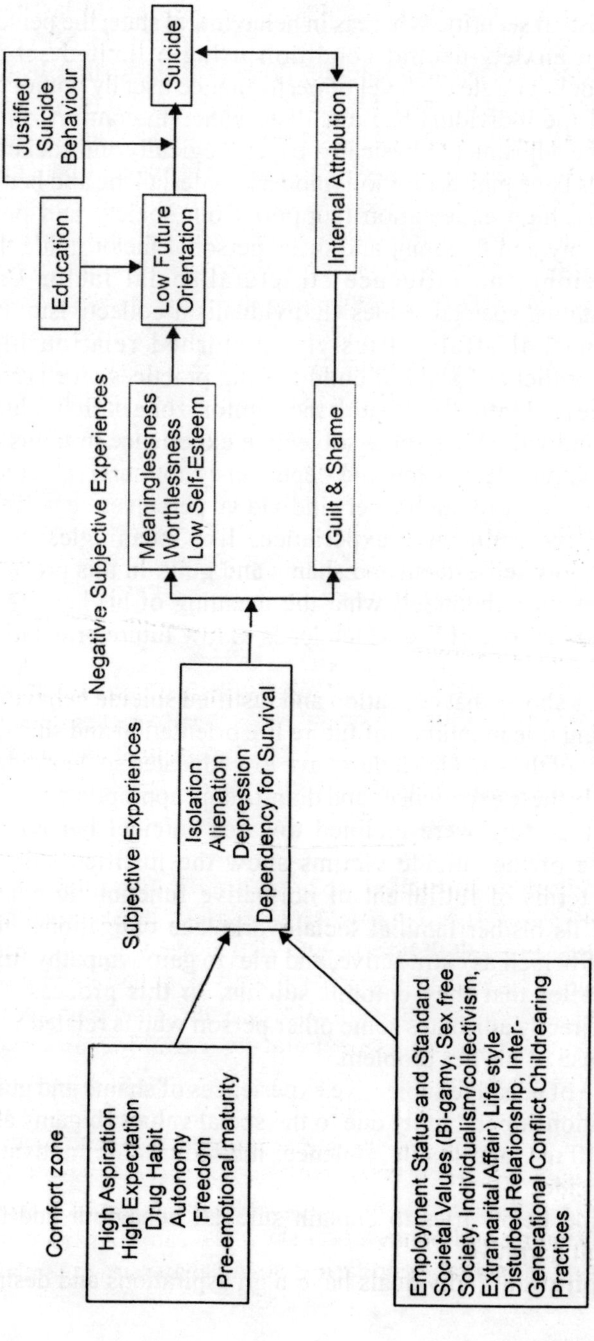

Fig. 14.1: Pictorial Presentation of Suicide behaviour in Sikkim

unfounded sense of security. Whereas in behavioural state, the person operates in an anxiety-neutral condition using a limited set of behaviours to deliver a steady level of performance usually without a sign of risk. If the individual had any disturbance in comfort zone, they try to make adjustment physically, psychologically and socially.

Individuals have high aspiration (modern/materialistic and better quality of life), high expectation (support from society and peer group), autonomy and freedom, and these personal factor guide the human behaviour and influence structural/social factor *i.e.*, employment status, societal values (individualism collectivism, bi-gamy, extramarital affair), lifestyle, disturbed relationship, generational conflict and style of child rearing practices ***vice versa***, and these process of influence disturb the comfort zone of individual.

Then the individual has some subjective experience in terms of isolation, alienation, depression and dependency for survival which are the emotional state of mind where individual perceives negatively and have negative subjective experiences like meaninglessness, worthlessness, low self-esteem and shame and guilt. In this process, individual questions about self what the meaning of his/her life is and what is the purpose of life which leads to low future orientation and suicide?

Figure 14.1 shows that education and justified suicide behaviour play a mediating role in journey of future life orientation and suicide. Primarily, most of the suicide victims have low educated so they didn't handle carefully these experiences and didn't adopt appropriate coping strategy and therefore were inclined towards suicidal behaviour. Besides, some of the suicide victims show the justified suicide behaviour in terms of fulfilment of normative functioning where individual fulfils his/her familial/social/workplace obligations, and shows himself/herself as extra active, and tries to gain sympathy from society, and after that they commit suicide. In this process, the individual indirectly attributes some other person who is related with him as the cause of his/her problem.

In the case of negative subjective experiences of shame and guilt, disturbed relationship in family due to the social values (bigamy and extramarital affair), and family violence, individuals are motivated to commit suicide.

The section below tries to explain suicidal behaviour and the process though narrative.

High Aspiration: Individuals have high aspirations and desires in terms of modern lifestyle, materialistic orientation and leisure and these aspirations influence the structural values and individual life.

Ramesh was 39-year old medical representative. He has four brothers and two younger sisters, they are all well settled. Sisters are settled in their own house after marriage and two elder brothers are government employees and are separated and having good financial conditions and quality of life. He was living with his father, mother and younger brother and his family. In his family, his wife is working and he has one child who is studying in class 6th.

"A class 10th educated he worked as Medical representative in a pharmacy company and his pay was not satisfactory, but he continued the job but had high aspiration which was not fulfilled by this job so one day he came home and next day after 10 a.m. he was not ready to go to office when his wife asks him go to office he tells her that he has quit his job. His wife tries to convince him but he is not willing, and in the evening he went outside home and came late night and he had taken alcohol. Before that he was a social drinker but after that he continued to take alcohol. He spent most of the time with his friend who are from rich family background. Beside this he started playing Lottery. His wife continuously pressurized him to join some job and quit alcohol but he didn't pay any heed to her. After that his wife wanted separation, and took transfer to another district in North Sikkim and tried to maintain distance from him. After this, he increased the frequency of taking alcohol and reduced the frequency of communication with family member. His father who is a very renowned politician in Sikkim, tried to convince him but he had bitter arguments with him which created generational conflict between father and son and this incidence 2 or 3 time take place between them after that he blocked the communication with all family member and family member also reduce the communication except his mother. He closed himself in a room and only watching T.V. and came outside during lunch and dinner time. He was also suffering from liver problem one he told with his younger brother, but he didn't inform another family member and he take for this LIV-52 without prescription of the doctor. He was emotionally very close to his wife After 3-4 month of incidence (separation) he went to meet with his wife and son in north Sikkim and after 3 days, he committed suicide. His brother told us after coming back from north Sikkim he was very sad and he didn't talk to anybody and didn't go outside."

The narrative reveals that the individual had high aspirations, due to which he had left the job which affected his family life and he felt alienated and isolated and subsequently committed suicide.

High Expectation and Societal values: Societal values can be perceived to be moving in the direction of individualism from collectivism. In such conditions, individual is witnessed to have orientation towards the self (husband, wife, and children) and if these are perceived negatively, it affects the individual behaviour. However, these disturbed relationships lead the individual to suicide.

For example, the case of 20 year old lady who had been married since 2-3 years and her husband was a driver by profession. She was staying in her maternal house. She had her mother, two brothers and sister-in-laws and an elder sister who had been married.

Her relation with her husband was not congenial, both of them were living separately and generally her husband used to be out for months together and whenever he came back he indulged in battering. Her husband's strange behaviour towards her was due to the fact that he had an extramarital relation and he was living with that woman. She along with her daughter lived in the house of her parents and although they gave her food she was subjected to a lot of emotional criticism from her sister-in-laws who accused her of being dependent on them and not adjusting with her husband. When these verbal altercations would become unbearable she would go to her elder sister house and live with them. This process continued for very long time and every time she visited her parents' place her sister in-laws always asked her to go back to her husband's house and this really disturbed her.

One day she visited her sister's house and told her brother-in-law that after my death please look after my daughter. Her brother-in- law was not happy on hearing this and she finally switched over the matter saying I am just having fun. She further added saying "you are my father, brother and brother-in-law and she burst into tears". That day she was very busy with the household chores. She prepared non-vegetarian food for everyone and was working continuously in comparison to other regular days. Later in late afternoon she consumed alcohol which was very surprising for her brother-in-law because she never drank and later that evening she committed suicide.

From this narrative it is clear that her sense of dependency on her brothers and sister-in-laws made her feel depressed because they were alienating her. She was strongly and negatively affected by their rejection, and this resulted in low self-esteem and finally suicide. However just before suicide, she was actively involved in the household work and trying to create a positive image of herself. Indirectly she was trying to gain the sympathy of the individuals around her which would finally justify her suicide.

The other case which also shows the influence of extramarital affairs on the life of the individual, and encouraged the suicidal behaviour is as follows:

For example 23 year old male married with a divorcee who had a two and half year old child also. He was deeply in love with his wife and always carried her photograph in his purse and flaunted in front of his friends saying that his wife is an actress. He deeply loved his daughter and also cared for her. After some time he started coming home late and one day his wife found the photograph of a lady under his pillow. This really angered his wife and she told her husband in clear terms that "I am your wife and it is your duty and responsibility to look after me and my daughter, you have to financially support me and I am not interested in your escapades outside the house". This incident marked a turning point in their relationship and henceforth he always started coming to the house in an inebriated state. There was always verbal exchange of words and he would even physically assault his wife. When the effect of alcohol would lessen he would always feel very sorry, guilty and apologise to his wife. It was in one of these drunken states that he assaulted his wife with the screwdriver following which she really fell ill. However, he continued to enquire about her health, and wheather she was taking medicines or not.

On the day of the suicide his wife was very ill, when he came home, he enquired about her health and told her that he would prepare some food for her. He went to the kitchen and all of a sudden came out and started beating his wife. The physical assault was so much that his wife had to take shelter in her cousin's house who lived in the neighbourhood. Following this incidence he left the house and did not returne at night. This did not trouble anyone because whenever such incidence happened he would not return home for weeks. However the next day his body was found hanging and people identified him by his tattoo.

This narrative explains that when he came back to his conscious mind the feeling of guilt and shame surrounded him and he blamed himself for the entire incident and this finally resulted in suicide.

Disturbed Relationship and Lifestyle

People have unpleasant relationships with family members and friends, which generally leads to use of drugs, alcohol, smoking and whiling away free time with friends. This becomes a pattern as seen in case of Savita. She was 20 years old, separated, belonged to Kalimpong. Savita migrated from Kalimpong, she basically left her home due to financial crisis. Her mother had left her father a long time back for her boyfriend and her father had become a drunkard. He is not financially well off and works as wood cutter.

The victim moved from Kalimpong to Gangtok two years ago in search of a job. She belonged to very poor family and her father was a woodcutter, her mother had left her in her childhood for another man and her father had taken to alcoholism. Initially she took up a small job in a restaurant and it was here she met this middle aged men who was a driver by profession. Driven by peer pressure she succumbed to it and finally married him. This marriage did not last for long because this man was not good looking and far beyond her age. She shifted jobs and started working in another restaurant. By nature she was an extrovert who loved to interact with people, she was very fond of dressing up and was very conscious about her looks. In her new workplace she slept in separate room from her friends and used to sleep talk. After she had moved in to her new job she attempted suicide by slashing her wrist, however with good counselling from the hotel owner she started enjoying her life again. She was very popular with the customer who visited the hotel and every evening a lot of school children would visit the hotel and she was very close and friendly to the boys.

According to the hotel owner she had started consuming alcohol and even stealing money from the counter on some pretext or the other. For example she would say her mother is hospitalized and in reality she had actually not seen her mother. She was a large hearted girl who never could save money because she spent always on others, for instance when her ex-husband relatives came to the hotel she fed them free of cost and got that money deducted from her salary.

A few months before suicide she went to her father and her sister who was living with her father, when she returned she was extremely disturbed and confessed to her friend that her father had asked her to come along with her husband next time and this really upset her because she had not apprised her father about her separation from her husband, after this incidence she had become very quiet and spent most of her time in seclusion. Her friends believed that she was in a relationship with one of the school children who frequented the hotel, she had approached him and probably the boy had refused her proposal. Because of examination the children were not visiting the hotel frequently but on the day of suicide that boy had come to the hotel and she had also talked to him. A few days back she was sitting near window and told her friend that she would want to jump out of the window and enjoy the site of her body falling in the valley.

On the day of the suicide she actively charged and appeared very happy she even helped her friends with their works and later in the afternoon see went in the bathroom and committed suicide by hanging herself from the ventilator. After her suicide when her father visited the hotel to collect her belongings he told the hotel owner that she was very depressed after her mother left her, she had even attempted suicide twice at home. And her friend also apprised that whenever she was sitting alone she always had her hand around her neck.

This narrative shows that due to disturbed relationship with the mother, husband and friend the victim feels isolated, and depression sets in which results in feeling of meaninglessness, worthlessness, and low future orientation which result in suicide.

Pre-Emotional maturity: defined in terms of emotional maturity before time. For example, individual begins to understand the aspects of physical intimacy (sex, love and hate) before the age of 14 years. Individuals who are actively involved in this process face disturbance in relationships, resulting in destructive behaviour and eventually suicide.

For example: *The case of Jiwan, 14 year old boy, studying in class 10th Todong school. Beside studies he was actively involved in a music band group and was also very good in singing and dancing. He was very extrovert by nature and was liked by everyone. His father was a bus driver and his mother ran a small tea stall, assisted by his elder sister. He was a very loving person and wanted to join the navy when he grew up. After his class 10th exam he was a little disturbed because he had not performed well in his maths paper. After his exam he joined a dance class in Deorali where he met a girl who was older than him, but he was instantly attracted toward her and even proposed her. She, however turned down his proposal saying that I am older than you and you are like my younger brother, despite that he* *continued to visit her house and also confided in his elder sister who also told him to forget about that girl. After this he became a loner and was not even talking to his friends at school and family members. One day before committing suicide he again went to propose the girl, who again turned down his proposal and on this he told the girl "Do you want to see what I can do for you, I can do anything for you, wait and watch". On the day of suicide he was actively involved with his mother in the hotel. Late afternoon when he finished all the work, he went up to his room and committed suicide. He however left a suicide note which read like this "Maa, Baba, Didi mujhe maaf kur do, main janta hoon ki mai galat kar raha hoon, lekin mujhe kuch accha nahi lag raha hai, mera jeevan bekar hai. (mother, father elder sister I know that I am doing something wrong, but I am not liking anything in this world and my life is worthless. Please forgive me.)*

It is clear from this narrative, how the pre-emotional maturity leads to negative subjective experience and eventually suicide.

Substance Abuse: Here emphasis is on the individuals involved in taking drugs, alcohol, and other narcotic analgesics. Such behaviour is the outcome of peer group pressure, socialization practices and curiosity of the individual and one of its negative consequences is suicide.

For example: Case Mohan 27 year old. Graduate from Scotish College in Kolkatta. He had one married elder sister. His Father and mother were government employees. In June 2009 his mother passed away. He also worked on Muster-roll in the Account department. He stayed away from his family, but along with his grandfather.

"He was very kind hearted, generous and believed in helping everybody in need. After his mother passed away his father divided his mother's assests between the two siblings which was deposited in their names. He used to take 100-500 rupees as pocket money from his father and he would always argue over this with his father. He would leave his house early in the morning and come back late at night, and some time never return. His father however felt that if got married his behaviour would change and this was another reason which generated intergenerational conflict.

Once a beggar came to his house asking for alms. His father instead of giving him any money gave the beggar a very long lecture and this really infuriated the boy and he said "if you don't want to give the money don't give it but don't preach the poor begger. It is all my money and I will be spend thrift and spend all the money". His father said that he never refused his son for anything, if he asked for 100 Rs. He always gave him extra and same was the case with his father's elder brother also (Tauji).

One day before committing suicide he told his father that he has to go to Delhi and he need 2-3 thousand rupees, which his father gave. He went to his uncle's house and told him that his girlfriend's mother is very ill and I need Rs. 1000 to take her to Delhi. This was the first time his father and uncle had both given him the exact amount of money he asked for. He looked quite upset that day and that night he went to stay with his friends. Next day in the evening he had committed suicide. From the postmortem report it was revealed that he had taken drugs and from his pocket was retrieved a list of persons who he owed money. His father could not come to terms with the fact that his son was taking drugs. After his son passed away his father always continued to insist that the government should control drugs in Sikkim.

This narrative explains that how child rearing practices leads to substance abuse and suicide.

On the basis of these narratives, it is found that how personal level factors, structural/social level factors, subjective experience and negative subjective experiences leads to suicide.

Main Findings of the Study

After 2002, the suicide rates in Sikkim has increased slightly. Most of the suicide victims belong to 15-44 years age cohort. Most of the suicide victims are youth and Middle aged. Also, most of the suicide victims are farmers (25.63%) followed by Self-employed (13.7%), unemployed 12.6 per cent, student 9.5 per cent and 12.99 per cent suicide victims are housewives. 93 per cent suicide victims had education below the matric level. Out of 835 suicide cases, the reason for suicide was not known for 29.72 per cent people, 25.51 per cent cases of suicides are caused by Insanity, 17.93 per cent suicides are due to family problems and 6.25 per cent due to prolonged illness.

In personal level factors: high aspiration, high expectation, substance abuse, pre-emotional maturity, autonomy and freedom are the cause for triggering suicide. In structural/societal level factors: employment status, modernization, lifestyle, child rearing practices, disturbed relationship, societal values, and generational conflict are the triggering cause of suicide. In subjective experience: loneliness, depression, isolation, and dependency for survival and in negative subjective experiences: Meaninglessness, worthlessness, low self-esteem, guilt, shame and low future orientation are the triggering causes of suicide. Internal attribution and justified suicide behaviour are the triggering cause of suicide. Low education can be a potential cause of suicide.

Conclusion

The objective of the study is to see the pattern of suicide in Sikkim and to see the role of Psycho-social factors in Suicide. The findings reveal that in personal causes: high aspiration, high expectation, substance abuse, autonomy and freedom are the causes of suicide. The trend of suicide shows that most of the suicide victims are farmers, self-employed, unemployed individuals and students. Here one major cause is identified i.e., nature of job and their income, how much they earn for livelihood. According to Sikkim Statistical Report (2006-07) the PER CAPITA INCOME (PCI) was Rs. 25872 per year, it means Rs. 2156 per month and that is not sufficient for running a livelihood. In this process the people are dependent on another family members for livelihood and have higher expectation for support. But structural level variable in terms of social values show that society is heading from collectivism towards individualism. So increase in consumption decreases support in the family (Versa-Sanso, 2007). Some of the studies have found that those who enjoy close relationship with others enjoy better psychological health (IOM, 2001; Sarason *et al.*, 1990) and Heikkeinn *et al.* (1997) found that interpersonal and job/finance related problem are causes of suicide.

Another cause of suicide in personal factor is substance abuse. In Sikkim there is no restriction on alcohol and there is social and cultural acceptance of alcohol so people consume alcohol. Research on substance abuse and suicide shows that substance abuse affects the suicidal risk and antisocial behaviour and the use of alcohol and other drugs increases suicidal tendencies (Putnins, 1995; Marttunen, *et al.*, 1994).

In context of age and suicide, most of the suicide victims belong to 15-44 years of age group. 36.15 per cent suicide victims belong to 15-29 years of age group and 28.6 per cent belong to 30-44 years of age group. If we see the personal and structural level factors which are functioning in middle and young age group, the major studies on age and suicide show that personality disorder, alcohol dependency, anxiety disorder and depression are causes of suicide (Foster *et al.*; 1997; Lesage, *et al.* 1994). But here we find that some structural and personal factors are functioning simultaneously and increasing the suicidal tendencies and rate like generational conflict, autonomy, freedom, life style, disturbed relationship and extra marital affair. Research on generational relations shows that decreased autonomy and freedom increases dissatisfaction and negative subjective experiences in terms of stress and strain in relationship in youth (Gangrade, 1976; Kagtcibasi, 1982; Verma & Satyanarayana, 2007).

Result also shows that subjective experiences as well as negative subjective experiences are the outcome of personal and structural level variable functioning. Subjective experience is psychological and emotional state where individual feels lonely, depressed and isolated, and this leads to negative subjective experiences in terms of meaninglessness, worthlessness, low self-esteem, shame and guilt. Mental illness, particularly those with psychological symptoms like depression, hopelessness, stress and guilt increase the probability of suicide (Rodomsky, *et al.*, 1999).

As the crisis in life becomes intensified over time, the actors feel or perceive more and more stress and pain and this deteriorates their social interaction, which reduces social esteem and increases depression which directs to meaninglessness. The intensified depression and reduction of self-esteem and deterioration of control on social interaction seems to be unbearable and suicide is seen as the only remedy. It leads to isolation and loneliness from other actors of social interaction and also results in shame and guilt at the level of self. This process leads to hopelessness which is a predictor of low future orientation and suicide (Abramson, Metalsky & Alloy, 1989; Abramson, Alloy & Hegan, 1998).

Other factors which are the causes of suicide are guilt and feeling of shame. Guilt can be described as a "bothered conscience" or a "feeling of culpability for offence" (Bales, 1998). When individual feels guilty, he feels responsible for an action that he regrets. People can feel ashamed, unworthy or embarrassed about action for which they are responsible. In this process individuals attribute themselves for the cause (Peterson *et al.,* 1982). However, if the individual externally attributes for his/her situation, then he/she tries to justify the suicide behaviour and tries to gain sympathy from society and indirectly blames people whom the individual perceives as a cause for their problems.

There is another cause which is playing the mediating variable role in the process of suicide *i.e.*, education. Data reveals that 93 per cent suicide victims have education below the matric level. However in Sikkim, the literacy rate is 83 per cent but the enrolment rate in high schools is only 5.15 per cent (Joint Director, PME, HRDD, Government of Sikkim 2008-09) and dropout rates in 2007 after 10th class was 25.42 per cent (Sikkim Development Report 2008 and Draft Annual Plan 2009-10, Part II). It means that most of the population of Sikkim is literate but they do not have sufficient education for their livelihood. When they don't have sufficient education they are not in the position to use the appropriate coping strategy for handling the stressful situation or are unable to handle properly the stressful situation which leads to suicide. Education and coping strategy are positively correlated. If the individuals have higher education, they use better coping strategies: problem focused coping, positive refraining, active coping, religion and instrumental support (Charles & Rudolf, 1987; Tuncau, Musabak, Gok, & Kutlu, 2008) which can act as an impediment to committing suicide.

REFERENCES

Abramson, L.Y.; Alloy, L.B.; Hogan, M.E.; Whitehouse, W.G.; Cornette, M.; Akhavan, S.; and Chiara, A. (1998). Suicidality and cognitive vulnerability to depression among college students: A perspective study. *Journal of Adolescence*, 21, 157-171.

Abramson, L.Y.; Metalsky, G.J. and Alloy, L.B. (1989). Hopelessness depression: A theory based subtype of depression, *Psychological Review.* 96 (2), 358-372.

Adam, K.S.; Bouckoms, A.; and Streiner, D. (1982). Parental loss and family stability in attempted suicide. *Archives of General Psychiatry*, 39, 1081-1085.

Assadi, M. (1998). "Farmers' Suicides: Signs of Distress in Rural Economy", *Economic and Political Weekly*, Vol. 33, No. 14, pp. 747-48.

Bales, N. (1998). "Coping with Shame and Guilt." http://fbg-church.org/articles/guilt. htm

Baumeister, R.F. (1990). Suicide as escape from self. *Psychological Review*. 90-113.

Bilton, T. (1996). *Introductory Sociology*, Macmillan Press.

Black, S.T. (1993). Comparing genuine and stimulated suicide notes: A new perspective. *Journal of Counselling & Clinical Psychology*, 61 (4), 699-702.

Bruner, J. (1990). *Acts of Meaning,* Cambridge: Harvard University Press.

Charles J.H.; Rudolf H.M. (1987). Personal and contextual determinants of coping strategy. *Journal of Personality and Social Psychology,* Vol. 52 (5), 946-955.

Deshpande, R.S. 2002: "Suicide by Farmers in Karnataka: Agrarian Distress and Possible Alleviatory Steps", *Economic and Political Weekly,* Vol. 37, No. 25, pp. 2601-10.

Douglas, J.D. (1967). *The Social Meanings of Suicide*, Princeton, N.J.: Princeton University Press.

Durkheim, E. (1951). *Suicide: A study in Sociology* (translation). By John A. Spaulding and George Simpson (New York: Free Press). (Originally published in 1897).

Fleer, J. and Pasewark, R.A. (1982). Prior public health agency contacts of individuals committing suicide. *Psychological Review*, 50 (3, Pt. 2), 1319-1324.

Foster, T.; Gillespie, K.; Mcclelland, R. and Patterson, C. (1999). Risk factors for suicide independent of DSM–III-R Axis I disorder. *British Journal of Psychiatry*, 175-179.

Freud, S. (1920). *A general introduction to psycho-analysis*. NewYork: Boni & Liveright.

Freud, S. (1936). *The basic writings of Sigmund Freud* (A.A. Brill, Ed. and Trans). New York. (Original work published in 1940).

Futterman, Samuel (1961). *Suicide* in Norman L. Farberow and Edwin S. Shneidman eds. *The Cry for Help* New York: McGraw-Hill.

Gangrade, K.D. (1976). *Crisis of values: A study in generation gap*, New Delhi: Chetana Publications.

Geertz, C. (1973). *The Interpretation of Cultures: Selected Essays*. New York: Basic Books.

Gibbs, J.P. and Martin, W.T. (1964). *Status Integration and Suicide: A Sociological Study*, (Eugene, Oregon: University of Oregon Books).

Halbwachs, M. (1930). *Les Causes du Suicide* (Paris: Alcan).

Harvey, J.H. (1996). *Embracing their Memory: Loss and the social psychology of storytelling*. Needham Heights, M. A: Allyn & Bacon.

Heikkin, M.E.; Henriksson, M.M.; Isomesta, E.T.; Marttunen, M.J. (1997). Recent life events and suicide in personality disorder. *Journal of Nervous & Mental Disease*, 185 (6), 373-381.

Heikkin, M.E.; Henriksson, M.M.; Isomesta, E.T. and Marttunen, M.J. (1997). Recent life events and suicide in personality disorder. *Journal of Nervous and Mental Disease*, 185 (6), 373-381.

Higgins, E.T. (1987). Self discrepancy. A theory relating self and affect. *Psychological Review*, 94, 319-340.

I.O.M. (Institute of Medicine). (2000). *Health and Behaviour: The Interplay of Biological, Behavioural and Societal Influence*. Washington, DC: National Academy Press.

Iyer K.G. and M.S. Manik. (2000). "*Indebtedness, Impoverishment and Suicides in Rural Punjab*", Indian Publishers and Distributors, Delhi.

Jacobs, D. and Klein, M.E. (1993). The Expanding role of psychological autopsies. In A.A. Leenars (Ed.), *Suicidology.* Northvale, NJ: Jason Aronson.

Jodhka, S. (2006). "Beyond Crises: Rethinking Contemporary Punjab Agriculture", *Economic and Political Weekly*, Vol. 16, No. 4, pp. 1530-1537.

Kagtcibasi, C. (1982b). *The Changing Values of Children in Turkey, Honolulu,* Hawaii: East-West Center, Publ. No. 60-E.

Kalingman, A., and Hocdorf, Z. (1993). Coping with distress and self harm: The Impact of primary preventation Program away adolescents. *Journal of Adolescence*, 16, 121-140.

Kumar, U.; Mandal, M.K. (Ed.) (2010). *Suicidal Behaviour: Assessment of People-at-Risk*, Sage, New Delhi.

Kumar, P. and Sharma, S.L. (1998). *Suicides in Rural Punjab,* Institute for Development and Communication, Chandigarh.

Leenaars, A.A. (1989). Suicide across the adult life-span: An archival study. Crisis, 10, 132-151.

Leenaars, A. (1992). Suicide notes of the older adult. *Suicide and Life-Threatening Behaviour*, 22 (1), 62-79.

Lesage, A.D.; Boyer, R.; Grunberg, F.; Vonier, C.; Morrisstte, R.; Menard-Buteau, C.; and Loyer, M. (1994). Suicide and mental disorder: a case-control study of young men. *American Journal of Psychiatry*, 151, 1063-1068.

Mann, J. J.; A. Apter, J.; Bertolote, A.; Beautrais, D.; Currier, A.; Hass *et al.*, (2005). Suicide Prevention Strategies: A Systematic Review. *Journal of American Medical Association*, 294 (16), 2064-74.

Marttunen, M.; Aro, H.; Henriksson, M., and Lonnquist, J.K. (1994). Psychosocial stressors more common in adolescent suicide with alcohol abuse compared with depressive adolescent suicide. *Journal of American Academy of Child & Adolescent Psychiatry*, 33: 490-497.

Marwaha, S. (2005). How best to tackle the problem of suicide. *The Tribune* Chandigarh, 25 June.

Menninger, K. (1938). *Man against himself.* New York: Harcourt, Brace & World.

Mishra, S. (2006). Suicides of Farmers in Maharashtra, Report Submitted to the Government of Maharashtra, IGIDR Mumbai. http://www.igidr.ac.in/suicide/suicide.htm. (accessed 8th June 2006).

Sikkim Annual Report 2004-05.

Sikkim Annual Report 2007-8.

Sikkim Development Report 2008.

Sikkim Draft Annual Plan 2009-10 Part II.

Sikkim Statistical Profile, 2006-07.

Sinsbury, P. (1956). *Suicide in London: An Ecological Study* (New York: Basic Books).

Stekel, W. (1910). Symposium on suicide. In: FRIEDMA, P. (Ed.). *On Suicide*. New York: International Universities Press, 1977. pp. 33-141.

Tuncay, T.; Musbak, I.; Gok, D.E., and Kuttu, M. (2008). The relationship between anxiety, coping strategies and characteristic of patients with diabetes. *Health and Quality of Life Outcome*. http: //www. hglo. com/ content/6/1/79.

Vasavi, A.R. (1999). "Agrarian Distress in Bidar: Market, State and Suicides", *Economic and Political Weekly*, Vol. 34, No. 32, pp. 2263-68.

Verma, S.K. and Satyanarayana, A. (2007). Influencing Factors of Intergenerational relations in Indian Family: A Narrative Approach?, *Journal of Research & Development*, HelpAge India.

Mohanakumar, S. and Sharma, R.K. (2006). Analyses of Farmer
Kerala, EPW, Vol. XLI, No. 16, pp. 1553-58.

Mohanty, B.B. (2005). "We are Like the Living Dead: Farmer S
Maharashtra, *Journal of Peasant Studies*, Vol 32, No. 2, pp.

Movement against State Repression. (1998). Cited in Singh, J. (Ed
in Rural Punjab, Monograph series IV.

Narasimha Rao, P. and Suri, K.C. (2006). Dimensions of Agrariar
in Andhra Pradesh, *EPW*, Vol. XLI, No. 16, pp. 1546-52.

Nisbet, A. Robert (1965*). Emile Durkheim*. Englewood Cliffs, Ne
Prentice Hall.

Paykel, E.S. (1991). Depression in Women. *British Journal of Psy*
158 (10), 22-29.

Personal Relationships, 7, 495–506.

Peterson; Samel; Baeyer, V.; Metalsky, A. and Seligman (1982). Attril
Style Questionnaire in Robinson, J.P., Shaver, P.R. & Wrightsm
(Ed.) *Measures of Personality and Social Psychological Attitua*
(1) Measures of Psychological Attitudes Series. Academic Pres

Putnins, A.L. (1995). Recent drug use and suicidal behaviour among
offenders. *Drug and Alcohol Review*, 14, 151-158.

Revathi, E. (1998). Farmers' Suicides: Missing Issues, *Economi*
Political Weekly, May 16, 1998.

Rodmsky, E.D.; Hass, G.L.; Mann, J.J. and John, A.S. (1999). Su
Behaviour in patients with schizophrenia and other psychotic di
American Journal of Psychiatry, 1956: 1590-1595.

Sanjay (2006). *Social Psychological study of Suicide among Cultiva*
Punjab. Unpublished manuscript. Department of Psychology, Al
University.

Sarason, I.G.; Pierce, G.R., and Sarason, B.R. (1990). Social sup
interactional processes: A triadic hypothesis. *Journal of Socia*

Schreiber, R.S. (2001). The 'How to' of grounded theory: Avoi
pitfalls. In R.S. Schreiber & P.N. Stern (Eds.), *Using ground*
in nursing, pp. 56-84. New York: Springer Publishing.

Shiva Vandana and Afsar H. Jafri. (1998). *Stronger than Steel*
Movement against Globalisation and the Gopalpur Steel P
Delhi: Research Foundation for Science, Technology and E

Shneidman, E. (1980). *Voices of death*. New York: Harper & Ro

Shneidman, E. (1993). *Suicide as Psychache: A clinical Appro*
Destructive Behaviour. London. Jason Aronson Inc.

Shridhar, V. (2006). "Why do Farmers Commit Suicide? The cas
Pradesh" *Economical & Political Weekly*, Vol. XLI, No.1
1565.

15

Knowledge, Attitude and Behaviour Change towards Safe Motherhood Practices—Findings of the Exploratory Study from Western Uttar Pradesh

Sasibala Rai Sharma

Introduction

Safe motherhood comprises of a series of initiatives, practices, protocols and service delivery guidelines designed to ensure that women receive high-quality gynaecological, family planning, prenatal, delivery and postpartum care, in order to achieve optimal health for the mother, foetus and infant during pregnancy and childbirth. Unsafe motherhood consists in maternal mortality or morbidity due to preventable pregnancy and childbirth-related causes. Safe motherhood decreases maternal and infant mortality and morbidity. Although, most maternal and infant deaths can be prevented through safe motherhood practices, millions of women worldwide are affected by maternal mortality and morbidity from preventable causes. Maternal mortality is an area of concern for the governments across the world and series of interventions are being carried out for the reduction of the same. The International Conference on Population and Development in 1994 had recommended reduction in maternal mortality by at least 50 per cent of the 1990 levels by the year 2000 and further one-half by the year 2015. The Millennium Development

Goals (MDG) of the United Nations has set the target of achieving 200 maternal deaths per lakh of live births by 2007 and 109 per lakh of live births by 2015.

There has been reduction in the maternal mortality rate in India yet the figure is far from national or internal targets. According to the United Nations Interagency Maternal Mortality Estimates for 1990–2008, released in September 2010, the absolute number of maternal deaths in India has fallen from 1,17,000 to 63,000.[1] This data is supported by a study published in *The Lancet* in April 2010, which shows that India's maternal mortality ratio (MMR) declined from 677 maternal deaths for every 1,00,000 live births in 1980 to 254 in 2008. The Government of India aimed to bring the MMR to below 100 by year 2012. The Ministry of Health and Family Welfare (MOHFW) reported that the number of Janani Suraksha Yojana (JSY) beneficiaries has increased greatly, from approximately 7,00,000 in 2005-06 to nearly 8.4 million in 2008-09.[2] The maternal health conditions, especially in the high focus states of Bihar, Madhya Pradesh, Orissa, Rajasthan and Uttar Pradesh continue to be unfavourable, resulting in higher MMR for the states, ranging from 303 in Orissa to 440 in Uttar Pradesh.

In order to meet the target of Millennium Development Goals (MDG) and to reduce MMR, Government of India launched Janani Suraksha Yojana (JSY) in April 2005 under National Rural Health Mission. JSY is being implemented in all states and Union Territories with special focus on low performing states. JSY is a safe motherhood intervention being implemented with the objective of reducing maternal and neo-natal mortality by promoting institutional delivery among the poor pregnant women. The Yojana, it integrates cash assistance with delivery and post-delivery care. The success of the scheme would be determined by the increase in institutional delivery among the poor families. The Yojana has identified ASHA, the accredited social health activist as an effective link between the Government and the poor pregnant women. The scheme focuses on the poor pregnant woman with special dispensation for states having low institutional delivery rates namely the states of Uttar Pradesh, Uttaranchal, Bihar, Jharkhand, Madhya Pradesh, Chhattisgarh, Assam, Rajasthan, Orissa and Jammu and Kashmir. While these states have been named as Low Performing States (LPS), the remaining states have been named as High performing States (HPS).

There is sharp increase in the number of beneficiaries of JSY. NRHM[3] website suggests that JSY has seen a sharp off take in the country, up from 7.39 lakhs, 31.58 lakhs and 73.29 lakh beneficiaries in 2005-06, 2006-07 and 2007-08 respectively. However, the increasing number of institutional deliveries indicates the success of the scheme, the vital statistics on MMR for the year 2011-2012 is yet awaited.

Attitude

Attitude is defined as enduring systems of beliefs. Consistent with the positions of other attitude theorists, we regard attitudes as general evaluations of people hold about themselves, other people, objects and issues. Such evaluations are often positive or negative, but they can also be uncertain at times. For example, you might have mixed feelings about a particular person or issue. These general evaluations are based on a variety of behavioural, affective, and cognitive processes. Affective or emotional component comprises of how the object, person, issue or event makes you feel. Individual thoughts and belief about the subject forms the cognitive component. How the attitude influences one's behaviour is a basis of the behavioural component. Attitudes can also be explicit and implicit. Explicit attitudes are those that we are consciously aware of and that clearly influence our behaviours and beliefs. Implicit attitudes are unconscious, but still have an effect on our beliefs and behaviours.

How Do Attitudes Form?

Past researches have indicated that there are several ways in which we acquire attitudes. One of our earliest agents of attitude formation is our parents, later followed by our peers and the media. When someone you admire greatly espouses a particular attitude, you are more likely to develop the same beliefs. For example, children spend a great deal of time observing the attitudes of their parents and usually begin to demonstrate similar outlooks. Sometimes, attitudes form directly because of one's experience. These experiences may be personal or they may result from observation. Our society, social roles and social norms can have a strong influence on one's attitudes. Social roles relate to how people are expected to behave in a particular role or context. Social norms involve society's rules for what behaviours are considered appropriate.

One can learn attitude through Classical and Operant Conditioning. The best example of learning attitude is exhibited by the use of classical conditioning by advertisers. They use classical conditioning to influence our attitude towards a particular product. Suppose someone is watching television commercial and sees young, beautiful people having fun in on a tropical beach while enjoying a sport drink. This attractive and appealing imagery causes to develop a positive association with this particular sport drink. Operant conditioning is also used to influence attitude formation. Imagine a college-going student has just started smoking. Whenever he lights up a cigarette among his peers, he is applauded and welcomed to the smokers club. However, when he lights up cigarette in public place, people complain, chastise him and ask him to leave their vicinity. This negative feedback from those around him eventually causes him to develop an unfavourable opinion of smoking and he decides to give up the habit.

How Do Attitudes Influence Behaviour?

It is our general assumption that people behave in accordance with their attitudes. However, social psychologists have found that attitudes and actual behaviour are not always perfectly aligned. After all, plenty of people support a particular candidate or political party and yet fail to go out and vote. Researchers have discovered that people are more likely to behave according to their attitudes under certain conditions:

- When your attitudes are the result of personal experience.
- When you are an expert in the subject.
- When you expect a favourable outcome.
- When the attitudes are repeatedly expressed.
- When you stand to win or lose something due to the issue.

In some cases, people may actually alter their attitudes in order to better align them with their behaviour. Cognitive dissonance is a phenomenon in which a person experiences psychological distress due to conflicting thoughts or beliefs. In order to reduce this tension, people may change their attitudes to reflect their other beliefs or actual behaviours.

Theories of Behaviour Change

Behaviour is a complex phenomenon and consists of many different factors, both internal to the individual as well as external. As Glanz, Lewis, and Rimers (1990) suggest, designing interventions to yield behaviour is best done with an understanding of behaviour change theories and an ability to use them in practice.

Social Cognitive Theory (Bandura, 1986) is a "theoretical framework for analysing human motivation, thought, and action" that "embraces an interactional model of causation in which environmental events, personal factors and behaviour—all operate as interactive determinants of each other". The key concept in this theory is perceived self-efficacy, which refers to the belief an individual, has his/her ability to successfully perform certain behaviour. Research has shown that an individual's self-efficacy has a direct influence on his/her choice of task and persistence in achieving the task. Low self-efficacy beliefs; for example, has been found to be negatively related to subsequent task performance.

Triandis' Model of Interpersonal Behaviour (Triandis, 1977) was based on the observations on the previous theories on attitude and behaviour change. It suggests that intentions – as in many of the other models – are immediate antecedents of behaviour. However, crucially, habits also mediate behaviour. In addition, both these influences are moderated by facilitating conditions.

*Transtheoretical Model or Stages of Change Model (*Prochaska *et al.*, 1998) deals with six stages involved in the behaviour change. These six stages are—*Pre-contemplation, Contemplation, Preparation, Action, Maintenance and Termination.*

Study Setting

FGDs were conducted in the *Bhangel* Village of Bisharkh block of Gautam Buddha Nagar district in the Western Uttar Pradesh. This village is located 7 km from the district hospital. It has mix demography dominated by Yadavs and is densely populated village. The population of this village is 15,000. There are twelve ASHA workers working actively in the village. There are eight Anganwadi Kendras in the village.

Sample

In order to gain insights into knowledge, attitude and its impact on behaviour change regarding safe motherhood practices among expectant mothers, focus group discussion (FGD) was conducted with groups of expectant mothers and ASHA/Anganwadi workers. The sample consisted of the expectant mothers in their second and third trimester of pregnancy. The rationale behind this sample selection is that the registration of the JSY beneficiary with the Anganwadi Kendra ideally begins with the confirmation of pregnancy. Discussion with the ASHA workers revealed that most of the women in the rural area are shy about disclosing/confirming their pregnancy in the first trimester. Most of them come for the registration with the JSY scheme in their second trimester of pregnancy. Thus, the expectant mothers in their second and third trimester of pregnancy were the ideal candidates for conducting this study. There were total 56 expectant mothers ranging from first trimester to third trimester of their pregnancy in this village at the time of study. Thirty-six expectant mothers in their second and third trimester were divided into three groups with each group having twelve members. Each group was invited at the three different Anganwadi Kendra at different schedule.

One of the key components of the National Rural Health Mission is to provide every village in the country with a trained female-community-health activist. The government has made efforts to identify such activists called ASHA from the village itself. They are being trained to work as an interface between the community and the public health system. The ASHA is envisaged to receive performance-based incentives for motivating women and children to receive services under the Reproductive and Child Health programme. As such, they have a vital role to play in implementing the JSY scheme at the grass roots level. Thus, in order to get insights into the supply side dynamics about JSY, ASHA workers were selected for conducting FGD. Out of twelve ASHA workers, ten ASHA workers participated in the FGD, as two of them were not available in the village at the time of FGD being conducted.

Measure

The FGDs were used to gain insights about knowledge, attitude and behaviour change about safe motherhood practices among expectant mothers. To understand the services provided under JSY, FGD with the first community level health workers *i.e.*, ASHA was also conducted. As this was the exploratory study, FGD was found to be most appropriate tool to capture the basic essence of the study. FGDs with the expectant mothers as well as ASHA workers were informal as well as targeted towards demand and supply side deliverables.

Procedure

ASHA plays a very important role in the JSY scheme. She is expected to disseminate information on JSY among the community members in general and to the pregnant women in particular, and motivate them for institutional delivery, accompany them to the hospital for delivery and stay with them at the institution. They were asked about the types of support they provided to assess the role they played in facilitative implementation of the JSY scheme at the grass roots level.

The FGD with the ASHA workers started as an informal discussion with them. Later on, it was focussed on services provided by them, support from the district and local administration in implementation of this scheme. After this, FGD was based on the close ended and direct questions on the following issues.

Type of help/support provided to expectant mothers such as:

- Arrangement of two Tetanus Toxoid injections
- Arrangement of at least three check-ups
- Arrange supply of 100 IFA (Folic Acid Supplements) tablets
- Arrangement of her registration for Institutional Delivery
- Information about JSY
- Decide and arrange place of delivery
- Accompany her for delivery
- Stay with her in hospital/institution
- Offer to take her to the institution
- Arrange transportation to reach the institution
- Help her identify the institution
- Advise her on having the baby delivered in hospital/clinic
- Advise her on post-natal care
- Arrange her JSY payment
- Inform her about JSY benefits
- Advise her on best breast feeding practices.

FGD with the expectant mothers initiated with the informal introduction of both the parties. The discussion was centred on number of children they have, whether it was their first pregnancy, family support and existing safe motherhood practices in the village. Later on participants were asked specific questions related to awareness/ knowledge about the various facilities under JSY and their attitude towards safe motherhood practices. Then they were asked question about first and second antenatal check-ups, Tetanus Toxoid vaccination, intake of folic acid supplements and other aspects of safe motherhood practices.

Findings of the Study

FGD with ASHA workers

90 per cent (9 out of 10) of the ASHA workers were aware about above facilities and assisted beneficiaries to avail the facilities.

FGD with the Expectant Mothers

It can be concluded from Table 15.1 that ASHA played crucial role in generating awareness about safe motherhood practices among

Table 15.1: Percentage of mothers aware about ASHA and services provided by them under JSY (Total number of respondents N-36)

Sr. No.	Indicator/variables	Response in %age
1.	Awareness About ASHA	100
2.	Visited me repeatedly during pregnancy	50
3.	Helped in registering for ANC services	90
4.	Counselled on the ANC services	85
5.	Referred for getting ANC services	70
6.	Accompanied for ANC services	70
7.	Told about Janani Suraksha	100
8.	Told about post natal services	60
9.	Counselled on breast feeding	50
10.	Satisfaction with the services of ASHA	80

Source: FGDs with the respondents of Bhangel Village in Gautam Buddha Nagar district.

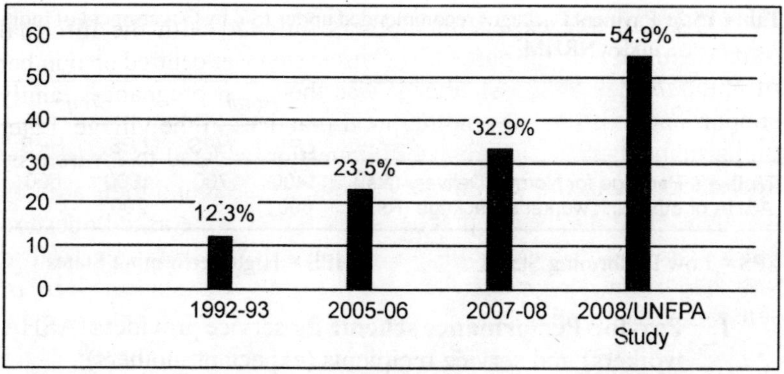

Fig. 15.1: Trends in Institutional delivery (in %) in Five States (Bihar, Madhya Pradesh, Rajasthan, Orissa and Uttar Pradesh

Sources: Data for 1992-93 and 2005-06 are from National Family Health Surveys. Data for 2007-08 are from District Level Household Survey.

the expectant mothers. The high level of awareness has lead to positive attitude towards safe motherhood among these women residing in the villages.

Most of the respondents agreed upon rise in institutional deliveries after implementation of JSY in their village. The extant literature on the trends in institutional delivery echoed the same. Institutional deliveries have increased in India over the past few years. Following figure shows data on the trend of institutional delivery over several years and includes data from a concurrent assessment of the JSY programme in five states (Bihar, Madhya Pradesh, Orissa, Rajasthan, and Uttar Pradesh) conducted in 2008 and sponsored by United Nations Population Fund (UNFPA) (Development and Research Services Ltd., May 2009).

Of course, many factors contributed to this increase, but it is likely that the JSY programme played a role in increasing the number of institutional deliveries, as beneficiaries have reported that the payments received as part of the JSY programme do help motivate them to deliver in health facilities.

Following factors seems to be playing major roles in generating knowledge, changing attitude and adoption of safe motherhood practices among the expectant mothers in the rural area;

Table 15.2: Payment Packages recommended under JSY by Government of India under NRHM

	Rural		*Urban*	
	LPS	*HPS*	*LPS*	*HPS*
Mother's Package for Normal Delivery (Rs.)	1400	700	1000	600
ASHA or other link worker's Package (Rs.)	600		200	

LPS = Low Performing States HPS = High Performing States

1. **Pay-for-Performance scheme** for service providers (ASHA workers) and service recipients (expectant mothers)
   Performance incentives to the service providers (ASHA) seem to motivate them to put their maximum efforts in reaching out to the beneficiaries. The socio-economic conditions of the beneficiary might be preventing them from accessing the safe-motherhood facilities and services previously. Since expectant mothers are paid for institutional delivery under JSY, the burden of going for institutional delivery might have been eased.
2. **Facilitating Conditions:** Most of the respondents of the FGD have agreed to the fact that the facilitating conditions available locally under JSY, have contributed largely in adoption of safe motherhood practices. These facilitating conditions include availability of community level health workers from local community, vaccination facility in the village, arrangement of transport facility for delivery, ASHA workers accompanying the expectant mothers for institutional delivery, ante-natal check-ups counselling by ASHA workers, availability of folic acid supplements and other provisions under JSY.
3. **Roles of ASHA workers in Awareness Generation and Service Delivery**: Discussion with the respondents revealed the fact that most of the ASHA workers acted as opinion leaders and change agent for safe motherhood practices among villagers. ASHA workers roles ranged from generating awareness about safe motherhood practices, informing about various provisions under JSY among expectant mothers and sometimes convincing family members of the expectant mothers to adopt safe motherhood practices.

Conclusion

The findings of the exploratory study suggest JSY is playing very crucial role in adoption of safe motherhood practices among expectant mothers in the rural areas. The community health workers roles are also commendable in delivering the services among the beneficiaries. At the time of the study, most of the respondents were in second and third trimester of pregnancy, it was difficult to capture all the aspects of behaviour change regarding safe motherhood practices.

REFERENCES

Bagozzi, R.P., and Edwards, E.A. (1998). Goal setting and goal pursuit in the regulation of body weight. *Psychology and Health.* (13) 593-621.

Bandura, A. (1989). Social cognitive theory. In R. Vasta (Ed.), *Annals of child development: Six theories of child development.* 6, 1-60. Greenwich, CT: JAI Press.

Bandura, A. (1992*).* Self-efficacy mechanism in psychobiologic functioning. In R. Schwarzer (Ed.), *Self-efficacy: Thought control of action.* 355-394. Washington, DC: Hemisphere.

Glanz, K.; Lewis, F.M., and Rimers, B.K. (Eds.). (1990). *Health Behaviour and Health Education: Theory, Research, and Practice.* SanFrancisco, CA: Jossey-Bass.

Development and Research Services Ltd. May 2009. Concurrent Assessment of Janani Suraksha Yojana Scheme in Selected States of India, 2008. New Delhi: UNFPA, GfK MODE.

Prochaska, J.; Johnson, S. and Lee, P. (1998). The transtheoretical model of behaviour change. In S. Schumaker, E. Schron, J. Ockene & W. McBee (Eds.), *The Handbook of Health Behaviour Change*, 2nd ed., New York, NY: Springer.

Triandis, H.C. (1977). *Interpersonal behaviour.* Monterey, CA: Brooks/ Cole.

NOTES

1. In 2005, the United Nations (U.N.) estimated that India had the largest number of maternal deaths in the world. U.N., TRENDS IN MATERNAL MORTALITY IN 2005: estimates developed by WHO, UNICEF, UNFPA, AND THE WORLD BANK 15 (2007), available at http: //www. unicef.org/vietnam/Maternal_Mortality_2005_24_9b. pdf.

In 2008, the U.N. estimated that though India still has the largest number of maternal deaths in the world, the overall number has dropped to 63,000. U.N., TRENDS IN MATERNAL MORTALITY: 1990-2008: ESTIMATES developed by WHO, UNICEF, UNFPA, AND THE WORLD BANK 17, 24 (2010), available at http://whqlibdoc.who.int/publications/2010/9789241500265_eng.pdf

2. http://mohfw.nic.in/NRHM.htm
3. http://mohfw.nic.in/NRHM.htm

Index